Carpe Diem

Charles B. Reeves, Jr.
Portrait for Kernan Hospital
by Elizabeth Byrd Mitchell, 1995

Carpe Diem

The Twentieth Century Pilgrimage of an Imparfit Knight

Show wisdom.
Life is brief.
Cut short hope.
Even while we speak,
Envious time has fled.
Seize the day.
Put little trust in the morrow.

—Horace, *Odes*, Book 1, No. 11

Charles B. Reeves, Jr.

GATEWAY PRESS, INC.
Baltimore, MD 2001

Originally printed, Baltimore, 1999
Reprinted with corrections and additions,
Baltimore, 2001

For book orders call Corporate 800
1-800-237-8400, ext. 54

Library of Congress Control Number 99-73583
International Standard Book Number 0-9674253-0-1

Published for the author by
Gateway Press, Inc.
1001 N. Calvert Street
Baltimore, MD 21202-3897

Printed in the United States of America

To Mother, who made it all possible

"And at a knyght than wol I first bigynne.
A knyght ther was, and that a worthy man, ..."

"And though that he were worthy, he was wys.
And of his port as meeke as is a mayde.
He nevere yet no vileynye ne sayde
In al his lyf unto no manner wight.
He was a verray, parfit gentil knyght."

—Geoffrey Chaucer: *The Canterbury Tales*,
General Prologue, Lines 42, 43, 68–72

TABLE OF CONTENTS

Preface

I started this collection of reminiscences in 1995 because I was urged to by various relatives, friends and even casual acquaintances. Shortly afterward in July 1995 I read a book by John Kotre, professor of psychology at the University of Michigan-Dearborn entitled *White Gloves—How We Create Ourselves Through Memory*. In the chapter on "Memory in the Mature," he encouraged having a "life review" before one attained the age of eighty. He stated, on page 179, "The feeling of satisfaction from a life review may be augmented by seeing your life as a part of a larger drama, as a variant of some archetypal tale. You may come to see your place in history." This encouraged me to continue and finish the job, to date.

On a similar plane of putting matters in perspective, the Summer 1998 Issue of *Maryland Humanities*—Chatauqua '98—American Humorists, has a section on Will Rogers by Doug Watson. At page 34, he gives an account of Will Durant's writing to Rogers asking for a statement of his philosophy. "Rogers' answer was brief and typically common sensed: 'Get a few laughs and do the best you can. … Believe in something for another world. but don't be too set on what it is. … Live your life so that whenever you lose, you are ahead.'"

Amen!

Acknowledgments

Mrs. Sue Chenowith, whom Jacques Schlenger graciously shared with me, blessedly suffered through whatever secretarial help I needed for this manuscript, which she put in first draft on the word processor. Then Stacey Howatt and the Support Center, particularly Mary Duffie, Gina Wilson, Diane Freeland and Tom Mallonga, took over. Molly Washburne in Charlottesville, Virginia had the manuscript printed and bound for preliminary distribution as a "rough draft" to immediate family and a few friends for Christmas 1997. Arthur Machen reviewed and edited the rough draft in his capacity as the permanent chairman of the Venable, Baetjer and Howard Committee on Style. His exercise on my behalf brought back to memory the days of yore. I was 14 or 15 years old, a Gilman student, when Arthur and Brad Jacobs, later editor of the *Evening Sun*, used to review my essays submitted to the *Blue and Gray*, the student literary magazine. Some things never seem to change. *Deo gratias!*

Jeff Price of the Baltimore *Sun* kindly put me in touch with his book editor, Michael Pakenham, who gave me suggestions as to publishing. After consulting with my lifelong friend Louise ("Peasie") Bruce, I chose Gateway Press as my publisher. It has been a pleasure working with the President, Ann Hughes, Janet Kratfel who designed the dust jacket, and the typesetter, Steven Meyer, Proprietor of The LetterEdge. They have all been most understanding in their work with a neophyte, and, as far as I am concerned, matters have gone "swimmingly"—a word that I used somewhere in the text and that had Steve scratching his head.

I acknowledge the erudite assistance of Robert R. Porter, Princeton Class of 1945, Oxford Rhodes Scholar and classicist *par exemplar,* who gave me the correct references to quotations from Virgil's *Aeneid* and the *Odes* of Horace.

I further acknowledge the tireless efforts of George Constable in July 1999 on Nantucket Island to dissuade me from using my title and subtitle for this opus. I have agreed with him that the quotation from Horace on the title page is a bit bleak, but Horace lived in tumultuous times in ancient Rome, not unlike our own. I have done a pretty fair job of following Horace's advice, "Carpe Diem" by "seizing the day" on many occasions.

As to the subtitle, I do not claim to be "a verray, *parfit* gentle knyght"—quite the contrary—but I have tried to convince George that my somewhat adventurous life during the twentieth century has had a good many aspects of a pilgrimage in the full medieval sense of the word, as portrayed by Chaucer in his *Canterbury Tales. Pace*, George. When you protest too much, you appear in the book!

Finally, in this Revised Edition, I express my thanks to Karen Chalonge, formerly of Paris, now living in Zermatt, for reading the "first edition" with a fine tooth comb, picking out a long list of typographical errors—mostly in French, German or Italian—and providing her usual Gallic over-all critique. Merci infiniment!

Also, for this edition, my new secretary, Shannon Campbell, has been most helpful and Leslie Scott of the Support Center has become a wizard at reading my writing. I am indebted to all of you.

Prologue

The following is a brief background of where I came from. It is not intended as research genealogy. It is presented simply to give a bit of background and color. It was suggested by my cousin Shanghai's wife, Charlotte, hereinafter more fully referred to, when I asked her recently about the "first edition" which I circulated among family and a few friends a year or two ago in rough draft.

The Reeves side of the family—my father's—came from Gloucestershire, England according to a book of Reeves genealogy, given me many years ago by Aunt Ella. The Reeves were among the early settlers of the southern part of New Jersey, circa 1650. Some of them had farms in Cape May County and others near Alloways, in the Salem and Millville areas. There was some migration to the Delaware Valley in the Gloucester and Burlington areas. Our branch of the Reeves family moved to Philadelphia around 1760, prior to the American Revolution.

Grandfather Charles Henry Reeves met his bride, Ella Tiers, in the 1870's at the then highly fashionable summer resort—for Philadelphians particularly—of Cape May, New Jersey. Grandfather and Grandmother moved to Baltimore shortly after they were married. He was a protégé of Mr. Platt, president of the Insurance Company of North America, and was made the representative in

Baltimore. Aunt Ella said that the company kept him on at full salary until the day he died, in recognition of his service during the Baltimore Fire of 1904. He took a horse and wagon down to his office on Commerce Street on the day of the fire, a Sunday. He and the driver had to put wet burlap on the horse because of the sparks and cinders. They brought the records up to the family house at 930 North Charles Street. Grandfather began paying claims on Monday morning.

Grandmother Reeves was born Ella Tiers and used to lord it over Grandfather since she was connected to the Carpenters, Chancellors, Englishes, Whartons et al. in Philadelphia. Her sister, Mary, was married to Colonel Frank Wister, who had a distinguished record in the Civil War. When Aunt Ella referred to her Philadelphia relatives, my brother, David, and I used to call it the Recital of the Litany of the Saints.

There was vague talk about the Tiers being related to the great Thiers, a President of the Republic of France. Aunt Ella's cousin, Gertrude Tiers Bell, was incensed when her daughter, Pauline Curtis, pooh-poohed the idea and stated that in her opinion, they were a "bunch of Portuguese adventurers."

Whatever the Tierses were, they were colorful. Aunt Mary Wister's husband said that Cousin Ethel Roberts "delighted in outraging polite society." My cousin Helen Tiers Houghton recalled that, as a young girl, she was on her Aunt Minnie Wanamaker's yacht in Palm Beach in the Roaring Twenties. A flamboyantly dressed lady, dripping jewels, insisted on being rowed in a dinghy from another yacht through a regatta which was in full swing. The lady was swearing profusely at the oarsman. Helen looked over the rail and to her horror said, "My God, it's Aunt Ethel."

When Aunt Ella decided to join the Colonial Dames of America, she went to the Historical Society in Philadelphia. She gave them all the information on Grandmother's side, the Tiers and their connections. Then the lady taking the information asked about the Reeves' connections. Aunt Ella said they would be of no interest. Grandfather had always been somewhat reticent about the Reeves side. His father had been divorced and Grandfather and his sister, Aunt Mary Banes, had been raised by their mother with no communication with the Reeveses. The lady asked for the maiden name of Aunt Ella's grandmother Reeves, and Aunt Ella somewhat condescendingly said, Anna Keene. After getting a little more information, the lady said, "Just a minute Mrs. Clotworthy, I would like to have you meet our director, Dr. Gregory Keene."

To Aunt Ella's amazement, Dr. Keene brushed aside the Litany of the Saints and said, "Mrs. Clotworthy, you don't have to give us any more information. Your grandmother, Anna Keene, is a direct descendant of Jöran Kujn from Sweden, one of the original settlors of Pennsylvania—before William Penn. We have all the information here." And he spread out a genealogical tree.

Aunt Ella was dumbfounded and wrote her sister, Aunt Nannie, who was a Sister of Charity at the Mother House, 140 Rue du Bac, in Paris, to tell her this bit of news. Aunt Nannie, like Aunt Ella, had been brought up on Grandmother Reeves somewhat lording it over Grandfather about her relations. When Aunt Nannie heard that Aunt Ella had gone into the Colonial Dames on Grandfather's side, she wrote back to Aunt Ella, "I can't believe it. Wouldn't Father be delighted!"

Cousin Shanghai Goodwin has provided a further interesting wrinkle. On a recent trip to the Philadelphia Historical Society, he said that my Swedish forebears, according to later research, were actually Finns who lived in territory subjugated by the Swedes. This could add another facet to the family history. It might also explain why they emigrated to America.

There were four Reeves children, Anne Tiers, Aunt Nannie, born August 15, 1875, who became Sister Mary, a Sister of Charity; Aunt Ella Clotworthy born October 13, 1876; Charles Henry, Jr., Uncle Harry, born in 1880; and my father, Charles Banes.

Aunt Nannie was a remarkable person. She was born on August 15, 1875, the Feast of the Assumption of the Blessed Virgin. She was at Atlantic City, New Jersey when she made her first communion at the age of 10. She turned to Grandmother Reeves and told her that she was going to become a nun, a religious sister. She grew up to be a beautiful young woman, blonde, with one blue eye and one brown. She made the usual debut in Baltimore —Bachelors' Cotillon ("Monday German"), etc.—and Grandmother doted on her. Aunt Ella says that she was always introduced as sort of "the other one."

Aunt Nannie dutifully took in all the social events up and down the East Coast, pleasing Grandmother, but, although she was having a good time, a real whirl, she was not completely happy. Finally she told Grandmother that she was going to become a Sister of Charity. She wanted to serve the poor. Aunt Ella said that, even after late partying, Aunt Nannie would go to seven o'clock Mass every morning at their parish church, St. Ignatius. She spent her last weekend at Belair Stud, the home of the Woodwards, the famous horse farm, in Prince George's County, Maryland.

She entered the Order in Philadelphia, at age 23, in 1898, and completed her novitiate at Emmitsburg, Maryland. Since she spoke French, she was sent to the Mother House of the Order of St. Vincent in Paris, 140 rue du Bac, originally built by Louis XIV for one of his mistresses, La Vallière. Aunt Nannie became the English-speaking secretary for the Most Revered Mother, particularly for the United States and Canada.

After World War I, she began taking care of refugees who arrived in Paris from the Bolshevik revolution in Russia. Eventually, the Order allowed her to open a small convent of her own at 56 rue d' Assas, where she distributed food to the poor, mostly White Russians. Two of her callers were Prince and Princess Lwow, he the last premier of Russia before the Bolsheviks. Although they were poor and their clothes threadbare, Aunt Ella said that instinctively everyone stood up when they entered.

Although she became ill, Aunt Nannie stayed on in Paris taking care of her poor, greatly assisted by the staff of the Paris *Herald*, who published appeals for her to the American community, particularly at Christmas time. World War II broke out on September 1, 1939 and the Cunard Line said that they had space for her whenever she wanted to leave. Everyone was urging her to go, and she finally did so that autumn. Deedie Massey, who had worked for her for years, told my sister-in-law Anne Reeves that Aunt Nannie had a deck chair on the ship next to an attractive gentleman named Arturo Toscanini. He was captivated by her. Aunt Nannie was a charmer to the last.

She came home to St. Agnes Hospital in Baltimore, where I last saw her at Christmastime, a frail old lady but still with a sparkle. On January 1, 1940 Aunt Ella went to the Mount Vernon Club New Year's Day reception, where everyone was asking for Aunt Nannie. Aunt Ella and Father were with her when she died that evening, also a holy day, the Feast of Mary, under the post-Vatican II liturgy.

Father was born in Baltimore, Maryland on November 9, 1881 in the family home that was then on the southwest corner of Charles and Madison Streets, on Mount Vernon Square or, more accurately, Washington Place. According to Aunt Ella, his birth was difficult. The attending midwife and physician wrapped him in a blanket and placed him by the open fire in the second floor bedroom while they strove to save my grandmother's life. In their endeavor, they completely forgot my father until he let out a wail. Fortunately, both Grandmother and Father survived.

My mother was Emily Fitzgerald Kenny. I have no details about her birth, in Baltimore on July 30, 1886. Presumably she was born in the family home, that was then on Eutaw Place. Later they moved to 12 East Madison Street, across from the house where

Father was born. Mother's background is interesting since nearly all her forebears are Irish or of Irish descent, commencing with William Plume. He was born Moran but changed it to Plume because he was in some sort of trouble with the English. He had to leave Ireland and landed in Norfolk, Virginia during the American Revolution. He was 19 years old and went immediately into the Continental Army. He wanted to have a chance to fight the English. According to Aunt Clara Brockenbrough in Richmond, Virginia, he served through the Revolution and its culmination at the Battle of Yorktown. He then went into business in Norfolk, owned a rope walk and was successful. He had a country place that he named Ghent, in honor of the treaty ending the War of 1812. Ghent is now a large section of the city of Norfolk. The financial street of Norfolk is Plume Street, named after him. His portrait hangs in my living room.

He was not the progenitor, as such, of Mother's line since he did not have any children, but he brought members of his family from Ireland to the United States. Mother's mother was a Doyle, and there were also Fitzgeralds and Herrons. The Norfolk relations are not as well documented as the Philadelphians since Norfolk suffered two catastrophes in the mid Nineteenth Century. In 1855, it was hit hard by yellow fever, losing one third of the its population. Then it suffered through the Civil War in 1861–1865.

One of the Fitzgeralds, Edward, was an officer in the U.S. Navy and was the first American officer ashore at Vera Cruz in the Mexican War of 1846–1847. He went to California where he made a name for himself as a vigilante in the civil unrest after the Gold Rush of 1848. When he died, the City of San Francisco declared a half-day holiday in his honor and the schools were closed. His portrait—by Alfred Jacob Miller, according to Stiles Colwill—also hangs in my living room.

Two of the Plume connections were a Professor and Mrs. James Behan. I have the professor's portrait and Anne Reeves has Mrs.

Behan's, in Princeton. The Behans returned to Ireland in 1861 at the time of the Civil War.

George Kenny, a third or fourth cousin of ours, lived at Ennis, County Clare, Ireland. He was discovered by Cousin Shanghai on a trip to Ireland in the 1960's. George was a lawyer and the local historian, whom the young of the district consulted for local lore. According to George, the Kennys were originally Danish Vikings who landed in Ireland in the Ninth or Tenth Century. They settled near Wexford on the southeast coast and stayed there until, as landowners, they were uprooted by Oliver Cromwell in the Seventeenth Century. They moved to County Clare to get as far away from the English as possible. Clare was the only county which was not occupied by Cromwell. The Kennys settled in the area of Miltown Malbay and Spanish Point, on the south side of Liscannor Bay.

George told me, when I met him in 1967, that my great-grandfather Cornelius Kenny said at the time of the Great Famine in the 1840's that Ireland was no place for a young man. He should go either to America or Australia. Fortunately Great Grandfather chose America. It is not clear whether Grandfather C.D. (Cornelius David) Kenny was born in Ireland and brought to this country as a child or whether he was born here. In any event Great Grandfather ended up in Rochester, New York and Grandfather Kenny moved down to Norfolk where he met the Plume line. My grandmother was born Clara Doyle.

Grandfather Kenny had a total of five children, four by my grandmother, namely Aunt Clara (Mrs. John M.) Brockenbrough; Aunt Eleanor, who became a Madame of the Sacred Heart; Mother; and Isidore who died at age 18. After Grandmother Kenny died, Grandfather married Frances Fant from Washington, and they had one child, Aunt Frances, later Goodwin. She was the mother of my cousins, Lawrence, Frances, Shanghai, and Emily. After my mother died Aunt Frances treated me almost like a fifth child.

Since I was so often at the Goodwins, Aunt Frances called me "Charles Reeves" and her own son "Charles Goodwin," to differentiate between the two Charleses. Charles Goodwin later became "Shanghai."

One of the Kennys, Matthew Kenny, went into the priesthood in the early Nineteenth Century and eventually became Dean of Killaloe. There is a plaque on the left side of the cathedral church at Ennis, County Clare, in his memory. The old cathedral is at Killaloe, a beautiful fourteenth or fifteenth century church, buried in the depths of the country. It is now Church of Ireland. According to George, the Dean of Killaloe was tantamount to being Bishop of Ennis. The new church at Ennis, built in the Nineteenth Century after the repeal of the penal laws, has a spire built by the Kennys in defiance of the English since Catholic churches were not allowed spires.

Aunt Eleanor Kenny's middle name was Sampson. Again, according to George, a young French girl appeared at Ennis, on the far west coast of Ireland, during the French Revolution, presumably at the time of "The Terror." She was taken in by a group of "religious women," the equivalent of nuns or sisters, since religious orders were suppressed by the English. She was raised by the nuns and married a man named Sampson. She was presumably an ancestor of ours since Aunt Eleanor was named after her. No one knew her background but she must have come from a prominent family if she was sent far away from France during the Revolution.

According to George, my great grandfather, Cornelius Kenny, was named for the legendary Cornelius—"Corney"—O'Brien, a close friend of my great-great-grandfather, David Kenny. My brother David's son, Cornelius David, perpetuates the name which, according to George, is not a "Kenny name." Our progenitor is David Kenny, buried near Miltown Malbay. Further, according to George, the O'Brien's ostensibly became Anglicans, "Church of Ireland,"

and preserved their wealth. The Kennys remained Catholic. If they wanted to be educated they had to go to France.

It is interesting that both sides of the family ended up in Baltimore because of the Civil War. Grandfather Reeves was sent here because the Insurance Company of North America was expanding into a booming Border State. Grandfather Kenny came north from Norfolk, according to my brother David, because his coffee, tea and sugar business was growing and he could not get adequate financing in the South immediately after the Civil War. The two families lived near each other and had pews in the same church, St. Ignatius.

Mother and Father were married on May 19, 1920 by James Cardinal Gibbons, the first Cardinal in the United States, since Baltimore is the primal see of the Roman Catholic Church in the United States. According to Aunt Ella, it was the last large "public" wedding which he performed. Two acolytes stood beside him with candles so that he could read the service.

As aforesaid, the foregoing is offered simply as background or color. It may not be accurate. It is not genealogical research, but it sets the stage for my entry on the scene. "Tantara!"

Emily Kenny Reeves, Charles B. Reeves, Sr., Charles B. Reeves, Jr.
4406 Greenway
Baltimore, 1923

1

Beginnings

I was born in Woman's Hospital on Bolton Hill on May 16, 1923. This was modern in those days since babies were usually born at home until well into the 20th Century. Father and Mother had bought 4406 Greenway in Guilford, one of the earliest planned suburbs in the United States. There I spent my childhood and live there today.

I have no idea of when I first spoke, but I would guess that it may have been early, based on subsequent experience. I was, however, slow in learning to walk, according to family accounts. My first memory, at the age of 14 months, is my first successful effort at walking. I climbed out of my crib at the rear of the second floor of the house and somehow navigated the steep back stairs into the kitchen. It caused an uproar from my nurse, the cook and the maids when I unexpectedly appeared in the kitchen from my afternoon nap.

As I picked up a little age, the memories become more frequent. I can remember at age three my mother leaving for the hospital to have my brother, David Kenny, born July 2, 1926. I remember running down the alley, Oakley Lane, to meet her when she returned with David. I was fascinated with a little baby. I also remember my mother two years later sitting on the terrace waiting to be taken to the hospital because her back was bothering her.

She and Father had gone to England to see Billy Barton run in the Grand National at Aintree, and she had been in pain ever since. She never returned from the hospital and died on June 7, 1928. She would have been 42 on July 30 of that year.

I have only a few memories of Mother—taking a ride in a Buick run-about with her and Father and going through a terrific hail-storm at University Parkway and 39th Street; being scolded for being a nuisance while she was trying to get ready to go out; being in St. Ignatius Church at Sunday Mass with her and Father and being generally obnoxious.

I was just five years old at the time, but I can clearly remember Father coming in to my bedroom about 2:30 P.M. while I was taking my nap and telling me that "God has taken Mother to heaven." I did not go to the funeral. David was not quite two years old and had not yet spoken. Aunt Ella said that he began to "chirp like a cricket" a few weeks after Mother died.

That summer my Mother's sister, Aunt Frances Goodwin, took David and me to Chatham, on Cape Cod, with her family. Memories are sketchy, but I do remember stepping on a broken clam shell while wading in to swim and cutting my left foot near the big toe. Uncle Lawrence swung me in the water to clean the cut, and I remember vividly having alcohol poured into it, when I reached the house.

Years later Aunt Frances recalled that my nurse, Minnie, was a pest, always getting in the way, washing baby bottles just at dinnertime when she had been specifically asked not to. Also, Aunt Frances said my hair had probably not been washed since Mother died. When Aunt Frances did so, my yells were so piercing that Uncle Lawrence came in off the water to see what had happened.

Father came up that summer to visit us, since I have a little picture which he took of David and me. My Cape Cod experiences actually began in 1924 when Aunt Frances and Mother took the

Warbasse house on the end of Penzance Point at Woods Hole. I have no memories of this at age one, but I do have a little picture taken of me on the terrace. My cousin Shanghai, actual name, Charles Goodwin, and his wife Charlotte now have a house on the same Point a few hundred yards away.

Charles B. Reeves, Jr. ("CBRJr"), Warbasse House,
Penzance Point, Woods Hole, Massachusetts
Summer, 1924

David K. Reeves and CBR Jr.
Chatham, Massachusetts
Summer, 1928

2

Calvert School

Mother had enrolled me at Calvert School before she died. I entered the Kindergarten in September 1928 but do not recall much of this, except that I was upset at going. Minnie used to walk me over in good weather, but Aunt Ella probably took me the first day.

I had better digress here to introduce Aunt Ella Clotworthy. She was my father's younger sister, born October 13, 1876. She had quite an active life. She was 75 years ahead of Woman's Lib. But here it will suffice to say that she was a widow in 1928, with a son, C. Baker Clotworthy, Jr., my first cousin, who was born on June 30, 1910 and was thus then 18 years old. Aunt Ella came out to take care of David and me when Mother went to the hospital and after Mother died, Father asked Aunt Ella to stay on, which she did. Baker moved to our house shortly thereafter and lived with us until he married in June 1940. We were a happy family. Baker was once asked what it was like, living with his Uncle Charlie. He said it was fine, so long as you were there on the dot of 7:00 P.M. when the dining room door opened for dinner.

As for Calvert, it was and remains today an excellent school. It was, however, difficult because it pushed the students in every subject. I particularly remember the phonetics which were crammed into us and which resulted in a greater than usual ability to spell in later life. Virgil Hillyer, the headmaster, was a brilliant person. He wrote textbooks used in the school—*A Child's History of the World* and *A Child's Geography of the World*—two excellent works that gave us a good grounding in those subjects. The facts were drilled into us, and to this day I encounter things I learned at Calvert. Thus, during the 1990–1991 Persian Gulf War, I remembered the Zigurrat of Ur when Saddam Hussein stationed some of his fighter planes around it, with no regard for his country's history or its monuments. Ur of the Chaldees, the Tigris and Euphrates Rivers and Babylon were all familiar names from my early education. At Calvert you had to fit the cookie cutter. If you did, all was well and you never forgot. Thus, for some reason, I still remember that the Battle of Zama was fought in 202 B.C. Things like that were drilled into us.

I do not have many other distinct memories of Calvert during the first two years, when I was five to seven years old, except that during the cold months, when we entered the building, we were met with a blast of hot, dry air. My personal thermostat has always been set for cold weather, possibly due to my English-Irish-Swedish background, plus maybe a touch of Viking through the Irish. One of the banes of my childhood existence was being buttoned into knee-high leather leggings that made my legs uncomfortably hot. In any event, whether it was the central heat or not, in my second grade year, called "Eighth Age" at Calvert, I came down with a series of ailments which nearly did me in. In February 1931, I first contracted measles and about a week later developed scarlet fever. Then in another week I came down with pneumonia. Finally, about another week later, I felt a pain behind my left ear when I was being bathed and was diagnosed as having a "mastoid," a common childhood ailment in those days before penicillin and various antibiotics. I was a very sick child indeed—so sick that I could not be moved to Sydenham Hospital for Infectious Diseases at Lake Montebello. In later years Aunt Ella said she realized how desperately sick I was when Dr. Dorsey or his assistant Dr. Tappan came in one day to see me three times—morning, afternoon and finally about eleven o'clock at night.

I was kept at home until I was strong enough to be moved to Union Memorial Hospital, where I remained for about six weeks. The first four weeks I was in Room 217, fronting on 33rd Street, and then after being operated on for the mastoid, I was moved to the fifth floor, back, a demotion which I did not like at all. I was thoroughly spoiled.

During my long illness and hospitalization, I had much attention, particularly from "Aunt Mildred" (Mrs. John C.B.) Pendleton, who was no relation but a very good friend of Aunt Ella. She often sounded as mad as a March hare but had a wonderful sense of humor and imagination, making up all kinds of imaginary characters for me, including one called Almyria, who purportedly suffered from the "epizootic." Aunt Mildred and I yarned about her for hours. In her more serious moments, Aunt Mildred had a shrewd estimate of life and its problems. She also gave me a grab-bag of small presents that I was allowed to open, one for each day. It gave me something to look forward to.

Also my stay at Union Memorial was brightened by the arrival of home-made ice cream, made by George Allen, who worked for our family for 45 years and was then employed at the Green Door Tea Room at 926 (now 930) North Charles Street, across from the Maryland Club. The Green Door was opened by Aunt Ella in the family's former residence, which she still owned. She and her son, Baker, lived there in the 1920's and she had a number of her friends, Sophie Ulrich, Frances and Jean Gilmor and others help her. This was in the days before the Mount Vernon Club and the Town Club (which eventually merged) were founded as women's clubs.

Having had minor operations before my mastoidectomy, I was well used to hospitals and had great confidence in the doctors. Dr. Edwin Broyles, my surgeon, lived near us, and his son, Edwin, was my brother's age and a close friend of his. I still have a vivid memory of the anesthesia. I was first given some sort of gas and then ether, and as I was going under, I had a sort of "Star Wars" experience with a circle of hard, sparkling lights, that seemed to rotate slowly. When I came out of the anesthetic, I was dreadfully nauseated, and, of course, my head hurt horribly from the operation. I had to have a strong bandage around my head to protect the wound and also keep the gauze drain in place. This drain had to be replaced frequently, an unpleasant experience.

I went home about the end of March and had to stay in bed for another week or two. When I was finally allowed up, I had forgotten how to walk and had to learn all over again. My recovery must have been rapid, since I can remember going outside for the first time, half-running across the lawn and clambering down the bushy bank to Greenway. During this recuperation, I was sent homework from Calvert. The class had started fractions, which were a complete mystery to me. Unable to decipher what the little dividing line meant, I simply added up the numbers, ignoring the line. I was soon straightened out by our teacher, Miss Stack.

Also during that year, as a part of our French class, we were learning the Marseillaise. To this day, I can sing it from "Allons, enfants de la patrie ..." through "l'étendard sanglant est levé." But then there is a hiatus caused by my absence from school. I subsequently picked up something about hearing "mugir les feroces soldats," but I have to hum along this part until finally we come out of the tunnel into "citoyens, formez vos battalions. Marchons, marchons ..." to the end. I admit that I am a bit fuzzy about the last few lines—probably because I had to make up a lot of work in the last two weeks of April and the month of May. Similarly, I suffered lacunae in other subjects, but, according to my classmate Pete (Eben D.) Finney, the school pushed me along and even gave me grades approaching those of Zandy (the Honorable Alexander II) Harvey. Zandy is now the retired Chief Judge of the United States District Court for the District of Maryland, but still working as hard as ever as a "senior judge."

3

Camp Wallula

My cousin, Lawrence Goodwin, was going to Camp Wallula in New London, New Hampshire in the summer of 1931 and I was possessed to go too. I would be eight years old, and Lawrence was 12 or 13. I imagine that Father and Aunt Ella were a bit dubious after my long illness, and pictures taken that summer show a decidedly frail-looking child. But I persevered and went off to Wallula around July 1. Among my tent mates were Nims Warren and Gus Hall. I used to row with Bill Lord from Philadelphia. We were the youngest boys in camp. We were divided into teams of "Army" and "Navy" and competed in everything, sailing, rowing, swimming, blueberry picking, "steal the old man's eggs," a sort of "prisoner's base." I was in the "Navy." Aunt Frances said that she would never have sent any of us there if she had seen it beforehand, because everything looked so beaten up—rowboats, sailboats, etc. But she said in later years she realized that this was its best advertisement since everything was used and not kept for show.

I loved every minute of it and received there my introduction to mountains, never having been even to Western Maryland to see the Blue Ridge Mountains or the Alleghenys. Accordingly, when we went in the camp truck, also well battered, to the base of Mt. Kearsarge, I saw my first mountain as we passed the outskirts of New London and descended toward it.

We drove part way up the base to a clearing, where we had a picture taken, then climbed up the trail to the summit. I cannot remember if we younger boys went up separately, but I do remember that we were told to walk steadily and slowly and not to speed ahead, get out of breath, and then make frequent stops, very good mountain advice, an initiation to the "guide's pace." Years later at age 72 trudging up to Namche Bazar on the Nepal side of Mount Everest I used the same technique.

We camped for a couple of nights on an island in Big Lake Sunapee and several nights on Bear Island in Lake Winnepesaukee. The latter was particularly memorable since we could clearly see rocks and pebbles on the bottom some forty or fifty feet down.

The summer had its traumatic side one evening when we were playing in a cabin near the tennis courts. I was racing around and brushed up against a two-man saw, which fell off its holder and put a four or five inch gash in my left leg. I still have the scar.

More serious was another roughhouse when I fell against the corner of a bureau and broke open my mastoid incision. A local doctor must have put in a drain which for some reason was forgotten. John Boyce, a counselor, took me over to George's Mills a couple of weeks later to another doctor. He cut out the drain and fixed me up in some fashion.* Years later John said it was the worst thing he had ever had to witness. Fortunately, I could not

* As a result of the damage incurred by me after the operation, I was partially deaf in my left ear. I could not hear a watch "tick," which they did in those days before digital watches. However, it was useful when Father gave dinner parties. I could literally turn my good ear to the pillow and "turn a deaf ear" to the party.
In recent years, I became deafer, and when I went to Johns Hopkins Hospital in March 1999 to look into hearing aids, I ended up with Dr. Niparko and Dr. Ng, who have a procedure to repair mastoid damage. I have just had this done on August 17, and the preliminary prognosis is optismistic. Maybe I won't have to tell Shanghai Goodwin and Nancy Marburg to "stop mumbling."

see what was going on.

The remaining two years at Calvert School passed without great incident, except that I did have a lengthy bout with bronchitis in the winter of 1932. I lost some time, but nothing like 1931.

Similarly, I had a good time at Wallula in the summers of 1932 and 1933, when I was respectively nine and ten. In those summers I had no more traumas and had a great time in all the activities. I climbed Mount Monadnock and Mount Cardigan. We had a fine canoe trip on the Pemigawasett River.

After camp, in 1932, I accompanied my cousins, Lawrence and Shanghai, to Chatham, where Uncle Lawrence and Aunt Frances again had a summer house. While there I contracted some sort of fever. Aunt Frances was afraid it might be polio. I cannot remember it, but subsequently she told me that she had had me pick up pennies, having read somewhere that if I could do this, I was not becoming paralyzed. Fortunately, I did not have polio, but I had to go to bed in the afternoon just as a total solar eclipse was developing. The birds were singing, preparing for their beds. When I awoke after the eclipse was over, I thought it was morning and was just as confused as the birds.

4

Gilman School

Aunt Ella's son, Baker, having gone to Gilman, she felt that I should go there too, particularly since the athletic facilities were better than any other schools in Baltimore. In any event, I must have liked the idea because in September 1932, I entered the Fourth Form of the Lower School. We were a small class of ten or twelve. I spent three years in the Lower School and then went into the Upper School in September 1935. There I was joined by Zandy Harvey and others from Calvert. I spent three years in the Upper School, the First, Second and Third Forms.

I had a good time at Gilman, enjoying both the studies and the athletics, and made many lifelong friends. The school had excellent spirit.

I played football on the 120's, coached by Miles Marion. We had a good team. I played lacrosse for two years on the Undersquad Team, coached by Edward Brown, the varsity football coach. Again we had a good team and I was captain in my second year, succeeding Ned Murray.

My favorite sport at Gilman was ice hockey, a program sponsored by Mr. Brown. We had some outdoor hockey since in those days we had cold winters, but mostly we played at the Sports Center on North Avenue, where I played on the Junior Varsity.

On Friday evenings when the Varsity was playing, David and I would take the Number Eleven trolley from Bedford Square, at the foot of our block on Greenway, and go early to the Sports Center. In that way, we could sit in the balcony directly over the north goal so that we could support our goalies, Bruce Baetjer, and later David Barrett. If we did not get these seats, some of the rougher elements were known to expectorate on the allegedly privileged boys from Gilman. There was no balcony over the goal at the North Avenue (the south) end, so our goalie was safe there.

Bobby Bordley, who had grown up in Canada, was the star of the varsity. Then Mr. Brown recruited Charlie Plitt, who was a remarkable athlete, in football (a fantastic passer), ice hockey and baseball (a very good pitcher). Charlie's father was in the painting business, and after hockey practice at the Sport Center in the late afternoon, we loved to get a ride back with him in the back of his automobile. We sat on the various cans of paint. It was like a modern pickup truck.

Also worthy of note in Gilman sports was our classmate, George Franke. He became so hefty and muscular and was so good at football, even in the Lower School, that in his Sixth Form year (Lower) he had to play on one of the smaller Upper School teams. He was a good hockey player, a defenseman, and an excellent catcher on the baseball team. He later starred on the Princeton varsity football team.

We have been lifelong friends, and he still reminisces about coming to our house for lunch on Saturdays and being cautioned by his mother about having to use a finger bowl. We used to walk over on Saturday to the Rex Theater on Greenmount Avenue to see a movie—in those days respectable ones, although in its last days as a theater it became known mostly for its X-rated films. It is now an evangelical chapel. After the movie we used to stop at Mrs. Griffith's drug store on the corner of Old Cold Spring Lane, next to the public school (that is now my voting place) and buy a rather watery ice cream soda. On this particular Saturday, George Franke, Staley Tregallas, Bobby Pickett and I bought some five cent cigars. We must have been about eleven or twelve years old, still in the Lower School, and David, aged eight or nine, who was with us, bought one for himself. When we arrived home we lit up the cigars. I was the guilty ringleader since David and I had on occasion pinched some of Father's Corona Coronas that he bought for his dinner parties. When any were missing Father may have suspected George Allen, although he never said so, since George was a devout Baptist and did not drink or smoke.

In any event, this time it was a different story with "tufers." We lit up in the garden, all of us, including David. I was the first to succumb and had to go upstairs to bed, feeling horrible. When Aunt Ella came home, she could not figure out what was wrong when she saw George, Staley and Bobby lying on the stone walkway by the fishpond in the garden and soaking their heads in the cold water. Finally, she saw David, the only one who did not get sick, sitting on the garden bench, calmly smoking a cigar. When Father came home he must have realized that it was not George Allen who had been to blame for the missing cigars.

In September 1936, I was involved in a memorable neighborhood incident with fireworks left over from the Fourth of July. Our neighbor across Greenway was Mr. Key Daingerfield, a bit of an eccentric who had a lovely wife, the daughter of General Felix Agnus. She was always kind to us children. In the days before traffic lights in the suburbs, Mr. Daingerfield would walk down to the intersection of Greenway, St. Paul Street and Charles Street and direct Sunday traffic in his plus fours and Norfolk jacket.

In my leftover fireworks, legal in those days, I had a triple salute mounted on a small wooden base. When lit, the first explosion would propel something like a cherry bomb about thirty or forty feet into the air and then the bomb would go off with a blast. Similarly with numbers two and three.

After dinner and on the way to practice the piano at our next-door neighbor's, Mabel Whiteley, a maiden lady, I thought that I might as well use up the salute. I placed it on the lawn, well away from our house and near Greenway, and lit the long fuse. Of course, the salute's base should have been firmly affixed to a board or something more substantial—but it was not—whereby this tale.

The first projectile went off as planned. The initial blast propelled the bomb into the branches of a large oak. The bomb let out its own flash and blast. But then the unforeseen occurred. The rest of the salute on its small base toppled over. As luck would have it, its remaining two projectiles pointed toward Greenway and the Daingerfields' house. Our house sits about ten feet above Greenway on an embankment. The Daingerfields' (now Margo Bates') is almost that much lower.

Number two salute went off with a blast. Lying on its side, it propelled the cherry bomb directly across Greenway at ground level. It went off with a flash and a blast just outside the Daingerfields' front door. Number three did the same. Shortly thereafter, I was inside Mabel's house and dutifully practicing "The Happy Farmer," about as high a musical level as I attained in my studies at the Peabody Conservatory.

Mr. Daingerfield, none too steady at best, thought that his house was under bombardment, probably by anarchists, and phoned for the constabulary. In a few minutes, Kate, Mabel's Irish maid and general factotum, came up to the second floor and announced to Miss Whiteley that the house was "surrounded by policemen." After a brief council of war, we decided that the best thing was to make a clean breast of it. I accordingly did so, and the police let it go at that. The only repercussion was a short article appearing in the next morning's *Sun* announcing the setting off of surplus fireworks in Guilford by a thirteen year old.

5

Canterbury School

Although the family is Catholic—i.e. Roman—I had never been to a Catholic school. Aunt Frances took David and me to Sunday School at the old St. Mary's behind Notre Dame College on Charles Street, where we made our First Communions and were confirmed. Sulpician Seminarians would come over from the Seminary on Roland Avenue to give us religious instruction at Gilman when we were in the Upper School, but Aunt Ella thought we should get some formal Catholic education. Accordingly I went to Canterbury School in New Milford, Connecticut, in September, 1938, for the last three years of my "high school" education. My cousin, Baker Clotworthy, had been there before me as had also my cousin Lawrence Goodwin. Jimmy Rowland from home, practically a member of the Goodwin family, also came with me, a class or two behind me. Lawrence drove us up. My Sixth Form sponsor or introducer was Peter Kiernan, later a Trustee and a loyal alumnus.

I roomed in the South House my Fourth Form year, at first with Newbold Lawrence from Lloyd Harbor, whose mother was a Cromwell from Baltimore. I had previously met Newbold at Fishers Island, when I was staying with Zandy Harvey, a connection of Newbold's by marriage.

Newbold and I did not room together long, since we were

involved in an incident on Halloween Night in which we set off a series of firecrackers, most of them deafening ones of the six-inch salute and cherry bomb category. We were banished to separate rooms. Next to us was Bob Corroon from New York. I cannot remember whether he aided and abetted us. In any event he wisely avoided any outright involvement. I think he was highly amused although he had to assume the pose of a stern "upper former."

I loved Canterbury. It was, and is, a beautiful place, located on a hilltop in the lower end of the Berkshire Hills, above New Milford and looking across to the Housatonic River and the hills surrounding Lake Candlewood. It is remarkable how little the view has changed. I was last there for our Fiftieth Reunion in 1991.

I particularly remember the first autumn that we were there because, although the foliage was beautiful in Maryland, in New England it was stunning. The reds and golds of the maples and gums against the dark green of the evergreens were breathtaking.

I played Number Three Back on the Junior Varsity football team in my Fourth and Fifth Form years. Tom Burke and John Murray were also backs, and we had a good team. The only particular incident that I remember was scoring a touchdown at South Kent School. The line had cleared out a big hole for me, and I was on Cloud Nine.

My chief delight was ice hockey. We had no artificial rink and skated and played almost exclusively on the Farm Pond, a trudge of about a quarter mile down hill and lying next to the road running towards Sherman and Lake Waramaug. We must have been fit as fiddles since the hockey squad was small. In my Sixth Form year when David appeared, we often played defense together when I needed a "rest" from playing right wing on the front line. I was usually so tired that I always tried to steer the opposing forwards to David so that he could knock them down. Also he was bigger than I. Of course our hockey was nothing like today's game that is much faster and rougher, with its bullet-like slap shots from curved sticks.

In addition we had to take care of the rink, no Zambonis. We shoveled the snow off by hand and occasionally used a snow plow on the farm truck. It was an outing to drive down at night on the farm truck and spray the rink. On one occasion the truck would not start for the trip back, and I can remember Bob "Obie" O'Brien cursing and kicking it and then ordering us to kneel down in the snow by the running board and say a "Hail Mary" out loud together. Something must have worked because we got it started for the ride back.

Meanwhile, on the world front, matters were deteriorating in Europe. Hitler reoccupied the Rhineland in 1936. In 1937 came the Anschluss in Austria; and finally in September 1938 Czechoslovakia fell to the Nazis. On September 1, 1939, while Helen Bruce and I, with Chauncey Hall, were visiting Betty Simpson and her parents on Lake Kiwassa in the Adirondacks, we heard that Hitler had attacked Poland, which gallantly defended itself with its cavalry against Stuka bombers and tanks. Polish radio played the Chopin March Militaire until Warsaw fell.

Stalin concluded a non-aggression pact with Hitler on September 22 and attacked Poland from the East. Events moved so rapidly that we did not receive our history books for Mr. Edward Macks' course in European History until some time in October. The final chapters had to be rewritten.

School and athletics went on as usual, but in the Spring of 1940 the pace quickened abroad. Hitler attacked Norway and Denmark, then fell on Holland and Belgium and moved through the Ardennes against France, an updated version of the Schlieffen Plan, as Mr. Mack explained to us. France fell quickly in June, and as she did, Italy attacked her from the South. We had finished our regular school exams, as I recall, and were studying for College Boards at the end of June when we heard Roosevelt give his famous speech about the Italian perfidy. Something like "the hand that held the dagger has struck it into the back of its neighbor." Listening to the radio in the North House Common Room before lunch, we felt that it was only a matter of time until we would be in the war.

That summer we had a house in Cape May, New Jersey on Queen Street for about a month and had two of our younger Philadelphia cousins, Wharton and Frank Tiers, down to visit us. Also I went up to Quissett and visited Helen and her parents, the Albert Bruces, who had the house that Aunt Frances usually rented.

In September, Hitler having disposed of France, turned the Luftwaffe loose with a vengeance on England for the Battle of Britain. Little did I know that one of my good ski friends at St. Anton in later years, Mouse Cleaver, was in the thick of it.

I played football on the varsity, as a substitute Number Three Back and saw very little action. Logan Bullitt from Philadelphia, Tony Cudahy from Lake Forest and Bill White were the stars. We had a good ice hockey season. Ed Cudahy was captain and Brother David joined me. We had a good "ice" winter, playing almost without interruption from December until the spring break in March. We went to Salisbury for a ski meet that turned out to be quite an experience since everyone had to compete in all four events—downhill, slalom, cross-country and jumping. They asked me if I wanted a practice jump, and I said "no thanks!" On my third jump of the series, I almost made it standing up to the bottom of the hill. Parker Matthai from Baltimore was the jumping star for Salisbury.

Since we were not let out for weekends it was a somewhat monastic life at Canterbury. On Sunday afternoons we took long walks, and I was lucky since an old friend of the family, Miss Edna Latrobe from Baltimore, a real character who traveled all over the world, had us over for lunch frequently at her little place at Roxbury, about six miles away. In good weather we often walked it one way or the other or sometimes both.

The remainder of the Spring at Canterbury was uneventful but, as usual, pleasant. One thing that was a regular fixture every May was a cold spell and a snowfall, only one inch, which melted by midday. It was beautiful on all the greenery.

Graduation came and went. We had a school dance. Helen Bruce came up from Foxcroft. Father and Aunt Ella were on hand for Graduation. I won the Headmaster's Prize for an essay on the Humanities and English, truckling a bit to Dr. Hume, I must confess.

The "Doc" was quite a person, cast in the mold of Father Sill at Kent, Dr. Endicott Peabody at Groton, and Dr. Boyden at Deerfield. They were autocrats. Dr. Hume was an amateur actor and an inspired English teacher. His Sixth Form readings were dramatic, and I particularly remember his reading of Keats' Odes, explaining the metaphors and imagery.

We had good teachers at Canterbury, Mr. Brodie, a Rhodes Scholar from Fort Smith, Arkansas, in Latin; Mr. Lindeman in Math; Mr. James Herlihy in French; Mr. Haskell, from Harvard, in our last year, in English (he liked my "spoof" review of Hamlet); and Mr. Degnan in Math, our hockey coach. Mr. Ed Mack was not only an extremely good history teacher; he was an accomplished organist, who played beautifully in chapel. Mr. Everett Mack was a good science teacher.

At the end of June 1941, Hitler scrapped his non-aggression pact with Stalin and launched a full scale assault on the U.S.S.R. They said that Stalin was so stunned that he could not surface for several days. Mr. Mack had always warned that if Hitler attacked Russia, he would be defeated. Eventually it would become a two-front war. He cited Napoleon's mistake in doing the same thing.

After we had completed College Boards at the end of June, I said good-bye to Canterbury—three very happy years for me—and went down to Wilmington, Delaware at Charlie Skelly's invitation to attend the wedding of Charlie's sister, Margaret, and

Bob Goheen, later to become President of Princeton University. The Friday night party was at Vic Mead, and, as I recall, Charlie's brother Max became engaged that night to Anne Layton. It was a great party.

Logan Bullitt was also on hand, and we had a wonderful time. The wedding reception the next day was at the Skellys' house, and I remember that Logan and I were farmed out to the McHughs' (whose three sons went to Canterbury) for dinner.

The next day, Sunday, Charlie, Logan and I drove up to Greenwich where the Skakels had a huge reception, something straight out of The Great Gatsby, to dedicate an enormous fountain, a real "jet d'eau"! Afterwards, I joined Newbold Lawrence and we journeyed down to Lloyd Harbor to have a little rest and recreation with his parents. This included some swimming at the Cold Spring Harbor Beach Club.

6

PRINCETON

Father had graduated from Princeton with the Class of 1903. It had been assumed that I would go there also. I had been interviewed at Canterbury by Dean Radcliffe Heermance, an imposing, mustachioed figure who arrived in a large Lincoln Continental. He reviewed my courses and marks and recommended that I enter the new Divisional Program in the Humanities, majoring in English. He accorded me advanced placement in some sophomore courses, English, Classics and French. Charlie Skelly had asked me to room with him. Because of all the religious background, I hesitated, wondering if I should go to Georgetown. I decided on Princeton in the summer, and, since Charlie had to have a decision, he had chosen to room with J. J. Kerrigan in 25 Campbell. This was probably a wise choice since Charlie and I might have had too good a time together. Father motored me up to Princeton in the summer and I was assigned a single room at 616 Pyne Hall, furnishing it from the Student Furniture Exchange.

In September Father drove me to Princeton to settle down in 616 Pyne Hall. He stayed at the Nassau Tavern. One thing I remember vividly is that when we came out into Palmer Square after dinner there was an incredible display of Northern Lights, aurora borealis. At first they started like shimmering curtains in the north, but eventually covered the whole sky and culminated in radiating in all directions from the zenith—directly overhead. I have never seen anything like it, even in the farthest reaches of subarctic Canada, Alaska or Siberia. Was it telling us something in that fateful 1941?

The next night I met Ed Cudahy to have a beer at the Nass. There we joined Larry Armour and Bill Douglas, both from Lake Forest and Class of 1945. We have been friends ever since, particularly Bill, through skiing, mountaineering, golf and general bonhomie.

The autumn proceeded pleasantly and interestingly. I played fall lacrosse under Bill Logan, the first I had played since Gilman. I enjoyed my studies. I was in Whitney Oates' precept in Classics, had Dean Robert Root's English 201 in 10 McCosh, which he ran like clockwork, and an early morning class in French 201 which I "cut" occasionally and which gave me nightmares for years afterwards. Also, because of the war, I took ROTC. The early Saturday morning class with teacher Moose Bliss of Pepper Constable's Class of 1936 football team was often hilarious, particularly one morning when a stray Army dog planted his paws on Tobie Hilliard's chest as he sat in his desk chair and began to bark in his face.

Saturday football games were fun in Palmer Stadium except for Navy, which beat us. We freshmen were sent down to protect the goal posts and were roundly thrashed by the Middies, en masse and very fit. I went to the infirmary with a split ear.

I went home for the weekend on Friday, December 5. On Sunday, December 7, we had finished the customary roast beef lunch and were listening on the radio to the New York Philharmonic. They interrupted the program for a special bulletin to announce that Japan had attacked Pearl Harbor. There were few details and, even now many years later, we realize that the authorities did not fully appreciate the extent of the damage to Battleship Row. We were lucky that the carriers were at sea. We subsequently heard that Jimmy Winants from Baltimore was taking a small plane flying lesson at the time and saw the Japanese planes coming in to attack. They had more important things to do than to bother him. And so we were in it!

I took the train back to Princeton that evening. There were lots of us on it, particularly the PJB (Princeton Junction and Back). I am sure we were all very somber but also at our age with a certain sense of elation and adventure.

The next day, Monday, about noon we gathered in 25 Campbell, Charlie Skelly and J. J. Kerrigan's room, to hear Roosevelt make his speech before the joint houses of Congress, the "day of infamy" speech asking for a declaration of war. As always, he was eloquent but very solemn. The Japanese had played into his hands. As one of their great leaders, Yamamoto, said, "I am afraid that we have awakened a sleeping giant." Indeed they had although the outlook became bleaker and bleaker as the year ended and we went into 1942.

One poignant event took place in Alexander Hall. The Trapp Family Singers came to Princeton shortly after Pearl Harbor and before we left for Christmas vacation. The place was packed. They sang by candlelight—Baroness von Trapp, their family priest, all the children down to Johannes who could not have been more than five.* It was "Sound of Music" but real. There was not a dry eye in the house.

When we returned from a Christmas vacation full of the old-fashioned debutante parties and also a trip to St. Sauveur skiing over New Year's (see the Chapter "Skiing" for further details), military matters were confusing. The University was gearing up for an all-out effort in support of military programs. Many of the more adventurous left for the Army Air Force or the Marines.

* According to an account in the *New York Times* concerning a revival of the stage play, Johannes must have been three!

The University and the ROTC urged us to stay put, and a lot of us did. It was a wise decision.

The University adopted an "accelerated" schedule. The new freshman class of 1946 entered in June. We all went to school through the summer. At the break in August, Newbold Lawrence and I decided to take a mountain climbing trip in New Hampshire. We took the train to Crawford Notch, hiked up the trail to the Mizpah Springs lean-to, then the next day to the Lake of the Clouds Hut, and finally up Mount Washington to the summit. We stayed at the Appalachian Mountain Club hut, next to the Observatory, with only the meteorologists in residence. We had the hut to ourselves. We stayed there several days, taking day trips down the various ravines, including Tuckerman's and Huntington. It was a perfect vacation.

We returned to the University in the fall with more studies and a bit more military confusion, with some of my friends, including Bill Douglas, leaving for the 10th Mountain Division. I reasoned that I would rather keep my skiing and mountaineering for fun, and I am glad that I did.

The eating clubs also decided to accelerate their schedules for Bicker Week and admission. Ivy Club, of which Father had been a member, decided to take no chances on their new "section" since they had lost out a bit on the class immediately ahead of us. Tom Hilliard, Tobie's older brother, Charlie Brown, Bob Blair's cousin, and others quietly lined up our section well in advance. Bonnie White asked me to join his "iron bound," which consisted of John Kinder, Tommy Ramseur and Nick Bell. When Bicker took place in September, we were supposed to wait for a night or two before being asked to join Ivy, but the pressure was too great with the usual proselytizing, politicking, etc. and I can still see Tom Hilliard coming in the first night of Bicker and saying, "Gentlemen, we would like you to join the Ivy Club."

We went to the Nass to celebrate. The first thing that I did was to go to the pay phone and call Father. He was delighted, Ivy having meant a tremendous amount to him. His friends there were lifelong: Frazor Harris and Ike Roberts from Philadelphia, Jack Perry from New York, et al. The names are all on his wedding present silver pitcher. We had kept our pre-bickering a deep, dark secret, and I imagine that Father did not expect me to become a member since I was rooming alone and a fairly serious student at that time, not the worldly Ivy type!

That fall I made the Editorial staff of the *Daily Princetonian*, the "Prince" as it was known. Bobby Carton was my mentor and Vince Brokerick the Editor. Don Durgin, later of CBS renown, was on the staff. It was hard work when we were on duty, sitting up with the printer, to all hours, but it was a lot of fun.

In August of 1942 we had gone to Newark to be officially examined by the Army, given shots and placed on the reserve roster. In March 1943 they took us to Fort Dix to take various tests, including the AGCT. 110 was passing for admission to OCS. Our average was something like 128. Dick Nash blew the register out when he scored 157 out of a possible 161. I had to stay over a couple of days, since my blood pressure went up, but then it came down to its usual level. One of the ROTC sergeants came for me and drove me back to Princeton. The gothic towers, green trees and lawns looked like heaven.

I moved over from Pyne into "barracks" in 1901 Hall on March 29, 1943. We fell out in the morning to roll call, marched to Commons for breakfast and then marched to lunch. I cannot remember all the details, but they made it as military as possible. We were in uniform, paid by the Army, sold our furnishings and sent all our belongings and civilian clothes home. We were "in the Army now."

There were other military programs at Princeton, Navy V-7 and V-12, and we eventually ended up in the ASTP, Army Specialized Training Program. But for now we were Field Artillery enlisted men.

7

THE ARMY—FIELD ARTILLERY

After classes were over in June, we were put on a troop train and hauled down to Fort Bragg, North Carolina. The only detail I can remember about the trip is being parked for at least an hour on the railroad bridge over the Schulkyll River in Philadelphia. Eventually we arrived at Fort Bragg and were placed in training batteries at the Replacement Center. We were divided among various platoons. Each platoon had a fair number of Princetonians in it. In nearby batteries were the Harvard and Yale ROTC units. It was straight basic training with tough marches with packs, "speed marches" i.e., six miles in an hour, "cannoneer's hop" with 105 mm howitzers, and some paper work such as map reading.

The heat was horrible. We were eaten each night by "red bugs," waking every morning at 5:30 with a series of welts. Having friends on hand made a huge difference. My bunk was on the ground floor, near the showers and latrine, between Harvey Kelsey and Bill Schill. Bob Maynard was on the second floor of our barracks, as was Hugh O'Neill. We also had a nice group of other fellows our age from all over the lot, and one "old timer," Al Conti. He for some reason was drafted at age 42 and ended up in our midst. Hugh O'Neill reported that Al's daily ritual on being awakened was to swing his legs over the side of the bunk, gaze dolefully at the floor and then very feelingly say, "Fuck me; I'm an Indian!"

I don't blame him, being with a bunch of 19 and 20 year olds.

Our sanity was preserved that long hot summer by the kindness of Tommy Ramseur's cousin, Steve Peck, at that time from Wilmington, North Carolina. Steve made it possible for us to stay on Saturday nights in the dormitory of the Carolina Club at Wrightsville Beach. We hitchhiked down on Saturday afternoons after our half-day chores and formations. It was a godsend to get away from Bragg and get into the ocean. We especially enjoyed Saturday buffet at the Carolina Hotel.

Towards the middle of September it began to cool off, and we were able to sleep better since the red bugs disappeared. For the last week of October and the first week in November we went on our two-week field problem, a sort of maneuvers out on the reservation. In the early morning we could hear the paratroopers of the 82nd and 101st Airborne being flown overhead to be dumped at the edge of the reservation. They were supposed to walk back 25 miles to their quarters before getting anything to eat. We regularly heard 8-inch shells going over us as the Field Artillery Board tested new weaponry. The 8-inch guns had a range of 10–12 miles and were extremely accurate. Bill Schill ran into Albie Merck from Far Hills, who was on the Board—an officer obviously. Also, in the "small world" category, my Battery Commander was Bill Woolverton, from Greenwich, who had been at St. Sauveur at the Leuchtenbergs' when we were all skiing. Needless to say, I distanced myself as far as possible.

When we went into the field for our two-week trip, the weather changed abruptly, and we had rain for 13 of the 14 days. It was cold. We had a drill where we had to stay awake with the guns all night. They were sheathed in ice by morning. We were dog tired, but we survived. About two days after we returned to heated barracks, we could hardly put our feet to the floor at Reveille. Having had cold, wet feet for two weeks we all came down with "trench foot," in varying degrees. I did not completely lose the tingle of the pins and needles for about five years.

At the end of November we finished basic training. We were well hardened and turned into real soldiers. We were supposed to go to Officer Candidate School (OCS) at Fort Sill, Oklahoma, the Field Artillery Center, but they did not have room for us right away. There was a certain amount of anxiety. They sent us back to Princeton, in the ASTP with the Aladdin's Lamp patch on our left shoulder. We were quartered in Campbell and Blair Halls. By now, wise to the ways of the world, when we fell out for Reveille formation in pitch black darkness, about one quarter of us would be present and answer for the others. When it was my turn to stand, I would unabashedly answer; "Post—here; Ramseur—here; Reeves—here; Root—here; Rose—here; etc."

We stayed at Princeton until about mid-January. We were given leave to go home for Christmas, a pleasant respite. I cannot remember what we did in the way of classes, but we must have had some sort of education—civilian and/or military. In January, we were sent to Fort Sill OCS by troop train, via Saint Louis, and I remember going across the flat lands of Missouri and Oklahoma on the "Katy"—the Missouri, Kansas and Texas Railroad. At Fort Sill we were put in OCS Class 107. Harvard and Yale units were in the vicinity. We were six to a hut. Bob Porter, Abbott Post, Tommy Ramseur, myself, Stan Root and Homer Rose were in ours, in alphabetical order.

OCS passed pleasantly, without too much stress. Gunnery week was the toughest. We fired the 105's with live ammunition. We had one unfortunate incident when a round dropped short, and Jerry McConnachie, who was directing fire from the bunker, got a piece of shrapnel right between the eyes. Fortunately, it must have come in "up and down" so it just made a narrow slit and was easily removed. That could have been a tragedy.

Also we had one week where we had to mark each other on all sorts of standards—known commonly as "fuck your buddy week."

We graduated in early May 1944. It was customary to put on a skit, which we did in style since there were quite a few Triangle Club members with us—Dick Scheuler, Wat Stewart, Harry McCauley, Harry Noyes, come to mind. They put on a spoof of *Oklahoma*, recently opened in New York, and it brought down the house.

After OCS we were given a two or three week leave and thus I was home for my 21st birthday on May 16, 1944, a brand new "shavetail" second lieutenant. It was great to be home. One thing that I had to do was to go down to the old Safe Deposit and Trust Company at 13 South Street, meet Mr. George Pausch and make a Will. My first lawyer was John Marshall Butler, but then Father's friend, Crossan Cooper, took over.

Also, on that trip, Father took me to lunch at the Maryland Club. We ate outside on the second floor porch. Butler, from the old Baltimore Club, was on the door. He told me with pride that he had been a guest at Father and Mother's wedding, on May 19, 1920, and that he had received the official invitation. Those old club servants were wonderful people and real friends of the members. The Baltimore Club, which folded during the Depression and was absorbed by the Maryland Club in 1933, must have been a delightful place. Father was Secretary for many years. The Club's employees included Emmanuel Chambers, William Brown, and James Penn.

After my leave, I was under orders to report to Camp Roberts, California, near Paso Robles, California. A number of us from OCS rendezvoused at Dallas and drove out in Tex Payne's car at night, to save gas and tires. We went out Route 66, via Flagstaff, Arizona, Needles, California and Bakersfield, which we reached about 3 A.M. nearly out of gas, "coming in on the fumes."

We stayed at Roberts only a few days since they were overstaffed. We were ordered back to Fort Sill to Officers' Communication School. Since we had some extra time, John Kinder and I took the train to San Francisco. He ran into an older friend of his from Wheeling, West Virginia, who took us to a grand dinner at Trader Vic's. We stayed at the St. Francis Hotel. We awoke the next morning to the news that the invasion of France had begun—D Day, June 6, 1944.

We regrouped in Los Angeles and drove back with Tex to Fort Sill, stopping en route at Bob Porter's family place in Tucson. It was an attractive town in those days, only 35,000 people. I remember going over to the D'Autremonts to swim. Cecily later married James Jesus Angleton, the obsessed counterspy of CIA.

We again drove at night, and as we crossed New Mexico, we came to a place in the desert called White Sands, near Almagordo. It was about 3 A.M., but the place was a blaze of light. We could not figure out what was going on. There was no room there to be had, and we were told to continue up into the mountains at Ruidoso. There we found a hotel and were delighted with the pine forests and the cool air. A year later we realized that White Sands was where they were working on the atomic bomb and set off the first atomic blast, on July 16, 1945, in the New Mexico desert north and west of there.

Back at Fort Sill we settled into the hutment area for officers' courses. We learned how to set up a headquarters battery, lay out the phone lines to the rear, to the battery firing centers and to the forward observers, all through manual switchboards. We learned radio procedure, CW (Morse Code), etc.

We had to tune our own radios, and the procedure was to open the wire door to one's small enclosure and call down to the monitor set for a frequency check. One hot afternoon I was doing this, leaned out of the enclosure, with the tuning fork still on the set, and grounded my arm across the radio set. The amperage was minuscule, so that the damage was slight, but at 600 volts it felt like someone had hit the underside of my arm with a baseball bat.

We finished the Communications Course in September, and I was assigned to a training battery in the Field Artillery Replacement Training Center at Fort Sill, the FART Center as locally known. We had a nice crowd of officers and I enjoyed training the soldiers. I was in good physical shape again since I led the Physical Training and took part in the marches and field exercises. Others preferred to do the increasingly cumbersome paper work, a bore to me, so I volunteered for their field work, RSOP's (Reconnaissance, Selection and Occupation of Position for battery and battery headquarters), and the longer field exercises. All this took place out on the reservation, which was part of the Wichita Mountains.

The sad side of this story was that one group of recruits that I trained was shipped overseas to France in November, sent up to the front in December, and put in the lines in a "quiet sector" with the 106th Division. It was in the Ardennes and was decimated by the Germans in their last great attack beginning December 16, 1944, the "Battle of the Bulge."

We had many Polish-American recruits from Hamtramck, Michigan, who were a delight—Bonyarczyk, Kryzminski, et al. If they liked you, they would do anything for you. I shudder to think of the opposite. I believe we got along fine.

One of my fellow officers interested me in flying. He had been in the Army Air Force taking flight training but left when he decided it was no place for a family man. Father had flown in World War I which was then the Army Signal Corps. I took some civilian lessons at Lawton, Oklahoma, just a few hours, and liked it. My first flying had been with Charlie Skelly in his plane at Princeton.

The war began to go successfully in Europe. I had a large map on the wall of my room in the BOQ, Bachelor Officers' Quarters, with a line of pins moving from Russia on the East and from France into Belgium, Luxembourg and finally the German border on the West. Suddenly the school for training of Field Artillery pilots opened up—i.e. Liaison Pilots. They knew how valuable they were in Europe and must have realized that they would need many more for the final battles in the Pacific, including the assault on the main islands of Japan.

I did not think I had a chance of passing the physical, particularly the eye exam, since my eyes had been about 20/40 when I left Princeton, but to my astonishment, I did. I applied for and was given leave to go home for Christmas. I flew home and had a good time. I started my leave on December 16, the day that the Battle of the Bulge began. We were all engrossed in it, since if it had been successful, it could have been disaster. But fortunately the German drive was contained under horrible winter conditions. Cuppy Fenwick was there, as a private in the infantry. Cat Rees from Princeton was there as an officer in the Fourth Armored, that made the swing up to Bastogne under then Colonel (later General and Chief of Staff) Creighton Abrams, as ordered by General Patton. Afterwards, Billy Reading from Harford County, whose father had been Uncle Lawrence's "general contractor" in restoring the farm at Mill Green, told Uncle Lawrence that when their armored unit moved up, they came upon a British unit, parked on the road, having tea. When the Brits would not move, they lowered the bulldozer blades on their tanks and cleared the road. They were under orders to move as fast as possible.

Ikey Iglehart was there as an infantryman and has written a fascinating account of it, titled ironically "ASTP" (Army Specialized Training Corps) the branch to which he was originally assigned.

8

Flying—Field Artillery Liaison Pilot

When I returned to Fort Sill, I received my orders to report to Sheppard Field, Texas, near Wichita Falls, just below the Red River and about 70 or 80 miles from Fort Sill. We were in the usual barracks with no private rooms such as BOQ but perfectly comfortable. We had a nice flight class. From Princeton 1945 there appeared Chan Brewer and Tommy Ramseur, Beverly McVeigh from VMI, Clarence Gilmore from Texas, Elmer Hagerty from Illinois, Joe Cardoza, Ben Oswalt, Princeton 1944.

Our flight instructor was a civilian, Mr. Scott, whom we of course called "Scotty." He had flown some of the first jets captured from the Germans, and when he described how they took off without any torque and that you could point them straight up to the sky, we simply could not believe him. The Germans were way ahead of us.

Scotty was a great flier, and he was good at showing us how to be smooth with our use of our engine and controls. It must have been a come down for him to teach small plane flying, Piper Cubs and L-5's, but he did it with a relish. He was a superb teacher.

We also did instrument training on the Steerman bi-planes, a very stable aeroplane. It was great fun recovering from "unusual positions," and of course the "idiot box," the Link trainer-simulator, drove us all up the wall at first.

We did "cross countries" over the flat Texas plains and always had the square-mile grid to guide us like a map. We flew to Abilene and other towns in the area, and also did some night flying, a hairy experience.

One warm afternoon they let us off early, and three or four of us were walking in Wichita Falls. A man in an automobile with his radio on, stopped at a red light, leaned over and said, "You boys have just lost your commander-in-chief." It was April 12, 1945 and Franklin D. Roosevelt had died in Warm Springs, Georgia.

We finished the Air Corps basic training in late April and were sent immediately to Fort Sill to receive our advanced training. The Air Force had insisted that they give us basic, but when we arrived at Fort Sill and the Department of Air Training, one of the first things they asked us was, "How high did you fly down there at Sheppard Field?" We said, "Never below 500 feet." They said, "Forget what they told you. We'll teach you to fly the way we want you to. You probably won't fly here **above** 500 feet." It was almost true.

We were called "grasshopper pilots" and had a grasshopper insignia on our flight jacket. It was appropriate particularly when a bunch of us were coming in to land in the late afternoon. The field was a large grass-covered one of irregular size without runways. We simply flew in to the perimeter and followed it around counter-clockwise until the tower in turn gave each of us a green light, at which time we would turn left, cut the engine and come in to land. It looked like a cloud of grasshoppers.

My instructor at Sill was nowhere near as friendly as Scotty. He was more of the "bully" type, but we had a fascinating time learning to fly the field artillery way. We landed in fields, on dirt strips, on paved roads and dirt roads, straight and curved; we landed and took off everywhere. There was one strip on the edge of the lake beyond the Main Post where we had to duck around a large tree to come in to land on a short, narrow dirt strip. Depending on the wind, it could get pretty exciting.

As the weather grew warmer, we came into tornado season. One very threatening morning, we were supposed to take a triangular cross-country. One group was to head straight north to a small town, possibly Chickasha, while our group was to fly east to another town, Vernon I believe. From there we were due to cross over the base of the triangle and fly back.

We were amazed that they would send us up in such weather. It was oppressively humid and the sky had a green tinge to it in the north. As soon as our group took off and headed east, we could look to our left and see a line of tornadoes, not huge ones but substantial ones, to the north. Needless to say, the north-bound group never made it. They made forced landings in fields all over the place. Our group made it to our town, but when we came in to land, men from the local flying service were there to grab our wings and keep us on the ground since the wind was already gusting over the flying speed of a Piper Cub, 38 miles per hour. Their comments about the crazy people at Sill were quite explicit.

We finished our course in July and were given leave. The war was over in Europe, a lot of people were home, mostly in transition, and preparing to be shipped to the Pacific. Bartie Harvey was there back from Tarawa and other Marine battles. He was in the same sort of training as I, but in the Marines. We decided to go up flying, hired a plane at Curtiss-Wright Airport on Smith Avenue, and flew over to pay Bartie's mother, Mrs. Harvey, "Iron Pants," a visit at their place on Brightside Road, off Bellona Avenue. She was waiting on the back terrace by the door and waved a towel at us. Bartie took the controls and headed right for her; she hesitated in her waving, then ran into the house and slammed the door. I grabbed the controls from Bartie and we just made it over the roof of the house.

When it was time to return to Sill, I left from National Airport in Washington, D.C. Mr. Harry Baetjer was there, putting Bruce on the plane to go back to Sill. Bruce was a captain and Secretary of the Department of Air Training, one of my superior officers. He chided me about being very chicken shit when I saluted him.

It was a serious time for Mr. Baetjer. His youngest son, Ned, two years older than I, had been killed in China flying with the B-29's. His son Howard, shot down once in Yugoslavia and rescued by Mihaelovic's Partisans, had been shot down again over Hungary and was in a prisoner-of-war camp somewhere. His son, Norman, the eldest, was in a Joint Assault Signal Company, JASCO, in the Pacific. They led the way on the island assaults, directing artillery fire, etc. Norman's wife, Jean, was at the airport with us, as was Miss Rutledge, who had run the Baetjer household for many years, after Mrs. Baetjer died of typhoid in the 1920's.

Bruce Baetjer had had quite a time in Africa. He qualified as a liaison pilot, and then, when they went up to Italy, near Monte Cassino, he was flying a colonel observer on some mission when he and another liaison plane were jumped by six Messerschmidts, Focke-Wulffs, according to Norman Baetjer. The flying sergeant in the other plane saw them first and dived for the ground in the approved fashion, i.e. straight down, turned toward the attacking plane and watching through the Plexiglas top. Bruce was a little behind and the ME's or FW's came in one after another at him. The first five missed, but the sixth riddled the plane. None of the shells hit Bruce or his passenger. Bruce said he called out, "Hold on to your hat, Colonel. We're going to crash!" which they did, in an olive grove. The plane was demolished but they escaped, Bruce with only a nasty gash on his skull.

Meanwhile, the sixth ME or FW had been so intent on shooting Bruce down that he came in too low and crashed into a hillside. Thus Bruce Baetjer, flying an artillery liaison plane, was given official credit for downing a Messerschmidt or FW, for which he received the Silver Star.

We flew back to Sill and had more specialized flight training. We learned to fly sea-planes on the lake, making a circle first to break up the flat water before taking off. We also learned how to take off and land on the Brodie Rig, essentially a clothes line, a long wire to be affixed to the side of a landing craft ("LST") in the invasion of Japan. Attached to the wire was a traveling assembly of wire loops, hanging down like arrester wires on an aircraft carrier. The airplane had a long, extendible hook device on its top that hooked into the wire loops. To take off, the plane was pulled back to the end of the wire, the stick was jammed forward to keep the nose down, the engine was revved full speed while the plane was held back, and then the plane was released. It picked up flying speed going down the wire. The pilot popped open the hook when he reached flying speed, and the plane dropped down and soared away.

The same principles applied on landing. We "dragged" in as close to stalling speed as possible, hooked the wire loops, cut the motor and kept the nose down. It was a strange looking contraption, but it worked. Flying off it in an invasion would have been something else.

July wore on with its heat and turned into August. We had classic thunder storms, one of which gave us hail as large as hen eggs. We had to leave some of the planes out when the storm came up, and the big hail stones went straight through the fabric wings. We used to "dope" these wings in the hangar work shop. I do not remember getting a "high," but in the summer heat they certainly were strong.

We were waiting for orders to go to the Pacific since it was an open secret that we were supposed to invade Japan in the Fall. Iwo Jima had been terrible. Okinawa was, if anything, worse since more people were involved. There were heavy casualties in the navy because of the kamikazes. I cannot vouch for the truth of it, but John Kinder has told me in recent years that Bob Porter, who was in the 77th Division Artillery as a forward observer on Okinawa, called down fire on his own position. John said that someone had told him that you could not mistake Bob's calm, scholarly voice. This was not "friendly fire," by mistake, as often happened in Vietnam, but was deliberately done by a forward observer who was overrun by the enemy. It was part of our training as forward observers.

One morning in early August, as we were getting ready for the day, in our barracks, someone said that they had heard the news that a special sort of bomb had been dropped on Japan. We all sensed something unusual but could not figure it out. We knew that the firebombs had decimated Tokyo, Osaka, Nagoya, and other cities, but this was evidently something completely new. As the day wore on, the news began to trickle in, and we eventually learned that an atomic bomb had been dropped on Hiroshima. Suddenly, absolutely incredulous, we began to realize that this could mean the end of the war and that we would live. It was August 6, 1945. The *New York Times* carried an aerial photo of Hiroshima on its front page a day or so later.

On August 9, the second bomb was dropped on Nagasaki, and we knew that the war was over. The Emperor ordered the Japanese military to surrender, and they agreed on August 14. The formal surrender was held on September 2 on the USS *Missouri* in Tokyo Harbor. General MacArthur declared that "These proceedings are now closed." It had all happened so fast that it was hard to believe. The war was over.

Everything came to a grinding halt while it was decided what to do next. Rumors were rife that we were going to turn on the Russians. Finally we were ordered to proceed to Fort Ord, California, outside Monterey, California. I cannot remember going home on leave probably because all transport was jammed with the war's end and we had just had leave. We arrived at Ord in September to await further orders, and ended up having a delightful time.

Jack O'Donovan, who was married to my cousin, Anna Reeves, was there. He was a major, but, even though I was only a second lieutenant, I regularly went down to Cadamartori's for dinner in Monterey with Jack and his field officer friends. It was a heady time.

Through Bob Porter, when we went to California after OCS, I had met Mr. and Mrs. Arthur Brown and their daughters, Sylvia and Victoria, in Hillsborough (Burlingame). Mr. Brown was a delightful person, a Beaux Arts architect who had designed most of the San Francisco Civic Center, including the Opera House, as well as lots of Stanford University. I reestablished contact there, and, since we were just sitting around Ord waiting for orders, I went up to the Peninsula more and more frequently and squired Sylvia Brown. It couldn't have been more delightful. The Brown house at 808 Irwin Drive was a treasure, filled with Mr. Brown's wonderful library.

We went to the opera, and Mr. Brown took me to the Pacific Union. It reminded me of the Maryland Club. We also did a bit of flying at Ord, and one day I was contouring by plane along the Seventeen Mile Drive. I popped over a little rise and was face-to-face with an automobile. I zoomed up and must have given the driver quite a scare.

9

Occupation of Japan

We finally received orders to move out in October. When we reached our transport in San Francisco, it was the SS *Lurline* of the Matson Line. We went overseas with the West Point graduating class of 1945, ate in the grand salon and had a wonderful trip to Manila, taking about ten days. I still have a mental picture of the albatrosses wheeling behind the stern, following us hour after hour.

At Manila, they trucked us through the city, which was badly smashed up, and took us to a camp at San Fernando del Norte, about 40 miles north. It was warm, but not unpleasantly so. We had tents, adequate showers, etc. The one thing that we were warned not to do was to go into the hills about ten miles away since they were occupied by the Hukbalahaps or "Huks," who were in rebellion and could not be controlled. We avoided the Huks, but did make one excursion over to Clark Field, where we saw literally thousands of planes lined up, most brand new with masking tape still on the windshields.

Many of the West Pointers took a trip to Baguio, since some of them had been there as "army brats" before the war. I enrolled in a good correspondence course, run by the Army. My textbook was Professor Carlton Hayes' big volume on European History, and I was able to make some good use of my time. I used to write papers and send them in. They would come back with comments. When I had to sign off, my unseen instructor was very sad.

Orders came through in about two weeks, and this time a bunch of us were off for Japan. We flew in a C-54 from Manila to Naha, Okinawa. They kept us overnight, and we flew to Japan early the next morning. Fujiyama was a beautiful sight as we neared Tokyo. It seemed unreal after the years of inaccessibility during the war. It had been only a picture on a calendar.

We landed at Atsugi and were driven to the transient officers' quarters in downtown Tokyo. We went to the Officers' Club, and I saw a Red Cross girl across the way, who looked familiar but whom I did not know at that time but now know very well as set forth in detail in a much later chapter. It was Kitty Hoffman, on her way to Hokkaido.

They split our pilot group among the divisions, and I was ordered off with two or three others to the 24th Division Artillery, stationed at Matsuyama, on Shikoku. We went by steam train down the coast. Around Hamamatsu we were allowed to go into the cab of the engine and had a ball shoveling coal into the firebox. The Japanese engineer and fireman must have thought we were crazy, but we had a grand time playing train. We went via Nagoya, Kyoto and Osaka to Takamatsu, where we took a ferry over to Shikoku and then continued by train to Matsuyama. It was a long trip but beautiful. We probably had to take K-or C-rations with us, since Japan was short of food.

Our stay at Matsuyama was short since they had enough pilots in the 24th. The airfield was on the waterfront, near the hotspring baths for which the city was famous.

Someone told me one day to fly over to Kure, across the Inland Sea, to pick up something. I asked for a map and was told I did not need one—stupid!—so they pointed out the direction. As I was winging my way across the Inland Sea, the unforeseen occurred.

A geyser of smoke began to arise from a large naval vessel at anchor and was soon higher than I. Evidently they had started to blow up one of the captured Japanese battleships, possibly the Yamato, since it was huge. I bore off to the left to avoid the smoke. When I reached the main island of Honshu, I realized that I had arrived over Hiroshima, recognizing it from the picture on the front page of the *New York Times* in August. Knowing that Kure was east, I flew in that direction and landed on the end of a huge dock, which was our landing field. It was probably used later to build giant supertankers. The return trip to Matsuyama was mercifully uneventful.

I was next ordered, in early December, to report to the 25th Division Air Section north of Nagoya, near Komaki. This was fortunate since the living conditions in a former Japanese barracks were much more comfortable and away from the city. I roomed with John Harman. Wiley Fancher, Ted Becker and John Mack were also there. We were waited on by Miya and Tatami, and we had young Japanese who served as KP's just to obtain the food. We were across country from Division Artillery headquarters, meaning that we could get away from the "brass" and be informal. We did, however, go over to headquarters for Christmas dinner and other parties and had a good time.

We also had a good Japanese friend, "Richard" Sakamoto, who lived across the road, near Komaki, who took us under his wing, introduced us to some of the locals, took us to Japanese country inns which we were not supposed to frequent and even organized a wild boar hunt in the hills. Fortunately we never saw a boar but had a good outing.

Finding out that I liked to ski, Richard drove with me to Kashiwabara, in the mountains toward Kyoto, where the Chief of Police and/or Mayor was his friend. We stayed in the Mayor's house and went "skiing" the next day. We, of course, did not have proper equipment, but we did work our way part way up the local mountain and generally had a good time.

This in turn led to a frightening experience. I decided to fly back one day to Kashiwabara and buzz the town to show my appreciation to my hosts. All went well until I started to return to Komaki, was leaving the mountains, and the engine began to miss. I did not know that water had seeped into our airplane gasoline from barrels which had been sitting too long. Wiley Fancher had a similar experience and managed to bring his plane home by using the hand-pump fueler. I decided to make a landing on a road, as trained by Fort Sill. There were people, farm carts, bicycles, etc on it. I could not get a clear enough space to land, so I ended up by kicking her over into a rice paddy. She turned upside down, but fortunately I always wore my heavy Air Force-type lap seat belt so was held well in place during the ensuing crash. My only damage was when I undid the seat belt and dropped on my head into the top of the plane.

We had picked up a bit of Japanese during our occupation, so I hitched a ride into the nearest town, near the city of Gifu, and managed to get through the civilian Japanese telephone system to the switchboard at Komaki. They contacted Richard, who in turn came out with Ted Becker and the other pilots to survey the wreckage. Wiley Fancher was particularly delighted since I had smashed up the plane which our newly assigned West Point Commander, Major Nesbitt, had chosen as his own. It had an adjustable-pitch propeller and other refinements not found on our other planes. Before Major Nesbitt left on a long leave stateside, he left strict orders with Ted Becker, who was in charge, that no one was to use his plane except Ted. Fortunately we had all left for the States before the Major returned. When we moved down to the Yamato Valley in the spring, we brought the wreckage with us for the Major's benefit.

In March 1946, they decided to move 25th Division Artillery to Nara. I don't know where the Division Headquarters was, but we wanted to make sure that we steered clear of garrison life with its attendant "chicken shit." The 25th Division formerly, a part of the old Hawaiian Division, had as its insignia a very attractive shoulder patch, a palmetto leaf in red with a yellow lightning bolt in the middle. It was known informally as a "mass of red tape, split by a bolt of chicken shit."

We made a survey of the Nara area, even looking at the small race track outside of town, on which we subsequently landed. But we told Div Arty that it was too small and that we would have to be on a big field, below Tambaichi. I led the advance party in March, and when John Moerls, an old-time NCO converted into an officer, questioned my arrangements, a telephone call to Ted Becker confirming that I was in charge quickly straightened him out.

We settled in comfortably in former Japanese barracks above the airfield. The water heater was a monster which looked as if it would blow up at any minute, but it gave us plenty of hot water, particularly for showers. The neighborhood was vintage rural Japan. We were surrounded by farms. Little old women would bring down great bundles of brushwood from the forests above. The valley was filled with rice paddies around the airfield, and the hillsides were terraced with paddies as high as they would go. Tea bushes were planted on the dividing banks. Later on in the spring the farmers, returning from work, would bring sprigs of azalea, *tsutsugi*, or other flowers. We always bowed politely to each other and said "Konitchiwa" or other suitable greeting. It was a bucolic setting, almost unbelievable with the war only six months behind us.

We had a pleasant life, a bit stultifying I suppose, but almost serene. We flew anywhere we wanted, and did whatever small tasks were assigned to us. We assiduously avoided garrison life.

We flew a regular mail route across the peninsula to Tsu on Nagoya Bay. Overland it would have been a three or four hour journey from Nara, but we hopped over in about twenty-five minutes. Occasionally we took a visiting VIP and that was fun.

Tsu was a former Japanese army cantonment. It was divided into squares with one main street, quite broad, everything of coarse gravel. The camp sloped upward toward the small mountain behind it. The only way to land was from the Bay side, going up hill on the main street. The kicker was that there was a set of electric or telephone wires at the bottom of the street, and to land one had to duck under them. With a passenger it was always fun to feel him tense up as we commenced our approach. Sometimes he would say, "Lieutenant, do you see those wires?" "Yes, sir. We'll go under them." It was too late for the passenger to get out.

Taking off also was fun. The easy way was to start at the uphill end of the main street and take off downhill toward the Bay. But it was more sporting to take off uphill and try to make it over the pass in the mountain without turning. Sometimes we were almost scraping the tree tops with our wheels. We never did this with passengers.

Kyoto was also interesting. We had to fly up there frequently since First, or "I," Corps was headquartered there. Since the city occupied all the usable land between the hills or mountains, we landed in the center of it on the broad walls of the Imperial Palace. This was not as horrendous as it looked since the tops of the walls were broad and level, thirty or forty feet, and were covered with gravel. The walls were sloped outward, with no parapets, and must have been forty or fifty feet above street level. Admittedly, the first landing or takeoff was a bit hairy and of course passengers were quite tense, but we were well trained and soon passed it off as nothing.

Life was given a lift when Bonnie White phoned me from Kobe, where he was stationed in the Signal Corps. As usual he had landed on his feet and was ensconced in a comfortable hotel on the hillside overlooking the harbor. My driver at that time was a Dupont, Maurice, from Pawtucket, Rhode Island not Wilmington so Bonnie welcomed me warmly when I went to visit him. He was living in luxury compared to our Spartan living and Dupont was suitably impressed. Dupont convinced me that we needed a new jeep to replace the contraband one that the Air Section had picked up with a crane off the dock in Manila. Bonnie White said that was easy and told Dupont how to pick one up at the supply depot near him.

I was terrified when we drove past the guard into the huge vehicle depot at Nishinomiya, near Kobe, with row after row of brand new jeeps, command cars, trucks of all kinds. We drove down to the far end of the jeeps; unscrewed the hoods on our old jeep and one of the new ones; Dupont said, "Now, Lieutenant" and we switched the hoods. We drove the new jeep out of its line and backed our old one into it. We drove the new jeep out with the old hood and numbers on it. As the guard saluted, I was frozen with fear. A couple of Bonnie's drinks at the Field Officers' bar helped quiet my nerves.

One day I had a telephone call from one of my flying school classmates, Beverly McVeigh, a VMI "Brother Rat" and a delightful person, asking if I would like to fly to Yokohama with him to "get some parts." This was a euphemism for taking an excursion, and I accepted with alacrity.

Beverly ("Buster") duly arrived at our field in his L-5. Although the weather did not look too good, gray with a lowering sky, we decided to give it a go, particularly since we would be going generally east, with a bit of north. We figured that the weather would be coming in from the west.

We flew across the small mountains of the Tsu peninsula, passed over Nagoya Bay and continued toward Hamamatsu and the other cities of the coast. Instead of getting better as we went east, the weather worsened. We were forced lower and lower. As we flew past Fujiyama, we were down to a few hundred feet and anxiously looked at the Ise Peninsula which juts into the ocean below the Hakone resort area, just east of Fiji and west of

Yokohama and Tokyo. There is a low pass next to the land side and we flew into it. The overcast was below the crest of the ridge. We found ourselves flying into a cul-de-sac. Although we were running low on fuel, we decided we had better turn around and take our chances flying around the coast. This we did with Beverly piloting in the front seat. We had enough room to turn around within the walls of the pass, flew back to the seashore, turned left and flew south along the shore, consisting mostly of cliffs dropping into the sea. We reached the end of the peninsula and turned north along the west shore of Sagami Bay, with the gas gauge sinking lower and lower. When we reached the beaches at the top of the peninsula, we breathed a sigh of relief. We knew that if we suddenly ran out of gas, we could set her down. We made it to Yokohama on "empty" and landed on the air strip in the center of the city. When the ground crew greeted us they said we were lucky. Three A-26's, the hottest twin-engine, single-pilot attack plane, had been flying up the same route that day and crashed in the mountains that we avoided.

I visited my friend, John Kinder, in the First Cavalry Division north of Tokyo. One day when John was duty officer, his commander asked him who this Lieutenant Reeves was. John said I was "weathered in." The Colonel said, "Kinder, there hasn't been a cloud in the sky. Get him out of here."

When Beverly and I flew back home, I piloted in beautiful weather, and we made it to our field on a single tank of gas. I remember that we had the Lalo Symphony playing on the radio as we flew down the coast in the late afternoon. It was beautiful.

The Yamato Valley below Nara is the most historic place in Japan, filled with imperial tombs, key-hole shape hillocks, wooded and surrounded by moats. There are also temples scattered through the valley, a beautiful area. One of our KP's, whom Wiley Fancher wickedly nick-named "Nesbitt" after our regular army Major, was a university student, and he and I took many short trips together.

We would go by jeep to various places in the valley, including the temples in Nara itself. We also flew to neighboring towns.

One day we drove to Yoshino-yama for the cherry blossom festival. It and Arachi-yama, near Kyoto, are the most famous in Japan. I was informally dressed in a flight suit without any insignia. We drove into town and were in a large crowd assembled for the first cherry blossom festival since the war. Some of the Japanese had had quite a bit of *saki* to drink, and Nesby spotted a nice inn-keeper who thought it was better for us to come in from the crowd. We went out on his verandah, to view the large slopes of cherry trees in full blossom. They had been planted by a *daimyo* two or three hundred years ago. It was a beautiful sight.

This was the only time that I had the slightest feeling of unease in Japan and it was understandable on such an occasion. It is a wonder that we did not encounter more resentment. Of course MacArthur sent the combat troops home from Japan as quickly as possible. He knew that they could not forget what they had been through. Sergeant Harriman, of our Air Section, who took care of my planes at Nagoya, and who had been with the 32nd Division through some of the worst fighting coming up the islands, said he could not reconcile himself to the Japanese at that time. We of course had a different attitude since we had never been in combat.

We went to Mass on Sundays in Nara. The building was more like a converted house than a church. If my memory is correct, this cell of Catholicism in Nara had its original roots in the work of St. Francis Xavier. He had come to Nagasaki and had made it as far as "Miyako," Kyoto. Some of his converts had migrated to Nara and had kept the faith for over three hundred years, with no priests to guide them.

During my stay in Japan, I paid a visit to the Sacred Heart Religious Order. I had a letter of introduction from Aunt Eleanor Kenny, Mother's sister, who had been a member of the Order for many years. I cannot remember whether my visit was at their house in Tokyo, or in Takarasuka, near Kobe, but in any event it was fascinating. The nun to whom I talked had been in Japan throughout the war. Toward the end the Japanese moved them for safety to Nagasaki, on Kyushu. They were there when the second atomic bomb dropped. What saved them was that the bomb was a bit off-target, falling behind a small hill, and the blast was deflected. They were covered in glass but not hurt. She talked about it quite matter-of-factly. Later one of their students became the Empress of Japan.

Our numbers to go home began to come up, at last. Ted Becker and some others, who had been in a long time, left for home. The weather became hot as June wore on. Early in July several of us were ordered to the staging area at Yokosuka. Before we left, we said good-bye to our Japanese friends who had worked for us. I still have the letter from Nesby, thanking us for showing him the meaning of democracy. The Occupation opened a whole new world to the Japanese, who had been under the thumb of the military for so long. MacArthur gave them a new Constitution.

After a brief stay in the camp, we were loaded on the *Milford Victory* and sailed from Yokohama for Seattle. Fortunately, I had one bottle of Canadian whiskey left from my Stateside supply. We sipped it each evening on deck before dinner, about a thimbleful each. There were fourteen of us from the Princeton Class of 1945 and Kay Gilpin '44, since we all had the same points and were eligible to go home at the same time. We were in tiers of bunks in the bow. The ship was packed, but we didn't mind. We were fed two meals a day. Off the Aleutians the old tub practically broke down, but we kept up some headway. We had an overcast about 1500 feet up and it was cold. After two days of wallowing we picked up speed and finally made it to Seattle. Our first view of the States was when we entered the Straits of Juan de Fuca in the evening and saw the glaciers and snowfields on the Olympic Peninsula and Vancouver Island lit up by the setting sun.

It was a lovely sight.

We landed, had a day or two in Seattle, were put on a troop train and four days later branched off at Harrisburg, came down through Glencoe and Timonium and were deposited at Fort Meade. We were mustered out. We were civilians again. It was the end of July 1946, and we had been on active service since April 1, 1943. We had been in the Army three years and four months. We were lucky.

Air Section
25th Division Artillery
Yamato Valley, Nara, Japan, April, 1946
(CBR Jr not present –visiting Bonsal White in Kobe, Japan)

10

Return to Princeton

I applied for and was readmitted to Princeton in September. They gave us every conceivable credit since the place was jammed. I was going to room in '79 Hall with Bonnie White, Rufe Barringer and John Kinder, but Kay Gilpin turned up without a room, and I magnanimously offered him my bunk, one of four in a two-room suite. I then moved into a large single room at the top of the fifth entry of 1903 Hall with Brother David. We were lucky since we were "legacies" of the Class of 1903, of which Father was a member. We were far more comfortable than most in post-war Princeton.

I took a variety of courses including Greek and Music, plus Jinks Harbison's "Ren and Ref," Renaissance and Reformation, and others which I cannot remember. Carlos Baker had taken over as my faculty advisor since Asher Hinds, who was the best teacher and mentor I ever had, a father figure to me, had died just before we went into the Army. I wrote my thesis on Hilaire Belloc, not a bad job on re-reading it in recent years. I graduated with honors. I probably should have done better, but Princeton after the war was different than before, and we had been through a lot at a rather tender age.

We took our meals at Ivy. We were short of civilian clothing, notably white shirts. David was able to buy an automobile in the spring of 1947 thanks to Mr. Jack Fassett, a friend of the family, who had a Ford dealership in Philadelphia.

We had one great experience during the football season when we journeyed to Philadelphia for the University of Pennsylvania game. Penn was a 28-point favorite since they had players like Bednarik on the line and Skip Minisi in the backfield, both of whom later went on to star in professional football. We took the special train which had a bar fixed up in something like a box car, simply to give the team support with no hope of victory. To everyone's delight and astonishment, the "Implausible Brats," as Stanley Woodward of the *New York Times* named us, beat Penn 17 to 14. Dick West was the captain, and he and Matt Atkinson from Baltimore were the heroes.

The loudspeakers at the end of the game at Franklin Field warned everyone to stay off the field to protect the turf. We of course ignored them and rushed the goal posts. The mounted police, on horses, came on the field to drive us off, and they did a good job themselves on the turf. The Philadelphia and New York papers were full of it the next day, with pictures of the police riding down the students. We were the heroes of Philadelphia at the parties that night. I don't know how or when we returned to Princeton.

Graduation in June 1947 coincided with the 200th Anniversary of Princeton, and at Harvard General Marshall gave his speech calling for the Marshall Plan. Europe, as well as Japan, was devastated. Father and Aunt Ella came up, and I remember that we lunched with Rufe Barringer and his parents at Ivy. John Kinder's parents and Charlie Allen's father entertained us with a wonderful dinner at the Tow Path Inn in New Hope the night before.

Before the War, I had assumed that I would go into teaching, at least for awhile, since I had done well at school. But the War had broadened our horizons, and I wasn't sure what I wanted to do. Carlos Baker told me about some tests that had been devised by

Gordon Sikes, the rowing coach. They were not aptitude tests as such but designed to match work and life style preferences. To my astonishment I scored in the highest grouping. Mr. Sikes said this indicated that I would be best suited as a lawyer, in advertising, or as president of a manufacturing company. In any event, he advised, get as much education as possible. I was floored. The results and recommendations were completely different from anything I had expected.

A lot of my friends, John Kinder, Paul Funkhouser, Rufe Barringer, et al., with lawyer backgrounds, had applied for law school. I wasn't sure, and I was too late anyway.

Temporizing, I took a delightful automobile trip in the summer through the west with Courtenay and Chilly Jenkins, Peter and Gary Winants and David. We had the Jenkins' old Packard station wagon, Denbigh, and David's new wood-body Ford convertible. The trip was hilarious, out to Lake Forest, where David and I stayed in luxury with the Washburnes, while the others slept on the beach; up through Wisconsin; the Dakotas; Deadwood on Rodeo Night was not to be believed; then out through Montana, the Big Horns, and to Glacier National Park and the Canadian Rockies. David and I took a slightly divergent route since we wanted to do Vancouver and Victoria. We met the others at the St. Francis Hotel in San Francisco. David and I came back via Burlingame, with a visit to the Arthur Browns, Monterey, Salt Lake City, Colorado Springs to see the Mulletts, who went to Canterbury, and home.

It was during this trip that Courtenay and Chilly began calling me "young Sprat." I couldn't figure out what they meant, but then they explained that their mother and father and a small group of friends called my father "Sprat." Its exact origin is mercifully obscured by the mists of time, but, as with Father, it stuck with me. It was widely disseminated by the likes of Mikey Smithwick in the equine field and by others. Some years later, my first boss-to-be,

Nick Shriver, did not like it at all. He didn't consider it dignified enough for an attorney. Tom Washburne, my future law partner, and I dubbed Nick the Chairman of the Committee to Eradicate the Use of the Name "Sprat." Nick never had a chance. It spread world-wide.

I was still up in the air when I returned home. There was a debutante party in September at the Jack Franklins' for Laura, at Hayfields. I ran into Harry Slack's fiancé-to-be, Betty Mellick from Far Hills. She had an excellent suggestion. She and four other girls who had just graduated from Foxcroft were going to the University of Geneva. "Why didn't I join them?"

This seemed like a capital idea. I figured that if I had spent three and a half years at the behest of the Army, there was no reason why I shouldn't take another year at my behest. Looking back from a vantage point of fifty years, thank heaven that I did it. In those days young people did not take off all over the world as they do now. Years later, Aunt Frances said that Aunt Ella disapproved violently. She said it would be demoralizing, as I suppose it was, but it certainly was fun and also fascinating, after my nine months in Japan.

Father was mollified by my being at the University of Geneva. Probably he envied me since he had had a good time in the Air Service in World War I in France, and he and Mother went to Europe at every opportunity.

In any event, I decided to go. I applied to the University of Geneva for admission in the October Term. Around October 15, 1947 Father, Aunt Ella and David, saw me off from LaGuardia Field on a TWA Constellation, similar to the C-54 which we had flown from Manila to Tokyo. I was off on my travels again.

11

WANDERJAHRE—EUROPE

The flight over in 1947 was far different than today. First, planes had not been flying the North Atlantic on a regular basis for all that many years. Fife Symington and his pals at Pan American had pioneered the Clipper routes just before the War ("World War II"). Then, during the War, the Allies began to ferry bombers to England. Teddy Gorman told me that it was a risky business. That is why Gander and Goose Bay bases were built in Newfoundland and Labrador and why Prestwick on the West Coast of Scotland was so important. Ireland was of course off limits to the Allies, particularly the British.

Accordingly we flew from La Guardia in late afternoon to Boston. I phoned Aunt Eleanor at Newton College. We fueled up and then set off for Gander. From Gander we flew to Shannon; then to Paris; and finally to Geneva, arriving about one A.M. the second day.

TWA billeted us at the Hotel Metropole, recently reopened on the Quai des Anglais. It was off season, quiet and most comfortable. A fellow passenger, Seth Bohn, about my age, was put in the same room, and we both fell exhausted into our beds. It had been a long trip.

I quickly established contact with the "girls," probably through the University since I had no idea where they were. It turned out that they were in a comfortable "pension" run by Mme. Florinetti on the Rue Ferdinand Hodler. I stayed on at the Metropole after Seth left for Berne and looked at a number of places before settling for Mlle. Lussy's pension at 14 Boulevard des Tranchées. I arranged to take my dinners at Mme. Guibentif's, a floor above. I had the usual continental breakfast in my room, and we took lunch out on our own. It was a satisfactory arrangement. At our dinner table there was a Swiss girl learning to be a florist, "Mlle. la fleuriste," and an Iranian student, M. Nassipur. Conversation was in French, good practice for me.

Classes at the University did not start until November 1. I bought a good bicycle, so that I could get around. I enrolled at the University, obtained a "carte d' étudiant," signed up for some lectures including M. Bourquin's on international law, and was all set to go.

Meanwhile, the girls, with their chaperone, Nancy Rockefeller's "Aunt Audi" Gratz, took off for Florence. They said to join them. That sounded like a good idea. I had to wait a day or so, to get an Italian visa, and then followed them. Harley Eldridge, from Philadelphia, and I went first to Interlaken, where we put up at the Weisses Kreuz, practically the only hotel open, in the center of town. Harley left for Jungfraujoch the next day, and I took a lovely trip up over the Brunig to Lucerne and then through the Gotthard to Cernobbio on Lake Como. I was going to stay at the Villa d'Este, but it was closed for the season, so I took a local train to Milano.

A young passenger, Michele Costa, befriended me and told me that Milan was crowded for some sort of industrial show. When I could not get a room at the Hotel du Nord, he invited me home to his family's flat. We had dinner at one of the restaurants in the Gran Galleria. It was interesting staying with Michele since his building was still smashed up from the bombing. He and his family were most hospitable, and I kept in touch with him for several years.

I took the train to Florence the next day; ensconced myself in the Savoy with the girls, who, in addition to Nancy, were Mamie Williams from St. Louis; Betty Mellick from Far Hills, who had originally made the suggestion of my joining them; Nancy Thomas from Washington; and Laura Wick, from Youngstown, Ohio. We did the usual touristy things, the Pitti Palace, the Duomo, the Ponte Vecchio, etc., plus dining out in various restaurants. We came back to Geneva after about a week.

Upon arrival at my pension, who should be there to greet me but Bruce Baetjer. Needless to say, this would liven things up a bit. He had taken a room at the Mirabeau Hotel across from the University. Life fell into a pleasant routine. I had classes at the University; Bruce found something to keep himself occupied; we met each evening with the girls at La Clémence on the Bourg du Four to have some *vermouth sec* and eat roasted chestnuts; we all went home to our various places for dinner; and often we would reconvene at La Clémence or some other spot for a quiet evening. Maria, Olga and Angelo at La Clémence took good care of us.

On the weekends Bruce and I would take off on our bicycles for some fairly strenuous touring. One time we left Geneva in a dreary fog, bicycled out to the cable car up Mont Salève, just over the border in France, and emerged into a perfectly beautiful morning at the top—above *la mer de brouillard*. After lunch, we cycled leisurely down to Annecy, which I had heard Father describe after World War I, and cycled back on Sunday.

Another time we took the train around the lake to Montreux, took the Montreux-Oberland Bernois ("MOB") to Mont Bovon; cycled down to Gruyères, where we had a fabulous trout lunch at a restaurant on the old town square; then cycled down to Chatel St. Denis. I went to Mass the next morning, which happened to be Armistice Day, and a Swiss military brass band was playing during the service in the old stone church. The acoustics were fabulous.

Still another time we took the MOB through Gstaad to Saanen, unloaded our bicycles in the evening, and in rain and drizzle slogged toward Saanenmöser. There were plenty of "zimmer zu vermieten" (rooms to rent) but we persevered until finally we reached the Bahnhof Hotel, then run by Frau Susie Wehren, a friend of Field Marshall Montgomery, so the locals informed us, who liked to have English speaking people around.

She gave us a good dinner, with wonderful Swiss puréed spinach. When we awoke in the morning it was cold and crystal clear, and we had a fabulous view of Wildstrubel, Oldenhorn, etc., just like a Swiss calendar.

We cycled down to Boltigen, all downhill, where we were serenaded by a brass band playing at the station. We boarded the train for Zweissimen, where we changed and went on to Interlaken. We cycled around the north side of the Lake of Thun to Beatushohlen, and then took the ski lifts to the top of Beatenberg. It was a glorious day, and we sat in the sun with all the Sunday Swiss, drank *dunkels bier* and ate *bratwurst*. The view across the lake to the giants of the Bernese Oberland was stupendous, Eiger, Monch, Jungfrau and countless other snowy peaks against an azure sky. Little did I know then how well known they would become to me.

A final bicycle trip the next weekend took us by train to Montreux, where we cycled up to the Chateau de Chillon on the lake, visited the Chateau, and then pedaled to Martigny. That part was hard work since there was a strong wind coming down the gorge of the Rhone Valley. We spent the night at Martigny; took the spectacular train ride to Valorcine; crossed the Col du Montets into France; and then had an incredible run downhill to Argentière, with the Chamonix Valley and the Mont Blanc chain of the Alps before us.

We had lunch in a delightful French hotel at Argentière, then cycled down through Chamonix, les Houches and finally to

Cluses, where we put the bicycles on the train and rode back to Geneva. It had been a stupendous trip.

By now it was the end of November. We all celebrated Thanksgiving together. Suddenly the weather changed; it was winter; and that weekend we took our first Swiss ski trip—up to St. Cergues in the Jura. It was simple skiing, but we had a ball. Harry Slack had come over to be with his then-official fiancé, Betty Mellick, and that added greatly to the festivity.

The next weekend we went to Rocher de Naye, above Vevey and Montreux and stayed at a little hotel at Caux. The skiing was spotty but we had a good time and began to get our ski legs. The bicycling had been good training.

The final weekend we went to Villars, at the end of the lake, near Aigle and the end of the Rhone Valley. On Thursday night in Geneva we had put on fancy dress and did the round of festivities in connection with the Escalade, the commemoration of the repulse of the Savoyards by the Genevois. Mère Royaume had dumped a marmite of hot soup on the Savoyards as they tried to scale the city wall by ladder, the "escalade." Bruce and I first took in Rigoletto by the Paris Opera, in French, at the Opera House near the University. The high point was when the audience demanded an encore of "La donn' e mobile" in Italian. It brought down the house.

Bruce had a Gay Nineties uniform, with bowler, and all I could find was a bear suit, the head of which kept shifting and made it difficult to ride a bicycle. I was reduced to looking out one of the ears.

We joined the girls and Harry Slack at La Clémence and took in various parties, particularly the Ball at the Hotel des Bergues. I arrived home very late and then had to catch a train early on Friday morning to Montreux, to pay a call on Miss Luti Pendleton, a friend of the family and Aunt Mildred's sister-in-law. My health was a bit fragile, but I made it for lunch and then left in the afternoon to join some of the group at Bex, en route to Villars. We continued up to Bretaye, La Chamossaire, and found a charming brand-new little hotel, run by a congenial "patron." The next day, Saturday, the rest of the group showed up, and we had good skiing, although the lift did not run until Sunday. Mamie and I went down to Mass at Glion, I by ski with a local. My ski diary reveals a nice trip down, except for an "egg beater" on the outskirts of town. By now we had good powder snow on the mountain.

The next week I arranged to buy a used Peugot 202, through the offices of "Monsieur Allen," an Englishman who lived at Mme. Florinetti's pension and who worked at the Rolls Royce dealership. I paid 5,000 Swiss francs for it, the equivalent of about $1200, at the 1947 rate of 4.25 Swiss francs to the dollar. I took a driving test; obtained my Swiss license; and Bruce and I drove out to Davos, despite the warnings of everyone about the wintry road conditions. We took our time, Christmas shopping along the way, and carrying luggage and skis for the girls. At one place where we had dinner, Bad Ragaz, the locals thought we were part of the American Olympic Team because of the number of skis on the roof of the car. We spent one night in Berne, stopped for a high lunch in Zurich, spent a second night in Sargans, and reached Davos in time for late lunch the third day. Despite the dire predictions, we had no problem driving from Kublis, in the valley, to Wolfgang at the top of the pass between Klosters and Davos.

We checked in at the Parsenn Sport Hotel, run by Hans Fopp, directly across from the Parsennbahn, the funicula to the Weissflujoch, the start of all the major ski runs. Hans greeted us warmly, arranged for us to ski with his brother, Martin, the next day, and we were off to the races. Davos was the big time. We had arrived.

The girls duly showed up with Aunt Audie, as did Harry Slack and also David Clark from New York, who was pursuing Laura Wick. We had a big table in the dining room, and a picture of our

Christmas lunch shows that we also invited some other Americans in the hotel to join us. Bruce and I skied with a guide almost every day and began to improve. One day Anton Pichler decided to take us on the nine-mile run down to Kublis. The weather was questionable, and when we dropped off the back and headed toward Kreuzweg, it socked in, snowing and blowing. We could not see more than ten yards ahead. Toni went ahead from one trail marker, long poles about eight feet high, to another and then called for Bruce and me to come to him separately. The wind was roaring, and if we had not been with a guide, it would have been dangerous. When we arrived at Kreuzweg, about a third of the way down, Toni telephoned to the ski patrol to tell them about the conditions and to advise them to close the run. After we warmed up a bit, we continued, and, after we reached the end of the Derby Schuss, which we skirted, we suddenly came down out of the storm and had a normal descent from there down to Kublis. It was a good experience for us and showed us the danger of the mountains.

We of course regaled the girls with tales of our derring-do, and they insisted on making the trip. This we did two or three days later in beautiful weather. I forget how many hours it took, but we must have set the record for length of time to make the run. We finally reached Kublis, led by the ski patrol with lanterns, in practically pitch dark night. At one place not far above the Schwendi Hut, it took a lot of coaxing to get the girls down one little slope.

We had a grand time at Christmas, taking in Midnight Mass in the little church in Davos Dorf, near our hotel. At the end the congregation sang "Stille Nacht, Heilige Nacht" and there was not a dry eye in the house. We had a Christmas tree, piles of gifts and a big Christmas lunch in the hotel. Afterwards we went down to the ice rink and skated it off.

At New Year's we had another big celebration and ended up at the Chami Bar, which we had opened a few nights before. Soon after New Year's, Dave Clark and Harry Slack departed, and then the girls returned to Geneva. It was a sad time. Bruce and I stayed and skied a lot with Bob Kent and Charlotte King, both good skiers. One day they suggested a cross-country, so we rented some seal skins from the Ettinger Sport Shop, picked up a Belgian friend of Bob and Char's, took the Parsennbahn to Weissflujoch, and then skied down to Langwies. We covered the last part on a commandeered hay wagon that I piloted down an icy track, facing forward, hanging onto the upward-curved runners, and steering with my feet. Mercifully, I lived to tell the tale.

We caught the train from Langwies to Arosa, took the ski lift to Hornli, had a leisurely drink and a bite to eat, then donned the seal skins and climbed the pass which gave us a run down to Tiefencastel. Looking back on it, I wonder if it was not dangerous since I remember years later reading about an avalanche in that area. As I recall, it was quite warm when we skied down the sunny upper snow fields in the afternoon. From Tiefencastel, we caught the train to Filisur, then back to Davos, on the Rhätische Bahn, all of which was included in our ski abonnement. We each had a 30-day pass, which came to about $1.35 a day. No wonder we usually took a long run at the end of each day, so that we could beat the railroad out of more of its money. Many an evening we rode back in pitch darkness from Kublis to Davos, filling the third-class rattler with heart-rending songs like "Rose Climb Up to Her Window."

The Canadian Olympic Team was training in Davos, under Emile Allais, and they became friends. One day they went over to St. Moritz to look over the venue, and Char, Bob, Bruce and I were invited to join them, traveling on our abonnements. These passes were good from Fideris at one end of the Rhatisch railroad, all the way to Scuol' Tarasp, far down the Engadine Valley, almost to the Austrian border.

We took the Corviglia funicula with the Canadians and watched Emile take off on the downhill run in bad visibility with Pierre Jalbert, his best downhiller, immediately behind. Suddenly we saw Emile take a leap and land on a sort of knoll. Pierre, slightly to his left, also leaped but hit the side of the knoll. Unfortunately he had broken his leg. We traversed over to the funicula and finally notified the ski patrol, which came down and loaded Pierre on a toboggan. It was a tough bit of luck and put a cloud over everything.

We separated from the team and called on a friend of Char who had a house on the millionaires' row near the Suvretta Slopes. I suppose that now it is billionaires' row. It was a lovely house with a view of what was going to be the bottom of the Olympic slalom runs.

Bruce and I took the car out of storage in Davos and drove back to Geneva about the middle of January. We tidied things up in Geneva, and then returned to Davos for more skiing. Mamie and Rocky came back for awhile, but their attentions were taken up mostly by their ski instructor, Hans. Also, Bill Douglas and Larry Armour showed up to go to the Olympics. They stayed at the Derby Hotel, near us, and we had a festive time—as well as excellent skiing.

Toward the end of January we trekked over to St. Moritz for the Olympics. Bruce and I and the girls stayed in the Chesa sur l'En, in St. Moritz Bad. Bill and Larry were in St. Moritz Platz. Squab Reed, an older friend of various families, showed up as did Wogs Morgan and Susie Cooper from the Foster Place in Vermont, Dottsy Smith and Ally Pyne from New York and also various Olympic folk, Bruce's friend Knobby Rogers on one of two American ice hockey teams, AAU and AHA; Lew Preston; Alice Kiaer and the American Women's team; so on ad infinitum. Looking back on it, it was close to the real Olympic spirit, commercial and jammed but also informal in many ways, and, above all, sporting.

The opening ceremony and everything else took place out of doors. Barbara Ann Scott led the Canadian team, and Dick Button was one of our leaders. They were the top two figure skaters in the world and received perfect marks. Barbara Ann was more cautious, whereas Dick let it all hang out.

We had great fun with the skiing since we had become friends with many of the Americans and Canadians, as well as some of the Europeans. Unfortunately, Paul Valaer, who was training for Switzerland at Davos and whom we knew, broke his leg on the Derby Schuss and was out of the competition. Parenthetically, Fritz Stäger, my great friend and guide at Lauterbrunnen and Mürren in later years, recently told me that Alfred Stäger, guide and friend, of whom more later, was a regular on the Swiss team but was hurt just before the Games.

At first the Americans were far outclassed, particularly in the downhill, by the Swiss and Austrians. But the American women came on strong and Gretchen Frazier won the gold in the downhill. Andy Mead at age 15 was doing fine, but had a fall in the transition gully in the downhill. Alice Kiaer had hired their own trainer, Walter Hänsli, from Davos, and it paid off.

We had a great time, and I remember the weather and the snow as being just about perfect. One night we gave Bruce a going-away party in the Chesa Veglia and managed to obtain a table in the Grill Room. It was a fabulous evening since we had three musicians, one of whom played the harp and zither and was, I am almost certain, Ernst Nasser of "The Third Man" fame. There were six of us for dinner, and the whole bill came to 272.50 Swiss francs, with tip, which, at $4.25 to the dollar, was $64. The dinner picked up momentum when two of the Norwegian ski team spotted the girls, and, needless to say, the girls did not discourage them. Bruce and I had a hard time protecting our turf. I remember throwing one of the Norwegians out of the horse sleigh on the way home. Also we ran into some of their teammates, obviously

CBR Jr
Meierhoftäli Run — Davos, Switzerland
January, 1948

Mamie Williams (von Gontard), Laura Wick (Howes),
Betty Mellick (Slack), Nancy Rockefeller (McFadden-Copp)
Parsenn, Davos, Switzerland
December, 1947

From left: Laura Wick, CBR Jr, Nancy Thomas (Rees), member Norwegian Olympic team, Nancy Rockefeller, Bruce Baetjer, Mamie Williams, "Arnie"–Norwegian team Going away party for Bruce – Grill Room.
Chesa Veglia – St. Moritz, Switzerland
February, 1948

feeling no pain, doing back flips down a steep snow bank.

We cheered the American ice hockey team, but they did not do well. The final event was the ski jump, below our inn in St. Moritz Bad. It was won by Peter Hugsted from Norway, but Gordy Wren, from Steamboat Springs, whom we had known in Davos, came in fifth, quite a surprise. The closing ceremonies rang down the curtain, and I went back to Davos with what remained of our little band. We had had a great time.

The various racing teams had been invited to St. Anton for the Hannes Schneider Pokol "Cup," the first major ski races in Austria since the war. A lot of us went with them, after obtaining military permits, since the Arlberg was occupied by the French. Our food had to be supplemented from Switzerland since Austria was in bad shape, but shortage of food did not dampen the Austrian hospitality. They put on terrific races. Jack Reddish from Utah surprised everyone by winning the downhill, by virtue of schussing the Osthang. Edi Mall won the combined despite falling at the bridge in the downhill.

The parties in the evening were great fun. The teams and the locals were intermingled. The whole set-up was a bit unusual since the French were our war-time allies and were occupying St. Anton. Their troops had less to eat than the Austrians, a fact which may explain why they shot up all the game, ordinarily so carefully protected and allotted to the hunters. M. le General et Mme. Badois were in Alice Kiaer's flat at the Haus Angelika but somehow it was arranged for them to move. The Austrians had been our war-time enemies but were also our friends through skiing. Hannes Schneider, the founder of modern skiing and the Arlberg Ski School of St. Anton, had been thrown in jail by the Nazis when a ski instructor whom he had fired from the ski school became head gauleiter of the area. Alice Kiaer had put the pressure on Harvey Gibson, head of Manufacturers Trust and Chairman of a consortium of banks holding frozen Nazi assets. Mr. Gibson, who was from North Conway, told the German representatives that they would not even discuss the release of the assets until the Schneider family was safely in Zurich. The son, Herbert Schneider, ended up in the American Army, 10th Mountain Division, as a scout in the Reconnaissance Company with Bill Douglas as fellow scout. Many of the other Austrians, including quite a number from St. Anton, ended up in the United States and the 10th Mountain. So it was a well mixed-up affair.

One evening Herman and Alice Kiaer entertained M. le General et Mme. Badois for dinner at the Post Hotel. Since I was at the University of Geneva, I was put next to Madame, who spoke not one word of English. I struggled manfully with my schoolboy French. Throughout the evening I desperately tried to catch the eye of some of my supposed friends, my fellow diners, but they all skillfully avoided me.

The day after the races, when I awoke in my fifth floor room in the Post Hotel, it was strangely quiet. I realized that the Galzigbahn, the big cable-car lift up the mountain, was not working. When we gathered at the ski school, we were told that a gear was broken. We asked how we were going to get up the mountain. Rudi Matt, the head of ski school, replied, "The same way that we did before the lift was built in 1937." The spoiled young Americans asked, "How?" and were told that they would be taken by truck, there were no buses, up to St. Christoph and then would walk up on seal skins attached to the bottoms of the skis. There were howls of protest, but to no avail. Rudi Matt may have been on the losing side in the war, but he was in charge here and his word was our command.

Pictures in my old ski diary show that the first day I went up with Bill Douglas, Weir Stewart, Hal Gifford and Ottmar Alber as guide. Thereafter I was paired with Lew Preston and his guide, Rudolf Wöhrli. The first day it took us about an hour-and-a-half to climb from St. Christoph to the Galzig, and we arrived

Herman Tschol,
Seppel Fahrner, (hidden),
Herman Kiaer. Saumspitze,
St. Anton-am-Arlberg,
Tirol, Austria, 1948

Below: from left:
Lew Preston, Seppel Fahrner,
Rudolph Wöerli, Herman
Kiaer, Herman Tschol
Wolfagerjoch – En route the
Valluga – Pateriol
in background
St. Anton, February, 1948

Sir Arnold Lunn
Arlberg - Kandahar Races
Chamonix, France
March, 1948

Below: left to right:
Lew Preston, CBR Jr,
Herman and Alice Kiaer–
Langen-am-Arlberg
Vorarlberg, Austria
February, 1948

exhausted. The lift was broken for a week, a blessing in disguise, and the last day Lew and I were determined not to be caught by Rudolf, who had stayed behind to fix something. We made it to the top of the Galzig in thirty-five minutes.

After that we were trained, and the guides took us on most of the area tours. Bill, Weir and I did the Schindlerkar and Mattunjoch, in beautiful conditions of deep powder snow. We would go on foot from the Galzig, past the Ulmer Hutte until the slope became steep, and then we would climb up to the Wolfagerjoch on skins. Another day we climbed the SCA-kopf, now called Gampen and Kapall, ate a sandwich on top and then had a lovely run down in powder.

One morning Wogs Morgan and Suzie Cooper invited me to come with them and their guide, Johann Fahrner, to do the Gampberg, now part of the Rendl ski area. We had a lovely climb of three-and-a-half or four hours, then a beautiful ski down over the powder slopes and a run down the wood road to St. Anton.

The next day, Herman Kiaer asked me to join him on an overnight tour to the Saumspitze. Hermann Tschol and Seppel Fahrner wanted to take him since it is a classic. I was in tip-top shape, about as skinny as a rail, and accepted with pleasure. We left in early afternoon, climbed up the road into the Moos-tal and spent the night at the Moos-tal Hut of the Arlberg Ski Club. Hermann and Seppel fed us well. We left the next morning about eight o'clock and reached the top about noon. The snow was a bit wind-blown on top, but it was a good climb. We had a wonderful view back across the valley to the Galzig and Valluga. In the other direction, it dropped sheer toward the Paznaun-tal and the Montafon-tal and thence into Switzerland. It was a fabulous panorama. We had a long run back down to the hut, with the first slopes very steep. After a short break at the hut, we skied all the way down the Moos-tal to St. Anton.

Our final tour at St. Anton took place on a Sunday. We took

the early lift up to Galzig, probably the eight o'clock, walked up past the Ulmer-hutte, put on the skins and climbed up to Wolfagerjoch, then turned left and traversed the very steep slopes which lead to what is now the top station (not the gipfel) of the Vallugabahn. Hermann Tschol and Seppel Fahrner showed us no mercy since they wanted us across those slopes as early as possible. When it warmed up later, they could be dangerous.

We climbed on skins to a point where the lift station is today. Then we climbed on foot, carrying the skis, up a set of steps cut in the snow to a point on the ridge. As we did so, a group of Austrians, on the peak of the Valluga above us, broke into song with yodels. It was the perfect setting. Pictures show that the guides carried the skis down the first pitch off the ridge, since it was very steep and there were no fixed ropes or steps as there are today.

We put on the skis and had a long, left-handed run, mostly traverse, around the mountain to Zurs, which we passed high above. At this stage of the game, I do not believe that Zurs was open. We kept high on the mountainside and eventually came down to the mouth of the tunnel, traversing the Flexen Pass. My diary reveals that at one point in the dark tunnel we nearly had a head-onner with a horse and sleigh. Through the pass, we came out on the fields and skied down to Stüben. There we had a large champagne-bowler in the Post Hotel, where we were met by Alice Kiaer. From there we skied down to Langen and took the train back to St. Anton.

I returned to Geneva, picked up the car and a day or so later drove with Dodie Post and Lew Preston to Chamonix for the Arlberg-Kandahar races, the first time they had been held in France. The downhill on the Brevent was terrifying, according to the participants. Many racers fell. It was won by James Couttet. The slalom was won by Henri Oreiller, "Rubber Legs," a real character. There was a big closing dinner in the Savoy Hotel, at which

Sir Arnold Lunn spoke in four languages, English, French, German and Italian. Years later Alfred Stäger from Mürren, a member of the Swiss team, and I compared notes. We figured that we sat within a few tables of each other.

Lew and I bade Dodie good-bye from Geneva, and then we had a gala dinner at Le Plat d'Argent, a watering spot near the Bourg du Four, which Bruce and I used to frequent. The next day I saw him off to London to stay with the Lewis Douglases and to squire Sharman around.

I packed at Mlle. Lussy's and took off for Kleine Scheidegg to meet Bill Douglas, Dottsy Smith and Ally Pyne. It was a lovely drive via Interlaken to Grindelwald, where I left the car and took the train to Scheidegg. Again, little did I know how well I would get to know this area in the years to come.

Our guide was Fritz Steuri. He took us on the regular ski runs around the area, and then one day took us up to the Eismeer station on the Jungfraubahn. We walked down the tunnel and came out onto the glacier, where we put on the skis. We had a great run down, in fabulous scenery, stopping to have a bite to eat at the "Fruhstucksplatz." We then skied all the way down to Grund and took the train back up to Scheidegg.

Another day we took the train up to Jungfraujoch, toured the ice palace, had lunch at the hotel, then went down to the glacier, put on the skis and skied down to Concordiaplatz, where all the glaciers meet and the Aletsch Glacier flows down to the Rhone Valley. We put on the skins and had a long leisurely climb up to the Lotschenlucke and the Hollandia Hut. Fritz had brought along Fritz Meyer from the hotel as porter, and they took excellent care of us.

The next morning we left early for the Ebnefluh, probably about six o'clock, and were on top about ten. It was a gorgeous day, and we could see everything from Mont Blanc to the Pennine

Alps, including the Matterhorn, and to the Bernina Gruppe. Fritz told Bill that he could see the Gross Glockner in Austria where Bill had been at Heiligenblut with the 10th Mountain after the war. Closer at hand, I asked Fritz to identify a sharp peak to the north and east and was told that it was the Finsteraarhorn, the highest peak in the Bernese Oberland and a wonderful ski tour in May, one of the highest in Europe. I remembered it twenty-one years later.

It was a bit hard on top, but we had a lovely run back to the hut, had something to eat, and then had a beautiful run down the pass and into the Lotschental, at first powder snow and then spring snow. Fritz went wild with joy. We eventually reached the little towns of Kippel, Blatten and Ried and stopped at one of the wirtschaft to have some wine and to sample Swiss cigars, stumpen. Eventually we ran out of snow and hired a horse and wagon to haul us down to Goppenstein. There we caught the train back through the Lotschberg Tunnel, and went via Kandersteg and Spiez, to Interlaken; thence via Lauterbrunnen to Scheidegg. It was dark when we arrived, and I remember Fritz pointing out the lights of Mürren across the valley as we climbed past Wengen.

From Scheidegg we went around to Zermatt, where I ensconced myself in the Zermatterhof and went down to have dinner at the Mont Cervin with Bob and Lassie Simonds. I was a bit early, and went in to Elsie's Bar to have a drink. A couple sitting at the bar were chatting back and forth with Elsie, and soon we were all engaged in conversation. Then the couple looked at the time and said they had to return to the children. After they left, Elsie asked if I had any idea with whom we were chatting, and I of course said, "No." Elsie informed me that they were Princess Juliana of the Netherlands and Prince Bernhard. Some years later Jeanne van der Valk said that this was what they liked best, to be somewhere unrecognized where they could act naturally. Princess Juliana became Queen that spring.

Bill had tried to engage Otto Furrer as a guide, on his father's recommendation, but he was tied up, so we obtained Emil Perren, a nice man and an excellent mountain guide. We skied all the usual places and then one day we took the Gornergratbahn up to Riffelboden, skied down to a steep, rocky slope, had to take the skis off and carried them down to the glacier. There we put on the skins and climbed up the Theodule Glacier to the Theodule Pass and the Italian frontier. There was a Swiss customs guard on duty but no Italian. Toward the top it became cold and windy. We had something to eat at the top, then had a long lovely ski around the Italian side of the Matterhorn down to Cervinia (Breuil). We put up at the Hotel Alberto Maquinaz, adequate but not up to Swiss standards.

The next morning, March 19, was the Feast of St. Joseph, a holy day of obligation in most of Europe. Emil went to Mass, and I accompanied him. At the Gospel, I was delighted when the priest simply took the Latin missal off the altar, turned around and read the Gospel in Italian to the congregation.

We took the lift to Testa Grigia, a rather long and fragile one, and were each given a little bottle of vermouth as an advertisement. When we reached the top, the wind was blowing a gale, so Emil said it was impossible to do the Breithorn. We therefore took a longer, more leisurely run down over the glaciers and traversed around to Schwarzsee, where we saw the little chapel of Maria zum Schnee and had something to eat. We then traversed farther to the left and came down Staffelalp to the road that runs down to Zmutt. We had snow all the way down until we had to traverse over to Zmutt and the sunny side. There we had to take off the skis and walk down across the fields, filled with crocuses. Our ski season was complete. It had been a wonderful winter.

The next stage was Holy Week in Rome. Easter was early in 1948, March 29, and Bill Douglas, Dottsy Smith and I drove in my car. We put the car on the train in Brig and retrieved it in

Domodossola. From there we drove south and eventually ended up in a delightful little hotel in Bagna di Lucca, not far from Bill's battlefields coming up the Apennines. The next day we traversed Pisa, Livorno and went down the coast. We ended up that evening in Mont' Alto, a dreary place on the coast, and drove into Rome the next morning, putting up at the Eden Hotel. The girls were at the Savoy, and they had engaged Mr. Tortora as guide on the advice of Buddy Trumbull from Boston. He was a great find, very knowledgeable, had worked for Stars and Stripes at the end of the war, and could not have been more pleasant. He took us all over Rome in the daytime. I had a top-drawer ecclesiastical connection in the person of Monsignor William Hemmick from Washington, who had been a great friend of Aunt Nannie's in Paris and also Aunt Ella. He had a lovely flat in the Palazzo Doria, and I took Bill, Dotsy, Wogs Morgan et al. there to cocktails. He clued us in on the various ceremonies and obtained tickets for us for the Pope's Easter Mass in St. Peter's. Rome was a surprising mixture of church-going and social functions. One evening we went to the Villa Taverna, behind the Borghese Gardens, to have cocktails with Ambassador and Mrs. James Dunn, friends of Bill's parents in Chicago.

Bill, Dotsy and I drove down to Naples, did the Amalfi Drive and went over to Capri. Naples was a bit dirty and crowded, but we enjoyed the trip. After we returned to Rome, they departed for Paris, London and then home.

One day before Easter I had bumped into Bob Porter in the middle of St. Peter's by the Pieta. He was down from Oxford with Jim Hester. Both were Rhodes Scholars. After Bill and Dotsy left, I joined Bob and Jim and moved into their "pensione" with them. It was a change of pace from the Hotel Eden but adequate, and it showed me a different facet of Roman life. The first evening was revealing since I started to park my car on the street. The padrone demurred and made me drive it into his courtyard, where it would be safe.

We spent a few more days in Rome, sightseeing with Mr. Tortora, and the last day we had a private audience with the Pope, about 150–200 in our room, lined up around the walls. Jim Hester, son of a Baptist minister and somewhat of a doubter, told us he refused to kneel and kiss the Pope's ring when he came in. Bob and I said "perfectly all right; just shake his hand." When the Pope entered, Pius XII, a very austere and aristocratic figure, Jim was the first person on his knees. The Pope made the usual circuit, speaking briefly to everyone. Jim kissed his ring.

Afterwards we went to Alfredo's and had fettucine and *Frascati*. We started out for Orvieto in the early afternoon in a golden glow. Naturally I relied on my two Rhodes scholar "brains" for the navigation. They failed me miserably. Unable to follow the map, they successively routed me through Terni and Rieti and finally Todi, with Jim Hester singing a refrain about "coming into Todi." We finally reached Orvieto at dusk. It looked like a Pinturicchio, olive gray and diffused with a golden light.

We worked our way north through Siena and Assisi and over to Venice, where we stayed on a side canal. We did the usual sightseeing, but one added touch was attending the Communist political rallies for the coming election. The orator always began with a sweeping "Amici."

I was a bit nervous about the car, since I wanted to have it out of Italy before the election. It was conceivable that Italy would go Communist and there might be trouble. Accordingly, we left Venice in time to reach the border into France. We had a lovely dinner in Alessandro, outside Genoa, a waiter having flagged us down in the street with a napkin. The next day we drove along the Italian Riviera, via San Remo, and crossed over into France at Menthon the day before the election.

We put up at the Hotel Rives d'Azur on the waterfront. Bob and Jim had to return to Oxford, and I established contact with Mme. Guerin, in Monte Carlo. She had been a friend of Aunt

Nannie, while she was in the Sisters of Charity Hospital there, and later Aunt Ella. I stayed on at the Rives d'Azur for a few days, eating dinner at a nice little restaurant on the old town square. I took trips around the neighborhood.

I left Menthon and drove via the Alpes Maritimes and Vercors to Geneva. In Geneva, I stopped at Mlle. Lussy's; then drove on to Paris, stopping at the Moulin des Ruats, near Vézelay. It was gorgeous in the spring, driving through the Burgundy countryside. It was on this trip that I stopped for lunch in a small town at a local bistro and ordered the usual "omelette aux fines herbes, une salade verte, et du vin blanc." They brought me a small cold bottle with no label on it, and when they poured it for me it was sparkling. I thought, "Uh oh. They've spotted me for an American and are sticking me for champagne." I was resigned to it and enjoyed the wine, but when the bill came, the charge for the wine was something like 50 cents. It must have been a local sparkling wine, *vin étincelant*.

I stopped off in Sens to see the cathedral that I remembered from Art & Architecture 202 at Princeton. It was probably a Saturday, since they were hearing confessions, and in those days everyone went to confession. I accordingly did so in French, and when I came to the end, I asked the priest if he would mind if I said the Act of Contrition in English. He replied "Mais non, mon fils. Le bon Dieu comprend toutes les langues—même l'anglais." Hark back to the days when Thomas à Becket stayed there to escape Henry II.

In Paris I stayed with Curtis Cate at his parents' house at 25 Avenue Francois 1er. Shortly after my arrival it was May 8, and we walked to the Etoile to see the V-E Day ceremonies at the Arc de Triomphe. At one point I had to move back and trod on someone's foot. I turned and said, "Pardon. Je m'excuse" and found I was apologizing to Sam Bell, a cousin from Philadelphia and member of the Ivy Club.

On my birthday, May 16th, I invited Laura Wick, the last of the Foxcroft girls to be in Europe, to join me for dinner. We had a drink with her parents at the Lotti or Meurice and then went to the Tour d'Argent for dinner. Princess Elizabeth and Prince Philip were in town on a state visit. On that night they were supposed to be on their own so that they could go out to a restaurant. My fears were confirmed when I drove up to the Quai d'Orsay and found it lined with Daimlers. We went in and said we wanted to go up for dinner, but they said no more guests were being accepted. They gave no reason. I explained that I was not interested in the Prince and Princess but that it was my birthday, and I wanted dinner, to no avail. So Wiggle and I, not amused, decided to try Maxim's.

That was the perfect choice since they and every top restaurant in Paris were hoping that they would be the royal choice, Maxim's particularly on account of Edward VII and shades of "The Merry Widow." When we flounced in and said we had been turned down at La Tour d'Argent, they were just as angry at not being the royal choice. We were ushered in as kindred spirits and were given a wonderful dinner, with most solicitous attention. All this on my 25th birthday! I doubt if I could afford to walk in the front door nowadays.

From Paris I drove to Oxford to visit Bob Porter, proceeding via Amiens and Beauvais and visiting both cathedrals; again memories of Art and Architecture 202. I had dinner at a good restaurant near the cathedral in Amiens, which was still largely in ruins except for the cathedral, and then on to Dunkerque, where I took the midnight ferry, sleeping on a bench. I arrived at Dover and have a very foggy memory of driving up to and through London, down the Mall, and past Buckingham Palace. There was no "ring road" in those days. A policeman, not a "Bobby," flagged me down for a lift as I left London. I let him off in High Wycombe. I don't know if I looked suspicious in my French car with Swiss license plates, but it was nice to have someone to talk to and keep me awake.

I reached the spires of Oxford and went straight to Christ Church, "House," where I was met by Roget and ensconced in the "butler's pantry" in the main quadrangle. I was attended to by a "scout." I had a great time there since it was the week of the "bumping races" and the Pembroke Ball, where Jim Hester lived. Lester Youngblood was very much on the scene as was Nick Katzenbach. I met members of the rugby team, who took me to the Trout, a lovely old inn near Blenheim. Speaking of the latter, one evening we were shooed out of "Hall" as we were drinking our port, since the Duke of Marlborough wanted to come in with surviving members of his Bullingdon Club. We protested to no avail, saying that we were simply carrying on the traditions of His Grace's club in his undergraduate days.

One morning I was summoned to Bob Bates' quarters in Peckwater Quad, since he was on the second floor facing the cathedral. Princess Elizabeth was making a visit. As she walked slowly through with various dignitaries in attendance, suddenly there was a fanfare. Sir Francis Dashwood, a friend of hers, was on the roof blowing a trumpet in her honor. She couldn't resist turning and waving.

One Sunday Father Ronald Knox, one of the famous "converts" to Roman Catholicism, said Mass and gave a brilliant, yet understandable, sermon. That evening he gave a talk, on "Enthusiasms," a discourse far over my head. He was most impressive, the epitome of English scholarship.

Mac Campbell from Baltimore appeared on the scene, and we took a trip through the West Country—Exeter, Winchester, Somerset, Devon, Clovelly, Tintagel, St. Michael's Mount, etc. We also went to Burwell, near New Market, to call on a Colonel and Mrs. O'Callaghan. Mac had a letter of introduction from Mrs. Jack Symington. I had not a clue and simply tagged along. When Mrs. O'Callaghan heard my name, she was a bit puzzled and asked if I were any relation to a Charles Reeves in Baltimore who was a friend of hers. I replied that he was my father. She welcomed me warmly. I suddenly realized who she was when she said she had been Margaret Cottman, the widow of Tom Cottman. They had been fox-hunting friends of Father and Mother's in the old Elkridge and Green Spring days.

Mac and I drove to London and checked in at the Cavendish, on the recommendation of Sam Small. After Mac left, I proceeded to Paris, where I encountered Westy Fenhagen, checked out the Left Bank and ended up at the France et Choiseul, that became my home-away-from-home. Westy was a wonderful guide, showing me around the Place des Vosges, le Marais, the Musée Carnavalet, the Musée Rodin and other places that I would probably have missed.

Somewhere along the line I took a jaunt back to Geneva, possibly to get money sent to my account at the Union de Banques Suisses. On the way, I ignored a little red light on my dashboard, which said "Huile," and shortly thereafter, in the neighborhood of Auxerre or Dijon, there was an ominous clanking. I drove on a short bit to a roadside filling station, i.e. solitary gas pump, and local garage, where the trouble was diagnosed, by what appeared to be a knowledgeable mechanic, as a burned-out bearing.

There was nothing to do but get the thing fixed, and the mechanic did an excellent job. I had to stay two nights in rather spartan quarters and learned how to use the local plumbing, something like a slit trench in army days. The people were most obliging, and the experience turned out to be interesting. I saw a side of rural French life which I would not otherwise have seen.

I returned to Paris in mid-June, since David was arriving for the summer. We were ensconced in rooms Nos. 1 and 42 on the *premier étage*, second floor, of the France et Choiseul and had a sitting room so that we could receive people such as those of Aunt Nannie's group who remained. These included M. Ignace, the Hungarian shoemaker, and Mme. Schirinsky, the Princess who used to vet the refugees for Aunt Nannie. Also we went out to see Mrs. Mathilda Whitridge, at Vineuil-St. Firmin, near Chantilly.

Anne Morgan, "Wogs," appeared again, and one evening we had a delightful joint cocktail party in the reception rooms of M. Derché, the manager-owner and a great friend of Trafford Klots, who insisted that we use them. The party spilled over into the courtyard and was a wonderful mixture of Wog's friends from the Morgan Bank and other acquaintances whom we both had accumulated along the way.

One day shortly after his arrival, David and I were sitting in the Café de la Paix having a glass of wine, and I asked him why he had come over. He said that Father had urged him to. We both wondered whether Father had sent David to bring me home. Then we agreed that if David decided to stay and Father came over to get us both, probably all three of us would have stayed on—indefinitely!

It was a lovely "dolce far niente," "douce faire rien," I suppose, in French. We went often to the races at Longchamps and Auteuil, particularly the latter for the steeplechases. Mac Campbell and I had gone to the Derby at Ascot in June and saw My Love win for Marcel Boussac. David and I went to Longchamps to see the Grand Prix, which My Love also won. In addition, who should be there but Princess Elizabeth in the royal box. We seemed to run into her everywhere. It was very Gallic to hear all the French women around us—for we were just below the royal box—remarking "Mais c'est charmant. Elle est enceinte."

One day we went to Notre Dame. There was an old Sister of Charity sitting quietly at the door with a little basket in her lap for donations. David and I asked her if she had known Aunt Nannie. Her eyes brightened up, and she said, "La soeur Américaine." We also went to 140 rue du Bac, the mother house, and were given a tour. We did not go to 56 rue d'Assas, where Aunt Nannie had had her own little "convent" to take care of her refugees.

We were about to take off on a trip when I was bothered by a hernia and decided to have it taken care of at the American Hospital at Neuilly. They had taken excellent care of Aunt Nannie when she became ill. The hospital could not have been better, and I had a battery of visitors, Bruce Baetjer, Bill Shellman, Peter Wolf (from the Foster Place), Perry Morgan, Wogs, David, et al. I asked them please to be quiet since it especially hurt if I laughed. Of course the inevitable always happened, one smile started a smirk, then a titter, and then an uproar of laughter. Finally, in agony, I begged them to get out. Also, the nurses asked us to be quiet since Georges Bernanos, the famous French Catholic author, was dying, across the hall.

After I left the hospital, Mrs. Whitridge insisted that I visit her for my recuperation. This was a god-send. She had one of the two small chateaux at the foot of the Foret de Chantilly. Her house was on the main street of Vineuil-St. Firmin, but when one drove in off the street through her heavy gate and came around her outbuildings, one was suddenly on the edge of a terrace and lawn which sloped down to a little river and abutted the Foret. At the end of her flower and vegetable garden, there was a locked gate, to which Mrs. Whitridge ("Tilly"—though not to her face) had a key. This led to the far end of the grounds of the Chateau de Chantilly with its waterways by Le Notre. A pond and waterfall were just outside her garden gate.

The Duff Coopers had the corresponding chateau. Tilly had been provided hers through her boyfriend, le Comte Foret-Divonne. It was owned by the Institut de France and rented for a pittance. When she took it over, it was in bad shape, and she did a lot to fix it up, including putting in extra bathrooms, something that the French considered an extravagance.

Mrs. Whitridge had been a good horsewoman and after her divorce from Mr. Horatio Whitridge, went to France to live. She was asked to go out with the Chantilly hunt, which she did. She said that she used to take her own sandwiches with her, and when they stopped for lunch, she would retire to her car and eat alone. Seeing that she was not a "thrusting" American, the French soon took her in, and she was, I believe, the first American to be asked to wear the "tricorne," the three-corned blue hat of the hunt.

During World War II, Tilly remained at Chantilly and was not interned. Shortly thereafter, the hunt was invited down to the Auvergne in southwest France, an area over-run by wild boar. The two masters of the hunt were M. le duc de Noailles and M. le duc de Roualles. Tilly said that they had fabulous hunting but were warned not to leave horseback since the boar were so dangerous. They stayed in wonderful old chateaux, but of course the plumbing facilities would be one "petit coin" at the end of a long hall. It was the "ancien régime."

I had a wonderful recuperation at Chantilly. My bedroom looked out across the lawn and meadows to the Foret. Yvonne would bring my breakfast. Marthe, the cook, was a bit more taciturn but also a character. One day Tilly took me calling on a Mme. de Savigny, who lived near Chantilly in a lovely little tumble-down, overgrown chateau, surrounded by a moat. Her hands were gnarled from years of horseback riding. She was charming. Tilly said she had been a top-notch horsewoman. She reminded me of Miss Fanny McLane at home.

One Sunday Tilly had my friends out for lunch—David, Bruce Baetjer, Perry Morgan, Wogs, Bill Shellman and maybe others. We had cocktails on the terrace, probably with absinthe, and champagne I am sure. The lunch was lovely. I was at one end of the long table. David was at the other, next to Mrs. Whitridge. During the fish course, Mrs. Whitridge asked David when I was going to go to work. At precisely this moment, I had a bone stick in my throat. I began to cough and finally had to leave the room. Mrs. Whitridge asked David what was wrong with me. David very kindly remarked, "Mrs. Whitridge, please don't mention work to

Charles. This always happens to him." Thanks, pal!

Because of my hospitalization, I had to curtail my activities a bit. David took a side trip through Northern France with Peter Wolf and others. Then David and I set forth for England; stayed in London at the Cavendish, where Rosa Lewis confused him with Father from World War I days; and then drove to the O'Callaghans. The Colonel (who was a member of the Jockey Club and a racing steward) took us out to the Downs at daybreak to watch the horses work out. Shades of Dick Francis! It was particularly fascinating to see the strings of top-notch thoroughbreds come out of their stables in single file and slowly parade through the center of town out to the Downs. There was no brooking of any nonsense or cutting up the way American race horses might do.

From there we wended our way up to Scotland via Otterburn on the Border; Edinburgh where the temperature was 89° one day and David in his seersucker suit was looked at on Prince's Street as if he were in his pajamas; Inverness, Garve; and then over to the Kyle of Lochalsh and the Isle of Skye. On the way to Inverness, we crossed from Deeside over the moors, via Tomintoul. Little did I know that 21 years later I would be shooting grouse on Revack, one of the Seafield Estates, outside of Grantown. The road from Tomintoul went past one of the beats, "the Pulpit Beat," which we shot on a fabulous day years later.

When we reached the top of the moor, admiring the view between Balmoral and Tomintoul, we suddenly saw a huge Daimler heave into sight over the crest of the ridge. We rushed back to our car to move it to the side of the narrow road to let the leviathan pass. As we did so the occupants graciously bowed, including one stately elderly lady. We waved back. After they had gone, we both said that the people in the Daimler looked familiar, one of them in particular looking like the (then, 1948) Queen Mother. When we saw the evening papers in Inverness or Garve, we were right. The Royal Family had flown that afternoon to Inverness from London after opening the summer Olympic Games at the White City Stadium. Small world; I seemed to bump into Princess Elizabeth everywhere. I don't think she recognized **me**.

We circled the Isle of Skye, lovely weather, spending one night at a little hotel at Dunvegan, where everyone at Sunday lunch spoke in hushed whispers. The next day, at the northern end of the island, we stopped at a small croft with a sign on the road saying, "Teas." It was about that time, so we drove in. The lady serving us asked if we would like "bacon or ham with our eggs." We were dumbfounded since everything was still tightly rationed on the mainland. The lady explained to us that, even during the war, they had not been rationed since they were so far from everything. I guess they lived on what they had.

We had a similar surprise when we arrived at Sligachan and checked in at the hotel, which is frequented by mountain climbers. There was no limit on whiskey, which again had been tightly rationed elsewhere. We liked the Isle of Skye.

Embarking at Portree, we motored south through the West, Oban, Glasgow, Ayrshire, and Dumfrieshire, lovely country. Eventually we reached Liverpool, which we fled since there was a strike going on and the atmosphere was ugly; then on to Chester, where we stayed.

The next day we stopped for oil and gas at Ross-on-Wye, just over the Welsh border. They had a small pub, in the rear of the filling station. When it closed at three, we stayed in and had sandwiches and beer as "bona fide" visitors.

We drove back through London, stopped at the Cavendish, then to Dover and took the night ferry to Dunkerque. Debarking very early, we espied a small, rather dingy cafe in the town, which was still badly beaten up. But, grubby as it looked, it was France. We had a delicious omelet, and a glass of wine. No question of rationing the eggs, and certainly not the wine!

We checked in at the France et Choiseul. Paris was quiet, since by then it was August. But it was pleasant. We drove to Chartres, a lovely town. Again, Art & Architecture 202 and shades of Bannister Fletcher, the art historian. It was a hot day, and we had a lovely lunch in a restaurant on the second ("premier étage") floor with plenty of wine, after touring the cathedral. We called another old friend of the family, Mrs. Charles (Louise Warfield) Morgan who lived at Beaumont-les-Autels. She said please come and visit since her son, Dicky, was there with two or three girls, who needed entertaining.

We followed directions and, after an hour or so, arrived at the gates of the Chateau d'Oursières. We looked at each other and knew we should not arrive hot and disheveled in grungy tee shirts. Out came the suitcases on the hood of the car, and we did a quick change at the gates. We arrived in good order.

Mrs. Morgan welcomed us warmly and ensconced us in a lovely room. The chateau was small (as chateaux go) but charming, surrounded by lovely fields and woods. Eure-et-Loir, a garden spot of France.

Dicky Morgan was most pleased to see us since he had Chalonge Batsell and two other girls there. We had a wonderful stay. Mrs. Morgan was fascinating since she had stayed there throughout the war. The chateau had been occupied by the Germans, and I later heard from her niece, Barbara Shreve, that the General had fallen in love with her. Toward the end of the war she moved to a small house on the place. After the Americans arrived, the road that ran by her gates was part of the "Red Ball Highway."

From Oursières we drove down through Brittany and Normandy, gorging on the seafood, particularly oysters and lobsters. We visited Mont St. Michel, and had an omelet at Mère Poulard's.

When we came to Vannes, the weather turned bad, and David suggested that we call Trafford and Isabel Klots. I did not know them then, but knew that Father and Aunt Ella were good friends of Isabel's mother, Mrs. Hulings. Isabel said please come, particularly since Jacqueline de Grammont was staying there. We arrived for tea and departed three days later partially because the Peugeot was "en panne" when we tried to leave the first time.

Trafford's father, Alfred Klots, had been a renowned portrait painter, and he had bought the chateau at Rochefort-en-terre as a ruin, pulled down by Richelieu when he was consolidating the hold of Louis XIV on the nobility. Mr. Klots rebuilt one wing, and it was charming, overhanging the town. Trafford also owned the town bar, a lovely little building with a Gothic arched doorway. We went there for drinks.

The chateau had been occupied by the Germans, and when Trafford arrived on the scene in July 1944 with the American army, it was in perfect condition. He left a note, advising that it was owned by an American and welcoming whomever might occupy it. When the advance stalled in the autumn, Trafford returned to find it occupied by the Americans and in a mess, trucks parked on the lawn, etc. He found a sergeant and ordered him to fall the men out at once. He gave them living hell for mistreating the property, and the men were chagrined. They cleaned things up at once.

Time was beginning to run short for David and me, since we were due to fly home from Geneva around mid-September. We did not have enough time to go completely around the south and west of France, so Trafford sent us through the Dordogne—Sarlat, Rocamadour, Gorges du Tarn, etc., a lovely trip. We came out at Avignon and Aix-les-Bains, toured Nimes, etc. Aix was jammed, Churchill visiting, so we camped out. We drove down to Menthon; stayed at the Rives d'Azur; paid a call on Mme. Guerin; toured the hill towns, Eze, etc. and the Corniche; then drove up through the Alpes Maritimes and Haute Savoie to Annecy. We spent two or three days in Geneva getting ready to leave and trying to sell the car, which had certainly been through the wars. Somewhere we took a jaunt through the mountains, driving over the new road through the Susten Pass. We paid a final call on la Clémence, saying good-bye to Maria, Olga and Angelo. I left the car with M. Allen to sell. Father said that I would never see the money, but he was wrong, and I eventually received about $1100, not bad for the amount of use that I had from it.

David and I flew back to New York, and it was thump-bump back to reality. It had been a wonderful year, and I was sadly spoiled.

Law School, University of Virginia, Student Legal Forum, 1951.
Left to right: CBR Jr., Endicott P. Davison, Robert F. Kennedy,
Justice William O. Douglas, Livingston Fairbank, James Slaughter.

12

Law School

When at Geneva, I had talked with Bruce Baetjer about my future, and when he heard about my career-testing at Princeton, he encouraged me to go to law school. I applied at Harvard and Virginia and was accepted at both. I opted for the latter and am glad that I did. It was a pleasant place to get a legal education.

The first year I roomed in a basement apartment with Rufus Barringer, John Kinder and Frank Parker, at Mr. Rimel's, on Oxford Road. We had a good time, and I quickly picked up with Brac Valentine from Richmond and Andy Peck from New York and Princeton. Andy had been on the championship Princeton golf team with Bill Campbell, Jacques Houdry and Dick Nash. Andy and I went over to Hot Springs for a weekend to play golf, and I have been going back ever since.

I also met Teddy Stettinius, a cousin of the Baltimore Stettinii. He was in the College, but not for long. He introduced me to the Middleburg-Warrenton run-and-jump set. Bobby Kennedy turned up in our class, and we became friends. We had a good class, and I had a good time, probably a bit too good, since my marks should have been better and I am afraid I was a bit "demoralized," in Aunt Ella's words, by my "wanderjahre" in Europe. I was thoroughly spoiled.

I had a disastrous first term, but then I pulled myself together, thanks in part to studying with Harry Montgomery from Farmville, Virginia, and by the end of first year managed to pull myself up to about the middle of the class. There I remained for the rest of law school. Bobby Kennedy had about the same marks, and he, too, could have done far better.

In the 1949–1950 school year I moved to Mr. William White's, at Farmington. Brac Valentine from Richmond and I roomed together, and Paul Funkhouser and Henry Valentine were in single rooms in the same wing of the house.

In January 1950, between terms, I went to Sun Valley to ski at Sam Meek's suggestion. We roomed in a sort of dormitory section on the ground floor of the Sun Valley Lodge, near the open-air heated swimming pool. We were the only two in a six-man room, with shower and bathroom facilities across the hall. We paid $6.00 a night.

Sam's mother was in the Lodge with Mrs. Godfrey Rockefeller, Nancy's aunt. Sam's Uncle Mac Mitchell was there, skiing on one leg, having lost the other in the war. We had a jolly group, Lou and Ann Werner, Mamie Williams, Bobby Kennedy and his by-now-fiancé Ethel Skakel, her friend, Courtney Murphy, Jean Kennedy, et al.

The snow was superb, and we had a terrific time. I recall dinners in the Ram, where the food was good. We took a horse-and-sleigh ride and dinner at Trail Creek Lodge. I was in ski class with Les Outz, one of the few holders of the Diamond Sun, who was a top instructor and a nice person. I remember one sparkling morning that I remarked on the cold when I skied off the lift at the top of Baldy. The attendant said it was 35° below zero at the bottom of the lift when I skied on and that it had been 47° below at the stables earlier. There was no wind, but we had to be careful of frost-bite.

When I flew back, I ran into Ed Cudahy on the plane. We had to circle Chicago a long time. When I arrived home I was late for my party at 4406 Greenway for Bonnie White and Molly Brent Johnston, an affair that I was giving jointly with Petie Finney and Dice Waters.

That spring Rufus Barringer asked me to be a member of the Student Legal Forum, a small group that brought speakers to the Law School.

In June 1950 Bobby Kennedy and Ethel Skakel were married. I stayed with Frank Parker in Greenwich. The nuptial Mass was in the Catholic Church in Greenwich and the reception was at the Skakels', including a seated, filet mignon lunch for 750 people.

On June 25, 1950 Shanghai and Emily Goodwin gave a "going away" party at the Farm, "Mill Green," before they left for Europe. Somewhere through the haze we vaguely heard something about Korea. The next day, Sunday, we learned that the North had attacked the South. President Truman quickly committed the United States with the backing of the United Nations.

I felt sick. Here we were at war again after not quite five full years of peace. I had spent three and a half years in the army, and my feeling was that that was enough. Fortunately, I had taken up flying again in the Reserves and was assigned to an active unit in Charlottesville that was not called up. That saved the day for me. I did, however, take the precaution of getting cleared for the CIA so that, if I were called up, I would be doing something interesting. Also, thank heavens that I had not been accepted for helicopter school, for which I had applied as a lark, the same idea as the Army Reserve Mountain Climbing program the year before. If I had been, I would have been snatched up for Korea fast.

In early July I went to Asheville, North Carolina to pick up Aunt Ella, who was visiting Mrs. Johnston, Sr. We did the usual sightseeing, including Biltmore and the George Vanderbilt place, and then had a lovely drive home over the Skyline Drive. We stopped in Roanoke to have dinner with Tom Leas and Kingsley (Houghton).

When I arrived home, I was at loose ends with no plans for the summer. At lunch one day with Father at Miss Minnie's, Mr. Gaylord Clark, one of the regulars at the table, said that I had just missed "Son," i.e., Gaylord, Jr., who had left for Toronto with Key Murray on their way to Timagami to go canoeing. Mr. Clark said he was sure they would like a third.

Somehow I managed to reach Gaylord in Toronto, and arranged to fly up and meet Key and him there. We rendezvoused, took the night train to Timagami, took a boat out to the Bear Island Hudson Bay Post, and were picked up by George Small and taken to the Fisher-Small place on their island, a lovely spot.

We hired two canoes and a Scotch-Indian guide, one John Turner, aged 71. We took a little warm-up, overnight paddle down the lake toward Timagami. The only thing that I can remember is that we started to camp in a site that had been used so often that it was near a huge dump of tin cans. We told John that this would never do and moved.

Next we set out for Lady Evelyn and Florence Lakes and the trout streams. We had a long paddle up the lake from Bear Island, and then had the first of what would turn out to be 42 portages in all. I had a good "tump line" with a large leather forehead plate, and I took pride in humping our canoe over all 42 portages. George Turner usually took the grub box. Key and Gaylord sorted out the other canoe and its load.

We were lucky on the weather, and I recall only one bad period when we had rain for about three days. I also remember one lovely camp at a large waterfall, which had a real whirlpool bath at its bottom, a wonderful cure for tired muscles.

A few miles below Florence Lake we took a detour into an isolated smaller lake, "Dry Lake" according to the map. A group from one of the boys' camps from Timagami was camped near us, but George Turner never breathed a word to them as we paddled off the main route early one morning and then had a rather hairy portage of a few hundred yards into the hidden lake. We paddled down to the end; it was about ten o'clock; and we began to fish. Nothing happened for about half an hour, and then they began to bite, lovely trout about eight or nine inches long, rainbows I believe and native. We had fish constantly on the line for about forty-five minutes, and then just as abruptly they stopped biting. It was some of the loveliest fishing I have ever had, and when we took them back to camp and cooked them, they were delicious.

Toward the end of the trip, as we descended the Sterling River and began to work our way through another series of lakes toward home, we began to run low on food. The last two or three days we subsisted mainly on George's bannock that reminded Key Murray of the shape, size and texture of a Bolton Hill manhole cover. When we returned to Bear Island, Key had definitely had enough and decided to head back to the friendly pavements of Baltimore, enough wilderness for him. Gaylord and I were having the time of our lives, particularly with Key as foil, and our appetites were whetted by George's tales of his youth, of freighter canoes on the Ottawa River, and of ferrying goods down river to Moosenee on James Bay before the ice went out on Hudson Bay. We made arrangements to go north and continue our trip. We had a farewell dinner with Key at the Minnewassee Hotel in Timagami and ate our way through the menu after our diet of bannock. When we had finished, Gaylord went back to the beginning and ate through the whole menu again. Key was aghast.

After a farewell to Key, we took the train to Cochrane, having arranged through the Hudson Bay Company to have two guides sent up from Moosenee, presumably with canoes. We had our own paddles and tump lines. We reached Cochrane on the last train before a strike closed everything down. We had planned to get there before the Indians. One of them was Johnny Smallboy, who had previously guided George and Sam Small. The Smalls warned us not to let him and the other guide get near liquor.

Unfortunately Johnny and the other guide, Abraham Chichou, who lived on the reservation upriver from Moosenee, arrived at Cochrane ahead of us and went straight to the De Gagnés' hotel, noted for serving Indians, with the expected result. Not surprisingly, Johnny and Abraham got into trouble and were thrown in jail. We told the Mounties to keep them there and not let them out until we had lined up canoes because the guides had arrived without them, despite our orders.

It was almost impossible to rent a canoe in Cochrane, and somehow we were referred to a Tac Tasker, who lived with his parents in the bush. He had been in some sort of trouble with the Canadian army and was "holed up." He was sympathetic to us since, as Gaylord reminded me only recently, he had thought that we were fleeing military service because of the Korean War. Otherwise he couldn't understand why Gaylord and I wanted to paddle down the Abitibi and Moose Rivers to James Bay with two Indians. We had to be on the lam.

We inspected the canoe, about a sixteen footer, wooden of course in those days, and arranged to rent her. We assured Tac that we would avoid rapids, even though this was just what we were looking for. He and his father invited us to stay for supper and brought up from the cellar some preserved moose meat, illegal of course, but delicious.

We took the canoe back to town, picked up provisions and went to the jail to get the guides. Unfortunately the Mounties had let them go. I believe De Gagné had bailed them out. We hightailed it around to the hotel, and there they were, slightly drunk, looking sheepish, but able to navigate. We somehow got them out of the hotel, down to the river and the four of us took off in the canoe, terribly cramped, but able to carry us to where the guides said they knew we could get a second canoe. Once in the water they were back in their element, absolute professionals.

We paddled down to the location of the second canoe, a much better one, about eighteen feet, with higher sides. Abraham and Gaylord took over this one and had a lot of the provisions and duffel. Johnny and I had the smaller one that leaked a bit. Abraham patched it with pine tar melted over a fire.

We camped the first night beside the river, and the next day as we were paddling along in placid water, we heard a motor boat approaching us. As it neared, we recognized the DeGagné son, who was about our age, in his twenties. He was angry because the Indians had left without paying. He wanted them to come back with him and pay up, and then, when we declined his demands, he suggested we go ashore and talk it over. I remembered Aunt Ella describing her trip in 1909 with Augusta Poe and Mrs. Murray to Timagami, then the end of the railroad. She was surprised that none of the guides could swim.

Reasonably sure that De Gagné could not swim, I signaled to Gaylord that we would stay in mid-stream for our negotiations. If De Gagné made a false move I had every intention of grabbing him and pulling him into the water. Fortunately we convinced him to go back with the assurance that he would be paid when we returned to Cochrane. This we did, and neither De Gagné, *père or fils*, was in evidence at the hotel when we came back.

Johnny and Abraham were chastened as we continued on our way. I am able to refresh my memory with a large framed map of our trip with dates appropriately entered. I remember portaging around the huge dams at Island Falls and Fraserdale, although the latter is not shown as such on my map. It shows "Abitibi Hydro." Later we hit Coral Rapids, a tricky challenge, now covered by another dam. Then we hit what the map calls "Long Rapids," that George Turner called "Nine Mile Rapids." It was a terrific trip, and we covered 210 miles in seven days. Some of it was lake paddling, particularly above the dams, but most of it was river paddling with long stretches of rapids.

We encountered the most serious rapids at the junction of the Abitibi with the Moose. This was no joke, and Johnny and Abraham looked at it a long time from the bank. It was on the order of the Missouri pouring into the Mississippi, and ordinarily there would have been the safety of the railroad nearby if anything untoward had happened. But the railroad was on strike, and we were on our own.

I don't know what the fall is in feet, but we had hugged the left shore, and the guides decided to shoot the rapids there where the waves were high but the current ran fast and free of obstructions. Johnny and I went first. Once committed there was no turning back. We stretched the tarpaulins over everything—food, i.e. grub boxes, duffel, etc., making ourselves as watertight as possible. As we hit the big swells, the bow, with me in it, plowed through them, and the wave amidships folded over from both sides and then bounced back into the river. I took a couple of solid lap-fulls from the biggest swells.

It was over in a flash, and Johnny skillfully steered us in a curve into the beach. We congratulated each other and signaled Abraham and Gaylord to come through. This they did in excellent fashion and were soon beside us on the beach. It was fascinating to see them race through with white water washing over the tarps. We bailed the canoes, and we must have had four to six inches of water in each.

We camped one more night on the banks of the Moose and then had an uneventful paddle down to Moose Factory. We rigged up tarps as sails to use the following wind to propel us. We reached Moose Factory, where Gaylord and I put up at the small hotel run by the Hudson Bay Company. Johnny went to his house and Abraham stayed with him before returning to the reservation. One day we went by motorboat with the guides down to the mouth of Moose River at James Bay and set up a blind with clumps-of-mud-and-toilet-paper decoys to watch the geese, then beginning to congregate for the autumn migration.

It had been a terrific trip fraught with some excitement and danger. We left the big canoe for Abraham to return to its owner. By then, the railroad strike had ended, and we took the train back to Cochrane, left Tac's canoe with a nice present for him and his father, paid off the De Gagné hotel, bade good-bye to the Mounties who were highly amused about our encounter on the river with De Gagné, and took the train back to Timagami, Bear Island, and the Smalls where we told our tales of adventure and derring-do.

I picked up the third year of Law School, rooming with Tom Washburne and Humpy Schock (from St. Louis) in a little rented house across from Fry's Springs. Jack O'Mara (Omar) from Cincinnati joined us for dinner. Our faithful factotum was Gladys, who hated cold weather and could regularly be found on winter mornings with her head in the oven. She couldn't understand our names, Mr. Washed-bird, Mr. Humpy and Mr. Sprat.

One morning Gladys called in late. Tom had to go down and bail her out of jail. When he asked what had happened, she said, "Me and my lady friend had a disagreement, so I buss (*sic*) her in de mouf." Gladys was sizable, so she must have sent her friend sprawling.

As the fall wore on, the U.S. and U.N. forces in Korea pushed above the 38th parallel under MacArthur. Some of our forces advanced north to the Chongin Reservoir. Then like a thunderclap, the Chinese army came in, overrunning everything. Our forces reeled back. Joe Huesman, a lawyer from Baltimore, whom I later knew quite well, was in the Marines and was at the Reservoir. They had a terrible retreat in the snow and ice.

Aunt Ella had said that she would like to go to Rome for the end of Holy Year 1950. It sounded like a good idea and we decided to make a tour by air, first to Paris to see Aunt Nannie's old friends, then to Rome for the Holy Year festivities, then return via Madrid and Lisbon, which had just opened up for tourists. Miss Einstein, formerly of Raymond Whitcomb and then at American Express, made all the arrangements. She was a superb, old-time travel agent.

At Thanksgiving, with all the arrangements made, we were at Aunt Ella's house, 4404 Sedgwick Road for dinner one night, and had a counsel of war as to whether or not to go. Father and Edith were there. We decided to, Chinese or no. By this time, the U.N. and U.S. troops had been pushed back to a tiny perimeter around Pusan, far in the south.

We took a BOAC (British Overseas Airway Company) Stratocruiser from New York to London and on to Paris. We put up at the France et Choiseul. Mrs. Deedie Massie, who had worked for Aunt Nannie and later for Miss Anne Morgan's relief work in Northern France, came from Vic-sur-Aisne. We had lunch at Prunier's.

We went out one day to "Tilly" Whitridge's, where I had a fine time seeing Marthe and Yvonne again. Young Dallas Johnson, Mrs. W's grandson, about six years old, was also there. His "argot" French was "formidable."

One day, the concierge phoned our rooms and said that "la Comtesse de Bouillé" was downstairs. I rushed down and started to struggle with my schoolboy and University of Geneva French. She said, "That's all right, Charles, I am your Aunt Ella's friend Daisy Polk from San Francisco." I breathed a sigh of relief. She had worked for Aunt Nannie and had married a Frenchman. Several years later, I was talking to Sylvia Brown and she said, "Oh, Aunt Daisy." We also saw the Princess Schirinsky and Monsieur Ignace, both wonderful people, in very different ways. M. Ignace was a well-educated Hungarian shoemaker who had fled Hungary after World War I to escape the Communists. For details on the Princess Schirinsky, see the Section entitled "Warfield Fund."

From Paris we flew to Rome on Alitalia. The view of the Alps was spectacular, a beautiful day. They also served a very good hot lunch. In Rome, we stayed at the Hotel Eden. We contacted Msgr. Hemmick, who was delighted to see Aunt Ella again. We went to his flat in the Palazzo Doria. We met his friend, young Charles Grace, who was traveling with his priest.

We attended the various services and events that were still done in the old style, Pope brought in on the sedia gestatoria, wildly cheering crowds, etc. Msgr. Hemmick provided us good seats in the tribune for Christmas Mass in St. Peter's. We had Christmas lunch at the hotel. I surprised Aunt Ella with a Christmas stocking, since she had always given one to Baker, David and me. We even brought over "The Night Before Christmas" to read, something which we always did in her room as children.

We flew to Madrid on December 26, staying at the Ritz. We contacted David's and my friend from Princeton, Peter Schultz. His father had been in our fathers' class. Peter spoke beautiful Spanish; natives thought he might be from the Canary Islands. He was studying at the University of Madrid. One night Peter and I went out to try the new green wine, known as corriente. When we were at El Escorial the next day, freezing cold with ice on all the fountains, I would gladly have crawled into one of the royal sarcophagi, if I had been strong enough to move the lid. At Aunt Ella's suggestion that evening at Lhardi's, reminiscent of Irvin's in the old days in Baltimore, a nice dry martini fixed me up beautifully.

One evening we took Peter and his friends Pepe Gallastro and "Gonzalo" to dinner at the Jockey. We had a cocktail, dinner, wine, cigar, brandy, all for about $20 for six persons. I hate to think what it would cost today.

One day we went to Toledo, and Peter Schultz had us detour into Illescas to see the church and the paintings that El Greco had done there to thank the nuns for care given him. Our guide had his nose a bit out of joint since he did not know about it, but afterwards I am sure he took his tourists there.

We left on December 30 for Lisbon, staying at the Aviz Hotel at my suggestion since I had recently read about it in *Life* Magazine. It was beautiful. Aunt Ella and I had a suite, which I believe was Nubar Gulbenkian's. We had an entrance hall, a sitting room and then each of us had a large bedroom, dressing room and bath. On New Year's Eve at the table next to us was old Calouste Gulbenkian, "Mr. Five Percent," reputedly the richest man in the world. He was alone, and I twitted Aunt Ella about being nice to him so that the family would be fixed for generations. She spurned the idea, but the next evening, after dinner, she told the waiter to put the cork back in her bottled water so that she could have it the following night. When I upbraided her for trying to save about three cents, her reply was, "If Mr. Gulbenkian can do it, I can do it."

One day we drove out to Fatima, via the Cathedral at Batalha. We had a car and driver and a guide, Mr. Wrangell, who was very religious. Fatima was, fortunately, deserted and we paid a call on one of the surviving three "children" to whom the Virgin Mary had appeared in 1917. She looked about 80 but was probably only about 55, based on her age at the date of the apparitions.

We took a trip to Cintra and to Queluz Palace, which is pink and white. If I had to be royalty and live in a palace, Queluz would be my choice. It seemed livable. We flew home January 5, in time for me to return to law school. It had been a fabulous trip, rather unusual for those days in being a seventeen day trip around Europe, all by airplane.

In the Legal Forum, we had brought in Livingston (Livy) Fairbank; Endicott Peabody (Cottie) Davison an Eli friend of Zandy Harvey; Jim Slaughter, who personally and through his family's foundation has subsequently given millions to the Law School; and Bobby Kennedy. We decided to make Bobby President because of his connections, and I became Secretary. In 1950–1951 we had a superb year, thanks to Bobby's ability to get outstanding speakers.

Recently, the Law School has sent me a list of our speakers, and after a lapse of 40 years, I find that some of my recollections differ from theirs. Thurman Arnold spoke on "Why the McCarran Bill and Loyalty Checks are a Bad Idea." Seth Richardson, Chairman of the Subversive Activities Control Board, which never amounted to much, spoke for that bill and loyalty checks. Supreme Court Justice William O. Douglas, "Willo," spoke on the Court and its problems. After this speech, we had our picture taken with him.

The future President of the United States, John F. ("Jack") Kennedy, then a U.S. Senator, gave a speech on European Defenses. It was a good talk and, of course, presented with characteristic charm. Arthur Krock of the *New York Times* and Bob Blair's step-father spoke on Major Issues in the National Election. Frank Folsom, President of RCA, spoke on Business and the Defense Effort in April 1951.

Bobby's father, Joseph P. Kennedy, spoke just before we left for Christmas vacation in December 1950. As aforesaid, the Korean War had started on June 25, 1950, and the Chinese Army attacked across the Yalu River in November, quickly overrunning the peninsula and forcing the United Nations forces to the Pusan perimeter. It was a grim time.

Mr. Kennedy made himself charming but he gave an isolationist speech, urging us to "cut and run" in Korea. This was reminiscent of his urging Great Britain to throw in the towel and capitulate to Hitler before World War II, when he was U.S. Ambassador to the Court of St. James. Franklin Roosevelt had recalled him at once.

His speech created an uproar that was quickly dubbed the "Great Debate." I left shortly thereafter with Aunt Ella for our flying tour of Europe. Everywhere we went the newspapers were full of the Kennedy speech. The Student Legal Forum was "on the map."

I remember that Abba Eban, Israel's Ambassador (Delegate) to the United Nations, gave an excellent and sensitive speech on the status of Israel. The list which the Law School recently gave me says that he was on a panel with Selim Harper, Chief Turkish Delegate to the U.N. and James Landis, former U.S. Envoy to the Middle East, as Moderator. I don't remember these latter two.

In the spring, Senator Joseph McCarthy gave a speech. As I recall he was rather temperate and did not make any of his wild claims. We went back to Bobby and Ethel's house on Cameron Road after the speech, and Joe McCarthy made himself quite agreeable. At that stage of the game, he was chummy with the Kennedys and had stayed with them at Hyannisport. Later, they disavowed him as he became wilder and wilder in his accusations. His topic to us was "The World-Wide Communist Conspiracy."

There was one speaker whom I particularly remember, not necessarily because of the content of his speech but because of the circumstances surrounding it. Bobby Kennedy one day had asked me, "What would you think of inviting Ralph Bunche to speak?" I thought for a split second, recalling my Aunt Ella's admiration for Mrs. Eleanor Roosevelt's efforts on behalf of the Negro race, and said, "I think it would be fine." We discussed the matter at length, consulting I am sure with the other members of the Forum, and probably also with Dean Ribble for the Law School and with the University administration. The invitation was issued and accepted.

Mr. Bunche was then United States Ambassador to the United Nations and a wonderful person. We had dinner at Bobby and Ethel's house. During dinner, I asked Tom Washburne, a new Forum member, of the Class of 1952, if he would go over to check the auditorium in Clark Hall (then the Law School) to see if everything was in order. He had not been gone long when the phone rang. It was Tom, saying, "Charlie, we've got problems." I feared some sort of protest, but it was the opposite. Tom said, "We can't stay here in Clark Hall. The auditorium is packed and people are still pouring in." Then he said that they had arranged to move over to the big University auditorium, Cabell Hall.

When we arrived it was jammed. Mr. Bunche gave a good speech on "Why Isolationism is Bad for the United States." At the end, he received a standing ovation. It was a heartwarming occasion and did the Student Legal Forum proud. One must remember that this was in the days of segregation in the South, including Virginia.

A few days before the mid-winter break in late January 1951, I telephoned Bruce Baetjer, who was in Landscape Architecture School at Harvard, and asked if he would like to go skiing in Aspen. Catching him without warning was the best thing to do, and he readily assented. I made all the arrangements and told him to meet me on an appointed day at National Airport in Washington. He later told me that he called up his father's office and had one of the firm's messengers bring him some money at Penn Station. He said he calculated how much he would probably need for the trip, and then, since he was traveling with me, doubled it.

We flew to Stapleton Field in Denver, which was then a small airport, caught an overnight bus to Glenwood Springs and then on to Aspen. We stayed in a flat at the brand-new Four-Plex of the Jerome Hotel. We went skiing that day. That evening, obviously tired, we had a quiet dinner at the Four Seasons Club, that John Kinder and I had frequented in the Summer of 1949.

We had a nice dinner and took a taxi back to town. When the taxi driver heard us talking about being tired and going straight to bed, he said, "Ridiculous. You boys should go to the Fraternal Order of Eagles. They're having a big party." Our arms were easily twisted, and I am glad that they were since we had a priceless evening and met every character in town.

About the third day it clouded over, and that night it began to snow. It continued all night, through the next day and then the next night. We had close to three feet of new snow, and when I went up the lift the morning that it cleared, it was like skiing on feathers. At the bottom of Ruthie's Run I could point my skis straight down the fall line and had no trouble turning. That was "Colorado champagne powder."

We had a wonderful time. Aspen was a small place, and we came to know everyone. Nina Paepcke, whose father had re-discovered and re-vitalized Aspen as a ski resort, and later as a cultural center with the Aspen Institute, was married to Leonard Wood, Wogs Morgan's cousin. Steve Knowlton of the 1948 St. Moritz Olympics was there touting his new restaurant, the Golden Horn. When we learned that his chef Guido was Swiss, we had him make us a fondue. Later Steve passed out handbills in the town advertising Sunday February 11 as "Baetjer-Reeves Fondue Night at the Golden Horn."

Botts Alexander from Princeton '44 showed up, as did Bobby Flanagan, Peter '45's younger brother; a Coolidge couple from Boston, whom Bruce knew; et al. We gave a cocktail party in our flat, a howling success, particularly at that altitude, with martinis.

Since it was Lent, I used to walk to early Mass and often followed Mrs. Gary Cooper and her daughter, Maria, who was about 12 and lanky like a young colt. Eero and Eliel Saraanen, the famous Finnish architects were in one of the four-plexes; as was Thornton Wilder. We bought prints of a painting by Herbert Bayer, one of the original Bauhaus set in Germany, an Aspen resident. In the ski fraternity I met Fred and Ellie Iselin. She was always twitting me about searching out scraps of powder snow. We also met Friedel Pfeiffer, whom Mr. Paepcke brought over from St. Anton and who made a fortune in real estate, according to Benno Rybiszka years later.

One day Steve Knowlton appeared at the bottom of the

mountain on a pair of shiny, silvery metal skis. We asked Steve what in heaven they were, and he said not to laugh at them, that they turned fantastically in powder snow and, incidentally, that they were made in our home town, Baltimore, by a man named Howard Head. Bruce and I visited his shop in the 1100 block of Morton's Alley after we returned home. After I started the practice of law, Bruce and I made him a proposition when he decided to raise money, but unfortunately he obtained his financing elsewhere. Howard and I ran into each other from time to time for many years. He was an inventive genius who revolutionized the manufacture of skis from wood to metal and eventually to "plastic." He did the same with tennis rackets.

Some time in the spring of 1951 a notice appeared on the bulletin board at Law School stating that Cross and Shriver, i.e., Nicholas Shriver, a Johns Hopkins friend of Baker Clotworthy, was looking for an associate. He had one other person with him, Jay Bright, Mr. Eben Cross having died. I responded, and after talking to some of the other firms, decided to take the job. Looking back on it from a vantage point of 48 years, it was fortuitous. I would not have traded that experience for anything. Nick was a hard taskmaster but fair and treated his associates well. He was an excellent teacher.

Bruce Baetjer and I had planned a final trip before I put my nose to the grindstone. We had booked passage to Europe after I took the Maryland State Bar Exams in July, going over on the Nieuw Amsterdam and returning on the Ile de France, the two best ships on the Atlantic. When I told Nick, in typical fashion he said "No," that he needed me right away and that is why he had hired me. In those days one did not set one's own terms, so I meekly assented to ten days vacation after the Bar Exams and canceled our reservations. I did, however, ask one concession. If I came to work right away, could I take my vacation in winter? Nick agreed, and that was one of the saving things of my life. It meant that I could keep on skiing on a regular basis.

I took my final exams and then took the cram course given by Hyman and Isidore Ginsberg for the Maryland State Bar Examinations. David Green, who had a job with Venable, Baetjer and Howard, John Mudd with Semmes, Bowen & Semmes, Joe Young with one of the predecessor firms of Piper & Marbury, and I would join for supper about 5 P.M. in the cafeteria of the Southern Hotel and then go up to the old University of Baltimore building on Howard Street, opposite the Stanley Theater. The sessions lasted from 6:30 to 10:30 P.M. There was no air conditioning in those days; the clang of the trolley cars came in with the general din and the heat; but the Ginsbergs managed to outshout it all.

It was a scene out of Dickens. I feverishly took down everything in my notes, whether or not I understood it at the time. Thus, one night a Ginsberg was bellowing about the "Bolivar Rule." I couldn't make much sense out of it since the only Bolivar that I knew was a cigar that Bruce Baetjer and I used to smoke at La Clémence in Geneva. When I pored over my notes the next day in my office at Cross and Shriver, I suddenly realized that it was the "Boulevard Rule," governing automobile traffic.

As luck would have it, Teddy Stettinius was due to be married at the end of June, right in the middle of the Bar Review course. He had asked me to be best man. His twin bothers, Joe and Wallace, Hugh O'Donovan, et al. were ushers. Kitty Douglas, later to marry Nick Brady, who became Secretary of the Treasury under George Bush, was maid of honor. It was quite a wedding. The nights which I would miss, Friday and Saturday, were Real Estate, probably the most complicated, if not most important, segment of the cram course. I was panicky and asked Dave Green if he would take carbon copy notes, which he most graciously did. They saved my life. Each day I studied nearly the entire day in Cross and Shriver, going over all the notes and also looking up the reports of the cases cited. In retrospect, I wish that I had studied as diligently in law school.

The Bar exams were given in early July, and I did not try to cram the night before. I had done all of my studying in advance. I may even have gone to a movie, as classically recommended. The exams were held in a large room above the old Richmond Market on Howard Street at Read. The room was well ventilated and not hot. The exams lasted two days, and the only specific that I can remember was the real estate section. This called for an answer involving a case entitled *Auer v. Penn.* David Green had taken the case down in his notes, and I had carefully reviewed it. In any event, being well prepared, I finished early, did not second-guess any answers and left before the period ended. There was no point in hanging around and messing things up. In some ways it was reminiscent of College Board exams, the Army AGCT test and some of Mr. Mack's history exams at Canterbury, in all of which, being under pressure, I did well. Whether it showed any intelligence or not, I do not know. In any event, I suppose that I was good at what they now call "test taking." I must have been able to spot what the examiner wanted, and quickly. This had been true of my cramming at Canterbury for mid-year exams in my senior year after having two extra weeks skiing at St. Sauveur. That put me under the guns. Also, I will never forget a Classics exam at Princeton when I overslept, ran up to McCosh Hall and did a three-hour exam in one-and-a-half hours, coming out with a one-minus (1-).

I took my ten day leave by driving up with Aunt Ella, Randi and Georgette Clotworthy to Essex, New York to stay at our cousins', the Tiers', on Lake Champlain. We had a fine time, and Morrie Klick and his wife, Teter (Tiers), were there. Morrie was a lovely person whom Teter had met in the Army in Germany after the war. It was a tragedy that both of them died young. They both had a delightful sense of humor.

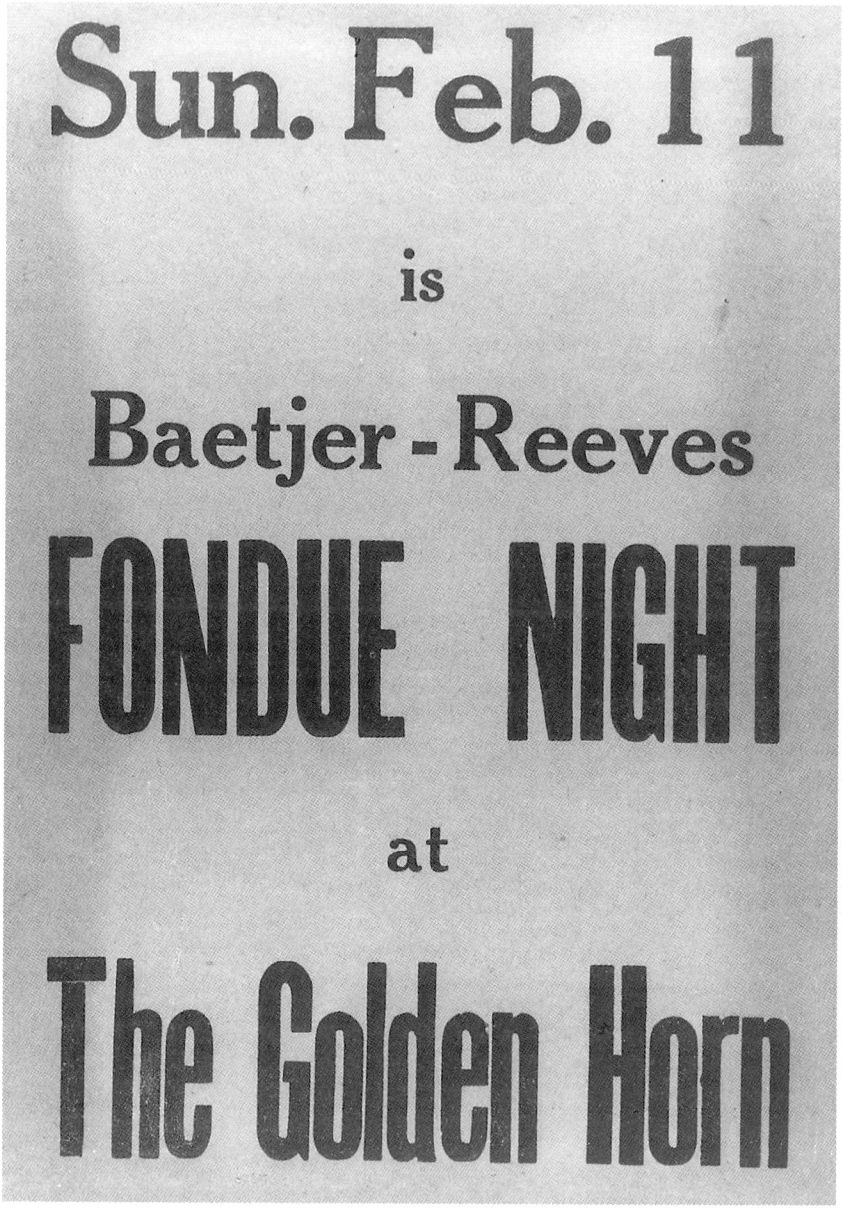

Handbill circulated in Aspen, Colorado by Steve Knowlton, ski racer 1948 Olympics and owner of the Golden Horn. February, 1951

13

CROSS AND SHRIVER

We drove back to Baltimore, and I went to work on July 21. We were on the sixth floor of the old Mercantile Building, on Calvert Street at Baltimore, across from Alex. Brown & Sons. There was no air conditioning. When the temperature reached 90°, it was almost impossible to work, with the papers sticking to one's perspiring arms.

Nick's first assignment was for me to go to Washington to look up the estate of Gertrude Lanahan Welker, who had recently died. She was the last life beneficiary of a trust established by her father, Samuel J. Lanahan in 1858. She had no will, and I eventually ended up with a monumental "trust construction" task, unraveling the devolution and inheritance of Mr. Lanahan's nine children. The trust of Catherine C. (Kate Carroll) Lanahan, one of the children, was a nightmare, one that I unraveled in the dusty files of the Circuit Court of Baltimore County in Towson.

Pending the publication of the results of the Bar exam in November, I was on a temporary salary of $35.00 a week. I lived at Aunt Ella's at 4404 Sedgwick Road. Most of my clothes and belongings were at 4406 Greenway. Gertrude Saunders, who had been with Aunt Ella since 1903, the year that Father graduated from Princeton, took care of us. I dined frequently at 4406 with Father and Edith.

It was hot that summer, particularly at the end of August, and I was delighted when Howard and Bruce Baetjer suggested that I join them at Fisher's Island for the Labor Day weekend. Howard and I flew up in the Mathieson Corporation's DC-3, at Tom Nichols' invitation, since it was going to pick him up at Southampton. We asked the pilot to make a quick tour of Fisher's so that we could show off to our friends before we landed at the air strip by the old fort. We stayed at the "Big Club," played golf, swam, took in all the parties and had a generally delightful time. Maggie Hillman and Dick Purnell were there. On Monday night we went down to Rennie (Reynolds) DuPont's for a drink and then boarded Rennie's yacht, the Goddess, for New London, where we took the "sleeper" for Wilmington, Baltimore, etc. This was a pleasant respite, to say the least, living very high on the hog.

It was a pleasant life in Baltimore. I saw a lot of Bonnie and Molly Brent White, Cuppy and Rosalie Fenwick, Bruce Baetjer, Howard and Kitty Baetjer, swam often at Norman and Jean Baetjer's, played golf at Green Spring, etc.

One day in November, out of the blue, came a letter from the State Bar Examiners. I can't remember whether I was apprehensive or not. The passing grade in those days was 210. My mark was 242. I compared grades with John Mudd, Notes Editor of the Law Review. He had 245. Dave Green, also on the Law Review, had 239. I was stunned.

One of my extra curricular activities was duck shooting, which I had done since boyhood with Father, first at Miss Mary Thom's Blakeford on the east bank of the Chester River on the Maryland Eastern Shore and later at the Philadelphia Club on East Neck Island. I also shot with Eddie Johnston at his father's place on East Neck Island. Eddie's sister, Molly Brent, who married Bonnie White, inherited the place, and I was invited down. The first trip was in late November or early December 1951, in the days before the Chesapeake Bay bridges. I remember a long drive complicated by a dusting of snow and a glaze of ice which had Baltimore in grid-lock just as I was leaving the office to drive around the head of the Bay. I managed to drive only as far as the Little Inn, run by Frances and Jean Gilmor, opposite Hopkins Hospital. I had dinner there, and afterwards things improved. I arrived at the ducking shore at 11 P.M.

Mr. Ed Shea, Mollie Brent's father-in-law at that time, was there, and he had a rough time in the blind the next day since it was cold and windy and spray was freezing over everything. But living at the Lodge made up for any discomfort in the ducking blinds since it was a long, low building, built by Mr. Johnston in the 1930's with all the comforts, including Beatrice as cook, Emmons as butler and "Splint," Maurice Downey, as head guide. Bernard Hepburn served as assistant. Splint and Amos Waterfield, who had served as guide at Miss Thom's and later at Cedar Point, next door to Molly Brent's, were the deans of the duck guiding community.

As winter approached, I had a lot of work with Nick Shriver including litigation. I had arranged with Bruce Baetjer to go to the Winter Olympics in Oslo and then down to Davos for a few days skiing, two weeks in all. I was terrified to mention my plans to Nick, but things kept falling into place, including finishing the litigation with only a few days to go. I summoned up my nerve, asked Nick if I could speak with him and reminded him of his consent to have me take my vacation in winter. He harrumphed his assent and asked me where I was going, probably expecting something like a long weekend at Wisp in Western Maryland or a few days in New England. When I said that Bruce Baetjer and I were going to the Winter Olympics in Oslo, he was speechless. Actually, I think he took vicarious pleasure in it since he asked me to give his friend, Henry Marx, a lawyer in New York, a telephone call as we passed through. Also when a client called for me while I was away, she later told me that Nick seemed to take pleasure in saying that I was in Oslo at the Olympics.

The Olympics themselves were great fun, very much like St. Moritz, smaller and more intimate than today, with no strict security. We stayed in a private house since we had been told that all the hotels were booked solid, which they weren't. It was better to stay in a house to see how the Norwegians lived at home. I liked that big Norwegian breakfast with herring and yett ost, a goat cheese that looked like a bar of old fashioned, yellow laundry soap. One night we had a lovely dinner at Henry's in the Continental Hotel, reminiscent of an English club, on the second floor. I had seen some herring that looked pretty "high." The waiter sought to dissuade me, but Bruce said, "He'll eat anything," and I did. It was delicious, probably like an extreme form of gravalox.

We paid a call on a friend of Emily Goodwin's from Vassar, Fanny Hoeg. The family had finished dinner in the late afternoon as it was growing dark, about four o'clock, and they had the first corner-set open fireplace, under a metal hood, which I had seen.

Andy Mead, whom we had known in 1948 at St. Moritz, St. Anton and Chamonix, won two gold medals in the skiing. Then we went to the men's downhill, quite a way out of town, at Norefjell. It was so informal that we walked down along the bottom portion of the course through the forest. One S-turn was quite difficult. The great hero was Stein Erikson, who won several golds.

After this race, as we were about to enter our car, driven by our chauffeur Johannsen, Bruce turned to a stranger standing nearby to find out the time. Bruce asked, "Do you speak any English?" The man replied, "A little." Bruce asked the time, and we departed. As soon as we were in the car, I said rather truculently, "Bruce, do you have any idea whom you asked for the time?" When Bruce replied "No," I said "Bruce, that was Gary Cooper." I had recognized him from Aspen. When he answered Bruce, his voice could have come right out of one of his movies, that nonchalant drawl.

We took in the ski-jumping at Holmenkollen, the mecca of jumping, on the outskirts of Oslo. We went to Bislett Stadium, outdoors, in the city to watch Hjalmar Andersen, "Jallis," a great national hero in speed skating. It was thrilling to hear the crowd, as he was skating to win a gold medal, chant in unison with his skating—"Hup, Jallis—Hup, Jallis."

We flew to Zurich, took the train to Davos, stayed at the Parsenn Sporthotel and had several days of good skiing. The two weeks came to an end too quickly, and I flew back to Cross and Shriver. But the precedent had been established, and skiing continued to play an important part in my life. I remember one year that I said to Walter Buck, my doctor, that I was so busy that I did not think I could get away. Walter said, "You have to, especially if you work for someone like Nick."

CBR Jr.
Portrait, 1996
by Elizabeth Byrd Mitchell

Ludwig Schweiger, Skiführer, and CBR Jr.
Mattunjoch, St. Anton-am-Arlberg, Tirol, Austria.
Photo taken by William Canby, circa 1986. (Used as background for portrait)

14

Special Interests

Here I will leave the strictly chronological format since the general stage is now set, within the framework of the practice of law. This commenced in July 1951, and finished with my retirement at the end of 1993. It has continued with a sort of coda from 1994 onwards, since I still have an office at Venable, Baetjer and Howard.

Skiing

Skiing has meant a tremendous amount to me throughout my life. I have met many friends, worldwide, through it and have been to many wonderful places because of it, from Europe to New Zealand.

I often wonder how I happened to pick it up, living in Baltimore. The hard winters which we had in the 1930's were probably a big factor, possibly also the Winter Olympics at Lake Placid in 1932. In any event, I bought my first pair of skis in approximately 1933. They are still in the attic, about four feet long with toe straps, impossible to turn on. My first ski mountain was the Sunken Gardens, across Charles Street from Bedford Square. We would start on Mr. DeMuth's lawn, coast down through his hedge and end up at the bottom, a vertical drop of about thirty feet. It was here that I saw my first snow plow turn, done by Clark Barrett, a counselor at Camp Wallula and a student at Dartmouth, who lived on Whitfield Road.

I graduated to the Whedbee's Hill on Lake Avenue, still in my toe straps. The run down the front hill was no problem since there was a wide runout at the bottom, like a ski jump. Here I marveled as Palmer Futcher, with a Canadian background, made a series of linked snow plow or stem turns.

The Whedbees' back hill was a different situation, since it was steep and there were wire fences at the bottom. It was turn or else. Manly Jenkins had a pair of skis with real bindings. He could turn. I don't know how I managed to keep from hitting the fence.

In 1939 Zandy Harvey and I went to Lake Placid, but we put on skis only a few times since most of the action was on the ice rink at the Club with the school and college hockey tournaments. Then in 1940 Mrs. Crimmins, "Ethel," told Father that she was taking her sons, Tom and Hugh, to St. Sauveur for skiing and asked me to come along. This was my introduction to "real" skiing.

St. Sauveur, about fifty miles north of Montreal, in the Laurentians, was a small town with practically no automobiles. I took the night sleeper from Baltimore, the Montrealer; changed in Montreal early in the morning; and caught the Laurentian (or Laurentide) to Piedmont. There one took a horse-drawn sleigh over the hill to St. Sauveur to the house run by the Duke and Duchess of Leuchtenberg, refugees from the Russian Revolution and the Bolsheviks.

The sleigh drivers loved to play a joke when they picked up people obviously going to the Duke's, e.g., New Yorkers swathed in furs. The guests would ask to be taken to "Monsieur le Duc." The driver would drive to the famous Pub, across the street from the church and a couple of doors from the Leuchtenbergs'. If the passengers did not know the correct house, the driver would stop since the Pub was owned and run by one "Monsieur Leduc." This caused some consternation since the Pub was a bit grungy. When the visitors looked puzzled at being taken to such a place, the driver would say, "Oh, you mean M. le **Duc**" and would drive on a few doors to the Duke's.

I bunked in the basement in a dormitory next to the ski room. Two of my roommates were Bill Woolverton, later my Battery Commander at Fort Bragg, and a friend of his, Fred Griswold. Other guests included Morrie Shepherd, the ski artist; Betty Dumaine, from Boston; Bill and Fred Rockefeller and their sister, Elsie; Elliott Richardson, later the hero of President Nixon's "Saturday Night Massacre," with his father, a nurse, and two brothers; Patty Moore, who married Serge Gagarin; and other emigré Russian friends of the Duke and Duchess.

The skiing was on rope tows on Hills 69, 70 and 71. The Duke struggled for years building a T-Bar on the Marquis' Hill, which only occasionally worked. The weather was wretched, warm with rain, but we had parties, including a fancy-dress one at New Years. Then it turned bitterly cold and snowed. Tom had to get back to Exeter, but just as Hugh and I were due to leave, the news leaked out that someone in the house had contracted measles and we were "quarantined." To this day I do not for certain know if that was true or a guileful scheme of Mrs. Crimmins'. Whatever the case, it was fortuitous that Hugh, at least, had this extra vacation. A few years later Tom died of wounds on Okinawa as a marine lieutenant and Hugh disappeared over the English Channel as a P-51 fighter pilot. They died within a short time of each other, and the plaques of remembrance hang in Johns Hopkins Hospital.

We had fabulous skiing. One night the temperature fell to -35° Fahrenheit. Late one afternoon Hugh and I skied back against the wind from Hill 70 with the temperature at 10 below. I returned to Canterbury, two weeks' late, just before mid-year exams. I was sunburned and people were puzzled.

I skied two more years at St. Sauveur, and in 1943 George Small and I went from there for a few days at Mont Tremblant with Boy and Amy Wickes, Kitty Wickes and Carrie Brooks Johnston. On the way back, George and I left the train at St. Adele and skied down the Maple Leaf Trail to Chiriotto's, where the Duchess and her daughters, Irina and Elena, met us for dinner. We took a sleigh ride home.

That was the end of skiing until after World War II, with the exception of one day's effort at Kashiwabara in Japan, after which I cracked up the Major's airplane, as hereinabove set forth.

One evening in January 1947, in a break between terms at Princeton, I ran into Bill Douglas at the Nassau Tavern. He had been through the war with the 10th Mountain Division. Herbert Schneider, son of Hannes Schneider, the founder of modern skiing at St. Anton, had been his fellow scout in the Reconnaissance Platoon. Bill suggested that we take a few days skiing at North Conway, the home of the Schneiders. I readily assented since I had had a pair of ski boots custom made by the Tirol Shoe Company in Montreal, for $32, and I had bought a snappy ski outfit from Abercrombie & Fitch.

We left at midnight in Bill's car and arrived at 9:30 A.M., as ski school was meeting. Bill took his mountain climbing ice axe and rope out of his car and walked on his crampons to Mr. Schneider ("Hannes," although he was always "Mr. Schneider" to me) at the ski school meeting place. Everything was covered by New England sheet ice. Hannes was delighted.

We took a room at Mabel and Otto Tschol's. I went to ski school and learned the Arlberg technique. We had a delightful time, a lot of which we spent at the Schneiders' with Hannes, Herbert and Herta. Mrs. Schneider had died not long after they had arrived in the States from St. Anton in 1938. Hannes told us many tales of the early days of St. Anton and of his experiences in the Austrian mountain troops on the Italian front, near the

Ortler, Konigspitze, et al., in World War I.

I remember one incident which typified what a gentleman Hannes Schneider was. I came in to Mass at North Conway just before it began and Mr. Schneider was already seated. The church was full; he saw me; and, despite my protests, insisted that I take his seat, since I was the guest. I never dreamed that the next winter I would be skiing in St. Anton.

After my first winter vacation in 1952, I arranged to meet Bruce in Davos in February 1953. He was in Rome at the American Academy, but after the snow fell, he could be found in the Alps. After we had been at Davos a few days, I told him that this was not what I had come for since the place was full of friends from New York and there was a party every night. I had come for skiing. Accordingly we hired Peter Ettinger, a mountain guide, and took off across the mountains for St. Anton.

We took a horse sleigh from Davos to Durboden and then climbed on seal skins to the Grialetsch Hut. Peter went at a blistering pace. I took it easy in the afternoon while Bruce, Peter and George Artamanenko, a Canadian whom Bruce invited, took a subsidiary climb up the Grialetschhorn. That evening at the hut was fantastic since there was a full moon which lit up the glaciers like midday. It was an incredible scene looking over the peaks and glaciers into the Engadine.

The next day we skied down to a valley where the glaciers met and then climbed up the Sarsura Glacier to the Piz Sarsura. From the peak, we had a beautiful run down over the glacier in settled powder snow a long way until we reached the forest, after which we followed a road down into the Engadine and reached the main highway between Susch and Zernez. There Peter had a taxi waiting for us, which took us to Guarda, a beautiful little town above the main valley. That night the townspeople had a party in our hotel, lasting till all hours with dancing, from children to old people. The night was February 28–March 1, and many years later I read in the *New York Times* Travel Section that this was the celebration of Kalenda März which is held only in the Engadine and neighboring Romansch and Ladenisch speaking valleys marking the beginning of the end of winter. It goes back to pre-Christian days.

The next morning there was not a soul stirring as we left about eight o'clock on skis and began a long toiling climb up the Val Tuoi toward the pass, between the two Iamspitze, on the Austrian frontier. The valley was facing south and felt like an oven as the sun rose high. I did not think I would make it, but toward the top, when I thought that I had reached my limit, Peter enticed me to come up to him and gave me a piece of sugar soaked in brandy. I vaulted up the last few yards.

At the top we climbed one of the little spitze and then descended the Austrian side to the Iamtalhütte, the oldest mountain hut in Austria, a huge one, built about 1888. The snow was windpacked, but we made it down. We left early the next morning; skied down to Galtur* in the Paznauntal; I rode in a horse sleigh to Seinisjoch to rest my legs; then we climbed up to the Neueheilbrunner Hut, where we had lunch about two o'clock. We left about three, had a short additional climb, then had a long ski down the Schonferwall to the Ferwalltal, passing the Pateriol on our right. When we hit the forest it was tough going, because the trail was negligible. But somehow we made it and reached St. Anton about six o'clock in pitch darkness.

Since Herta Schneider had no room at the Schneider Haus, we put up at Herta's cousin's, Haus Lina, and sent Peter back to St. Anton the next day. He was a good, old-time guide. His pace was fast, and we accused him of taking the round-about way through Guarda so that he could buy a cow, but I would not have had it any other way. It was a ski tour. Before I left St. Anton, I joined

* Galtur is the town that was hit by avalanches in 1999. 28 people died. I was in St. Anton at the time, as noted hereinafter.

the Ski Club Arlberg, founded in 1901, the oldest in the world. I used Alice Kiaer and Rudi Matt as my sponsors.

Fifteen years later Franz Fahrner saw that I was awarded the silver medal of the SCA and then some time in the early 1980's, I was awarded the gold, of which I am very proud. "Ich bin ganz stolz darauf" in Tiroler deutsch. When I received the gold, Franz sternly admonished, "Charlie, when you go to Switzerland with this medal you have to ski well. Otherwise, you will ruin our reputation. No murxing!"—i.e., sloppy skiing.

The next year in late February, 1954, after Emily Goodwin's wedding to Phil Kemp, I met Bruce at St. Anton. We had a few days training, and then we set off for the Ötztal with Schani Bombardelli from Landeck, who taught in the ski school at St. Anton and was a first-rate mountain guide. He spoke almost no English, so we made out in German and Italian. We took the train to Imst, a bus to Zwiesselstein and then to Obergurgl, where we spent the night. The next day we climbed up to the Neuekarlsruhe Hut, where we stopped for lunch and a view of the glacier, then climbed up to the Hochwildehaus, that was full of Germans. The facilities were filthy, for which the Germans were known in those days.

From there we had a long climb up to the Miederjoch and then a long ski down to the Samoar-hutte, the old Hermann Goering Hut, in the days of the Deutsche-Osterreiche Ski Verein. There we were very comfortable, they called it a "Hotel" and we even had a shower. The snow was beautiful, about six or eight inches of new powder over the glaciers.

We climbed the Hintere Schwärze, 3636 meters, on a beautiful day. The last part, up the gipfel, was quite steep over the rocks. Bruce said he did not like the height, but he made it, and we had a fantastic long glacier ski back down to the hut in the powder snow.

One day, when the weather was bad, a Sunday, we climbed up the Similaun Glacier to the Similaun Hut, just over the border into Italy. The glacier was covered with a pea-soup fog. We christened it the "Vino Rosso Abfahrt" since the skiers, German and Austrian, came hurtling down the glacier from the hut, singing, yodeling and taking crashing falls. They were not hurt because they were full of good Italian red wine. We had a good lunch in the Similaun Hut, were smitten with the fair Annie who served us and even took a climb part way up the Similaun after lunch at the insistence of some of the Germans, with Schani leading the way. The ski back to the Similaun Hut was hilarious. I took a slow-motion fall as I came out of a graceful turn. The location of this climb and run must have been close to where "Ötzi," the 7,000 year old man, was found a few years ago.

After most of the Germans had departed, we prevailed upon the *hutten-wirt* to play the zither for us. It was beautiful. He was Italian by nationality but a true Sud-tiroler, blond and blue-eyed.

The next morning we started about seven o'clock in beautiful weather and climbed to the top of the Similaun with lovely snow. We skied back to the hut, had a good breakfast, picked up the rucksacks and skied down into another valley. From there we had a long climb up to the Hochjoch Hospiz, where we had lunch. It was then about three o'clock and Schani asked us if we could do some more and make it up to the Vernagthütte. We asked how the climb was, and he said "immer eben," "always even," not "level" we later found out. Thinking he meant fairly flat, we started out and ended up with a grueling three-hour, quite steep climb. We kept exclaiming "immer eben!" with appropriate epithets but we finally made it to the hut just before seven. With time out for meals, we had been almost continuously on skis for nearly twelve hours. It was the longest ski day I have ever had, but we were fit, and survived.

There was reason in Schani's madness, because he saw that the

Bruce Baetjer and CBR Jr
Lech-am-Arlberg
Austria, 1954

Below:
Sandra Malfatti and CBR Jr
St. Anton, Austria
1954

CBR Jr and Benno Rybizka
St. Anton, Austria
March, 1957

Below: left to right:
Herbert Matt,
Anna Davidson (Thompson),
CBR Jr
St. Anton, Austria
February, 1957

weather was changing and wanted to have us in a position to do the Wildspitze, the highest peak in the Otztaler Alpen, in good conditions, the next day. It was a wonderful climb up, including the gipfel, and then a lovely powder snow run down. We did not go on to the Braun-schweiger Hut at Schani's recommendation but returned to the Vernagt Hut. We had a celebration that night with red wine. The next day we skied down to Vend in fog and bad conditions. Schani had been right on the money.

We returned to St. Anton. Looking at my old diary, I see a picture of Sandra Malfatti, from Rome, and me in my Austrian garb taken in the Post Hotel Keller, the night spot. Sandra sent a copy to her father, the Baron, who was something high in the Knights of Malta, and he was alarmed that Sandra had fallen in love with a ski instructor.

The next year, 1955, Bruce and I again hired Schani, this time to take us to the Ortler Group in Italy. At Landeck we took a bus over the Reschen Pass, where the last fighting of World War II took place between the Germans and Italian guerrillas, down into Mals and then up to Solda, near the Stelvio Pass. Aunt Ella somehow negotiated the latter before the war in a Daimler with Mrs. Johnston, Senior, chauffeur-driven of course.

It was gorgeous scenery, and every time we stopped we were besieged by the locals who implored us to tell our President that they, the South Tirol, whom Woodrow Wilson had given to Italy after World War I, wanted to be back with Austria. I hear today that they are not so insistent.

The next day we started for the mountains, taking the road part way from Solda, then climbed on skins to the Rifugio Città di Milano and on to the Casati Hut, between the Monte Cevedale and the Königsspitze (Gran Zebru). For some reason Schani took it easy in the afternoon and told Bruce and me to go ahead and climb the Cevedale, which we did. It was a big rolling glacier with apparently no crevasses.

The next morning we set out early for the Königsspitze, since it was according to Schani "eine echte berg," a real mountain. It was here, as we left the hut in the cold early morning, that an incident occurred that Bruce never let me forget. On these mountain tours when one is climbing, it is quite warm and one nearly always takes off one's gloves. But a descent is cold and naturally gloves are de rigeur. I did not know what the drill called for that day on leaving the hut, whether we would begin with a climb or have a ski down at first. Therefore in all innocence I turned to Schani at the door of the hut and asked him if I should put on my gloves. Something must have snapped in Bruce because he turned on me quite fiercely and said, "For Christ's sweet sake, Sprat, don't you know whether your goddam hands are hot or cold? Do you have to ask the guide?" It was no use trying to explain.

We did start with quite a long run down, and I did have my gloves on. Then we climbed on skins up the flank of the mountain. It finally became so steep that we took the skis off on the side of the summit ridge. We then climbed on foot to the top. Schani had us on the rope, and I was glad of the additional safety. Bruce did not particularly like the height but he persevered gamely. The view on top was spectacular, particularly over to the Ortler, a few meters higher and looking grim with its cliffs and rock faces.

In 1956 I came over earlier to St. Anton, at the end of January, since Bruce and I had made plans to go to Cortina d'Ampezzo to see the Winter Olympics. Just before we left St. Anton, we were skiing with Benno Rybizka in his "special group." It was the first full year of the new cable car to the top of the Valluga, a mountain which previously we had to climb on skins. We had had a two day snowstorm, and to our surprise they opened the upper section of the lift to the Valluga in the afternoon. On the way up I said to Benno that I did not like the looks of the snow. It seemed windblown and unsettled. Benno agreed. I asked him which run he intended to take us down. He said "Mattunjoch," a choice that surprised me since it is very steep, very open and prone to avalanches. He said it should be the safest.

We had a fantastic run down, deep powder without a track on it, but I was apprehensive all the way down. When we finally reached the Steissbachtal, the main run down a valley to St. Anton, an instructor came streaking down the valley and shouted something to Benno. When I asked Benno what was up, he said "Avalanche" and took off at top speed. The instructor was Walter Poehl, a close friend of Franz Fahrner. He had a ski school class and had taken them out on the steep slopes to the left below Walfagehrjoch, the Schindler "hänge" that we had pioneered with Benno. When we crossed them, we went one at a time. Walter had taken his class across, two or three went down the slopes to the bottom and then the avalanche came down from one of the gullies to the right of Walfagehrjoch, looking up. The class was buried and four or five died, including one American girl. Toni Marth and other ski instructors who arrived on the scene first dug several out. It cast a pall over St. Anton, and we were glad to get away to Cortina.

Margaret Crawford from Australia had been invited by Bruce Baetjer to go with us, and at first I was not pleased since we had made our plans a year earlier. But, as it turned out, Margaret made the trip. We took the train to Innsbruck, changed to the diner over the Brenner Pass and had such a high old Tirolean lunch with red wine that we had to leap off the diner at Fortezza, race back to our carriage and pull the luggage off in the nick of time. Bruce and I were well ensconced at the Albergo Francheschi and fortunately Margaret found accommodations at what she called the "dog doctor's," i.e., the veterinarian's. She found Alfred Stäger from Mürren, who was training Denis Feron, the only Belgian in the Winter Olympics. We had what we called the Belgian training table at the Hotel Flora and had such a generally jovial time that they arranged a bank of potted palms around us to protect the other guests.

We took in the various skiing events, of which Toni Sailer from Kitzbühel was the star, "the blitz from Kitz." He took golds in slalom, giant slalom and downhill. Bruce and I also haunted the beautiful outdoor ice rink that fitted in with the towering Dolomites behind it. The American and Canadian ice hockey teams knocked each other out and the Russians, who were making their first-ever appearance in the Olympics, went on to win the gold. The Russians were a pleasure to watch with their fast skating, precision-passing and generally clean play.

When we returned to St. Anton, it was still subdued. It was also cold, since a Siberian front had come down. One day it was -22° Celsius at the top, and we had to be careful of frostbite.

In 1957 I went to St. Anton alone since Bruce had succumbed to matrimony and his wife, Mimi, did not ski. That was "the" social winter. All the hohheiten, "highnesses," descended on St. Anton en masse. I said that one had to have sixteen quarterings on one's shield to be allowed to say at the Schneider Haus. Charlie and Adelaide Luxembourg were there, with their cousin, Christa d'Aosta, the granddaughter of Victor Emmanuel of Italy, plus the Württemberg princesses and various lesser nobility. Wonnie Hohenlohe was Charlie Lux's pal, and they had quite a coterie of friends who kept the Gasthof Poste in an uproar at dinner. When we asked Ludwig, the headwaiter, why he permitted such carryings-on, his remark, with respect to Wonnie, was, with a shrug of the shoulders, "Ach! Der Prinz!" Wonnie could do no wrong, and he was a strong skier too.

The weather was terrible. It rained nearly every day, but nobody cared. There was a party every night. Sandra Malfatti had one, which put me on the circuit with the Middle Europeans. Gina Liechtenstein had one the next night and told me to come in my Austrian outfit. Also one night through Bruce's friends, Bobby and Dawn Peacock, I found myself with the "Jolly Brits," Angus Ogilvie, Carrie Coke and company. I ducked out early since there was good skiing promised for the next day.

I had heard Mouse Cleaver expostulate about high life at the Palace Hotel in St. Moritz with his friend Andrea Badrutt, one of the owners. Having had enough of the St. Anton rain, we trained down to Landeck and then caught the German bus from Munich to St. Moritz. At the border, Mouse phoned Andrea and invited him for blinis in the Grill Room. "Don't worry, Charles," said Mouse, "the rest of the dinner will be on Andrea," and it was.

I had asked Mouse, quite seriously, if we should take our skis. To our pleasant surprise the conditions in St. Moritz were excellent and we had fine skiing. Charles Oppenheim, an acquaintance of Mouse, was there with his family, and Mouse and I were invited to join his entourage, that included Max Robi, the top guide in the Engadine, and a Bentley. We were in clover.

The new cable car up the Diavolezza had just opened, and Max pioneered a lot of shoots and gullies to see if they could be classified as ski runs. Some obviously were not since they turned out to be steep, narrow and rocky, quite "hairy" but fun. Also the general life at the Palace with Andrea was easy to take.

1958 and 1959 do not figure in the skiing section since I became an Assistant Attorney General of the State of Maryland in July 1957 and our case load in the courts, particularly the Court of Appeals of Maryland, our highest court, made it impossible to get away in the winter. But I had other strings to my bow, as hereinafter set forth in the section entitled Mountain Climbing.

My return to the ski slopes was in February 1960 in St. Anton. By that time the ski school was in the throes of the Kruckenhauser revolution, a new technique which had been developed at St. Christoph, on the Arlberg Pass above St. Anton, by the famed Dr. K and which, in its extreme form, involved a lot of "hopping." This mania in time died down and became a more relaxed modern parallel technique. Franz Fahrner insisted that I make the transition to the more moderate form, saying that I would be able to ski to an older age with it since it was much easier, especially with the new equipment. In time even that has been modified and now the St. Anton Ski School advocates keeping one's skis a little bit apart. I now tell my teachers and guides that I spent years of my life and a small fortune learning the St. Anton-Austrian skis-together, stylish, "modische," technique and I am not about to change. Actually, some years before he died, Alfred Stäger said, "Charlie, don't ever let anybody try to change the way you ski." I doubt if they could.

I was back in St. Anton in 1961, but the highlight of that winter was that Margaret Crawford invited me over to Kleine Scheidegg to join her and her twin sister, Frances McDermott, and their friend Keith Hyland for a week of "flying." The Swiss had asked the twins if we would be guinea pigs for a series of flights up to the glaciers with the Pilatus Porter, a wheel-and-ski equipped air plane, and also by helicopter so that they could see what could be used for ski runs. Our pilots were either Hermann Geiger, the famous pioneer of glacier flying, or his assistant, Martignoni.

We assembled at the Belvedere Hotel at Kleine Scheidegg. Alfred Stäger from Mürren was our guide. The first day we did the Eismeer Glacier from Eigergletscher, a station on the Jungfrau Railway. I had done this previously in 1948. This was the last year that it was open for regular parties since the glacier had changed so much. When we reached the ice fall, the seracs were huge, and we had to clamber over them on foot, have our skis hauled up and then we were lowered down by ropes. It was quite an exercise.

The next day they ran the Lauberhorn Lift at the Scheidegg early for us, and then we skied down to the landing place for the airplane. The slope had been tracked up by skiers late the afternoon before and the tracks froze like iron overnight. Skiing the next morning was like traversing a railroad marshalling yard. It shook up the liver.

The plane came in and picked us up. We flew first to the Rosenegg, a subsidiary saddle on the top of the Wetterhorn, above Grindelwald. It was a spectacular flight over the Lauterbrunnen and Grindelwald Valleys and then up to the saddle. We landed on a steep uphill slope, just below the ridge between the peaks of the Wetterhorn. Geiger gunned the engine to turn the plane around and face downhill for his takeoff. There was no response, and the plane started to slide back. I was in the co-pilot's seat, and jumped out to hold the wing.

We unloaded, turned the plane around and Geiger took off. We walked up to the little col, which opened to the northeast, behind the Wetterhorn, and skied down the Gauli Glacier, past the Gauli Hut and on to the level glacier. It was a beautiful scene with the big peaks all around us. Geiger flew in, picked us up and flew us up to the Wetterlimme, which is a col on the flank of the Wetterhorn peaks. From there we had a long ski down in good snow over the glaciers until we dropped down into the forest. Then it became a struggle, "chaiber krampf," "what a cramp" as the Swiss would say. Some very amusing Italians with their guide had joined us, and they were continually chattering back and forth. When the way became extremely tortuous, it really wasn't a ski run as such, one of them said, "Che dice di questa pista?" "What do you think of this run?" and one of the others replied, "Troppe curve!" "Too many turns!" We were convulsed as we struggled over the roots and through the branches.

Somehow we came down to Rosenlaui, took a car to Meiringen and back by train to Scheidegg. Along the Brienzersee I turned to the Italians and asked, "Che dice di questo lago." Their reply, "Molto bello!" The whole trip was beautiful, from beginning to end.

We included the Ebnefluh—Fafleralp—Petersgrat—Stechelberg tour in this week, a gorgeous trip. Flying up to the Ebnefluh, a peak we had climbed on foot in 1948, we had a long ski down over the glaciers and snowfields to Fafleralp in the Lotschental. We then flew up to the Petersgrat, a long glacial ridge between the Gspaltenhorn and the Lötschental, and had a long ski down over the glaciers, the snowfields and through the forests to Stechelberg at the bottom of the Lauterbrunnen Valley.

We closed the week with a flight from the Lauberhorn to the Wetterlücke, a glacier pass between the Lauterbrunnen Breithorn and the Tschingelhorn at the southwest end of the Lauterbrunnen Valley. We roped up, first Alfred, then Margaret, next Frances, then me and finally Keith on the end. Although the Italians were not with us we had become quite Italianized and became respectively "Alfredo, Margareta, Francesca, Carlo e Kicci," nicknames which became part of us and which we the survivors, Margaret and I, use to this day.

It was serious business and we followed Alfred carefully, but we did have occasional lapses which resulted in Kicci being snatched off his feet a couple of times. It was a beautiful run, quite steep in parts. We ended up at Stechelberg. All roads seemed to lead there, as will be seen in the Mountain Climbing section.

In the winter of 1962 I was working with Arthur Machen at Venable, Baetjer and Howard on a number of underwritings (IPO's) and then my brother, David, was married on April 24. This meant that I could not get away skiing at the regular time, so I arranged with Margaret Crawford to come over late and do the Haute Route, the ski tour from Zermatt to Chamonix.

I finished up the last underwriting with Arthur, Schenuit & Co. for Robert Garrett & Sons, took the train to New York and flew Swissair to Zurich. I arrived at Zermatt, met Margaret, Elias Julen and Alfred Stäger, had two or three days of skiing at Zermatt, mostly on the Gornergrat, since it was the end of April, and took off on April 30 for the Haute Route, fortunately using an airplane, the Pilatus Porter again, with Martignone at the stick. We felt quite ritzy, getting off the cog railway at the top of the

Gornergrat, skiing down to Riffelboden and being met by our plane on the side of the regular ski runs.

We flew to the Tète Blanche, had a long, beautiful glacier run in new snow to a spot above Arolla, climbed to the Bertol Hut, skied down the glacier, were picked up and flew to the head of the Otemma Glacier and had another long ski down. The plane was waiting for us somewhat nervously, since it was by now about 3:30 in the afternoon and the clouds were beginning to roll in. We took off in the nick of time, flew past the clouds, across to the Trient Glacier, and landed below the hut. The plane wheeled around and took off just as the clouds closed in and it began to snow.

We climbed up to the hut, finding it unoccupied, unheated and freezing cold. Elias and Alfred built a fire in the stove. Margaret piled on the blankets and went to bed. I put on some wooden hut shoes and warmed up by pacing up and down on the terrace in the snow.

Alfred and Elias gave us a substantial dinner, and we turned in early. I awoke at dawn the next morning and clomped my way up behind the hut in the wooden hut shoes to see the sunrise lighting up the Aiguilles Dorées. The guides packed oatmeal with butter and sugar into us, and then we climbed up to the pass at the French frontier. Before we left, we signed the hut book indicating where we had come from, where we were going, and the date. Since it was May 1, under "Remarks" I duly noted, in the best Virginia tradition, "Hooray, Hooray, the First of May." I suppose in later years, some scholar poring over the records in Geneva, Berne or Zurich must have tried to puzzle out the meaning, unless he or she had Virginia connections.

At the col on the frontier we were roped up and gently lowered down into France. Once there, we donned the skis and had a gorgeous run down to the Albert Premier Refuge, lovely powder snow. There we paused about ten o'clock and waited for a half hour. When we continued, we had equally lovely spring snow conditions, "firn schnee" or in France "neige de printemps." Years later Elias was quoted as saying that in all the years he had done the Haute Route, these were the best conditions he had ever seen. I can believe it. We skied all the way to the bottom at LeTour, where we had lunch in the open at a restaurant at the end of the run. That indeed was the "Haute Route."

We went down to Chamonix and the next day took the lift up the Aigulle du Midi, then the highest lift in Europe. We clambered down the narrow ridge to the head of the glacier and had a spectacular run down the Mer de Glace and the Vallée Blanche, stopping for a bite at a spot on the glacier. The scenery was stupendous with all the Aiguilles, Dru, Vert, Géant, etc., looming over the glaciers. We skied down to the end and then had only a short scratch down the right-hand wall of the snout of the glacier to terra firma.

Margaret Crawford had to return to England and Alfred to Mürren, so I took Elias down to Val d'Isère for some spring skiing. One small incident sticks in my mind. We took some sort of transportation, probably bus, to Albertville, where we changed about nine A.M. to take the bus up to Val d'Isère. Elias and I were waiting outside a cafè when a large camion loaded with logs rolled up and three stocky Frenchmen got out, went in to the café and walked up to the bar. For some reason, I suppose out of curiosity and having nothing better to do, I followed them in. The patron said "Messieurs?" and without further ado one of them said, "Trois grands rouges." M. le patron set what looked like a toothbrush tumbler of red wine before each, and turned to me with a "Monsieur?" to which I quickly replied, "Moi aussi, merci," and promptly had my own tumbler of inky red set before me. The three truck men tossed theirs off, jumped into the truck and sped off, all at 9 A.M. It was not bad wine.

When we reached Val d' Isère, a wonderful drive up into the mountains, Elias asked if I wanted to stay in a big hotel or a pension that he recommended. I elected the latter, and we ended up at the Pension Hellrob, owned and run by the Goitschel family, probably of Austrian origin a few generations ago. They had three daughters, Marielle about 16, Christine 14, and a smaller one. The two older girls were big, solidly built, and were excellent ski racers. In the 1964 Olympics at Innsbruck they came into their own and at the 1968 Olympics in Grenoble they cleaned up. At the time of our stay they were bouncing French teenagers, full of beans and teasing. They used to wait on us at table, particularly breakfast, and delighted in trying to teach me teenage slang. Marielle would say, "Bon jour, Monsieur," and after my reply would rejoin with "Etes-vous grinche?" or "Etes-vous poignu ce matin?" and Mme. Goitschel would scoldingly say, "Pas ça, Marielle!" One morning Marielle went skiing with us. It was easy to see that she was going to be really good.

Elias and I had a week of terrific spring skiing and then went back to Zermatt. We stopped at Geneva overnight and had a fine dinner at Le Plat d' Argent in the old quarter near the Bourg du Four. It was a lovely spring night and the windows were open. On the train the next day Elias asked if I would like to climb the Matterhorn if the conditions were right. He said that he could get the key to the Belvedere Hut, and we might be the first climbers that season to make it. This meant that Herr Seiler of the Mont Cervin would give us a dinner. I said I was game. When Elias looked at the Matterhorn the next day he said it was not possible. There was too much new snow. We made the most of it.

I stayed at Elias's house, Chalet Felderhof, in the flat on the top floor. Every day Elias and I would go skiing in powder snow. His daughter, Ernla, who taught in the ski school, came with us at least one day, as did Annie, Elias's wife. I was in tip top shape. On my birthday, May 16, we skied in good powder. The next day Elias and I flew up with a little plane to the Breithorn, climbed the peak, something we had been unable to do in 1948, and skied all the way down the valley to a pub above Zermatt. There we fed francs into the music box and played the SchneeWalzer and other appropriate tunes. A horse sleigh brought us back to town.

Since Annie had a resident's permit and could park below the town, the next day we drove down the valley, put the car on the train at Brig for the trip through the Lötschberg Tunnel and took it off at Kandersteg. I was becoming hungry but Annie said to hold on until we reached Esche, a beautiful spot high up looking down on the Lake of Thun with the lilacs in bloom. It was one of the prettiest sights I have ever seen. Annie was going to come up to Mürren but had to turn around at Lauterbrunnen because of some family news she had received.

I went on up to Mürren, stayed a night or so at the Hotel Edelweiss, the Eiger being closed, and then flew home, just in time for the stock market crash of 1962, which put an end to our underwritings for awhile.

In 1963 I went to Switzerland in late March. About two or three weeks before I had seen a small item in the newspaper about an outbreak of typhoid at Zermatt, where I was supposed to meet Margaret and Alfred. I took the precaution of getting a typhoid "booster" before I left home since I had not had any shots since Army days. I can't remember whether I called Margaret before coming over, but I clearly remember going to the main tourist office when I reached Zurich Hauptbahnhof and was told there was nothing to worry about. I called Margaret in Zermatt, and she was a bit evasive but said it was all right to come up, in other words, one could get into Zermatt. When I arrived, I learned the truth.

The first case of typhoid had been discovered about January 25, but the town powers hushed it up so as not to lose the ski season. One English girl returned home and died. Another person also died. I don't know how many people became ill. The news finally broke in early March, six weeks after the first case was diagnosed. The locals blamed the typhoid on Italians working on the dam system known as La Grande Dixence. The truth was that Zermatt had been warned some years before about the deficiency of their water system as the town grew in size. The two rival factions in town politics temporized, and the outbreak occurred.

With that background, I met Margaret and Alfred. The consensus was that since we were here we might as well stay and enjoy the skiing. The town had emptied out in a panic, and the snow was fantastic. We put up at the Hotel Alex, owned by Alex Perren, a great friend and climbing partner of my mountain guide, Josef Petrig. We felt queasy about the typhoid. Clay Frick, a physician friend whom I had known at the Foster Place in Stowe, was there with several of his children. He warned us not to touch raw vegetables, salads, fruit, tap water, not even for brushing teeth. The next morning we decided to try to get some shots and went up to the "Notspital," the emergency hospital, about 9:30. We stayed about 15 minutes, without any perceptible progress, unanimously decided to chuck it since it was so depressing and went down to Le Centrale, the main local pub, and had a bottle of white wine. We walked down to the Gornergrat Bahn, stepped aboard without waiting, even took seats, unheard of in high season, and went up to the Gornergrat.

There we took one of the high mountain lifts, cablecars to Hochtäli or Stockhorn. At the top we had absolutely untouched snow in front of us, about three feet of it over a huge base. We shoved off and were having a glorious run when suddenly Margaret sat down, not fell, just simply sat and began to laugh. Alfred was at first scared and then angry, "Get up, Margaret. What's the matter with you?" Margaret, through her laughter replied in her best high-Australian-English accents, "Alfred, I cahnt (*sic!*). You boys are used to this drinking in the morning. I'm not." Finally Alfred talked her into resuming her descent.

We had a week of some of the finest skiing that I will ever see. Each time we went to Stockhorn or Hochtäli we would decide on a route and say, "Let's save this other one for the next time." When we came up for the next run, there would not be a track on it. After one run, we took the lift up to Sunegga, on the mountain opposite our tracks. Alfred counted my turns and said that I had done 69 without stopping. We looked over from the lift and could see our tracks all the way down the huge slope.

But it had its other side, and we could not get away from the gnawing feeling of the typhoid. Finally the authorities closed the town, and all visitors were told to leave. Margaret phoned Mürren but Annelies von Allmen said we could not come up from Lauterbrunnen. If we did, her entire staff would leave. She met us at the Lauterbrunnen Station, with fresh laundry for Margaret and a couple of bottles of Spiezer wine for me. We took the train up to Wengen.

There we checked in at the Silberhorn Hotel. The next morning they found out that we had come from Zermatt and asked us to leave. All Switzerland had panicked.

We traveled to Bourg St. Pierre, which is part way up to the Grand Saint Bernard and stayed in a new little place called the Relais du Napoleon. We were joined by Elias Julen and Laura Leonard. We men gave the two single rooms to Laura and Margaret. We took the third room, which we christened the "dog room." It looked like a kennel. We were still pariahs, but when someone asked where we came from, we could say "Wengen," which was a true reply, as far as it went.

They had installed a new *teleferique* at the Col, where we skied. We looked longingly at the gorgeous run down to Etroubles and the Val d'Aosta, but we were warned that if we skied down there, we might be stopped at the Italian border and made to climb back up.

The bright spot was the little pub about a quarter mile up the path to the village. We trudged up at cocktail time, having changed appropriately for dinner. Laura was turned out in a black velvet dress with strings of pearls and jewelry, straight off East 72nd Street. She asked for some whiskey, and the dignified old lady behind the bar did not think there was any. Laura spotted a cob-webby bottle on the top shelf and asked for a drink. The old lady poured her about half a tumbler full and charged her one Swiss franc, then about 23 U.S. cents. Laura came back for more.

Elias went back to Zermatt but rejoined us at Chamonix. Margaret reminded me recently that we hired a ski guide in Chamonix and reconnoitered the area where we were to meet Elias. The skiing was absolutely appalling, breakable crust over bad snow. Elias was due the next day and the guide asked us where we wanted to ski on that day. When we told him that we wanted to ski the same area, because we were to meet Elias, a fact that the guide did not know, he thought we had gone completely mad. Elias had to remove his Zermatt-Matterhorn insignia from his ski jacket before he crossed the border.

In 1964 I was prepared to return to St. Anton but read about the lack of snow in Innsbruck, where the Olympics were being held. I called Margaret and she said not to come. So I did a "180°" and went to Vail with Dick and Sheila Jackson and Gay (Gary, Jr.) Black. Vail was just starting its second season and had great skiing. Bill Peterson, a water skiing acrobat, was our class guide. It was like a private group, and we lived in the back bowls. We had nice soft Head skis and the powder snow was superb.

In 1965 after Randi Clotworthy's wedding I joined Cuppy and Betty Fenwick in Kitzbühel. To my surprise we had excellent powder snow and I was in Class 1 in the ski school. It was like the old days in St. Anton in Class 1 with Robert Falch. I stayed on a few days after the Fenwicks left, then went on up to St. Anton. Jack and Jeanne van der Valk were in their new house and kindly invited me to stay in one of the two lower rooms. Sveva Orsini had the other.

In 1966, I was back at the Schneider Haus. After some skiing at St. Anton, I took a taxi to St. Moritz with Herbert, who worked on the railroad, moon-lighting as a driver for "Harry Taxi." I can hear Harry's raspy voice on the radio, as we drove down the valley toward Landeck saying, "Macht ihm ein gute trinkgeld dir geben" "Make him give you a good tip." The trip in those days cost about $35.00.

We stayed at the Privat Hotel Au Reduit, owned and run by the Knauses. Herr Knaus was a quiet little man who was related to the Badrutts, the owners of the Palace Hotel. Frau Knaus was a real "Auntie Mame." We had Mario Ramponi as a guide, and I skied with Catharine Black and her daughter Wildy. Pete Whitman was there, as were Kathy and Anne Stewart and Winky Foster. Gracie Mc Millan and Eleanor completed the "extended family" and we had a hilarious time.

In 1967, Cathy Black gave her son Gary a present of two weeks of skiing with Mario. Gary kindly asked me to join him along with Henry Wheelright and the two Wellers, Josie and Sam. Since I was about twenty years their senior, I went to St. Anton a week early to toughen up. I taxied over to St. Anton, and when I came down to dinner the first night in all my Tirolean finery, Gary asked me if I would do him a favor. I readily assented, and then he said, "Sprat, the Wellers are in Europe for the first time. When they arrive, would you pretend that you are Austrian?" I protested but eventually gave in. When Josie and Sam arrived, I was introduced as "the Count." The story was that I could understand English, but I was embarrassed about speaking it because of my accent. Pete Whitman, who had majored in languages at Yale, was my interpreter. I felt like a snake-in-the-grass being such an impostor, and my chickens came home to roost the first night.

A nice old-fashioned German couple staying in the hotel ate dinner earlier than we, and when they left the dining room, they bowed to me. I accosted Frau Knaus after dinner and she admitted that they had asked her which was the Count and she said that it was I. When they asked why I spoke such bad German with such a heavy Austrian accent, she never batted an eye, explaining that my mother was a wealthy American from Chicago and my father was an impoverished Austrian count who had a large schloss in Nieder Osterreich. We took in shooting parties of rich Americans and I had spent most of my life in the United States. I thanked Frau Knaus for getting me in so deep.

We kept up the deception during skiing. I feigned difficulty getting the Wellers' names straight. I finally understood "Josie" and said, with great relief, "Ah, Josl." The nickname has stuck to this day. At dinner the truth finally emerged. We had been in to cocktails in the bar with the bar maids, Annie and Doris, and they were into the deception with relish. We went into dinner and the wine was a bit slow in coming, so I leaned over the table and said to Pete Whitman, "Peterli, der wein fliesst wie leim." One of the Wellers turned to Pete and asked "Mr. Whitman, what did the Count say?" Pete had tears rolling down his cheeks by this time and said, "Josie, the Count says that the wine is flowing like glue." That ripped it. Nobody could keep a straight face, and the cat was out of the bag. The Wellers seemed disappointed that I was not a real Austrian count.

We had excellent skiing with Mario, and he was pushed with such good skiers. One morning when we went over to catch the spring snow on the Suvretta Hänge, it was just right, thawed out an inch or so with a firm base. After several runs we were surprised to see that the surface did not soften up. The sun angle was right and a light wind came down from the north to keep it cool enough. Each time we would say "Let's make another." We skied till after two o'clock, at which time we were so tired that we had to call it quits and have lunch at the little restaurant on the Suvretta slopes.

At the end of the time with Mario, we hired a small airplane to fly from Samaden, the airport for St. Moritz, up to the Piz Sarsura, where Bruce Baetjer and I had been on foot in 1953. We had to wait a bit and it was amusing to see the traffic at the airport, Gianni Agnelli and entourage helicoptering up to the Diavolezza; the young Aga Khan arriving to fly in his jet to Gstaad, with his luggage following him in a second jet. Our little puddle jumper came in and Gary, Mario, Josie and I flew to the top of the Sarsura glacier. We climbed to the little peak, that I had surmounted 14 years before.

We had a lovely ski down, powder snow on the glacier, then becoming softer as we approached the forest. We were able to ski almost all the way down the woods road to the main road in the Engadine. When we arrived, we had no taxi and had to hoof it up the road in ski boots to Zernez. Gary had on a brand new pair of Heirling boots, and they were so stiff that he took them off with an oath and walked up the road in his stocking feet. When we reached the outskirts of Zernez we went in to the first wirts-schaft and had a bottle of Aigle white wine while we waited for a taxi to the train station. Before the train station we stopped the taxi at another wirtschaft and had another Aigle. Finally we decided "to hell with the train," bought another bottle of Aigle to take with us and drove to St. Moritz. It was just in time for evening Mass, so I told them to let me off at the church. The sermon was mostly in Italian and Romansch but I seemed to understand every word of it. At the end of the Mass, Easter Sunday, the big door at the end of the nave was opened, and the view down to the lake and across to the mountains, with a full moon, was breathtaking.

In 1968 I went to St. Anton to train for a week, and then taxied over to St. Moritz again with a view to doing the Piz Palu. I engaged Arno Grass, a mountain guide from Pontresina, and drove to il Fuorn and Buffolora in the National Park south of Zernez to practice climbing on skins. Then we took a small plane in to the Val Fedoz, climbed in deep snow over the ridge to the east and skied over into and down the Val Fex. The snow was so deep on the climb up that at the top pitch I had to take my skis off and turn them around in the snow. It was impossible to make a kick turn. Later, when I asked Arno if we should have been roped up, he said it would have done no good if the snow had avalanched.

One day in training, Arno took me up Piz Lagalb to see if steep slopes bothered me. We went far over on the left side, looking up, and made some turns about half-way down. It went all right. It was almost as steep as Tuckerman's Ravine. When we stopped to catch our breath, I looked down into the bottom of the bowl and said, "Arno, be careful going down there because I can see Farah Diba, the Empress of Iran, with her ski guide and her bodyguards." That was like waving a red flag at a bull, to tell a Swiss guide not to go somewhere. The next thing I knew, Arno had pushed off and I followed in pursuit. Soon we were tangled up in the Iranian entourage, weaving in and out, Swiss guide, Farah Diba, two tall thin bodyguards looking like something out of a James Bond film. I was sure that I would be drilled on the spot by a "burp gun" or an automatic pistol, but we made it through somehow.

We took the lift up the Diavolezza late one afternoon and bedded down in the Hut. We arose early the next morning, broke the fast and skied down to the glacier. Putting on skins, we climbed up about three hours in beautiful weather and with good snow. We left the skis at the saddle and climbed in ski boots another hour up a snow ridge. We were careful of the cornice when we reached the top since a group of Italians had come too close to the cornice in the not-too-distant past and eleven of them fell down to the glacier. I had wanted to do the Piz Palu ever since I had heard of the Leni Riefenstahl film "The White Hell of Piz Palu" made in the 1930's. I may even have seen it. But in any event we made the climb and it was beautiful. The Bernina Gruppe was magnificent, Piz Berina, Bianco Grat, Bella Vista, etc.

We tramped back to the saddle, put on the skis and favored the right side of the glacier to avoid some seracs and crevasses. Then we traversed left, climbed up the little pitch and squeezed around the corner that Catherine Black hated, on to the Isla Perse and down to the Morterartsch Glacier and Morterartsch. It was a glorious trip in excellent conditions.

Arno came to dinner on Saturday night, and when he left it had begun to snow. I left the next morning for Mürren, and it snowed all the way to Zurich; again between Zurich and Berne; and after Berne all the way to Interlaken, Lauterbrunnen and up to Mürren. When we took the little train from Grütchalp, at the top of the funicula, around the shoulder to Mürren, the engineer and conductor crept along and looked anxiously up the mountain every time we crossed a gully. We made it in to Mürren about six o'clock and they closed the train. It was too dangerous from avalanches.

The next morning at least three feet of fresh snow had fallen, and I had Kari von Allmen, a mountain guide, as my ski instructor. We rented some deep snow skis and set out on the Schiltgrat. At first the snow was so heavy that we could hardly push through it but by afternoon it began to dry out and became fun. Gradually we worked around the lower slopes Schiltgrat, Gimmelen, Fineln, Maulerhübel and Winteregg. We may even have made a run to Lauterbrunnen, since there was plenty of snow all the way down to the valley floor. When the Schilthorn Bahn opened we went to Birg and eventually to the Schilthorn. Whenever I see Kari, I am now skiing with his son, Bruno, we still talk about that week of powder snow skiing. It was superb, the kind of thing that they dream of in Colorado, Utah and the Canadian Rockies, but the difference was, and is, that in those days, even in 1968, practically no one skied the deep snow.

One day the son of the hotel family, Beat von Allmen, joined us. He was on the Swiss National Ski Team. Kari, Beat and I were skiing the Engetal Hänge from Birg. We made run after run in untouched powder, a bit different from our Western powder which can be like skiing through angel dust. It practically blows away. The European powder, when it settles and is untouched, is more like skiing through cream, a bit fuller-bodied. In any event, we were skiing in it to perfection on a cloudless March day. Each one took turns leading and obviously we were doing our best to show off. On one of Beat's turns to lead, we were about half way across the main slope from Birg facing toward Schilthorn. The slope down was quite narrow since there were outcroppings of rock on both sides. Beat took off like a streak, making beautiful carved turns. He reached the narrow throat and dropped over the edge toward the valley. Kari and I, standing on the traversing track above, waited for him to come out on the valley floor. No Beat. Finally Kari said, "Charlie, wait here. I'll see what's happened." Kari skied down carefully, making lovely rounded turns in his own track. At the narrow spot he stopped and looked down. I heard him laugh and then he motioned me down. When I reached the spot where he was standing, I realized what had happened. It looked like an automobile accident. Beat had shot into the narrow space at high speed and had hit a buried stone. The whole slope is nothing but talus in the summertime. He said that he had turned three somersaults and lost everything, skis, poles, gloves, hat, glasses, et al. He was not hurt. In today's parlance it looked like he was holding a "yard sale."

The last day was unforgettable. Kari and I took the Schiltgrat lift, traversed and climbed a little bit and came up into the Blumenlücke, a saddle overlooking the Blümen-tal and facing toward Allmend-hübel. There was not a track on it. It was a cloudless morning about ten-thirty or eleven. Kari asked if I would like to go first and of course I said "yes." I shoved off, making nice rounded, Benno Rybizka-style turns. It was heaven. I reached the valley floor, slightly above the Suppen-alp restaurant. Kari came down, making his own track. We admired the tracks and congratulated each other, preening in the sunshine like a couple of peacocks. Then we took off down the Kandahar run. When we had reached the slope where the Rad-lift used to be, we stopped and suddenly Alfred, who was head of the ski school, came up behind us. "Well," he said, "I figured it was you two." He had been at the top of the Allmendhübel, organizing the ski school classes, when he saw two little specks come up over the skyline at the top of the Blumenlücke, "Charles and Kari," he said to himself. He watched us ski down and then tore down himself, into the Blumen-tal, down the Bob Run and through the woods to the Kandahar. He was skiing behind us when he caught us at the Rad-slope where we stopped. "Charles," he said, "I think you ski better in the deep snow than on the piste." That was quite a compliment.

In 1969 during the winter we were swamped with securities work, representing underwriters and also doing a "company" offering. There was no getting away at the regular time, but finally the bubble burst in April. It had been a hectic time, and I had to get away. I harked back to 1948 when I had stood on the Ebnefluh with Fritz Steuri and pointed to the Finsteraar-horn. I remembered that he had said it was the best ski-mountaineering climb in the Alps and that May was the time to do it. Kaspar and Erica von Allmen had closed Wengernalp for the season when I phoned, but they arranged for me to go to the Regina in Grindelwald. I was able to engage Hermann Steuri, "Steurimantl," as guide. One couldn't do better than that since Hermann was soon to become President of the International Mountain Guides' Association.

There was no snow in Grindelwald, and we trained by walking. One rainy day we entered the Wetterhorn Hotel, the little mountain hotel at the end of the Upper Grindelwald Glacier, and it was there that I learned the expression "flatsch nass." "Soaked to the skin" is about the closest in English. We took our ski training by picking up young Hans Schlunegger and a friend and taking them with us on a jaunt. We rode by jeep to Bussalp, then climbed on foot and skis when we hit snow to the top of the ridge which includes the Faulhorn. We had a ski down to and around a small dam-lake, "stausee," climbed and traversed around another one on the north side of the ridge, and eventually ran out of snow a bit above Giessbach. We trudged down to a phone, summoned a car to drive us to Interlaken, and caught the train back to Grindelwald.

In a day or so the weather looked propitious, but not for long, according to Hermann, so we drove down to Reichenbach, had some lunch in the charming old inn there and had a tour of the ultra-modern stainless-steel kitchen, which was in remarkable contrast to the hundreds-of-years-old chalet. Hans Boss, the butcher from Grindelwald and one of the "Boss Bua," renowned for their singing, was invited by Hermann, and we had permission to fly with the provisions plane up to the Finsteraarhorn Hut, perched on a ridge above the glacier.

The next morning, May 13, we left the hut about 6 A.M. and climbed on skins up the glacier. We crossed over a ridge to the glacier on the left leading up to the Hüggi-sattel. It was warm and I left my skis a bit below the saddle and continued on foot. At the saddle, which is over 4,000 meters high, Hermann and Hans left their skis, and we roped up. It was spectacular, to say the least, a far cry from the thirteenth floor of the Mercantile Trust Building and IPO's. On the far side of the saddle the cliffs and ice plunged almost sheer down to the glacier. On our right the peak of the Finsteraarhorn towered overhead. Hermann wanted to take the left hand side of the wall, but I demurred because of the horrible exposure. We took the wall farther to the right, a bit more difficult, but I did not have to look down that yawning abyss to the left. We clambered up the rocks in a half hour or so and were on top, 4274 meters, the highest point in the Bernese Oberland. I could look over to the Ebnefluh where I had stood in 1948 with Fritz Steuri, Fritz Meyer, Dottsie Smith and Bill Douglas. We were above everything, including Eiger, Mönch and Jungfrau. It was a gorgeous day, no wind, quite warm in the sun.

We stayed on top about half an hour; then went down the rocks, with me leading on the rope and Hermann and Hans making sure that I did not plunge down. They put on their skis at the saddle; I did a sitting glissade to the spot where mine were; and then we skied down to the hut.

We left early the next morning, about 3:30 A.M., because it was warm. The temperature at the hut, an aerie perched on a ledge hundreds of feet above the glacier, had not dropped below freezing during the night. We skied down to the glacier proper, then had a long ski on the level to where the walls began to narrow and make it impossible to descend directly. We turned righthanded and climbed up to the Galmilücke, passing by an oddly shaped outcropping of rock that looked like a bird with neck outstretched. From there we skied down the Galmi Glacier in to the Upper Rhone Valley as the weather became increasingly hot.

We had to take the skis off a little above Münster and walk into the town, then down to the railroad station. I was dying of thirst and dripping with perspiration in my ski clothes. I would gladly have taken off my skin-tight, stylish Habicher custom-made trousers and walked in my underwear if Hermann would have let me. We took the train down to Brig and entered the main Bahnhof Restaurant. We wanted to order white wine but Hermann would not let any of us—we had picked up a few extra people at the hut who wanted to come down with us—until we had had something to eat. I took asparagus since they had just come in season and the usual European asparagus-mania was on. Hermann said that if we had started in on the wine, it was then about noon, we were so dehydrated that we would have been swinging on the chandeliers. I am sure we would have, gladly.

It was a beautiful ride to Goppenstein, through the Lötschberg Tunnel to Kandersteg, Spiez, the lakes, Interlaken, Zweilütschinen and up to Grindelwald, in mid-May with everything green and in blossom. Margaret and James Crawford appeared to help me celebrate my birthday on May 16, and then we drove via Berne, stopping for lunch with Margaret's friends the Matheys, to Solothurn to take a swim and see Urs and Ursula Sieber. From there we motored up into the Black Forest; spent a night at Titisee; then down the Rhone to Boppard; and over to the Mosel Valley the next day, with a splendid lunch at Berncastel with plenty of Berncastel Doktor. We spent the next night in a charming half-timbered inn in the Ardennes. From there we drove on to Waterloo and to Brussels, where Margaret and James turned me over to Pan American for my flight home.

In 1970 Frances McDermott and Margaret Crawford were in St. Anton with their "chicks" and I followed them over to St. Moritz. I phoned Mrs. Huder, who ran the private guides service, to hire a guide. She told me that they were very busy, but that she would do what she could. She called back and said she had a guide. When I said, "Great," she rejoined that it was a female guide. I re-rejoined, "How old?" "About 25." "I'll take her."

The next morning I was wondering if some great galloping beast would appear. Instead a Volkswagen drove up and out stepped a petite blonde named Heidi Michel. Margaret Crawford was furious. That year at St. Moritz people fawned on me who ordinarily wouldn't give me the time of day. Ellie Kahn bumped into us one day in a ski shop, and when I introduced Heidi as my ski guide, Ellie gave me an arch look which spoke volumes.

The Cresta

Heidi was an excellent skier and was a great friend of Gunther Sachs, who put her in one of his movies riding a huge motorcycle, and all the English Cresta crowd, including Sonny Blandford, Duke-of-Marlborough-to-be. Her friend, Peter Trainen, was a Cresta rider, and Heidi said I should try it, with Peter as my trainer. I, of course, demurred, just as I did with Mikey Smithwick in 1974 when I said that I did not want another horse, as herein below more specifically set forth. And, just as with Mikey, the inevitable occurred. Early one morning I found myself in the starting gate by the club house, face down on a heavy "skeleton" with a helmet on my head, incidentally sporting the Union Jack, metal protectors on my hands and elbows, iron rakes on my shoes for braking, etc. I thought, "Sprat, you've done a lot of dumb things in your life, but this has to be about the dumbest." I wanted to get off and run away, but that would not be "cricket." I could not "let the side down."

Off I shoved, braking furiously, made it through Shuttlecock and, when I picked up speed, rocketed through the turns above the bridge without knowing what I had done. I was hooked.

One morning Peter was giving me his instructions and he said later that I didn't pay one bit of attention to him. All I wanted to do was jump on the sled and go. As soon as I started off, he raced for the club house porch to see what would happen. He knew I was in for trouble. I eschewed braking and flew through the first turn or so. Then as I hurtled into Shuttlecock, which is the one turn in the course which is designed to throw the rider out, I thought, "Something doesn't look right." I was too high on the wall, and the next thing I knew I was flying through the air and across an expanse of snow covered with hay. I had asked Peter what to do in an emergency. I jettisoned the sled, but it caught up with me as I slid across the banked-up hay and gave me a nasty crack in the arm.

I stood up and waved that I was all right, dragged myself and the sled to the road and clambered into the return truck with my sweater festooned with hay. A Brit asked as I came aboard, "Yank aren't you?" "Yes." "Where from?" "Maryland." "Where?" "Baltimore." "Know the Griswolds?" Small world.

A night or so later, I went to the Cresta Ball at the Palace, sporting my shuttlecock pin which Heidi and Peter had given me. Sol and Ellie Kahn and I were at a table with the lady who owned the Folies Bergeres. She had on what I suppose is called a spray of diamonds, about six rows wide and five inches long. For once, Ellie was one-upped. She leaned over and said, "Charlie, look at that ice."

Bill Douglas' father and mother used to stay at the Palace every winter, all winter. They were both excellent skiers, and Mr. Douglas had done not only the Cresta, but the bobsled run as well. He was proud of me for doing the Cresta, and particularly for being entitled to wear the shuttlecock pin.

Skiing Continued

From 1969 on skiing settled into a more set pattern. I would go to St. Anton about February 15, ski there for two weeks, then take an additional week at Mürren. I varied this two or three years by joining Paul and Kitty Swett at Gstaad, both a change of scenery and rather "up market" for social life.

When I arrived at St. Anton in 1973, Alfred Tschol, in charge of private guides at the ski school, said he did not have a guide but to come back after lunch. When I did so, Alfred introduced me to Bobby Fahrner, whom I subsequently learned was one of the top skiers in St. Anton. I lucked into him because he had been engaged by some Californians who wanted to ski only on the "piste," i.e. the runs or slopes where the snow was packed and groomed by machines. That was not Bobby's bag, and he ditched them.

I went up with Bobby that afternoon. He was trying me out on the Kandahar when someone almost ran into him. I said, "Bobby, that's why I don't like the piste." He looked at me a bit quizzically and said, "Do you mean that?" When I replied in the affirmative we went up the Galzig again, climbed up a little way and dropped over the back toward the Arlbergstrasse between St. Chrisoph and Rauz. This was in the days before the new Rauz lift up to the Galzig and the other supplementary lifts on that side. The visibility was not good but the snow was superb, deep powder, possibly a little heavy.

At one point Bobby fell into a hole but without incident. When we reached the bottom, we congratulated each other. We walked the road back to St. Christoph. We had done the Film Run, which had been pioneered for a movie but was rarely used in those days. From then on we did them all, Arlenmäder, Pfanni, everything "off piste." Usually it was fabulous, but when it was not, it was horrible, no in-between.

One of our regular runs was to go up the Valluga, ski down over Walfagehrjoch past the Ulmer Hutte to Rauz and on down to Steuben. Then we took the lift up the Albona and either traversed left and skied down to the Ferwall or else climbed the Maroikopf which took about twenty-five minutes when I was trained. We would then ski down over the Maroi slopes to the forest and thrash down through the trees to the Ferwall, where Bobby's brother Kurt had a restaurant.

One day we did Knödl-Kopf and had a lovely light powder run to St. Christoph. Another day we did the Peischel-Kopf, going up the Albona, and then traversing over behind Knödel-Kopf and to the top of Peischel. It was a lovely view over toward the Valluga and all the St. Anton ski runs and similarly to the south and west past Pateriol and Kaltenberg. When we started down it was all right, but then as we traversed in a more southerly direction it became soft and finally, as we reached the upper scattered woods, it became sog. It was like slogging through liquid cement. Bobby became furious after awhile. "This is the worst snow that I have ever seen," he said. I replied that I thought that I had seen worse. This only made him more furious, and I could not help being amused, although I tried to keep it to myself. He tried taking off his skis and immediately sank in to his hips. I had to laugh, and kept my own skis on, even though they had four inches of snow glued to them with every step. Somehow we made it down. Bobby reached the Rasthaus Ferwall, the restaurant, and Kurt and Ingrid, his wife, asked, "Where's Charlie?" Bobby snarled, "Up there somewhere." Kurt and I laugh about it to this day.

Another day Bobby and I were slated to go helicoptering with Hansi Wolfram and Horti Bührli and were at the helipad at the curve in the Arlbergstrasse, below the Mooserkreuz, about 8:45 A.M. Hansi phoned in and said Horti didn't feel well. Bobby said, "What shall we do?" I said, "It's expensive, but let's go, just the two of us." Thank heaven we did. First of all, it was before the dollar's plunge against the Austrian schilling in the wake of OPEC, the Nixon cut from the gold standard, Jimmy Carter, trade deficits, inflation and a host of other things. Secondly, and by far the most important, it was a sparkling clear morning with the prospect of good powder snow.

We flew first to the Brulen-kopf, a shoulder on the southwest side of the Pateriol. Bobby stepped out of the helicopter and sank to his waist in fresh powder snow. He let out a broad grin and said, "I knew it would be good, but I didn't think it would be this good!" I descended and the helicopter flew off, leaving us in a paradise of sparkling powder snow, deep blue sky, mountains on every side and absolute silence.

Bobby asked if I would like to go first and pointed the way down the steep slopes. It was fantastic. We skied down past the "Kugelten Sta," a huge boulder as big as a small house which must have fallen off the Pateriol many years ago. We stopped farther on, before we reached the forest, and waited in the sun for the chopper. He came in and flew us around the corner of the cliffs and rock slopes that lead up to the Darmstadter Hutte and the Kuchenspitze, then flew up and landed on the Saumspitze. We lay down in the snow as he took off, and when we stood up, I shook Bobby by the hand. He looked a bit puzzled and then I said that for me it was an historic occasion. Bobby was going to be 25 years old in a few days, I was going to be exactly twice his age in the month of May, and I had stepped on this very spot almost exactly 25 years ago with Herman Tschol, Seppel Fahrner and Herman Kiaer, but coming by foot and not by helicopter.

Bobby and I sat on top for some time looking down the Moos-tal, past St. Anton and over to the Galzig and the Valluga. When we were ready to go, I again went first, and Bobby's last words as I shoved off were, "Don't fall. They can see us from St. Anton." I went down the steep slopes of the glacier in satisfactory fashion, not as nicely rounded as I would have liked, not like my turns with Benno on the Schongraben or the Schindler-hänge or with Alfred Stäger and Elias Julen on the Stockhorn and Höchtali ten years before, but they were all right since I had on fairly stiff Kneissl skis with Lange boots, not as supple as I would have liked. Bobby came down in beautiful turns alongside mine, and after we had preened a bit, admiring our tracks on the steep slopes above us, we turned down the valley for the long run to St. Anton. It had been an incredible day.

The next day was still beautiful, and we took the lift up the Galzig and Valluga and then the little cabin up to the Valluga-gipfel. We could see our tracks of the day before even with the naked eye. We fed one-schilling pieces into the telescope so that we could admire them at even closer hand, and undoubtedly brag about them to anyone who would listen. When I told Rudi Matt, he said, "Charlie, they will be there next summer!"

I skied with Bobby in the winters of 1973, 1974 and 1975. We had fantastic skiing, nearly all off piste. One day we did the usual Valluga, Rauz, bus to Zürs, Madlochjoch, Zug, Monnenfluh, Lech, Rüfikopf, Zurs run, nearly all in deep snow. But instead of going directly from Madlochjoch toward Lech, we climbed left up over the shoulder and skied down Stierloch. Bobby went first and appeared around a corner farther down. He told me to come over a bit to where I could see directly down to him. It was so steep that I could not see the slope. He assured me that it was possible and urged me to come down. I did a "nervous Nelly" and asked about avalanche, etc. He said, "It's o.k." and down I came. When I told Rudi Matt about it, his comment was, "Next I suppose you'll be doing the Arschloch!" (No translation supplied!)

One bright morning Bobby and I flew up to the Sulz-Kopf, a narrow summit with steep walls. Again we had to lie down while the chopper took off. There was little room. Bobby put on his skis, made a few quick turns in a narrow couloir and beckoned to me. I said, "Bobby, it looks awfully narrow to me, and if I fall you couldn't hold me, could you?" He said "no" so I said "I am going to side-step down" and he agreed. I am glad that I did because I have often looked at it across the Moos-tal from the new Rendl lift and it looks awfully steep. If I had fallen, I could have gone a long way down.

We had a spectacular run down into the valley, and when we neared the bottom, we ran into a ski instructor friend of Bobby's, Ziggy, who had a group from Vienna with him. We all had lunch at Tritt-alm, where there is a hut for cows, hay etc. Bobby packed an in-run above the roof of the hut and used the hut as a ski jump. After a few glasses of wine, I was tempted to try it but fortunately decided not to. Ziggy and Bobby decided to join forces, and a day or so later we all flew together to the Hohe Riffler, the highest peak in the area, about 3100 meters.

We landed in a saddle near the top and then had a long ski down around the top of the mountain, toward Flirsch and finally to a jagd—i.e. hunting—hut of Bobby's, in a subsidiary valley. There we cooked small steaks and had a bit of a rest. The helicopter came in about 1:30 and flew us up to the Rosfal-scharte, which descends to the west, to the Moos-tal. It really was too late, but we had to make it. The guides said to keep the skis flat, and to ski very gingerly, no sharp turns or weight on one ski. It was like skiing on egg shells, but we all made it safely down without breaking through. We breathed a sigh of relief when we finally hit a piste.

I debated with myself about including the following episode, but decided that it ought to be part of the record. In 1975 Gary Black and his wife, Mandy, appeared on the scene, and I took them on one of our tours. The only difference was that Bobby did not show up that morning and after waiting for him some time at the Valluga restaurant, we shoved off, with me leading. We skied down to Rauz, taking the spring snow slopes on the right as I had often done with Bobby. Gary and Mandy complimented me on my "guiding." We crossed the road, skied to Stüben, took the lift up the Albona and climbed the Maroi-Kopf. All in lovely conditions.

We then went down the other side of the Maroi intending to go to the Ferwall and have lunch at the Răsthaus Ferwall with Kurt and Ingrid. And that is where the trouble began because I led them too far to the right. We were following tracks, and it was nice snow. Then the tracks diverged to the far right, to a point where I knew we did not want to be. We went a bit left and skied down into a gully which narrowed to a throat and then disappeared over an edge. We could see ski tracks in the valley not two hundred yards from where we stood. I asked Gary to go down toward the edge and see if it would "go." He called up to us and said, "Sprat, I don't think so. It gets awfully steep and looks rocky." Later I found out that we were at Kräckerli, and many years later heard that it was mostly cliff in summertime.

We had a council of war. It was tempting to try to go down, but Gary and Mandy had two small children. I knew that we could climb back up to the Kaltenberg Hut, where there was a telephone and that we could then call St. Anton and let them know that we were safe. I told Gary and Mandy that it would be tough but that we would at least be alive. So about one o'clock we started to climb back up, sidestepping, since we had no skins. It was warm and as we climbed up the slope I looked over at the slopes that we would have traversed if we had been on the correct track to the Ferwall. I mused that, being in full sunlight, they could have been avalanche-dangerous since we would have been later than called for.

Hour after hour passed as we side-stepped back up the slope. It is amazing what you can do if you have to. The afternoon wore on, and Gary and Mandy were forging ahead. I told them to keep going and, when they reached the hut, to call Herta and Franz so that they could alert the ski school and the "dienst." Gary and Mandy reached the hut about 6, and I about 7, helped by some Austrians and Germans who were coming up from the valley, over the Albona and Maroi. When I reached the hut, Gary and Mandy said, "Sprat, the phone is broken, 'Kaputt.'" I was desperate and wanted to ski down to Stüben at once, despite the dark.

I knew that they would send out a search party from St. Anton if we did not appear by nightfall. Everyone said it was impossible, so we spent the night and left the hut in the morning, as soon as there was enough light to see. We made it down to Stüben about eight o'clock, went to the Post Hotel to phone and Franz Fahrner answered. At first he couldn't take in who was calling and then he was overwhelmed with relief. We took a taxi back to St. Anton.

When we reached St. Christoph, I suggested we go up the Galzig and ski down to St. Anton. I was soundly veto-ed. When we arrived at the Schneider Haus, we were greeted with relief and joy. The "dienst" had gone out to look for us the night before but, having no idea where to start, soon gave up. I talked to the head man and gave them a contribution for new lights before I left.

To this day Christian Marth calls me "Mr. Albona" and asks if I have been to the Kaltenberg Hut recently. André Traxl hints that one night's lodging at the Kaltenberg Hut cost me a lot of money, but I have never told him the true story. It is best that some things be left unsaid, unless buried in memoirs which no one will read.

I did not go skiing in 1976 since I had become involved with fox hunting, about which more in detail in a later section, and we had an "open winter" at home, practically no snow and not very cold. In 1977, I returned to St. Anton and moved across the street to the Schwarzer Adler. Herta had rented the Schneider Haus to Herr Kneissl, of ski manufacturing fame, and she and Franz had built a house up the hill, near the van der Valks and the Montjola. It was too far out of town for me. Hansi, a real character, was the "maitre d'" of the "Schwazi," and Charlie, who later took over the Senn Hut, was a waiter; a colorful group.

Margaret and Frances were there with the young Australians and asked me to join the tour. Fritz Gertsch from Wengen was their guide. I skied a bit in St. Anton to become acclimated and then joined them at Zermatt. From there we went over to Verbier, an area which I had not seen before, a rather unattractive sprawl of a town but good skiing. We did the north face of the Mont Gelé one day, which was quite an experience. Once into the gully it was steep but do-able, but the traverse into it was "hairy." One slip and you could go down about two thousand feet with no hope of stopping. The Australians said that they had seen somebody take such a fall the year before. Fritz would not let them turn back.

Having planned to leave from Verbier, I skied in the morning, said good-bye to Fritz Gertsch, packed up my skis and, at lunch with Margaret and Frances, called home to tell Aunt Frances of my arrival the next day. She said, "You can't come home. There's no water in your house." A main three feet under the alley concrete had frozen in the terrible cold of that winter. I was stunned. I told Aunt Frances I would call her later.

I returned to the table to confer with Margaret and Frances and they blithely said, "That's simple. Stay over and ski with us." I was torn, but eventually made the inevitable decision. I called Swissair, canceled the next day's reservation, since I had one of those 14–42 day tickets that one could get in those days, and said I would let them know when I wanted to fly back. The next day I called the office and also Aunt Frances, from the Club Mediteranée Hotel in the next valley after a gorgeous run down the back side of the Mont Gelé.

After Verbier we went to Val d'Isère where we had more good powder snow. One day we arose early after a big storm and were on the top slopes by nine o'clock. We made run after run just as the avalanche patrol and the ski lifts opened them. We went over to the glacier and eventually skied back to Val d' Isère through the Col Perse, a narrow gorge from the bottom of the glacier to the open slopes above town. Fritz asked me to stay back as "sweep" and we went through one at a time. We reached the town about three o'clock without having stopped for lunch. It was one of the best days of skiing that I have had.

Another day we did the Trois Vallées in France, Les Menuires, Courcheval and Meribel, good skiing with very few French out because it was partially overcast and lightly snowing, perfect conditions.

A final day we motored up to the Grand St. Bernard. We stopped in at the Relais Napoleon and said hello to "Monsieur et Madame les patrons." They remembered Margaret and me from 1963, the typhoid year. We skied a few runs on the *teleferique*. Then we took the run down to Étroubles in the Italian Val d'Aosta, the run which we were not permitted to take in 1963. It was beautiful, with only two tracks ahead of us. And at the end there was a restaurant with Italian food and red wine. We took the bus back over the pass to the Grand St. Bernard in the late afternoon twilight.

The crowd broke up at Verbier, and I went to Wengernalp for a few days with Margaret. Urs and Ursula Sieber were there, plus Ian Bonnas, who gave us wonderful piano music, and his wife Kate.

I returned home. When I made it back to the office and thought that I had sneaked in after such a long time away, Ronnie Reno had circulated a memo, similar to the ones which were issued in those days when a new associate joined us. He announced that I had returned to the firm and asked everyone to stop by my office and welcome me back. What a friend!

After those years of superb powder snow without anybody skiing it, the new generation with new boots, new skis and new techniques took over, and we ended up more and more on the piste, with the possible consolation that ski lifts proliferated everywhere and made it possible to get in many more miles of skiing and the slopes were beautifully groomed.

One exception was 1982 when I had Albert Klimmer as my guide at St. Anton. I skied with him three weeks, staying in the Alte Post, that Michael Zanner and Claudia, his wife, had taken over. I had room 105, a single, and it was so cold that some nights I had to sleep with my ski hat on since my head almost touched the outside wall at the end of the hall. Albert and I had day after day of deep powder. One was on the Bach-seite slopes in deep snow and terrible visibility. We saw only one class all day and had the place all to ourselves. It was snowing so hard that that after each run our tracks were obliterated and we had untouched powder the next time.

On another day, it had cleared and the troops poured out to take advantage of the powder. Albert and I took the cable car to the Valluga, skied the top slopes to the new stick lift and then over the Wolfagerjoch to the Schindler-Hänge. We traversed far over to our left, on the right looking up from the Ulmer-hütte run, to a ridge running up the slope with a gully next to it. Albert went down the gully in gorgeous powder and, when he reached the bottom, signaled me to come down since some people had followed us. I could hear California voices approaching and took off. It was fantastic, light powder, but so deep that the snow literally came up over my head. I stopped at the bottom and Albert and I wanted to see the Americans come down. First came a man, who stopped about half-way down and called back to his companions, "Wow! This is really deep!" Then a girl shoved off and came down nicely. At the end another man came down and we could tell that he was not going to make it. His turns kept getting faster and faster as he began to lose control, and finally he crashed and burned. We all had a good laugh.

Another memorable powder snow day was one which I skied with Toni Spiss, from St. Jacob, not the racer who was the protégé of Neal Starr. I had done a few runs with the racer at one time, and he was an incredible skier with his "bunny rabbit" leaps with the skis tucked up behind and the points down. "My" Toni Spiss and I enjoyed some extremely deep powder snow. When we pushed off the top of the Galzig toward the Steissbach-tal, we felt as if we would suffocate as we skied into a mulde, a sort of depression, and the snow would pass over our heads.

We skied many runs which are not usually ski-able, such as Versala, plus Fang, Schongraben, Maienwassen, Maienplat, Armeissinegg, Zwischen-abfahrt, "bird nesting" down through the trees beside Ost-hang, everywhere.

The first year I skied with Ludwig Schweiger was 1981 and we had the unpleasant experience of coming upon an elderly German who was skiing down the Schwarz-wang and was run into by a young Austrian from Landeck, schussing from the Arlen-sattel down to the Tanz-boden lift. There were no warning signs and the two runs simply crossed. I stayed with the injured man while Ludwig went down to call the Dienst. When they arrived and we left, I remarked to Ludwig that I hoped that they would check him for internal injuries since he was commencing to pale. We later heard that he died in the helicopter on the way to Innsbruck. He had a ruptured aorta.

One year I skied with Reinhard Schranz and we had a memorable late afternoon at the Senn Hutte with Christian Marth and his guest Pino, who was a vintner from Frascati. Charlie broke out a couple of big bottles of Frascati, Egon Ebster was there playing the squeeze box and when we left in the gathering dusk, it is a wonder that we made it down.

The first year I skied with Herbert Rofner was 1984, the year of the Winter Olympics at Sarajevo. We arranged our skiing so as to be in front of a good television set for each of the main skiing events. The Americans were cleaning up. The Austrians collected one bronze medal. We finally came to the men's downhill and were at the Alte Post to watch. Bill Johnson had number six starting position and was in the lead after his run. We waited until Number 20 or 25 had skied and Herbert said that no one would catch him. I ordered drinks for everyone, about a dozen or so persons in the bar area. When a couple of strangers looked puzzled, I explained that it was not every day that an American won the Olympic men's downhill. As a matter of fact, it was the first, and only, so far. Herbert said that if the Austrians had won as many medals as the Americans, the churchbells would have been ringing up and down the valley. That night at dinner at the Hotel Tirol with Franz and Herta some Austrian friends of the Fahrners sent us over a bottle of champagne.

After 1984 the ski school signed me up with Ludwig Schweiger regularly. We had wonderful skiing, and I tried to imitate his style. He was a joy to watch. We went everywhere, and I particularly remember one slightly overcast day when we went to do the Schindler with the "Engineer Hendler" traverse over to the Steissbachtal in order to avoid the notorious Schindler-kar lower mogul slope. The snow cats had pisted all the upper slopes and there was no one on them, probably because it looked "socked in" from below. It wasn't. The sun was shining through fitfully and there was an inch or two of fresh snow. We made run after run, taking the Schindler-grat lift up and never told a soul. We had it almost entirely to ourselves.

Bill Canby skied with Ludwig and me a few years, and whenever he was behind me it sounded like a run-away freight train. I continually warned him not to run over me. He was a delightful person, and we had many good times together. Bill was the one who took the little picture of Ludwig and me at the start of the Mattunjoch run. I had Polly Mitchell use this picture as the background for my portrait at home.

In most recent years, after two weeks at St. Anton, I would go over for a third week at Mürren. Margaret and I did a lot of skiing with Alfred Stäger after his morning ski school. I also skied one year with Hitti von Allmen, a couple of years with Stefan von Allmen, a year or two with Fritz Stäger while he was still a skiing instructor, one time with Fritz Lauener, including a memorable trip from the top of the Schilthorn, down into the Saustal and on to Isenfluh with David Winstead and his then "girl" Libby; and several years with Madelena von Allmen. Our favorite run was "paradiesli!" Now Bruno von Allmen, Kari's son, is my regular guide, with the exception of one year when he was injured and I skied with Mikki Spurri, the son of Baltz, the school master.

I have also skied twice with Michele Marchand at Leysin, but that more properly belongs in the section on Special Trips, i.e. New Zealand.

I continue to ski, with my doctors' blessings, and will as long as I can. To make sure that I do, each year as I prepare to leave St. Anton, I book Room 206 at the Alte Post with the new owner, Franz Tandl, and Sabena, his daughter, who runs the place. After I pay Helga, the cashier for the ski school, for my guide, I book him for the next year with Alfred Tschol. It is now Herbert Rofner on a regular basis since Ludwig Schweiger no longer teaches.

Thus when January comes around and I feel old, tired, creaky and full of flu, I think, "Oh, God, I've signed up and must go." Each year after Christmas and the New Year, someone asks "Are you going skiing this year?" and I answer, "Yes." "Where?"

"St. Anton." "Who're you going with?" "No one." "Do you know anyone there?" "The whole town." It's the same at Mürren, more so since it is so small.

As this ever-burgeoning opus goes to press I here interlineate the extraordinary winter of 1999, a remarkable close to the century of skiing, the Arlberg Ski Club at St. Anton having been founded in 1901.

I was due to fly from Dulles Airport on February 9. Swissair had to cancel its flight because Zurich Airport was closed by a meter of snow. I arrived two days later. I had met Oliver Schnyder, a Swiss and master pianist studying at the Peabody Conservatory in Baltimore, on the flight. He showed me pictures in the *Tages Anzeiger* of front-end loaders clearing the trolley lines in downtown Zurich. I was able to make it to St. Anton by train without incident, but I had not seen so much snow in the town since 1954 and some time around 1970.

Herbert Rofner and I had a few days of lovely skiing, fabulous snow. And then it began to snow again. The culmination was a three-day snow storm that Toni Eiter, owner of the bookstore where I pick up my *Herald Tribune*, warned me about. He said that the meteorologist in Innsbruck predicted three meters—ten feet—of additional snow. It was exactly as he said.

In town the total accumulation was four or five feet, since we had one day of rain, but, beginning a few hundred feet above town, it was ten feet. All lifts were closed for four days. The train, the main line between Zurich and Vienna, did not cross the Arlberg for one week. Barricades were put across the street a few hundred meters beyond the church, to the east, and short of the railroad crossing, to the west. Two hotels were evacuated at the east end of town—Arlberg and Tirol, I believe—and at our end the Café Seiler, Haus Jennewein and the Bergheim.

We had a nine o'clock curfew two nights. On the fourth day

that the lifts were closed, a beautiful sunny one, everyone went walking, many up the Moos, the bottom of the Galzig ski slopes. I walked up to the S'grubli, Ludwig Schweiger's inn and restaurant, for lunch. It seemed like something out of another century with everyone strolling, chatting, some sitting in the snow, others doing a little light snow boarding or skiing—but no hell bent tearing down the slope, cutting in and out as it usually is. It was remarkable.

After things returned to normal, I stayed the whole month in St. Anton since Switzerland also had lots of avalanches and damage. It was not worth going all the way over there for limited skiing. I had kept in touch with Fritz Stäger, Annelies von Allmen and Bruno von Allmen by phone and knew what the conditions were.

What now worries everyone is, was this the winter-of-a-century?, or is a new more violent weather pattern setting in? Herbert Rofner says we will see more avalanche fences on the mountains next winter.

Mountain Climbing

As I have previously stated in the general section of this saga, I was fascinated by mountains from the time that I first laid eyes on Mt. Kearsarge in New Hampshire. After the war, I was in the active Officers' Reserve and Zandy Harvey told me about a course in basic mountaineering that he had taken in the summer of 1948 at Camp Carson, Colorado, near Colorado Springs. John Kinder and I applied for it and in summer vacation 1949 drove out in July in my brand-new Ford convertible.

We had a good time, especially since I knew Aidan Mullett, and he introduced us to Cappy and Ginny Menary. We climbed in the morning, and stopped for lunch at twelve in a large shed in the Canyon. It invariably rained for a half-hour every day at lunch time. We climbed again in the afternoon. The course lasted two weeks and ended with a climb up something called Bald Mountain, about 12,000 feet high. I had blisters since our climbing boots were our G.I. boots from Army days.

John and I put in a good bit of time at the Broadmoor and also the Cheyenne Mountain Country Club, for which Dr. Mullett gave me a guest card. It reminded me very much of Elkridge, particularly the bar. In climbing we were taught basic rock training, including rappelling, overhangs, tension traverses, etc. We had practice falls in which your partner was well anchored on belay, above and out-of-sight. You climbed up regularly, then quickly took up a few feet of rope and without further warning let the slack go, pushed off and called out "falling." My partner, John Kinder, did the job, fortunately. We applied for the advanced course in the San Juan range, which would have included snow and ice climbing, but neither one of us could obtain clearance from the reserves at home, due to lack of funds. Even when we volunteered to foot our own expenses, they would not permit it.

We headed for Aspen, crossing South Park, one of the beauty spots of the Rockies, and spent a night in Fair Play, a real "Western" town. John was aghast in those days when I ordered a dry martini before dinner. He acidly informed me that it would be more appropriate to order a shot of red-eye in a tin cup. We drove over Independence Pass, 12,500 feet, on a gravel road, and, looking for Aspen, we drove through it and had to turn back at a line of cottonwoods on the edge of town because it was so small. We put up at the Jerome, ran into Sally Chapman and Nancy Atchinson, and arranged to pack in to Snowmass Lake.

We outfitted ourselves at Mike Magnifico's, hired Briggs the sheriff to pack us in, drove up to Maroon Lake and then had a beautiful trip up over Buckskin Pass, where the horses walked through snow banks, down into the beaver creek valley and up through the pine woods to Snowmass Lake, a spectacular setting in a glacial cirque, almost completely surrounded by Snowmass Mountain.

We set up camp in the woods a bit back from the lake. We caught a large lake trout and tried to "plank" it without success. In the morning, we would take a frying pan and some bacon and walk down to the stream dammed up by the beavers. The water was as clear as glass, about a foot to three feet deep. We caught a nice mess of little brown trout and cooked them in the bacon grease. I have never tasted anything better.

We wanted to take a real climb and were lucky that the Colorado Mountain Club came in and camped nearby. They were climbing Capital and Pyramid. One of their members, Jack Scudder from New York, had not done Snowmass so he guided John and me. It was a grunt up over the talus to the snowfield and then a long slog up the snow to the summit ridge, that consisted mostly of big loose boulders and slabs. At the top, that is over 14,000 feet high, the view in all directions was spectacular. To the west it extended to the deserts. On the descent John bounded ahead, but I took my time and Jack stayed with me. In later years John said that he thought that Jack had been a bit too footloose on the summit ridge. We saw an obituary in the *New York Times* about a year after our climb, saying that Jack had been killed when his rope became tangled and jammed in a carabiner and he accidently cut it, trying to free himself. He did a good job guiding us and was a pleasant fellow.

The Colorado training came in handy nine years later. As mentioned in the previous section, I could not go skiing in 1958 and 1959 because of the press of litigation in the Attorney General's office. Accordingly, having had my appetite whetted by H.E.G. Tyndale's *Mountain Paths* in which he described the classic climbs in the Alps made by a group of schoolboys from Winchester, including George Leigh Mallory of Everest fame, I decided to go climbing, particularly wanting to do the Matterhorn after having read Richard Haliburton's account of it as a boy. I had an arbitration in Rotterdam, of which more later, so I combined work and pleasure.

My friend Gaylord Clark had climbed in the west with Eddie Petrig from Zermatt. Eddie had told Gaylord that his brother, Josie, was a guide in Zermatt, so I wrote Josie and booked him. I went over in early August 1958 and checked in at the Mont Cervin Hotel. I trained with Josie every morning on the Riffelhorn, a small peak just off the Gornergrat railway, that dropped on the far side sheer for a thousand feet or so to the Gorner glacier. I did not tell Josie that I had had the Colorado training, but I was thankful for it, particularly on the technical places such as chimneys, overhangs, etc. Josie was impressed when he let me down facing out over the cliffs to the glacier. In the afternoons I would train by stiff walks, my favorite being the steep one out of the town and up the Trift Valley to the Hotel [*sic!*] du Trift, a dump which was used by the Italians working on the Grand Dixence dam project. Toward the end of my training period, I found that I could race up to it non-stop in about fifty minutes. I was becoming fit. About the last afternoon I burst open the door at the end of my training walk, in the fog and rain, and literally fell over Margaret Crawford and Alfred Stäger. They had known that I was in Europe but I hadn't a clue as to their whereabouts. We decided to join forces when I returned from Holland.

I flew to Amsterdam and stayed at the Pays-Bas, going to Rotterdam for my arbitration, about which more in the law section. I flew back to Zurich from Schiphol which is 14 feet below sea level, and 72 hours later I stood at nearly 14,000 above sea level. When I returned to Zermatt, Margaret and Alfred had moved into the Mont Cervin where I was staying, the weather had cleared up and Margaret announced that we were going to the Rothorn Hut the next day to do the Zinalrothorn, about which I had read in Tyndale's book, an excellent climb, in some respects better than the normal route on the Matterhorn.

Margaret did not want to do the Rothorn. She wanted to do only the Matterhorn. She said no one in Australia had heard of the "Zinnel"-rothorn, deliberately mispronouncing it. They had heard only of the Matterhorn. Elias Julen and Alfred, who were guiding Margaret, refused to take her up the Matterhorn unless she first did the Zinalrothorn. They said that Margaret's great uncle, "grande zio," as I explained to my friend from Milan, Stefano Gatti, had climbed the Zinalrothorn for the first time almost exactly 100 years ago to the day. They insisted that she make the climb in honor of this historic occasion.

Margaret, whose maiden name is Stephen, was connected to Sir Leslie Stephen, author of "The Playground of Europe" among others and a towering figure of the Golden Age of alpinism in the mid-19th Century. He had more first ascents than anyone. In any event, up we went to the Rothorn Hut the next day, Margaret and I walking while the guides took the materiel-bahn used by the Grand Dixence workmen. We made the walk in four hours, which is good time. We sailed past the Hotel du Trift. I had been well trained by my climbing with Josie and also by my strenuous walks. In addition, I think that my trip to Holland probably gave my system an extra boost of oxygen.

The next morning we left the hut at four-thirty. We climbed together for a long way, Elias leading two English boys; Alfred leading Margaret; and Josie towing me along. When we reached the main peak, Elias and Alfred with their charges bore off to the left, up the normal route. Josie bore off to the right, and when I asked him where we were going, he said nothing. Finally, as we started up our ridge to the right, I heard him calling over to Elias about a "hakke." I gave the rope a tug and said, "Hey, Josie. I heard hakke. Isn't that a piton?," i.e., *mauerhaken*. It was obvious that it was and that he was asking Elias where a fixed piton was. We found out as the ridge grew nearly vertical and we came to what amounted to an overhang. Josie stationed me firmly and said not to move. Then he climbed up to the piton, snapped in a snap-link, "karabiner," tested it with the rope and climbed up over it. He reached a good stance, went on belay and told me to climb. I called "climbing," as taught in Colorado, and climbed to the piton. I gathered up some spare rope, unhooked the snap link, hooked it on my belt and climbed to Josie, who had a tight belay on me. Then he paid me one of those funny little off-hand compliments which speak more than volumes. "You did that better than I did." Of course that was not true because he was leading, which was much more difficult, but I was pleased, and silently thanked the Colorado Mountain Climbing School.

We continued on with no more overhangs, and when we were on the final peak, the gipfel, we had to traverse to the right to reach the summit platform. There was a good grip on a large rock or shelf which stuck out over the edge, and Josie, who was firmly anchored around the corner, said "Charlie, do you want to look down?" I of course said, "Sure," and looked down toward Zinal. It looked sheer, and actually the top part was, a drop of four thousand feet down to the valley. I was so well trained and height-conditioned that I had no sense of fear.

As Josie and I came around the corner and over the top, the guides were congratulating themselves and us on the historic occasion. Margaret, who was seated on the little summit plateau, looked down at me as I came up the last few steps and in perfect clipped Anglo-Australian accents said, "Well, Charles, I guess we can scratch this one off the list." I thought the guides would pick her up and hurl her bodily over the edge down to Zinal. I rejoined softly with the expression attributed, I believe, to George Leigh Mallory, "Have we conquered an enemy? None but ourselves."

We had reached the top about 8:30 and the descent down the normal route was much quicker. We were at the hut about noon, had something to eat and then set off for Zermatt. I took off at a fast pace with a Cuban, and we galloped down to the town, probably too quickly. That evening Bill Hollenbeck from Philadelphia,

Princeton '40 and a friend of Bruce Baetjer showed up at the hotel, and we helped him and his friend drink his birthday champagne.

The next afternoon, Sunday, we took off for the Matterhorn. We took the lift to Schwarzee and then walked to the Hornli Hut, the Belvedere. I had Josie Petrig as guide, and Margaret had both Elias Julen and Alfred Stäger. Partway up to the hut, the guides met some friends who were coming down from the peak. They chatted awhile, no introductions for us, and then departed. It was Lionel Terray and Maurice Herzog from Chamonix, the first persons to climb an "eight thousander," Annapurna, in Nepal in 1953.

That night a bad storm blew in, thunder, lightning, hail, wind, shutters banging, etc. I had spent a restless night anyway, possibly from too much exertion in too short a time and maybe a touch of "colic." In any event, about four o'clock when it quieted down, I thought, "Thank, God. We can have the day off." No such luck, although at four-thirty, the normal departure time, the hut was strangely quiet.

About six a drama unfolded in the kitchen downstairs. Margaret had awakened, looked at her watch and was horrified at the late hour. She dressed and descended to the kitchen where she saw the three guides, the deans of the Alpine bergfuhrer verein, sitting placidly at the kitchen table drinking white wine. Her opening words were, "You filthy brutes! What are you doing?" They looked around, rather surprised at this outburst, and said, "Having a glass of white wine." At this Margaret burst into tears and said, "But we're supposed to climb the Matterhorn today." "Don't be silly, Margaret," they chorused. "Look out the window. Nobody can climb today." Margaret rejoined, "But I **have** to. I must leave for England tomorrow." Margaret had her car booked on the auto-ferry from Dunkerque to Dover and had to return on a certain date, probably for some toney party with her snappy relations.

A counsel of war was held. I was summoned and told to eat breakfast. I went upstairs, and the next thing I knew, Josie came into the room, rather crossly, had me raise my arms, tied on the rope as if he would cut me in two, turned me around, and led me down the stairs like a cow. It was quiet and gray outside with a light mist falling. It was fairly warm, in any event not freezing. Years later the story came out that the guides had decided to humor Margaret and thought that they would climb a few hundred yards up and then have to turn around and come down. Thus we started up, commencing to climb as soon as we left the hut.

We passed the Moseley Dalle, the first steep place, with the weather still not bad. We were the only people on the mountain, the only ones crazy enough to climb, and we made rapid progress. In two hours, we reached the Solvay Refuge, an aerie perched on the edge of an abyss, giving on the left down the east face of the Matterhorn, and to the right down the north face, overhung by the Zmuttgrat. The guides went inside the hut, leaving us standing outside in the mist and letting us rest for about five minutes. Then we continued. Afterwards they said that at the first sign of colder weather, that would lead to freezing and ice, they would have turned back. It could have been bad.

We came to the fixed ropes and the chains, then the roof, the steep snow field leading to the summit. The steps were huge and solid, and we clambered on up. About eleven o'clock we reached the summit. We had made good standard time, about four hours, and there wasn't another soul in sight. In this respect we were lucky, having the mountain all to ourselves. It was still relatively warm, with no wind, but wet snow began to fall, and I put on my sweater and light anorak. We walked over to the Italian summit with the cross on top. We shook hands all around and congratulated ourselves, particularly Margaret, since she could now tell her Australian friends about climbing the Matterhorn and also get to her party in England. After fifteen minutes on top we started down. When we reached the chains, I felt quite tired. I could hardly hold on to the ropes, but then, as we proceeded lower, I was able to obtain more oxygen and I began to feel fine again.

We reached the Solvay Hut and this time the guides asked us to come in. The overcast had begun to rise because for the first time we could see the valley. Elias and Alfred broke out bottles of white wine that they had left there on the way up and also bread, cheese and chocolate. We had a party, finishing off with the local Swiss cigars, "stumpen." The rest of our descent was hilarious, rolling down the ridge. When we reached the Moseley Dalle, the last steep place above the hut, they sent me down first on Josie's rope. I started down straight ahead, then one of them said, "A little more to the right, Charles." I complied. Then one said, "More left, Charles." Again I complied. Then a third said, "No. Back to the right and straight down." I leaned back on the rope, looked up at the three faces peering at me over the edge of the cliff, and said, "Will you three Swiss guides please make up your goddam minds where you want me to go!" I was greeted by shouts of derision. For years Alfred loved to tell this tale.

We reached the hut about three o'clock, then walked down to the Schwarzee lift and took it to Zermatt. The weather turned beautiful the next day, not a cloud in the sky, but it was just as well that we had had the bad weather and the mountain to ourselves. Margaret had to push off for England and, since I had no desire to go home, now that I was trained and the weather was good, she suggested that I go over to Mürren and do some more climbing with Alfred. "Mürren?" I said incredulously. "All I know about Mürren is what I have read in Sir Arnold Lunn's books, the Palace Hotel and belted earls." Margaret assured me that there was good climbing there, and I arranged to go over and stay at the Hotel Eiger. When I checked my bags with the old-time concierge at the Mont Cervin and told him where I was staying, his eyes lit up and he repeated, "Ah! Hotel Eiger." I felt that I would be in good hands.

It was a gorgeous trip over, and as soon as I met Adolf von Allmen and his wife, Mimi, and saw the Hotel Eiger, I fell in love with the place. As Margaret and Frances have often said, Mürren is a "coo-cuck-clock village at the back side of the moon." Small, cozy, old-fashioned and with absolutely incredible scenery as it sits on its shelf 2500 feet above the Lauterbrunnen Valley and opposite Eiger, Monch, Jungfrau and the western string of Oberland giants, it truly defies description.

I was ensconced in Room 3 in the Eiger, at the southwest corner of the hotel with stupendous views out my corner windows, across the valley to the sheer wall of the Schwarz Mönch and up the valley to Breithorn, Tschingelhorn, Gspaltenhorn and Bütlassen. All the immediate surroundings were a lush green and the village was bedecked with flowers.

The hotel itself in 1958 was priceless, time had stopped still in the 1920's and 30's. Lots of wicker furniture, an old-fashioned dining room with iron stanchions, a "stübli" that looked as if built for the railroad employees who frequented it, a fairly primitive upstairs bar with a place for dancing but no set entertainment, an old-fashioned sitting room, etc. I loved it.

I was a bit foot-sore and tired from my Zermatt exertions, so we took it easy for a couple of days. One afternoon Alfred led me up into the Blumental where he and his father were taking in the hay. Afterwards we had bread and cheese, coffee, white wine and a schnapps in the hay hut. On the way down Alfred stopped at a little shed to milk some goats for his children, of whom he eventually had six. When I re-entered the hotel, it was dark and Mimi was worried that I had been lost.

Another day Adolf took us looking for mushrooms, *la chasse aux champignons*. He was an expert and had a book as well. We collected quite a batch in the woods above the rail line toward Winteregg. When we had finished, we sat down to a little picnic with schnapps.

After my rest days, Alfred asked me where I would like to climb, on this side or across the valley. I elected for the latter. We took the funicula down to Lauterbrunnen and the train up to Wengen, Kleine Scheidegg and the Jungfraujoch, with view stops at Eigerwand and Eigergletscher. At the joch, we left most of our gear at the mountain hut adjacent to the hotel, and set out for the Mönch. I must have been in fantastic shape, because we walked up the glacier behind the Mönch to about Mönchjoch, then turned left up to the rocks of the Mönch, roped up and climbed almost without stopping to the top. The last ridge was quite steep, with big steps like a staircase, but the snow and ice were firm and the going was good. At the top there was no wind, and the view in all directions was spectacular. We looked over the edge to Mürren about six thousand feet below us on its shelf above the valley. I don't believe it took us more than three hours from Jungfraujoch to the top. We lolled around about a half-hour, then descended to the glacier, un-roped and walked back to Jungfraujoch. It had been a lovely day.

The next morning we were up about four, off by four-thirty from the hut and descended to the glacier, the Jungfraufirn. We walked across to the base of the Jungfrau, put on our crampons, roped up and started climbing the front of the glacier. The conditions were perfect, and after Alfred had cut a few steps going in a left-handed direction (looking up) we began to move simultaneously, I holding a few loops of the rope in my left hand and balancing myself against the slope with my ice axe in my right. Alfred's rhythm was a marvel to watch, a swing of the ice axe down and back, step up, chop another, step up, with me following right behind. We climbed steadily and reached the saddle between the Jungfrau and Rottalhorn in about three hours. We stopped to look over the edge. Alfred warned about the outcropping of hard, green ice to avoid on the summit ridge, and then we climbed straight to the top. We were on the summit about eight o'clock. It was wonderful, with all the peaks, glaciers and valleys of the

Bernese Oberland spread out below, excepting of course the spire of the Finsteraarhorn, which was a few meters above us in the distance over Concordia Platz, the Aletsch Glacier and the Grünhornlücke.

We stayed on top a half-hour or so, admiring the view and picking out the various peaks. Then Alfred said that we could go back the way we had come, to Jungfraujoch, or if I felt strong enough, we could take the longest downhill climb in the Alps, longer even than from the top of the Matterhorn to Zermatt. I of course said I felt fine and off we started, down the Hoch-firn. This is the top snow field of the Jungfrau, facing roughly southwest and at a steep angle. I adjusted my crampons and then led off with Alfred holding me on the rope. We moved together but he also took a movie of me with my camera, clomping steadily down like the Abominable Snowman.

After a while we came to rocks and took off the crampons. Then we came to quite a long and fairly sharp ridge with some fixed ropes in it. Alfred said not to touch them since they were rotten. We kept going down, down, down until finally we reached the Rottal Hut in the Rottal, a big high valley, almost a glacial cirque, under the Jungfrau, Rottal Horn and Ebnefluh. It was about eleven or twelve and beginning to heat up. We had something to eat and then started off again, without the rope.

We went down and down, seemingly forever. At one point on the right side of the Rottal, Alfred asked if I felt strong enough to climb up a little way since we might see some ibex. I said yes, and we climbed up toward a small ridge. The wind, such as it was, was in our faces. Alfred cautioned silence, told me to have my movie camera ready, and we crept up to the ridge. As we reached the top, I looked over and there were three ibex, lying down, sunning themselves. They jumped up and I took a fantastic picture of them moving away. When I showed the movies at Zermatt and Mürren the next year, people could not believe that I did not have a telephoto lens—no "zooms" in those days.

We continued on as it became hotter and hotter. I asked Alfred how far it was to Stechelberg, the little village at the head of the Lauterbrunnen Valley. He said "about an hour." We went on and on with no sign of civilization. Finally, about two-thirty, I stopped to ask how far it was. Alfred said "an hour." I asked, "A **good** hour?" I knew what that meant. Alfred said, "No, it really is just about an hour" I took my wristwatch, pointed to it, and said, "Alfred, I am hot and tired and I will walk exactly one hour and then if we are not in Stechelberg you will have to figure out how to get me there because I will **not** walk one step farther." Alfred snorted, "Chasch dänke, Charlie!" which in schweizer-deutsch means something like "Is that what you think?" or, "You say so!?"

On we went. After fifteen minutes, I said "Forty-five minutes left, Alfred." Another snort and an oath from Alfred. After all, I was carrying only myself, my ice axe and a light rucksack. Alfred had all his gear, safety and first aid equipment and the rope. I don't believe I could have lifted up what he was carrying. I was 35 years old. He was 30, about my height, and obviously as strong as an ox. He had asked me if I had wanted to make this trek down. He hadn't forced me to do it. So on we went.

Another fifteen minutes and the scene repeated itself. "Thirty minutes, Alfred." Snort—oath, etc. Then, "Another fifteen minutes to go, Alfred." Of course we both knew that it was a game, a sort of morale factor, but it was hot, I was tired and as Mikki Spurri, a young mountain guide at Mürren said many years later, it feels as if your knees are being driven into your armpits. Then we were down to, "Ten," "Five," and I began to count the minutes, "Four," "Three," and, just as I was about to say "Two," a little roof appeared down below. I stopped. "Alfred, is that Stechelberg?" "Yes." "Alfred you are one damn lucky guide." A look of derision, and probably a grin from Alfred. I could not keep a straight face. "Alfred, two more minutes and I would have stopped. I **mean** it."

"Chasch dänke, Charlie" followed by "Himmel donderli—himmel sternerli" and I don't know what other resounding Oberlander oaths.

We trudged down to the first houses of Stechelberg. We stopped at the Zimmerman pig trough, a bathtub, stripped to the waist and splashed ice water on our backs. It was heaven, after the inferno above. We walked a few more steps to the Ritti, the little pub by the road run by Hitti-Fritz von Allmen, and had a bottle of Spiezer wine with plenty of water. It was about three-thirty in the afternoon, and we had been under way for approximately eleven hours. Not bad for a "flackländer," a sea-level boy!

The weather held beautiful, cool at night, warm and sunny in the day. I even sounded Alfred out on doing the Eiger by the Mitteleggi Ridge, but he said there was too much ice and it was too late in the season. I think that I was up for it, but one can't do everything. We finished with a lovely climb on the Mürren side, the Gspaltenhorn and Bütlassen.

We left Mürren by the road to Spielbodenalp, and climbed up the Brünli, which is frequented by cows. Apparently they don't get height dizzy even though it is steep and exposed. Then we went on to the Sefinenfurka. Here we ran into two groups, or herds, of chamois, gemsen, about forty or fifty in all. I took good movies of them. We traversed around behind Bütlassen and, even though I was well trained and used to heights, I felt a bit queasy as we rounded a corner on a narrow, slippery cattle track with wet, grassy slopes heeling over into a void. Years later I found out that this is well known as the "nasse platte," the "wet place." We reached the Gspaltenhorn Hut, which had no resident keeper so late in the season, and Alfred cooked a wonderful risotto, on which one could have climbed for days.

We left the next morning at four-thirty and reached the summit about eight. We had arranged with Adolf and Mimi to wave at them at that time and they later said they had seen us clearly through the hotel telescope. The Gspaltenhorn is a lovely climb, mostly good rock, and quite a long way up a knife edge with a dizzying drop into Kilchbalm. It was another gorgeous day, and we had a wonderful view of the Oberland, with a different perspective on Eiger, Mönch and Jungfrau. We could see almost our entire descent of the Jungfrau into the Rottal.

We descended to the saddle where we had left our rucksacks, and then climbed the Bütlassen. At one point there is an overhang, and Alfred climbed it. When he sent the rope down to me for the rucksacks, they swung out over the void as I let go of them. I made it up unencumbered, with strong help from the rope. On the far side we had a long snowfield down which we could glissade. Then we had a long tramp down to Boganngen and finally Mürren. It was a lovely climax to a climbing summer. I could hardly believe that I had done what I did.

I left my climbing gear in Mürren in the hopes that I would be back the following summer, 1959, and I was. This was my first flight by jet, on Swissair, and it was hard to believe that we flew from New York to Geneva in less than seven hours. We hopped over to Zurich and I realized that we were going to cross the Bernese Oberland. We flew almost directly over Mürren, and we were at just about the height of Eiger, Monch and Jungfrau. When I reached Zurich and phoned Mimi to tell her she said, "Yes. We saw you."

I went first to Mürren and after a little conditioning, Alfred and I went to train on the Lobhörner, a set of teeth in one of the ridges behind Mürren. They are short but sheer and very exposed. Numbers 1 and 2, I did without difficulty, but I rebelled at the traverse of No. 3 because it bellied out over the precipices. No. 4 for some reason I did not mind, although it is the biggest. Then we had a fantastic rappel down the far end. In later years Hilti von Allmen used to kid me about the Lobhörner.

On Sunday morning I attended ten o'clock Mass in my climbing clothes, with my rucksack and ice axe. Alfred met me after Mass and we walked through Gimmelwald toward Stechelberg, but when we crossed the big stream, we bore right-handed up through the forest to Obersteinberg, a little mountain hotel at the far end of the forest. That climb up was hot and I sweated profusely. At Obersteinberg we had some lunch out on the terrace and I took off my wringing-wet shirt. When we started again it was much more comfortable and it became much cooler as we passed the Oberhornsee, a glacial tarn, and neared the glacier itself. A tramp over the ice and we reached the Mutthorn Hut, set in the middle of the glacier on an outcropping of rock that dropped into a cliff.

The hut was crowded with a contingent of Swiss army troops training in the area. But Alfred's friend, Fritz Gertsch, was in charge, so we were well taken care of. We left early the next morning to do the Lauterbrunnen Breithorn. We had good weather and climbed rapidly over the rocks, which were wet but not icy. When we approached the summit we ran into snow, and when we made it to the top we had a foot of soft new snow. As we were standing there on the peak ridge, a small Swiss army plane holding about six people, with a greenhouse type of canopy, flew quite close by us, and we all waved to each other. The trip back was uneventful and Alfred encouraged me to take a snooze after lunch.

The next day we climbed the Tschingelhorn, which is closer to the hut and not as high or as difficult as the Breithorn, but the temperature must have dropped overnight because the rocks were coated with ice. There was one spot that I did not like at all, but when we came down, the ice had melted. I couldn't even spot where the nasty place had been.

Since Alfred was meeting another client, I walked down to Stechelberg with a German couple who drove me to Lauterbrunnen to take the funicula, no cable car in those days. I packed and took the train to Zermatt to climb with Josie again. I loved the trip over, the little train from Mürren around the edge of the precipices to Grütsch, the funicula down to Lauterbrunnen, a train to Interlaken Ost, then change and down to Spiez with a coffee or a glass of wine on the terrace outside the station under the trees. From Spiez, the BLS, Berne-Lötschberg-Simplon, to Kandersteg, through the Lötschberg Tunnel to Goppenstein at the foot of the Lötschental, down through the avalanche tunnels to Brig, change to the little red train up to Zermatt—one of the loveliest trips in the world.

At Zermatt I ran into Stefano Gatti, Maria and Mrs. Gatti from Milan; Karen and Sonja Chalonge from Paris; Renata and Sonja Gessner from Milan, all of the 1958 group. Karen Chalonge and Renata Gessner were excellent climbers. Josie told me to meet him at the Rothorn Hut and the next morning we took off for the Wellenkuppe and Obergabelhorn, a twin classic. The Wellenkuppe, named by Sir Martin Conway the "White Cap," is a beautiful snow climb with a traverse of a large gendarme. There is a short climb down to a saddle and then a climb to the top of the Obergabelhorn, a spectacular ridge, looking over at the north face of the Matterhorn; then a long, long ridge down the Arbengrat. The parish priest accompanied us with his guide, and we had a wonderful climb.

A few days later Renata Gessner told us that she had done the Junggrat of the Breithorn, a long ice and rock ridge rising up the face of the Breithorn, opposite the Gornergrat. It was named for Geoffrey Winthrop Young, a Britisher who lost a leg in World War I but continued climbing afterwards with his guide, the famous Joseph Knubel. I had not heard of it as a climb and was told that it was difficult, but Renata said the conditions were excellent. I mentioned it to Josie, and he organized his brothers, Eddie, who had returned to Zermatt from Sun Valley, and Herman, who was head of the Mountain Rescue, plus a German couple.

One afternoon we took the Schwarzee lift as far as Füri and then traversed to the Gandegg Hut, small and a relic of the glory days of climbing. We arose the next morning at 2:30 and were underway by 3:15, climbing by candle lanterns down a steep slope to the glacier. We had a long traverse around the base of the Breithorn to the Young Ridge, the "Junggrat." We reached it about seven o'clock, had a bite to eat, and I took some spectacular movies as the sun came up over the cloud layer in the valley. We donned the crampons and began to climb, on three separate ropes. Josie explained that the ridge was so long that we would have not time to take off the crampons each time we left the ice and came to rock but would simply climb up the rock with crampons on. At first it felt like walking on stilts up a slate roof, but, as Josie said, I quickly became used to it and up we went.

We had a snow and ice ridge, then a scramble over a rock field or ridge, no real gendarme, then more snow and ice followed by rock, etc., etc. It warmed up but not insufferably, and we three ropes moved along in tandem. It was spectacular looking over at the Gornergrat where we hoped that the tourists were watching us with awe. When we reached the top of the ridge where it merged into the mountain, it was a bit tricky. First Herman crossed the top of a snow-filled couloir just below a large cornice, anchored his ice axe and the guides rigged up a fixed rope from axe to axe across the couloir. Then we each went over alone, but belayed. After we had all passed over, we stood fast while Herman went up to the over-hanging cornice and chopped a way through it. He passed down a rope and one by one we climbed and suddenly stood in the sun on the rounded summit of the Breithorn. It was about noon.

After enjoying the view, we walked down the summit snowfields and glacier toward Testa Grigia, then bore off down the Theodule Glacier to the Gandegg Hut. There we had a beer, most welcome since it had been a long day, by now about two o'clock. Herman and I, feeling quite refreshed, galloped down to the Füri station. When we reached it, Herman took a small round flask with a long neck out of his rucksack and passed it to me. I took a swig and the tears came to my eyes, homemade absinthe, bootleg for which Zermatt is famous.

I returned to Mürren and Alfred was miffed that I had stayed so long in Zermatt. I had time for another climb and he suggested the Wetterhorn. We took the train over to Grindelwald and took a lift to the Milchbach pub at the edge of the forest. We then climbed to a tunnel through the rocks, the Milchbach loch, at the end of which was the lower Grindelwald glacier. It heeled over to the left into nothingness and when I questioned Alfred about a rope he snorted, no crampons either; we simply walked across the ice in "vibram" soles. We turned right on the other side and climbed gradually over rock slopes to the Gleckstein Hut.

We made the usual early start the next morning and had a long gradual climb up to the ridge. It did not look particularly impressive, but Alfred assured me that it was known for ice and rock falls and avalanches. We reached the ridge connecting the various summits, traversed on the reverse side to the highest peak and then Alfred chopped a way through the cornice and we were on top. Another beautiful day, not a breath of wind, and when we sat near the precipices plunging down to Grindelwald and the Grosse Scheidegg, we could clearly hear the cowbells in the valley nearly ten thousand feet below us.

1958 and 1959 were my big years of climbing, but I did continue sporadically in smaller doses. I came to Switzerland in the summer of 1965 and went to the Engelhörner Hut with Hilti von Allmen and Margaret. I was out of condition and not used to heights and froze on the Ochsenplatte. The weather worsened each day. We had light snow at the hut. Each morning we stayed later and later in bed while Arnold Glatthard and his climbing school clattered through our bunk room to go climbing in the freezing rain, mist and snow. The last morning Margaret and I from our bunks said, "Hilti, we think we have found the perfect guide." Hilti's reply was, "Margaret, I think that I have found the perfect guests."

Hilti was killed in March 1966 in an avalanche near Tres Fluos in St. Moritz, and Margaret and I were lucky that we had this delightful sojourn with him. At his death there was no finer climber in Switzerland, and I still have the letter which he wrote me offering to take me to the Dolomites in the summer of 1966 when he had his vacation. Margaret Crawford wrote a tribute to Hilti in the British Ski Year Book of 1966 and alluded to our mutual comments with Hilti about guides and guests in the Engelhorner hut. The Editor, Sir Arnold Lunn, in his Review of the Year, stated:

> "I am very grateful to Mrs. Crawford for her remarkable tribute to a remarkable man. In all Alpine literature I remember few more moving and convincing tributes of a great guide."

In 1969, after grouse shooting in Scotland, I did not want to go home, called down to the von Allmens, found that the weather was perfect, and flew down and did some hiking with Alfred, including another climb of the Gspaltenhorn and Bütlassen. That climb illustrates how strange a thing acrophobia, fear of heights, is. Alfred and I took an easy way up to Sefinenfurka, not up the harrowing path over Brünli. After we crossed the furka and came to the slippery corner that I did not like in 1958, the "nasse platte," Alfred was aghast when I practically froze. "Charlie, if you can't walk around this, how can I possibly get you up the Laitergrat tomorrow?" i.e. the narrowest part of the summit knife-edge ridge on the Gspaltenhorn. I told him I didn't know but to keep on going. The next day after a good night's sleep, breakfast and a bit of a grunt up the scree slope to the saddle, where we left the rucksacks, we climbed on up and after we had gone quite a way Alfred suddenly stopped and said, "Charlie, I don't understand you. Yesterday you froze on a part (*sic*)—i.e. path—that I could have led a cow up. Today you just walked across the Laitergrat." I laughed and said, "Alfred, it beats the hell out of me." We had a lovely climb the rest of the way; then, after a brief rest and look-around, descended to the col, picked up the rucksacks and started up the Bütlassen. Just below the overhang, in the shadow of the mountain, there was still a light dusting of snow. Alfred had worn his nailed boots, tricounis, because he had seen the snow from the valley. As he was climbing up a steep bit with me firmly standing on a good platform, he had trouble raising his right foot to a stance that he wanted. Without thinking, I put out the palm of my hand and hoisted him up. Not a word was spoken, but I often wonder how I could have done it. It was over in a flash.

Somewhere in these years, Alfred Stäger and Fritz Stäger—not related—had me made a member of the Swiss Alpine Club, in the Lauterbrunnen section. As soon as I was eligible, Fritz Stäger obtained my senior, gold club medal for me. My investiture was to have taken place on the Mauler Hubel, where the English officer prisoners of war in World War I used to drink champagne by moonlight. Hans Josi, the section president, came up from Lauterbrunnen for the ceremony, but on that day it was snowing too hard, so we had the ceremony in the employees' room of the Winteregg ski lift station. We then went over and had a high lunch with Martha Schmidt in the new Winteregg restaurant.

As with my golden Ski Club Arlberg medal, "Ich bin sehr stolz darauf." I am very proud of it. Both medals are featured in my St. Anton mountain portrait.

In August 1977 I received a call out of the blue from Bill Douglas, who wanted to go climbing in the Wind River Mountains in Wyoming. I flew to Denver, we did some light training at Breckenridge, Bill's house being just under 10,000 feet above sea level, and drove to Phelps and Sally Swift's at Pinedale, Wyoming. There we were met by Wayne and Stan Misch from Bill Thompson's Jackson Hole Mountain Guides. Wayne had his guitar strapped to his back and Stan, clad in sneakers, about 17 years old with a pig-tail down his back, looked like the quintessential hippie. Sally wondered what Bill and I had let ourselves in for.

We packed in to a lake from the road head and then had a long grunt up through the forest to our camp site. The weather was bad. The next day we tried to climb Temple Mountain in the fog. But as we climbed higher, the rain turned to snow and we retreated. The following day we awakened to a real snowstorm, packed up and walked out. If we had stayed, we would have had a foot of snow at our campsite.

Stan was one of the best climbers in the Tetons and Bill and I had several delightful trips with him, Bill Thompson, and the other guides. We stayed at Teton Village. Stan was my guide, and we continually surprised Bill Thompson with our exploits. In 1979 Stan and I were just hiking around and casually climbed up to the Indian sanctuary on the subsidiary peak behind and slightly lower than the Grand Teton. We both agreed that the "Grand" looked feasible for me, and in 1980 we did it with Bill Douglas, Bill Thompson, Squeaky Meket, et al.

In 1983 Margaret and I decided to have a 25th Reunion of our big climbs in Switzerland. I took my nephew Charlie with me. Charlie and I went up to the Monchsjoch and made an attempt on the Monch with a guide from Jungfraujoch. Charlie could have made it but I was too old and out of training. We went over to Zermatt, picked up Eddie Petrig, and did Pollux with the help of the new lift up the Kleine Matterhorn. Before we left, Charlie's mother, Anne, had said to me, "Now, Uncle Charles, you won't take Charlie into anything dangerous, will you?" To which I replied, "Of course not, Anne." As we ascended Pollux, we came to a rock face. Eddie was ahead. Charlie was below him on the rope, standing on a foothold about six inches long, and not terribly deep. I was below Charlie, looking up, when I suddenly recalled Anne's admonition. Inwardly, I said fervently, "Dear God, please don't let anything happen to that child." We reached the top without incident and descended by a much easier route.

That is the last real climb that I have done, but Fritz Stäger and

Charles D. Reeves
("Charlie") and CBR Jr.
Schwarzee, Zermatt,
Switzerland at the foot
of the Matterhorn

Below:
Charlie and CBR Jr.
Summit of Pollux,
Zermatt, Switzerland
September, 1983

Charles D. Reeves, "Charlie," and Eddie Petrig
Pollux, Zermatt, Switzerland
September, 1983

Emmi Stäger, Oeli Stäger, (Grandson), Alfred Stäger and Charlie
Spielboden Alp, Mürren, Switzerland
August, 1983

I still do some "walks," some of them quite strenuous. We look nostalgically at the big peaks and reminisce:

"Forsitan et haec olim meminisse juvabit."

Roughly translated from Virgil's *Aeneid*—"Perhaps sometime in the future it will give us pleasure to look back on these things." That's putting it mildly.

Kernan Hospital

In 1895 Dr. R. Tunstall Taylor founded the Hospital for the Relief of Crippled and Deformed Children on 20th Street in Baltimore City, the first hospital south of Philadelphia exclusively for children. Miss Ada Mosby, a daughter of General John Singleton Mosby, the "Grey Ghost," a famous fighter for the Confederacy in the Civil War, had worked in various capacities to assist Dr. Taylor with his hospital. She approached James Lawrence Kernan, a Baltimore theatrical and hotel entrepreneur, to ask him to lend a piano for the children. He had been a childhood friend of John Wilkes Booth and a soldier under General Mosby. Mr. Kernan ended up by buying the Radnor Park estate, west of the City of Baltimore, and giving it to the hospital. In 1911 it changed its name to the James Lawrence Kernan Hospital and Industrial School of Maryland for Crippled Children.

The Kernan Theater and Hotel Company was the main support for the hospital until the time of the stock market crash of 1929 and the ensuing Great Depression of the 1930's. When the business went under, Mr. Redmond C. Stewart, a friend of Father's through fox hunting and the Maryland Hunt Cup, became President of the Board of Trustees of the hospital in 1932 and persuaded a number of his friends to join him on the Board; namely, Messrs. James Whedbee, Hambleton Ober, James Turner, Father, et al. Mr. Stewart died in 1936 and Father was elected President. He served until his resignation on January l, 1955 for reasons of health. He was devoted to Kernan and, in his letter of resignation, asked the Trustees never to forget "the crippled child." While he was President and until David and I grew up and went off to boarding school, college, etc., Father had a regular routine on most Sundays when he would take us first to 11:15 Mass at St. Vincent's on Front Street, the fastest Mass in town, under the old liturgy, and then out to Kernan to make what Bob Abrams, the Medical Director for many years, called Father's "grand rounds." David and I came to know some of the children personally, since they were there for weeks, months, even years. Most of them suffered from "polio," i.e., poliomyelitis.

During Father's time, the hospital was licensed for 126 beds and the old Board of Trustees' minutes of 1950 showed that there was a waiting list. In the early 1950's, about the time of Father's resignation, the Salk and Sabin vaccines were developed, which knocked out poliomyelitis. Streptomycin was developed about the same time and eliminated tuberculosis of the spine and similar orthopedic problems. Father died August 12, 1957. In 1959, after I finished my tour as Assistant Attorney General of Maryland, I was invited to go on the Board, and I accepted with pleasure.

I had not been in the hospital since the war and was surprised to see the changes. The census was only 44, mostly adult orthopedic surgical patients and few children. There were no more separate wards of white and black children, many of them bent on boards in those days to correct curved spines.

There would not even have been that many patients if the Board had not brought a "friendly suit" in the 1950's to eliminate the restrictions to a "children's hospital" in Mr. Kernan's deed of the hospital's property. Miss Pruitt was Administrator, having started out as a nurse. She remembered David and me as "little boys." By that time, Mr. James Turner had succeeded Father as President of the Board.

Bob Abrams succeeded Dr. Voshell as Medical Director. "K.K."

Stewart, Mr. Redmond Stewart's widow was on the Board, as were Mr. Eugene Williams, President of the Western Maryland Railroad, Jim McHenry, Bill Swope, Roger Hopkins, Charlie Wagner and later Bucky Turner.

My first duty was, as a member of the Memorials Committee, to work up a list of lawyers to whom we wrote soliciting financial support from their clients in wills, etc. I became Assistant Secretary to Rieman McIntosh, and then Secretary, a post which I held until I became President in 1987.

During those years we went through a remarkable series of accelerating changes in technology and health-care delivery. Somehow we managed to stay one jump ahead of the curve. When I first came on board, hospital stays were lengthy and we had plenty of money. Then in 1974 the Health Services Cost Review Commission ("HSCRC") came into being in Maryland, and the screws began to be tightened on length-of-stays. At that time, we learned of several large bequests which were coming our way, so we, like many other hospitals in view of HSCRC, spun off the securities of our endowment into a separate endowment corporation, with the members of the hospital board as Trustees of the endowment. At the same time, under the prodding of Joe Leahy, who had become the Administrator to succeed Miss Pruitt, we rewrote the hospital bylaws to comply with the standards of the new Joint Committee for the Accreditation of Hospitals ("JCAH"). Also we shortened the name of the Hospital to The James Lawrence Kernan Hospital. Although we had some children patients and wanted to maintain a pediatric presence, we were no longer a "children's hospital."

Joe Leahy had come to us from the Air Force health administrative system and a hospital building corporation which did some expansion work for us. He instituted a program of having one or two trustees attend each monthly meeting of the Medical Executive Committee ("MEC"). At one of these Bob Abrams asked for permission to buy an arthroscope, an instrument which enables an exploration and even an entire operation on a knee or other joint to be made through a tiny aperture, without opening up the entire limb. Bob made the understatement of the evening when he said that it "might have an effect on our census." Of course we had to have it to keep abreast of developments, but largely due to it we saw our surgery go from 100% in-patient to about 64% out-patient or "same day." Our "patient days" shrank from approximately 17,000 in 1981 to about 7,000 in 1987. I used to kid Bob and say we should never have allowed him to buy that first arthroscope.

The Maryland Legislature had proposed but did not pass legislation which would close some of the hospitals in the state because of over-bedding. The Maryland Health Resources Planning Commission (HRPC) began to push its Hospital Capacity Plan (HCP) under which HRPC had the authority to close hospitals. Also HSCRC turned up the heat in order to save its own neck since it operated under a "waiver" from Medicare regulation only so long as the growth in hospital costs in Maryland stayed below the national average. I stated repeatedly at our Board meetings that Kernan was like a sitting duck on a still pond and that any of the regulatory agencies would love to pick us off. Kernan was an excellent little orthopedic hospital with alumni all over the United States, had a growing endowment and was sitting on approximately 85 acres, nearly all just inside the western city limit of Baltimore. It was worth fighting for.

When I had gone on the Board in 1959, we were faced with a decision as to whether to accept a sizable bequest, which would entail additional construction. It would also involve the acceptance of Hill-Burton funds, a Federal program to finance hospital construction. I voted to accept the funds and proceed with construction. My reasons were that we were in a quadrant or sector of the metropolitan area not served by a hospital and also that Baltimore was starting the construction of a highway around the City, the Beltway or I-695, as part of the Federal Interstate Highway program. This should make us more accessible. Also, about the same time, we had offers to purchase small parcels of our land, all of which I opposed. In 1974 when a 12-acre parcel adjoining our land became available thanks to Joe Leahy's investigation, I urged that we snap it up, at least for protection, even if it could only be used for a goat farm. It bordered our back property which descended rather steeply through woods to Gwynn's Falls. We bought it at what would now be a low price.

As hospital length-of-stays shortened because of pressure by third party payors, Medicare, Medicaid, BlueCross/Blue Shield, insurance companies, etc., and because of bureaucratic action and technological progress, it became increasingly apparent that the days of Kernan's standing as an independent, specialty hospital were numbered. We had one early surprising overture from a comparable hospital looking toward a merger, but a thorough investigation and study with them confirmed what we had felt from the beginning, the staffs of the hospitals were oriented in different directions, and one hospital would have to close and move to the other. This neither wanted to do. But the exercise was a valuable experience for days soon to come.

As the heat was turned up in 1984 and 1985, Kernan had a number of prospective suitors, about 11 in all, and four or five of them were serious. I remarked at one of our Board meetings that we were blessed with plenty of money and were going to spend it on ourselves before making a decision which would seal the fate of the hospital for all time. Thus we undertook full scale surveys with four suitors. I used to say that they told us that they were interested in our soul, but I was afraid that it was our body that they were after, i.e., our real estate and the endowment fund.

In all these maneuverings there was one institution from which we had not heard, University of Maryland Hospital. I knew nothing about them internally but did know that we had had a long standing relationship with them. They had had their pediatric orthopedic residents at Kernan for as long as anyone could remember. Subsequently our historian, Shirley Cammack, found out that University had had a clinic at Kernan before it was "Kernan," since its founding, in order to study pediatric orthopedic problems. I kept asking the Administration, Dick Currie and Jon Harris, "Where is University?" Finally Ken Johnson, head of the University Neurological Department, interested the higher-ups of University because of his interest in rehabilitation. In our discussions with the other hospitals in the summer and fall of 1985 we were coming close to having to make a decision. Bill Swope was President of the Board, and the other members, with one exception, were solidly behind us.

Then one day in mid-September 1985, Dick Currie, the CEO, said that some of the top executives of University were coming out to look at Kernan. Subsequently we learned that Ken Johnson had told them that they had better come quick because we were serious about making a decision. I talked to Dick Currie on the phone after they had left, and he said, "Mr. Reeves, they made an appointment to come back next week." I felt that we had a "live one."

They did come back, Mort Rapoport, President and CEO of University of Maryland Medical System ("UMMS"), Frank Gunther, Chairman of the UMMS Board of Directors, and John Dennis, Dean of the University of Maryland Medical School. They must have liked what they saw because they asked that we set up a meeting with them the next week. Our team was basically Bill Swope, Dick Currie, Jon Harris, and I, as Secretary of the Board and counsel. At the preliminary meeting, which was at UMMS, downtown at 22 South Greene Street, we agreed that we would meet every week, alternating sites at UMMS and Kernan. The next meeting was scheduled for Kernan's.

We duly met and made rapid progress. They outlined why they were interested in us, location on the west side of town, their need for additional property, lower cost at Kernan, etc. When the meeting was about to end, I pointed out that the next one was scheduled to be held at Greene Street. Mort, Frank and John looked at each other and then said that they preferred that it be held at Kernan. I could hardly suppress a grin because up to that time Kernan had always been looked on as remote and hard to get to. It sent a strong message as to our desirability and accessibility.

At the next meeting they made the proposal that clinched it for me and I am sure the others. Whereas all our other suitors had cast longing eyes at our endowment, one of them forthrightly asking if it was "freely transferable," one of the UMMS three said, "We want you to keep your own endowment." I had a strong favorable "gut reaction."

They said we should have an "expediter," to which we had no objection. They suggested the accounting firm of Peat, Marwick, which was our accountant. We had a meeting each week at Kernan, and early in December we were at the point where we decided that we should have something in writing, a letter of intent. We set up a meeting at Piper & Marbury with Richard Tilghman. We explained our intentions and where we stood as to agreements on the part of each institution. Richard hesitated for a moment at the end of the discussion and then said that it looked to him as if we were beyond the letter of intent stage and that we were ready for a contract, simple if possible. We agreed. Rich drew up the contract and after very little fuss and feathers we signed it at Kernan on December 19, 1985. It happened to be the day of our Christmas lunch for the employees. We invited Mort, Frank and John down to the cafeteria for lunch, which they accepted. It was a "done deal" with only the details to be worked out. The announcement was made, and the medical community of the City and State were amazed. We had done it in two months.

At that time UMMS, the former University Hospital, had been privatized only about two years, which showed great foresight on the part of their management to take such a large step and so quickly. Also, they had plenty of internal problems, and I had any number of people ask me if we knew what we were doing. However, as usual, Aunt Frances had her finger on it. When I told her, to my surprise she said, "I'm glad to hear that." I asked "Why?" and she said, "I was afraid that you were going to go with one of those smaller hospitals. I'm glad you went with a teaching hospital." Right on the money, a more difficult course to take in many ways but also a more challenging and ultimately a more rewarding one.

In my naiveté I thought that UMMS could turn a faucet and send patients to Kernan. I soon learned that this was not the case. They had plenty of problems of their own with census, etc. Finally, Dr. Ed Kowaleski moved his "step down" program to Kernan. This was for patients discharged from hospitals but not yet ready to go home. Also UMMS later moved the headquarters for Dr. Dror Paley's "limb-lengthening" program, the Ilizirov procedure, to Kernan. Gradually things began to take hold.

Then we took a quantum leap. The State of Maryland, in its program to extricate itself from the health care business, asked UMMS to take over Montebello, the state rehabilitation hospital, that did a lot of rehab work for Shock Trauma. I assume that UMMS in effect told the State, "No more white elephants," i.e., the 22 South Greene Street old University Hospital which they took over from the State. They told the Governor that they would do it on the condition that they were given money to rebuild it and funds for some years of support because of "non--pay" patients, uncompensated care. The State agreed and UMMS told us that they did not want to rebuild at its then site. They asked our opinion on rebuilding it at Kernan. We agreed, and the rest is history.

They hired RTK&L, a top notch architectural firm, that produced a design which preserved as much as possible of Kernan's rural setting. Ground was broken in late 1994, and when Kernan had the celebration of its Centennial on October 7, 1995, we were able to use the Great Hall of the new structure for cocktails and then adjourned to a large tent for a dinner dance. The next day we used the tent and the surrounding grounds for a large party for the employees.

In April 1996, at our annual meeting I bowed out as Chairman of the Hospital Board, which was replaced by the management committee of UMMS with two or three of the former Kernan Trustees. I stayed on as President of the Endowment Fund corporation. I am invited to meetings of the UMMS Board of Directors and have been on the Steering Committee of their Long Range Planning Committee. Kernan is part of the UMMS Rehabilitation Network and is a state-of-the-art rehabilitation hospital as well as maintaining its position as a top-notch orthopedic hospital. I know that Father would be pleased with the way that it has developed. It has been a fascinating and a rewarding experience for me.

We opened the Kernan Museum in the Mansion House in June 1999, and in one room we have a copy of Mr. Redmond Stewart's portrait in his hunting scarlet as MFH of Green Spring, a photo blow up of Father when he was Treasurer of the Maryland Jockey Club of Pimlico, and a portrait photo of Miss Gardiner who was the Administrator of the Hospital. There is a portrait of Doctor Allen Voshell, and a picture of Dr. Moses Gellman. We had a lovely party with a tent and music on the front lawn. The "old timers" would have loved it.

Anna Emory Warfield Memorial Fund

Solomon Davies Warfield was President of the Continental Trust Company in Baltimore. This occupied the site of the of Mercantile Trust Building on Calvert Street, the first "sky scraper" in the city. It was the building in which I had my offices from 1951 through 1971. Mr. Warfield was also President of the Seaboard Airline

Railroad Company, now part of CSX, which in turn owned the Old Bay Line, The Baltimore Steam Packet Company. In addition, he was "Uncle Sol" to Wallis Warfield, who became the Duchess of Windsor.

Mr. Warfield died in 1927 and left the bulk of his estate to fund an old ladies' home in his country place, Manor Glen, in northern Baltimore County. This was to be in memory of his mother, Anna Emory Warfield. After the Depression there was not enough money for the home, and the provisions of the will were construed to establish a fund for the support of elderly ladies. This was incorporated as The Anna Emory Warfield Memorial Fund.

At first the grants were small, but gradually the investments of the fund grew. Mr. Henry Warfield, brother of Uncle Sol, was president, followed by Mr. William Casey of Maryland Trust Company and then by Lyttleton B. Purnell, III, who was married to Josephine (Jodie) Warfield, a niece of Uncle Sol.

Aunt Ella, as set forth elsewhere herein, was a friend of Sol Warfield. After his death she kept in close touch with Mr. Casey during his long tenure as President. She persuaded him to add Aunt Nannie's friend, Madame Schirinsky, the Countess, as a grantee. Mr. Casey visited her in Paris and saw how an emigré Countess lived in a cold water, fifth floor walk-up.

Dick Emory, of Venable, Baetjer and Howard, had handled the legal aspects of having the will construed and the Fund started. Bobby Harvey, then President and Chairman of Maryland National Bank, was on the Board as was Mr. Edward Dunn, Senior, managing partner of Robert Garrett & Sons. In the mid-1960's Lyt invited me to go on the Board, primarily because of Aunt Ella's interest, and when he decided to resign as President, Mr. Dunn and Bobby Harvey asked me to take over in 1969. I was swamped with securities work at the time, but Lyt kindly helped in getting the Fund set up with the accountants under the new ERISA rules.

We regularly meet at the Maryland Club and then have lunch, provided by the custodian bank, NationsBank. We always drink a toast to Uncle Sol.

We have about 42 grantees from time to time, mostly elderly women, and it is satisfying work. The expressions of thanks are heart-warming. The general purpose of the grants is to enable the grantees to continue to live in their own homes. We now have a substantial endowment enhanced by several bequests over the years.

Mrs. Meredith Dubor was the Secretary of the Board of Trustees for many years. She was followed by Mrs. Thelma O'Neal, who served for fifteen years. Cases are screened by Mrs. Esther Bonnet, formerly of Family and Childrens' Society, before assigning them to the individual trustees who then give their recommendations for approval. In the phrase of Crossan Cooper, it is the kind of charitable work that gives one "psychic mileage." A few years ago the Sunpapers did a deprecating article on Baltimore's "quirky little charities." The Warfield Fund led the list. If the lady writing the article had been a bit more sensitive and had verified her facts, she might have changed her tune. We did not dignify the article with a reply.

Here I think is the appropriate place for the account of an episode in Aunt Ella Clotworthy's life that arose out of her friendship with Mr. Warfield and that turned out to have world-wide implications many years later.

Aunt Ella had tremendous executive ability and Mr. Warfield recognized it after observing her activities in various roles at the time of World War I. At the end of that war, Mr. Warfield was President of the Seaboard Airline Railroad Company, that owned the Baltimore Steam Packet Company—the "Old Bay Line." The line carried freight, passengers, automobiles and trucks between Baltimore and Norfolk, Virginia. He told Aunt Ella that the U.S. Army had just returned the Bay Line's boats in bad shape, and asked Aunt Ella if she would take on the job of rehabilitating them. She at first refused, saying that she "would not think of working for men." Mr. Warfield persisted and Aunt Ella finally agreed. Later she said that her days of working for the Bay Line were some of the happiest times of her life.

She must have taken to business life like a duck to water because she cleaned up the boats, forced Mr. Warfield to reverse a salary decrease for the employees that he had just put in, and developed excellent food. She restored the $1.00 dinner, that was a full home-cooked meal of Maryland specialties.

Then after two years she told Mr. Warfield that she had done everything that she possibly could with the existing boats. If he wanted to further improve service, he would have to give her three new boats. She knew that he should have the money because every spring, in the days before trucking became competitive, the Bay Line cleared $300,000 on strawberries alone. They were off-loaded at Union Dock at the foot of Baltimore Harbor. She told him that he took her money—made by the Bay Line—and put it in his railroad. She wanted her money for the new boats.

Mr. Warfield replied that she would have to present her case to the Board of Directors of the railroad. Aunt Ella must have been terrified—appearing before a board of directors, all men of course in those days, the early 1920's. One of the Directors was a prominent Baltimore dry goods merchant, Mr. Jacob Epstein, who owned the Baltimore Bargain House.

One of my younger partners within the last few years provided me with a pertinent bit of information. He said that he had heard that Mr. Epstein's motto, or "mission statement" in today's parlance, for the Baltimore Bargain House was, "Give the lady what she wants." Tom Washburne tells me that that was also the motto for Marshall Field. Be that as it may, Aunt Ella duly appeared before the meeting of the Board of Directors of the railroad company to give her presentation. I am sure that she must have given a forceful one. By this time, she was Vice President of the Bay Line, in charge of all passenger operations. At the conclusion of her presentation there was silence—and then a single voice quietly spoke up—Mr. Epstein—"Give the lady what she wants."

The Board concurred. Aunt Ella had her three new steamboats. She supervised their construction at the Pusey, Jones shipyard in Wilmington. The first two were named the State of Maryland and the State of Virginia. Aunt Ella christened the third, the President Warfield, named for "Uncle Sol," who had died, in 1928.

The President Warfield fulfilled its mission for years on the Chesapeake Bay. Then it participated in the Normandy landings in 1944, transporting soldiers from England to France. After World War II a group of Jewish businessmen, including Baltimorean Jacop Blaustein, bought the then almost derelict vessel and converted it into a ship which could carry 4,000 Jews displaced by Hitler's Holocaust. It was renamed the "Exodus." It was denied entry to Israel to land its passengers, but it served its purpose in bringing world-wide recognition of the problem. I doubt if anyone knows today, 50 years after the founding of Israel, that the provenance of the Exodus owes much to the approval of a Baltimore Jewish businessman who quietly said, "Give the lady what she wants."

Clubs

Clubs have been a big factor in my life. The first one that I experienced was the Elkridge Club, where I took up golf at the urging of our next-door neighbor, Mabel Whiteley. Recently, Stewart McLean, working on a history of Elkridge, asked me to give him some anecdotes, which I accordingly did and which are set forth herein below.

Grandfather Charles H. Reeves must have joined Elkridge about the time of its move to its present location from Howard County, in 1884. Aunt Ella says she can remember playing on the lawn at the Club, when she was about eight years old. This would tie in with the date since she was born on October 13, 1876. She died on June 15, 1974.

We were members of the group of Thursday night, "cook's night out," regulars who attended Thursday night buffets. The others who come to mind were the Frederick Brunes, Crossan Coopers, Charles Marburgs, Hooper Miles, and William Marburys. Aunt Ella was able to make it to the Club for dinner until she was about 95 years of age. One night as I put her in the car she must have realized that she probably would not be back, and I could hear her distinctly say, "Good-bye, Elkridge."

One evening as we went from the lawn up to our table on the front porch, she looked up at one of the larger trees and said, "That tree shouldn't be there." I said, "Aunt Ella, it has certainly been there forty or fifty years." "I don't care," was her response. "It wasn't there when I was a child." That is when she said she had been coming to the Club since she was eight. When I asked Wallace Lanahan, who was then President, if this sounded right, he said that it was because he had recently been looking at the old records and the move was made in 1884.

Aunt Ella said that the family used to take an outing on Sunday to have lunch at the Club. Since they did not have their own horse and carriage, they would hire what she described as a "sea-going hack." This could hold them all, Grandfather and Grandmother and the four children, i.e., Aunt Nannie, who became a Sister of Charity and spent most of her career at the Mother House in Paris; Aunt Ella, Uncle Harry; and Father. The children would go to the kennels to watch the fox hounds being fed. Everyone would be summoned in to lunch by the ringing of a hand bell. George the maitre d' did this at the 100th Anniversary party in 1978. It was a full day excursion from their house at 926, now 930, North Charles Street, directly across from the Maryland Club.

When Aunt Ella was about 15 and Aunt Nannie 16, they would play golf at a small three-hole course on Lake Avenue, near Charles Street. In other words, just south of the present tenth green. Jimmy Roche was their caddy. He later became club professional and served for many years.

Mabel Whiteley, our next door neighbor on Greenway, urged me to take up golf when I was 14 or 15, in 1937 or 1938. I used to play with Zandy Harvey. The first hole ran south where the driving range is now. The second hole was the present eighteenth. The third hole went up the hill, present number one, etc. A caddy charged $1.00 for eighteen holes. I can remember a crew of men digging crab grass out of the greens, with strings stretched across to guide them.

During World War II, my brother David and Cabell Bruce occasionally worked on the grounds crew. Jimmy Roche was the golf professional, John Roche was the greenskeeper and Willy Roche was the caddy master.

One time, when Mr. Wallace Lanahan, Senior, was president he asked Father to investigate losses from the restaurant and other departments. When Father was querying one of the help, he was told that the Clubhouse had a lot of rats, of which Father duly took note. Then the speaker volunteered, "... and them Roches eats a lot." Father said, "Rats **and roaches**!" "Oh no sir. I don't mean them kind of roaches. I mean Mr. Jimmy, Mr. John and Mr. Willy."

When I took up golf, Father said that he had played at one time and to ask Jimmy if any of his clubs were still around. "Oh no," said Jimmy, "Your father broke all his clubs." Days of wooden shafts.

I continue to use the club regularly, usually for the Sunday night buffet dinners, where Nancy Marburg and I have the table which Aunt Ella and I used to have.

Next came the Green Spring Valley Hunt Club. Courtenay Jenkins urged me to join it after our trip in 1947. Having played golf at Elkridge, I naturally assumed that it had an 18-hole course. The first time I played, with a caddy of course, we played nine holes, and then I asked the caddy where was No. 10. He pointed out the tee, and I said, "but we have already played that one." "Yes," he said, "but that's also the tenth hole." It was a ten-hole course.

After I returned to Baltimore to work, Aunt Ella and I for several years rented a house on or near the Green Spring course. In 1952, we subletted from Anna O'Donovan the Atkinsons' on the west side of Reisterstown Road, south of Valley Road. This is now part of a huge development. In 1953 and 1954 we rented Mrs. Ravida Kennedy Johnson's on Garrison Forest Road across from the third green. In 1955 we had Mrs. Collins (Becky) Burgwin's brand new house on the fourth hole, complete with linen and china. In 1956, we had Kitty and Billy Alexanders', complete with swimming pool. It was a pleasant arrangement. We moved out about July 1 in time for Baker Clotworthy's and David's joint birthday parties. We usually stayed through October and then returned to town. It was also a good experience for me vis-a-vis domestic help because Gertrude Saunders was retiring and we could, but with difficulty, still obtain replacements.

About this time I was asked to go on the Board of Governors of Green Spring. I served from 1954 through 1966, most of it as Secretary. We had the usual club problems, mostly money, but not like it is today with all the threats of litigation. During my tenure, we expanded the golf course to 18 holes, largely because of Herbert Wagner's timely warning that, if we did not do it promptly, it might not be done at all. Also, thanks to Jess Sweetser, who was a member and the peer of Bobby Jones in their respective heydays, and to Roland McKenzie, the Walker Cup great, we engaged Robert Trent Jones as golf architect. He was in his prime and did a superlative job.

We put in the first watering system and bought the Ewing property, now serving as the practice range. When the Pennsylvania Railroad abandoned the track bed of the Green Spring Valley Branch of the Northern Central Railroad and tore up what remained of the rails, I worked out the details with Mr. Carracuzzo of the Title Guarantee Company so that the Club acquired all interests in its property. A claim to them had been set forth in correspondence between Latimer Stewart, when he was president of the club, and his cousin, Mr. Walter Franklin, who was then president of the Pennsylvania Railroad.

It is amusing to note that in the spring of 1996, CSX, as successor to the Pennsylvania Railroad, suddenly posted signs at several places in the Green Spring Valley along the former right-of-way advertising an auction of several pieces. This created an uproar, and after we informed CSX of the status quo, they backed off and cancelled the auction. I particularly remember one small piece that the Club bought from the Pennsylvania since it was subject to an unrecorded fee simple deed that affected the area of the 8th green. This deed was to the Baltimore and Susquehanna Railroad Company in 1832. The Green Spring Valley Branch had been active during World War I. During World War II it had been viewed as a possible vital link around Baltimore between the Pennsylvania and the Western Maryland systems.

I continue to play golf at Green Spring, and the course is in better condition than it has ever been. John Flattery was the pro for many years, a delightful person. I used to call him the Elsa Maxwell of the Green Spring Valley because of his ability and tact in arranging golf matches. When we golfers came in off the course proclaiming the usual woes, I would ask John if he was going to hear Confessions on Saturday night. Curtis Mabry has ably filled his shoes in recent years and has proved a master diplomat.

In 1951, when I went to work, I joined the Merchants Club at 206 East Redwood Street at Mr. Summerfield Baldwin's invitation. Zandy Harvey organized a table consisting of Bonnie White, Dice Waters, Teddy Gorman, et al. We eventually took over Mr. Baldwin's table on the fourth floor. The oak tables and chairs reminded me of the dining room at Gilman. Doris was our waitress for over 25 years. The club had wonderful old time help, but when it fell upon hard times and hired a management "expert" from Texas, that sounded its death knell. Various businesses and law firms had fixed tables. Barty Harvey had organized a table for his Alex. Brown & Sons group and friends, also on the fourth floor. When that group began to dwindle, George Constable came over and joined us, also Ed Northrup, when Zandy became a Federal judge. When the Merchants Club went under in the 1980's, George Constable and I moved the venue to the Maryland Club.

At Bonnie White's invitation, I joined the Maryland Club in 1952, according to the Club book. I played a bit of squash occasionally. I did not go there regularly for lunch since it took too much time from downtown. However, the parties were great fun: the Preakness party on the Friday night before the race, with its Calcutta followed by poker and crap games; the members' Christmas lunch, where we organized a table, at which I ate the same menu that Father and Grandfather Reeves had eaten, pickled oysters, roast pig, pig tails, sauerkraut, sweet potatoes, hominy, hot mince pie with ice cream, and lots of "bubbly." Louis Naumann, of Swiss origin and a graduate of the Lausanne Hotel School, took care of us well.

I was put on the Entertainment Committee and in 1961 ran the first Women's Reception in seventy years. Aunt Ella cautioned me to be careful since there had been some sort of brouhaha at the 1891 reception when they opened the "new" club house at One

East Eager Street. She would not go into details, but ladies had been invited to that function and were never allowed in again.

Dr. Edwin Broyles was the President and I planned the party with Louis Naumann along the lines of the Christmas lunch with lobster thermidor as the piece de resistance. Over 400 people showed up. I had a committee which included some young stalwarts such as Frank Riggs and Tom Burdette, in case there were any trouble. But everything went swimmingly and Dr. Broyles gave me a nice accolade in his annual report to the membership.

I was, and still am, on the Admissions Committee, which is the most amusing committee of the Club. For years its stalwarts were Mr. Gaylord Clark, Chairman, Irvine Keyser, Fife Symington, Bonnie White, Phil Hathaway, et al. In 1961 I was named to the Board of Governors to fill the vacancy caused by the resignation of Stuart Janney. Subsequently I was Assistant Secretary from 1964 to 1967 to Zandy Harvey and then became Secretary in 1967 when he went on the bench. I served until 1983 through some fairly tumultuous times. I became Vice President in 1983 and President from 1987 until 1991. During my Presidency we completed the "new" squash courts in 1988. The step of which I am proudest was our admission of the first Afro-American members.

In 1981, the Entertainment Committee recommended that we have a Children's Christmas party. I was not particularly enthusiastic but went along with the majority. Then the Committee came to me and said they needed a Santa Claus. I as much as said, "So what's that to me?" to which they rejoined, "You're it." It was strenuous ho-ho-ho-ing through a clamoring mob of children and then handing out candy canes behind the protection of a sturdy table. Each year I told Mrs. Mandaro, our manager, that this was absolutely the last year, for me. I finally "hung up my tack" after 1997. Nancy Marburg and Kitty Hoffman were the long-suffering Santa's helpers.

On Saturday night, August 19, 1995, I had retired early. The phone rang about 10:30 P.M. It was Jeff Price, head of the Foreign Department of the Sunpapers, a member of the Maryland Club and a regular, with his family, at St. Ignatius Church. "Charlie," he said, "The paper has just called me and from what they say I think the Maryland Club is burning to the ground." I couldn't believe what I was hearing, especially since the building looks like a stone fortress. I thanked Jeff and said that I had better go to the Club at once. It was a good thing that I did since all of the Club officers were out of town, on vacation.

As I walked through my living room I flicked on the TV, and there it was, on Channel 11, looking like London during the Blitz. It was a warm night, with a light southeast breeze, but not stiflingly hot. I drove down Maryland Avenue, and, at Chase Street where it makes a diagonal to the right and becomes Cathedral Street, I ran into the smoke. It was hard to breathe. I drove to the end of the block on Cathedral Street, at Eager Street, and parked behind a fire engine, which was blocking Eager Street. The fireman said not to worry about parking since they would be there "all night."

I started to walk down the north side of Eager toward Charles Street, but the smoke was too thick. I came back and asked the fireman if he had any sort of mask and he said "no" but that it would be better walking on the south side, which was more protected, and it was. With the searchlights, the smoke, the water and the hoses all over the streets it truly was a picture out of the London Blitz of 1940.

At that time, there was no fire line as such and I walked to the intersection of Charles and Eager. I approached the club entrance, where the Fire Chief and some others were standing in the middle of Eager Street. Bill Wingate, the head doorman, was there. Shortly after, Joan Blake, the maitre d' hotel, and Tony Lofton, the utility man, showed up. A few of the younger members, including Clark Griffin, who is on the Board and Chairman of the Squash Committee, also appeared. The firemen first asked Bill where the gas could be turned off, and then they asked us both how they could get to the fourth floor. We couldn't figure out why they wanted to know, but we explained as best we could. It was difficult because access to the fourth floor is up a small service staircase that is hard to find under the best conditions. Months later, we found out why this was so important. They had to get to the fourth floor to lay down a curtain of water to seal off the major portion of the Club from the old squash courts, where the blaze had started and was burning furiously.

When things quieted down a little I said to the Chief that I did not like to "bother him with trivia" but there was one object of historic interest that we would like to save, if possible. He asked what it was and I said "the portrait of our first president, Jerome Bonaparte, as in Napoleon." A fireman standing next to me with a special red helmet turned and said, "Tell me exactly where it is." I explained that it was on the first floor, toward the east end of the club, on the north side of the east pier in the Eager Street lounge, just off the café. I never gave it another thought until about fifteen or twenty minutes later, someone shouted, "Charlie, here's your portrait," and out came the man in the special helmet, holding the portrait of Jerome Bonaparte in his arms. I could not believe it and thanked him profusely. He was Captain Ronald Baker of the Baltimore City Fire Department, head of the Fire Investigation Bureau.

I turned it over to Walter Schamu, an architect and a member of the Board. Walter pointed out the smoke and water damage. The shellac had begun to melt. It was good that Captain Baker rescued it when he did. It has now been restored and is hanging in the Charles Street lounge, alongside Samuel Smith, second president of the Club.

Shortly after this the smoke began to pour out of the east end of the Club, the dining room and pantry on the second floor and the kitchen above, on the third. The flames shot out of the east gable above the porch, three or four feet into the open air. It was appalling. The firemen had a tower in Eager Street. They moved it east and elevated it to the level of the fire. There was a fireman in the "cherry picker." He directed two water cannon on the blaze, and gradually it died down. I was standing on the sidewalk on the north side of Eager Street just across from the café. It was hard to believe what we were seeing.

I finally left about two o'clock in the morning after things began to settle down. The streets were full of people as the night spots let out. By this time the police had fire lines up, and a policeman had rightly quizzed Walter Schamu and me when he saw me turn over the portrait of Jerome Bonaparte to Walter for safekeeping.

When I reached home, I called Dickie Riggs in Beaver Creek, Colorado. He had already heard from Mrs. Mandaro. The next morning, after church, I called George Constable. He never liked the Bonsparte portrait and always commented unfavorably on Jerome's dour countenance. I of course would counter by praising Jerome's benign look. I told George that we had saved Jerome just for him.

About two months later we had a meeting of the club members at Gilman School, and the firemen explained in detail what they had done. The first company arriving on the scene saw the severity of the blaze and immediately turned in six alarms. The big initial decision was whether to try to save the building or let it burn and protect the surrounding properties. Sizing up the massive construction of the building, they decided to try to save it. They then decided to let the old squash courts, where the fire had started, serve as the "ice box," i.e., the focal point of the fire to be left to burn. The fire had started there allegedly because of "faulty wiring." It now appears that it may have been caused by a faulty "light ballast," which was installed two years before the fire. A claim has been brought against the manufacturer by our insurer, USF&G, since there have been similar cases involving this particular equipment.

Someone asked what the temperatures in the building had been and they said 600–700°. It was possible to go in the building for a short time at these temperatures only because of the new protective materials which had been developed as a part of the space program.

In November 1996, the Club was back to almost full operation. It officially reopened in 1997. Dickie Riggs and his committee did a fabulous job in the restoration process. The *Sunpapers*, instead of criticizing the Maryland Club, as they usually do, wrote factual articles about the fire and had a complimentary editorial, praising the Club for its role in bringing young people downtown and helping preserve the City. At the same time, Dickie and his committee pushed through the settlement on the properties to the south of the club property, which the Club was in the process of buying, so that the Club now has a large area for member parking. It took courage to purchase the property in such circumstances.

Dickie Riggs and his cousin, Frank Riggs, also had the idea of converting part of the huge basement of the club into a state-of-the-art exercise and fitness facility, adjacent to the squash courts. It replaced storage areas, coal bins, a terrapin pen and God knows what else. It is a resounding success and has even recruited superannuated members like me, trying to condition myself for skiing and golf.

15

LAW PRACTICE

I have already covered part of my legal career, law school, Bar exams, employment by Nick Shriver, first experiences, and setting the stage for winter vacations, that I somehow managed almost every year. As I write these reminiscences, it is sad to hear the comments about present day law practice. I had my share of dull stuff and grinding away but mostly, from the perspective of many years, it was fulfilling and interesting. As I look back, I don't think that I would have wanted any other career. I will touch on the high points and let the dross settle to the bottom.

Nick Shriver used to be one of the counsel for the Baltimore Transit Company, and in *Joeckel v. BTC*, 208 Md. 586 (1955) we argued the last appeal of a trolley car case in Maryland. We naturally won because decades of BTC house counsel had tightened the screws down so that it was almost impossible for a plaintiff to win. I wonder if the old trolley car cases will have any relevance in the present day of "light rail."

In the spring of 1957, Zandy Harvey mentioned to me at a Bar Association meeting that he had been serving as Assistant Attorney General of the State of Maryland. He was about to return to private law practice and wondered if I would like to succeed him. I was intrigued because I had never thought of it. In those days it was like a post-graduate law course. The Attorney General was an elected official but the Deputy and the Assistants were taken from private practice. This is no longer possible because of extreme specialization and the impossible conflicts of interest for anyone in a large firm.

I was interviewed by the Attorney General, C. Ferdinand Sybert, and was offered the job. I started in early July and had one of the most challenging, interesting and rewarding times of my life. Since this was just before the explosion of litigation and the legal profession, there were only about five or six Assistant Attorneys General, plus the Deputy, Steadman (Nippy) Prescott. Ferd Sybert was a wonderful person under whom to work since he was quite shy, did not like to go into court and let his assistants take full responsibility for their cases.

I served from July 1957 through February 1959 and during that twenty months I argued 13 cases in the Court of Appeals, Maryland's highest court. One argument was a "double," the Martin and Rheem sales tax cases, and a number were criminal appeals, but recently someone at Venable said that we have senior litigators who have never been in the Court of Appeals. I was lucky.

One of my advisees was the Board of Supervisors of Elections of Baltimore City. As an incidental duty I had to "rewrite" the election manual for the elections in 1958, primarily because of changes in voting machines that were no longer in use. "Miss McSherry," who ran the office, held my feet to the fire on this one.

She was a remarkable person, nearing the end of her career, but I am glad that she was still running the office when I served. She was a grandmother, Mrs. Tyson Greer. To the office and everyone in the legal community she was still "Miss McSherry," her name when she had been hired in 1916 by Attorney General Albert C. Ritchie, later to be four-term Governor of the State of Maryland. She ran the office, assigning most of the cases, doling out the requests for opinions, codifying the opinions to be published in the annual volumes of Opinions of the Attorney General, dealing with the politicians, etc. We got along famously. My office, on the 12th floor, was at the west end of the building, No. 10 Light Street, then Maryland National Bank Building, now NationsBank, so that visitors to me had to pass by the entrance to the library, on the north side, where Miss McSherry held forth. Whenever the Board of Supervisors of Elections of Baltimore City came in to see me, she would stand in the doorway, with her head tilted back, and hold her nose. She did not have too high an opinion of "pols," the "b'hoy" type!

Aunt Ella and Aunt Frances were possessed to hear me argue a case. I relented under pressure and let them come to the Court of Appeals to hear an inheritance tax appeal from the Circuit Court of Kent County, involving the doctrine of "implied consideration." *Register of Wills for Kent County v. Herman Blackway*, 217 Md.1 (1957). Zandy Harvey had tried the case below and the Attorney General, and Zandy, wanted it appealed since the lower court in typical Eastern Shore informality had allowed counsel for the taxpayer to take the stand and present evidence for his client and the deceased transferor of real property.

Aunt Ella and Aunt Frances sat in the rear of the lovely old Court of Appeals courtroom, which was then in the old State House, the oldest in continuous use in the United States and the place where George Washington surrendered his commission as Commander-in-Chief after the American Revolution in 1783. The five judge Court of Appeals consisted of Chief Judge Frederick W. Brune, and Judges William Henderson and Hall Hammond, all friends of the family, plus Judge Charles Markell from Southern Maryland and Judge Horney from Chestertown, Kent County who had been the Circuit Court judge below. Judge Horney excused, or "recused," himself. In any event, the three judges who sat in the center knew me, and I am sure that they saw Aunt Ella and Aunt Frances, both of whom they knew well, sitting in the rear of the courtroom. They put me through my paces. Then to everyone's discomfiture Judge Brune laid out the local lawyer for taking the witness chair and testifying. But it turned out all right in the end for him since the Court of Appeals found in his favor and affirmed the lower court. Looking at the briefs today, forty years later, this looks fair under the equities, although the procedure at the lower court was slipshod. It also made good inheritance tax law since the doctrine of "implied consideration" was now blessed by the courts instead of being only an opinion of the Attorney General first enunciated in 1940 by Attorney General William C. Walsh and his Assistant Attorney General, Norwood B. Orrick, a few years later to be my partner.

By reason of my clients, the Election Board, the spring of 1958 was a busy one since it was the year of a general election. Three times that spring I was in the Court of Appeals on "typewritten briefs," which means that, being election cases, they were expedited and there was not time enough to have the briefs printed, as mine customarily were by the presses of the *Daily Record* under the supervision of Chester Watkins.

The first case was *Claude B. Hillman, Secretary of State, State of Maryland v. Louis V. Collier*, 217 Md. 93, which involved a section of the election laws that never should have been approved by counsel for the Maryland Legislature when it recodified the Election Law in 1957 or by the Attorney General's office. This was a provision requiring a candidate for election to the United States House of Representatives to "be a resident of the congressional district in which he seeks election." Louis V. Collier resided in the Second Congressional district but filed for election in the Fourth. Mr. Hillman's office refused to accept his certificate of candidacy because of the above provision of the law. The primaries were due to be held May 20, 1958. By letter of March 27, 1958 the Attorney General had expressed doubts about the law but could not advise Mr. Hillman to ignore it.

I did my best to uphold the law on the appeal. This involved going to the Library of Congress in Washington, D.C., and reviewing the Precedents of the House of Representatives, but I could not convince the Court of Appeals that this residency requirement was not an additional qualification. The most interesting precedent was one in which Joshua Barney, later to be the local naval hero of the War of 1812 in Maryland, tried to prevent the seating of one William McCreary because of a residency requirement. The House and Senate are the sole judges of the qualifications of their members, and the House simply seated McCreary by stating in a resolution that "the said William McCreary is entitled to his seat in this House." I tried to sow doubt with the Court of Appeals but to no avail.

I had a "ghost voter" case against Hyman Pressman when he challenged the right of people to vote from their old addresses on the site which was razed in Baltimore City to construct the present State Office Building on Preston Street. *Board of Supervisors of Elections of Baltimore City v. Weiss*, et al.—217 Md. 133, 141 A.2d 734 (1958).

We were also involved in the Theodore R. McKeldin suit to run for Mayor of Baltimore in 1959 after two terms as Governor of Maryland. Frank Gallagher sued the Election Board on the grounds that McKeldin had abandoned his Baltimore domicile by reason of his residence as Governor in Annapolis. Representing the Election Board, we argued that we had to accept the candidacy and let the opposing forces fight it out. McKeldin prevailed. *Francis K. Gallagher et al. v. Board of Supervisors of Elections and Theodore R. McKeldin*, 219 Md. 192, 148 2d 390 (1959).

We also had a number of lower court cases, that kept me hopping. One in particular was low comedy since it involved one Joe Bertalo who was "shanghaied" into running for State Senator in the Baltimore City First District against Joe Bertorelli, a well entrenched Democratic Senator. Mr. Bertalo worked on a tug boat in Baltimore Harbor and first one and then the other faction would get him "well oiled" first to file for election since his name would appear on the ballot just ahead of Joe Bertorelli's, then to withdraw his candidacy, again to reinstate it, etc. It was ward-heeler politics and gave the newspapers a field day. Mr. Bertalo was eventually allowed to withdraw his candidacy and Joe Bertorelli continued to represent the First District.

The biggest hassle in which I was involved was a sales and use tax case (or cases) involving the Glenn L. Martin [Aircraft] Company and Rheem Manufacturing Company. Ted (Dice) Waters would ordinarily have handled it, but because of potential conflicts of interest he could not. It was accordingly assigned to another assistant, who for obvious reasons shall go nameless. This assistant was strictly a political appointee, practically never wrote an opinion except on the most mundane level and, as it turned out, was totally incompetent to handle anything of a major nature. About all that I ever heard him do was give advice on a very low level to the police department. He was a nice person but—

With this as background, one day shortly before Christmas Ferd Sybert called me into his office and asked me if I would do him a favor and I of course said yes. He then told me that the above Assistant Attorney General had missed the deadline for filing the brief in the Court of Appeals for the Martin and Rheem cases. He hadn't even started to write it. Because of the parties involved and the millions in sales and use taxes, the Attorney General had obtained a special order from the Court of Appeals to extend the time for filing the briefs which was in about two weeks. Would I take over? That was a challenge.

Ed Englebert, Counsel for the Retail Sales Tax Division of the Comptroller of the Treasury, would help me with all the details. My opposition was formidable, William L. Marbury of Piper & Marbury with Mr. Charles Evans, Fred Cross, who had been house counsel for Martin, and Jack Jones, who later came into the A.G.'s office about the time that I was leaving. I went to work at once with

Ed Englebert, who was a diligent public servant. A lot of people, those who came up against him, thought he was arrogant, and maybe he was when you were on the other side. But he and I got along fine. After all, I was trying to pull his chestnuts out of the fire.

I began to find out what a fire it was. He was unaware that I knew Mr. Marbury personally and that the families had been friends for a long time, particularly the Slingluffs, two of whom were his aunts and great friends of Aunt Ella. Ed Englebert and Mr. Marbury had locked horns at least ten years before when Mr. Marbury began to carefully shepherd a number of defense-contractor cases through the sales and use tax maze. These involved "facilities contracts" and Mr. Marbury, when he was in government work in World War II, had had a hand in drafting the contracts so that title to the materials would pass immediately to the United States government, with no title passing through the contractors like Martin and Rheem. This resulted in no Maryland sales and use taxes. Ed had apparently lost one case after another against Mr. Marbury, as indeed who wouldn't? Finally in desperation he persuaded the Maryland Legislature to pass an act which purportedly would make this type of transaction subject to sales and use taxes and make it retroactive for ten years.

I pitched right in on the brief and Ed helped as much as possible. I remember working all New Year's Day of 1958. That evening I went out to Stone Hall at Trafford Klots' invitation, Isabel was away, to eat haggis and drink champagne with Kitty and Ethel Hoffman and Charles and Nancy Marburg. It was quite festive, a welcome respite to working on the brief.

Ed and I put the brief together as quickly as possible and made the second deadline. During the course of the writing of the various briefs, Mr. Marbury asked me to come over to his office one evening to discuss a point as to which he said that we were "disingenuous." I can remember Ed cautioning me to watch out since Mr. Marbury appeared so gentlemanly but "you can't trust that man." I didn't mention to Ed that I knew Mr. Marbury pretty well. But it is true that neither of us pulled any punches.

We lost on appeal in the Court of Appeals, as expected, but at least Mr. Marbury and his team knew that they had been in a battle. I petitioned the Supreme Court of the United States for **certiorari** since so much money was involved. One of the points in my brief was that the question of constitutionality of retroactive taxation under the U.S. Constitution should not be left to a state court. The case is reported as *Comptroller of the Treasury of Maryland v. Rheem Manufacturing Co.*, 358 U.S. 822 (1958) Reported below 216 Md. 259 (140 A.2d 301). The Supreme Court refused to grant **certiorari**, but Mr. Marbury gave me one of those off-hand little comments which mean so much. He said that my point about retroactivity was a good one. "Praise indeed!"

I also enjoyed a remark made by Chester Watkins, who was in charge of printing briefs at the *Daily Record*. He gave me my first brief in galley proofs, but after that he said, "Charlie, you make very few changes. I am going to give you page proofs from now on."

In the summer of 1958 I took off for Switzerland for some mountain climbing, as set forth hereinabove. I combined the trip with an arbitration hearing in Rotterdam for Nick Shriver for a firm client. I stayed in Amsterdam and one evening I visited my friend from St. Anton, Jeanne van der Valk. She was staying with friends of hers, the Burgerhouts, at Duindigt, near the Hague. After dinner, the host, Dolf, asked if I would like to take a "little tour." I said yes, and instead of taking an automobile tour, we drove down to his airfield which was part of a private race track, wheeled out an airplane and took an aerial tour of Holland. We flew over Roseborg, which was then swamps and estuaries, in which the Burgerhouts had interests. It became soon thereafter part of the huge new Europort of Rotterdam. Mrs. Burgerhout was connected to the Fokker aircraft family. I told them that their "little tour" outdid the Texans.

Their house was a new one, not far from the North Sea or English Channel. The old one had been bombed out by the British since the Germans had V-1 and V-2 rocket installations on the property.

At the end of my Attorney General tour, we were short-handed and they piled too much on us. In addition to our usual workload, we began writing answers to habeas corpus and post-conviction-procedure appeals. I started to feel the pressure physically and was glad to return to the relative security of Cross & Shriver.

Of course everything always happens at once in the law, and 1961 was no exception. A client of mine became involved in an oil exploration deal in Midland, Texas with a mutual friend of ours. His banker called me in and I had to blow the whistle. The figures were fairly substantial for an individual, so I flew down to Midland to try to sort things out. Fortunately my Princeton '45 and Ivy Club friend, Toby Hilliard, was there in the oil business. He was the uncrowned mayor of Midland. I had no idea who wore the white hats and who the black, so I laid the while thing before Toby. At the end he said, "So that's where the money went?"

He put me in touch with a good law firm, Lynch & Chappell, and we began to sort out the mess. In the process I met a number of characters, including J.P. "Bum" Gibbons, who was about 6' 8", wore a huge Stetson hat and boots and had the top of one ear cut off, bitten off, in a fight, they said. He had started out as a mule skinner and eventually made a fortune supplying wildcatters and, I suppose, doing some wild-catting himself. My client was on the hook as the "guarantor" of a substantial amount. All we had to do was pay up.

In the midst of all this, I received a call from Arthur Machen at Venable, Baetjer and Howard. I had heard that he was looking for help in the securities field and had contacted him. He was calling to say that they had checked me out and would like me to come over. I was just about to run back to Texas, so I said I would call him as soon as I returned. This I did, worked out all the details and switched as of November 1, 1961. Physically, it meant only a move from the sixth to the fourteenth floor in the Mercantile Building, but it was a soul-searching and wrenching experience, since lawyers were not fungibles in those days.

As soon as I checked into Venable, I disappeared for about two weeks to Midland, unscrambling the oil snarl. Mr. Eney, who ran the firm with Mr. Cooper, must have wondered what he had hired. On one of my Texas trips we had a true Texas-type experience, a bankruptcy hearing in the U.S. District Court for the Western District of Texas. Going to the District Court in Maryland meant walking two blocks up Calvert Street to the United States Court House, but in Texas it meant taking a Viscount prop-jet and flying an hour and a half from Midland to El Paso.

As the Midland matter wound down, the securities work picked up and Arthur Machen and I had a merry time with underwritings, IPO's, initial public offerings. They came to a grinding halt in May 1962 when the market collapsed, just about the time we finished the last of our deals. Brother David was married after Easter and I took off shortly thereafter for Zermatt to do the Haute Route with Margaret Crawford, as set forth hereinabove in the "Skiing" section.

When the securities business dried up for a while, I went to work for Mr. Eney and in 1963 we handled a case **pro bono** for the Republican Party in Maryland. Hyman Pressman was running for City Comptroller, had been defeated in the primary and wanted to change party allegiance for the general election. He was challenged by Frank Gallagher and the Democrats. Time was of the essence. Mr. Eney ran the show and organized a team consisting of Bob Thomas, Bob Bair, Joe Kaplan and me. The case took exactly one week from the initial filing in the Circuit Court for Baltimore, through a hearing, decision, appeal to the Court of Appeals and a decision by that court. We won. *Black v. Supervisors of Elections of Baltimore City*, 232 Md. 74, 191 A.2d 580 (1963).

In 1966 and 1967 I had an interesting time when Eddie Johnston decided to build a boat he could use for his marine navigation, particularly as escort for the Bermuda sailing races. Having found that Congress had passed a special law governing oceanographic research vessels, we made her into an "ORV" and took advantage of the various favorable provisions of the law. For me, it involved several trips to Norway, first drafting the contract with the Norwegians and then overseeing the final details of delivery of the vessel and payment for it. When there was a construction delay in May 1967, Eddie sent John Eareckson and me to the Förde Fjord for some salmon fishing. I caught, or "killed," the first salmon of the season, 9.6 kilos or 21.2 pounds. They offered to buy it from me to ship to Oslo for the restaurants. I had it smoked and airmailed home.

When John and I headed back to Bergen, we had an incredible bus trip over the mountains through 25 feet of snow at the summit and then a hairpin-turns descent to the Sogne Fjord at Balestrand where everything was green and the flowers and fruit trees in bloom. We went by boat through the fjords to Flom and by bus to Myrdal on the railroad on the Hardanger Vidda.

When we took delivery of the ORV Annandale, Eddie had imported a crew of his Bermuda sea-faring friends, and we sailed her to England and up the Thames to the Catherine Dock, where Sir Francis Chichester had recently landed after his solo round-the-world trip by sail. Eddie showed his navigational expertise by hitting the marker off the mouth of the Thames on the nose.

In London, we stayed at the Grosvernor House. I left them there and came home via Ireland. This included a visit to Cousin George Kenny at Ennis. He gave me a lot of family history and was the unofficial historian of the area. All the young consulted him. I also stayed two days at Riversfield, a lovely place near Kilmallock, with Peg Watt, a great friend of Ethel Crimmins. We had two days of racing at Mallow, straight out of *Experiences of an Irish R.M.* One evening, at Mrs. Watts', we had a notable dinner at which everyone had to sing a solo. I was about to panic when they came to me, but I gave them, "Some people like to hunt in Harford County." The applause was deafening, so I gave them an encore, "I'm always chasing tail hounds," two old Elkridge Fox Hunting Club songs which Father used to sing. The next day I drove Mrs. Watts' trainer, Willy O'Grady, to the Rock of Cashel and we had a high lunch at the restaurant in the old bishop's residence.

In 1969 I went grouse shooting in Scotland, beginning on "the glorious twelfth," as set forth hereinafter in the section on "Shooting." After the week's shooting was over, there was no compelling reason to dash home so I called down to Mürren. They said the climbing conditions and weather were beautiful, so down I went since I had left my climbing gear with the von Allmens. Alfred and I did the Gspaltenhorn and Butlassen again, and he remarked that I was in good condition, from climbing up the moors.

One evening I was at peace with the world, having had dinner, sitting at the bar, "um die ecke," i.e. "around the corner," chatting with Paul the bartender, when the phone rang. Paul said, "It's for you, Charlie," so I said, "Fine. I'll take it here." Paul said, "No. You'd better take it in the box by the office. It's international." I went out to "the box," wondering what it was all about, and to my surprise there was my then secretary, Marge Grossman, on the other end. "What's up, Miss G?" She then explained that she had just received a call from Nanny Martin who had told her that Kitty Hoffman and Carol Brewster had had a traffic accident in Hungary. Kitty was being detained. Either Nanny or Carol would call me in the morning. Thus began my "Hungarian caper," one of the most fascinating experiences of my life.

Carol called early the next morning and explained that she and Kitty were on their way back to Vienna to turn in their car after having toured Eastern Europe, Yugoslavia, Rumania, Bulgaria, Hungary, without incident. They were stopping for gas at Tatabanya, Hungary. The entrance was confusing and when they turned in, a motorcycle had hit them and the driver was killed. Carol was allowed to come home, but Kitty was detained since she was the driver. She had returned to Budapest and was staying there in a hotel. She had Hungarian lawyers and the U.S. Embassy had been most helpful.

By chance Mr. and Mrs. John Henry Lewin, Sr. were due at the Eiger that evening. I asked Annelies von Allmen to look into how I could fly to Budapest. After talking to Mr. Lewin, who said I should go down there right away, and after finding out from Annelies that I could get a visa in Berne and fly Swissair to Budapest, I called Kitty at the Hotel Royal on Lenin Korut and told her that I would be there within 48 hours. Later she told me that the Embassy had told her that I must be dreaming. But that's what I did.

I took the train to Berne, obtained my Hungarian visa with little delay, as a "tourist," and caught Swissair from Zurich in the afternoon. I took a taxi from the airport to the hotel, and called Kitty in her room. She asked where I was and I said "Downstairs, at the desk." She could not believe it. That evening she and Betty Walden, one of the Embassy people, took me to dinner at Gundel, a lovely introduction to the "old" Budapest that Father loved, with its gypsy music.

We went back to Betty's afterwards, and a bit later Kits said that she would have to go since she had to report at Kapok, the police, in the morning. I asked her how she was going to go home, since it was a little distance, and she replied that she was going to walk up the river a block or so and catch the bus to her hotel. Since it was nearly midnight, I asked Betty if it was safe for Kitty to go alone, and Betty replied that it was safe everywhere in

Budapest, with one area possibly excepted. This was of course the height, or the "depth," of the "Cold War," and the Communists, Russian and Hungarian, had a tight hold on the country and the city. In 1956 the Hungarians had tried to revolt and were brutally crushed. In 1968 the Czechs, next door, had tried to revolt and the Russians moved in with tanks, the "Prague Spring." But under a totalitarian regime crime is also ruthlessly suppressed.

The next day I went to the Embassy and was briefed by Gil Sperling, the Consul. I also met the Ambassador, Alfred Puhan, and the Deputy Charge of Mission, Francis Meehan. They were glad that I had shown up on Kitty's behalf, since that relieved them of a lot of responsibility.

The following day I met Kitty's lawyers, Gyula Simon and Gyula Gayer. The former was older, had been a corporate lawyer in Budapest before the war and looked like Mr. Punch. The latter was younger and resembled a contemporary American lawyer. They could not have been nicer, were very competent and were one hundred per cent behind Kitty. The one thing that became apparent was that it had to be an absolutely apolitical matter. I assured them we had no intention of escalating the matter and had complete respect for the Hungarian judiciary on a matter such as this. Throughout the entire proceeding we bent over backwards to respect their laws and their legal system.

I was convinced that the two Gyulas were doing everything possible for Kitty in preparing for trial. They outlined for me the probable schedule, and explained that the venue would be Esztergom, near the Czech border, on the Danube River, the seat of Komarom County, in which Tatabanya, the site of the accident, is located. I flew to Zurich, took the train to Mürren, packed and went home, expecting to have some time to pull things together before Kitty's trial came up. It was now early September.

To my surprise, about two weeks later, Gyula Gayer called to say that the lower court trial had been set for September 30 in

Esztergom. Fortunately I have saved my old office daybooks or "diaries" and can find the exact dates, which I never could do from memory after nearly 30 years.

I flew back on September 25, a Thursday, was briefed by the Gyulas with Kitty, and on Tuesday morning September 30 we drove to Esztergom in two cars, the two Gyulas, Kitty, myself and Gil Sperling, the consul. As we left the outskirts of Budapest, I noticed a camp or containment area on our left, with a red star flag flying from a flagpole. I asked what it was and was told that it was a Russian Red Army garrison. As we reached the outskirts of Esztergom there was a similar one on the right and I was given the same answer to the same question. The Russians kept a low profile in the City of Budapest. Occasionally one saw the soldiers off duty looking at the huge Red Army war memorial, but the body of troops were kept outside the cities and were stationed in a series of camps which reached across the country from the Czech or Polish border on the north to the Yugoslav border on the south. Apparently the Russians had the same system in all their occupied territories, Poland, Rumania, Bulgaria, East Germany and, I suppose, the Baltic States.

We arrived in Esztergom early. The trial was held in a plain court room that looked a bit like our old Peoples' Court in Baltimore except that it was not over the fish market, as ours used to be, and was clean. The building was a non-descript low modern one, a bit ramshackle, not bad, just poor-looking and threadbare. There was a single judge, young, solid-looking but not unfriendly. I can't remember all the details, but the two Gyulas, with an interpreter, took the testimony, including that of Kitty. We finished about one o'clock and then broke for lunch.

That day we ate in a restaurant near the river, and then walked down to see the ruined bridge, leading to Czechoslovakia on the opposite bank. It had been destroyed by the Germans in World War II to stop the Russian advance, and had not been restored.

The span was partly submerged in the river.

We readjourned in the courtroom after lunch, and the judge handed down his ruling, which was translated for us. He found Kitty guilty and handed down a jail sentence of fourteen months. He explained that with good behavior she would be free in eight months. Naturally, we were all depressed, but the lawyers had warned us not to get our hopes up. The sentence was in line with Hungarian law.

It was a beautiful afternoon, and we took the long way back to Budapest along the Danube, stopping off in Vizograd to see the archeological diggings going back to Roman times. I duly reported to the Ambassador and told him that we would file an appeal at once. I see from my calendar that when I arrived home I went down to the State Department on Wednesday, October 8, and must have reported to John Vought, who held down the Hungarian desk. Again, I expected to have some time before the appeal came on for hearing.

Suddenly, a day or so later, a call came in from Budapest advising me that the hearing on the appeal had been set for the next week. I made arrangements to return at once. On Sunday night, October 12, I was at the David Barretts' for cocktails, and there I ran into Ollie and Nancy Reeder, who were off on a business trip to Norway and then going down to Vienna. I said that if I had any delay, I would look them up. Little did I know how it would work out.

I flew back to Budapest, was briefed by the two Gyulas and up to Esztergom we went, ready to argue the appeal. There was a delay when we went into the courtroom and finally they said that they did not have an interpreter. We would have to wait approximately two weeks. I was sunk. There was hardly time to fly back to the States and return. At this juncture Herb Wilgis, economic officer for the Embassy, really blew up outside in the square. Here I was able to fly all the way back for the hearing and be ready on the appointed day, while the Hungarians couldn't even get an interpreter to Esztergom. Herb is a big man, and he was fuming.

Somehow we restrained him and we returned to Budapest. I talked matters over with Gil Sperling and the Ambassador and decided that I would stay in Europe. I could go out to Vienna and see the Hojos Bank people, to whom Benjie Griswold had introduced me, in case we ever needed immediate European funds. I could also meet up with the Reeders and maybe even, the thought crossed my mind, take the train to St. Anton and spend a few days there. I did just that.

I took the train, the Wienerwalzer, from Budapest to Vienna. I passed Gyor, where Howard Baetjer had been shot down in World War II. I was sitting in a compartment with a man who turned out to be a medical doctor in Budapest. We reached the border, which looked like something out of an Alfred Hitchcock movie, barbed wire fences for some distance back and then high watchtowers.

After we crossed the border, the doctor really opened up. He told about the revolt of 1956 against the Russians; how teenagers threw rocks at Russian tanks; the shooting of machine guns, etc. in Budapest, the pockmarks were still there at the time of my visits; and the terrible wounds that he had to treat at his clinic or hospital. It took two or three weeks for the Russians to seize complete control of the situation and then they came and demanded the medical records of all persons who had been treated. The doctor had received word of this beforehand and had immediately destroyed his records. They told the Russians that in the confusion of the battles they had not had time to keep records.

In Vienna I checked in at the Bristol, went to call on the Hojos Bank, had dinner one night at the Drei Hussaren and welcomed the Reeders. One day we took a trip by mini-bus to the Wachau, visited Melk Abbey and its fantastic library, stopped off at Durnstein for a glass of Durnsteiner at a riverside hotel terrace on the banks of the Danube and agreed that Richard-the-Lion-Hearted probably told the musician not to bother him when he heard that famous tune.

I took the Arlberg Express to St. Anton, a beautiful ride through Kitzbuhel, Salzburg and Innsbruck, stayed at the Alte Post, did lots of walking, sometimes meeting Pepi Gabl and Walter Schuler in a jeep observing game in the Fasul-tal, and generally had a relaxed time in beautiful autumn weather with Herta and Franz Fahrner and their friends. I even went to the tailor in Strengen and had a new "fake count suit," *falscher graf Tiroler trachten anzug,* made. Franz said I would be a "ganz modische hund," a "very stylish dog."

I flew back from Zurich to Budapest and again we drove to Esztergom for the appellate hearing. This time they had an interpreter, but she was totally inadequate. We insisted on a proper interpreter. They were not sure when the appeal would be rescheduled, so I flew home. I must have been in Budapest on November 1 or 2, all Saints Day or All Souls Day, because I went to the evening Mass in Szent Istvan, St. Stephen's, the big church in Pest, built at the height of prosperity around 1900. It was beautiful, lit entirely by candles. The church was packed.

Apropos of the Church, Kitty and I on Sundays always went to High Mass at the Cathedral on the Var, the Coronation Church on the Capitol hill. It was a bona fide pre-Vatican II, High Mass with three priests, acolytes, choir, organ, music, incense, the "works." The place would be jammed and afterwards we would stroll out on the Fisherman's Bastion to listen to the Red Army band, which tried to draw the people away from Mass, without success.

Life was complicated for the Embassy at this time since Cardinal Mindszenty, the primate of Hungary, was living on the third floor. He had sought refuge, political asylum, in 1956 and had been there ever since. I asked if I could see him or at least go to his Mass on Sunday. I was told that only the White House could give such permission. I teased Kitty Hoffman, an Episcopalian, because the Cardinal had heard of her plight, summoned her and invited her to his Masses. Later, as the Cold War thawed a bit and the Pope wanted to resume relations with Communist regimes, he negotiated Cardinal Mindszenty's release and moved him to Vienna, where he lived the few years of life left to him. Frank Meehan, the DCM, who was a Catholic, said that the Cardinal was probably tortured at some stage, since he had a misshapen foot.

I flew back to Baltimore in early November. I see from my daybook that I returned to Budapest on November 12 for the "final" hearing on the appeal, which was set for 9:30 A.M., November 14, in Esztergom. This time we brought our own interpreter, a courtly gentleman of the old school, who had been a professor and a lawyer. He had no use for the Communists.

Six of us were crowded into Gyula Gayer's car, and I was seated next to Gyula Simon. He asked if I minded if he read his mail and I of course said "go ahead." I didn't mean to eavesdrop, but I couldn't help it, because of the close quarters, when he opened a letter typed in English, from a friend of his who was Librarian at the University of Edinburgh. At the bottom of one of the pages, Gyula's friend said how sorry everyone was in his part of the country to lose a grande dame who had been a fixture for sixty years, etc. I said, "Gyula, when you turn the page, I think you will find out that that person was the Countess of Seafield." Gyula looked a bit puzzled, turned the page and it was. I explained that we had been shooting on her estates in Scotland three months previously. Small world.

When we entered the courtroom for the hearing there were three judges. The one in the middle was president of the court and seemed a decent sort, as did the one on his left (our right). But the one on the other side, our left, was a different sort, at least for appearance sake. He was thin-lipped, had steel rimmed glasses and Hollywood could not have done a better job casting a

Communist apparatchik. He reminded me a bit of Jack Pollack, one of the old-time political bosses in Baltimore. He was a tough cookie.

The Gyulas conducted the hearing for Kitty. It went on into the early afternoon. After a recess the judges delivered their opinion, Kitty's sentence was reduced to eight months, and the presiding judge carefully explained that with good behavior she would be out in 5½ months. This was a cruel blow, but we were prepared for it. Kitty stood and in English explained that she was a school teacher, a riding instructor at Garrison Forest School, and would need some time to wind up her affairs. The Ambassador had told me that he needed as much time as possible to see what he could do on the diplomatic level and said to ask for a 60-day grace period for Kitty before she had to go to jail. Otherwise she would have been incarcerated immediately. Also we would be filing a petition for executive clemency, which would take time to prepare, file and have processed. Kitty accordingly, in English, asked for a 60-day grace period before she reported to Czekesfehervar, where she would be imprisoned. There was not a flicker of understanding on the faces of the three judges while Kitty spoke, and then our interpreter put it into Hungarian. Their faces began to react as he progressed. As soon as he had finished, the presiding judge said something in Hungarian which I immediately interpreted as "Granted." He had said this before the party member could catch his breath, and catch it he did. He looked like a thunder cloud, but the presiding Judge had spoken. We left the courtroom fast.

In the square we consoled Kitty on her sentence, congratulated her on her composure and delivery, and were thankful for the period of grace. They could have made her report at once. The prison would not have been like the "Cut" at Jessup's, Maryland, and Kitty would probably have met some interesting political prisoners. But it was far better not to have to do it.

The next day I went to work with the two Gyulas and we began to hammer out the appeal for executive clemency to the Presidential Council of the Hungarian Peoples Republic. We wanted to do it fast because of the 60-day limit. We worked like American lawyers, and one day as we were having lunch at 3 P.M. in the Berlin Etterem, i.e., "East Berlin Restaurant" with pictures of East Berlin on the walls, Gyula Simon said, "Isn't it funny, Charles? We're supposed to be enemies." My reply was, "No, Gyula. We're just lawyers working for Kitty Hoffman."

Our appeal referred to the death of Kitty's sister Ethel in 1963 when a car struck her near Garrison Forrest School; Kitty's teaching at the school; the fact that she did not know any Hungarian and that imprisonment would be equivalent to "solitary confinement." All this was spelled out in English and then had to be translated into Hungarian for the Presidential Council. The Gyulas said there was no word for "solitary confinement" in Hungarian. I said, "There must be." When they asked "why?" I asked them if there was a brewery on the Danube River in Budapest. They said "Yes; why?" "Isn't there a prison next to it?" "Yes." "Well, my friend, Howard Baetjer was in solitary confinement for 30 days in that prison during the War." We somehow worked out the wording. After Howard was shot down over Gyor, he had been brought to Budapest, imprisoned by the Nazis and later placed in "solitary" for 30 days when he offended one of his jailers.

In the appeal, we explained that Kitty and Carol Brewster were on their way to Vienna to turn in the car after driving all over Yugoslavia, Rumania, Bulgaria and Hungary without incident. They were heading for Bratisalava, in Czechoslovakia when the accident occurred. The Gyulas pointed out that Bratislava was known as Pressburg when it was under the Austrians and as Poszonyi when it was Hungarian. What name should we use? I opted for Poszonyi with a bit of tongue-in-cheek. They concurred.

When we had finished and were about to file the appeal, the

Gyulas asked whether I wanted it filed direct with the Presidential Council or with the Lower Court which would start it on its way up to the Council. I asked which would be more considerate of the court or diplomatic, and they said the latter. So we filed it with the Court in Esztergom. We did it so promptly that the judges had not even written their opinion.

That was all I could do, so I packed up, said my good-byes all around, especially thanking Ambassador Puhan, DCM Francis Meehan, Consul Gil Sperling, Marian and Ross Titus, Betty Walden and other members of the staff for all they had done. I also paid the bills of the Gyulas, which were most reasonable by our standards, before I left. I took Malev to London, "over-nighted" at Claridge's, and flew home in time for Thanksgiving.

Life resumed its usual pace, and I kept an eye on the calendar. As December ticked away, I did all I could to find out about Kitty's possible incarceration, including visiting, sending food and/or clothing, letters, etc. I kept in touch with John Vought on the Hungarian desk in the State Department.

Toward the end of December it began to look gloomy. On New Year's Eve, 1969, our usual group was at Nick and Catherine Ballichs' for our black-tie dinner. We talked to Kitty by phone at Ross and Marian Titus's flat at 12 Szechenyi Rakpart. We tried to be cheerful. Kitty's time was about to run out, on Monday, January 12, 1970.

On that day the phone rang in my office, and John Vought said, "Charlie, I don't know what's going on, but we have just been advised that Kitty has been granted an eight day extension at the request of the Hungarian Foreign Minister." We tried not to be too hopeful, but something was in the wind. A week later, at 11 A.M., I will never forget the date, January 19, 1970, or the hour, I was at my desk when the phone rang. It was John Vought. "Charlie, I have some news for you." "Good or bad?" "Let me read you a cable we have just received—

"Presidential Council of the Hungarian People's Republic has granted complete clemency to Miss Katharine McLane Hoffman. Request no publicity. Even favorable publicity not helpful."

I said, "John, I can't believe it." John's reply was, "Neither can we." I was astounded. I had expected the worst. Kits later said that when she reported to Kapok, the police, the next day, the woman whom she usually saw would not believe her. She had not yet been officially informed.

I called Kitty's family, Mr. Hoffman, Dickie, a few close friends. We asked everyone to keep it quiet. We wanted Kitty to get out, before anything could go awry. Of course, dear Kits drove us up the wall by taking her time, particularly since she had to say good-bye to the "jolly Brits" since they had been so nice to her. But eventually she flew out and we welcomed her at BWI. We had a blast that night at Pete Whitman's, and then on February 14 we had a big dinner party at the Mount Vernon Club. Nick Ballich sardonically remarked that it was like the second coming of Christ.

The State Department wanted to see us, and we went over one day to meet with John Vought, his boss who was the man responsible for Eastern Europe and his boss, the Under Secretary of State for Europe. Everyone was there except William Rogers himself, the Secretary of State. It was a fantastic experience, now that it had come to a successful conclusion. When I had told Crossan Cooper he wrinkled up his nose and acknowledged the news, but Mr. Eney congratulated me. Friends of Kitty's took a collection to defray my out-of-pocket expenses, which were considerable, and Mr. Hoffman told Crossan Cooper that he wanted to pay us a fee. The detailed bill was a bit out of the ordinary as to the matters covered. I was told that Frank Murnaghan had said, "Only Charlie Reeves could have done it." I have never asked him to verify it. I gladly took it "on hearsay."

How it all came about is hard to say, but years later, quite recently actually, Herb Wilgis said that Ambassador Puhan had asked him if he should mention it at the Foreign Minister's 1970 New Year's Day party for all the diplomats. Herb said "no," that it was better to let the Foreign Minister enjoy his party. Looking back on it from the perspective of nearly thirty years, we kept it as low-key as possible. We bent over backwards not to have it escalate into a political matter. Kingdon Gould, then Ambassador to Luxembourg, had come down to visit Kitty, but he made it clear that it was a personal visit and had no other significance. From the way that the Hungarians in advising us of the clemency had asked for no publicity, not even favorable publicity, we concluded that this was their way of showing, in the depth of the Cold War, that they wanted to be helpful but they did not want the Russians to know of their action. Also we had done everything possible to comply with their laws and procedures, such as filing the appeal with the Lower Court rather than going over its head direct to the Presidential Council. With all the traveling back and forth it had been grueling, but fascinating, far from the ordinary daily grind of law practice.

Around March 1, 1970, I was in St. Moritz, having come over to see Margaret Crawford and her entourage. We were all staying in the Hotel Albana, and one evening I took one of Margaret's "chicks" down to the Palace for dinner. I was togged out in my new Austrian suit from Strengen, and after dinner we sat at the bar. It was quiet, just the orchestra. A nice looking gentleman came over and introduced himself. It turned out that he was Alexander, "Bandi," Eszterhazy, a friend of Jeanne van der Valk's in Rome. He was hired by Andrea Badrutt, owner of the Palace, to be a sort of welcomer for the guests. We discussed my recent Hungarian experiences, and I told him of one particular golden Sunday when I had gone out on the Diplomatic Shoot beyond the Buda Hills. He asked "where" and I said "Martonvasar." He said, "my grandmother's estate." Small world again.

On Labor Day weekend in 1972 I was taking it easy at home when the phone rang. A friend who lived fairly near me asked if I could come over on a legal matter. Thus started another adventure. The friend had been involved in an Irish bank, which was having difficulties. This entailed several trips to Ireland which were not "all bad" since my friend owned race horses in Ireland and we went to many steeple chases together.

One of my trips started rather abruptly with a telephone call from Dublin, just as I was about to go to Mass at St. Ignatius one Sunday. My friend, now "client," was meeting there with Irish attorneys and accountants and he was worrying about the securities aspects of a proposed refinancing which was coming up for approval by the Irish Court. I gave him my thoughts and went off to church. The situation continued to worry me, and when I returned home, I called Aer Lingus to see if they had any space available that night. My friend called again and asked if I could come over, since they were scheduled to have a hearing the next morning in the High Court in Dublin at 11 A.M. I told him I had already made a reservation.

I flew to New York that afternoon, caught Aer Lingus in the early evening, and, after the mandatory stop in Shannon the next morning, which had me biting my nails, I arrived in Dublin about 9:30 A.M., caught a taxi, went direct to the High Court, asked the porter in which courtroom Justice Kenny was sitting, left my suitcase and went to the courtroom to join client, attorneys, accountants, et al. After the hearing, which resulted in provisional liquidation of the bank, we adjourned to the Royal Hibernian Hotel and went into a marathon meeting. When it was over, late in the afternoon or early evening, I announced that I was going to bed. One of our attorneys, Andrew Curneen, would hear none of it. He said he wanted to take me out. He was a big, rugged Irish "footballer" type.

I did obtain his permission to get a shower and wash up and met him downstairs a bit later. After dinner, he took me to a real "shibeen." This was in the dark days of the "troubles" in Northern

Ireland. The shibeen was located in a neighborhood which was scruffy, to say the least. When we knocked on the door there was no answer. There was very little light in the street. We found a telephone box, much the worse for wear, and Andrew identified himself. This time they let him in. The place was run by an Irish woman who must have been active in IRA affairs. We met a number of characters, which would include the owner/manager of the shibeen. Andrew did not keep me out too late, and I would not have missed it for anything. It was something straight out of Brendan Behan.

A day or so later on this trip, we drove to Naas to see the steeplechases, in which my client's best horse ran a good second in the big race. It was cold, and there was snow on the mountains in the distance. My client's partner in the enterprise was a member of the Kildare Street Club, which reminded me strongly of the Maryland Club, so we had a lovely lunch there one day.

In addition, my client and his wife were great friends of Lord and Lady Dunsany, who lived in Dunsany Castle, a few miles outside of Dublin. We had a beautiful Sunday lunch there. The narcissus and other spring flowers were just coming out. The Earl was a member of the Plunkett family. One of his collaterals was Blessed Oliver Plunkett, the last martyr put to death by the English. He was canonized a few years after our visit and is now St. Oliver Plunkett.

I think it safe to say that during that brief trip, we had run the gamut of Irish living.

Thereafter, legal matters took a more mundane course. I had a slew of estate work plus IPO's, initial public offerings of common stock in the 1980's, and in the early 1990's I slid over into some bond work with Bob Shelton and Davis Sherman. After I had completed the mandatory five year "scale down" at the end of the year in which I was 70, I retired on December 31, 1993. The firm still gives me an office, for which I am most grateful, and any secretarial help which I need. I am content with the set up.

In my retired status I have plenty of non-legal matters to keep me busy. The insurance company, and ALAS, warn that a retired attorney should not give even free legal advice. That conveniently lets me off the hook whenever my opinion is asked on some legal or quasi-legal matter.

In looking over my appellate briefs and having John Nixdorff of our library staff check the citations, I came across one which had almost a circus aspect because of the dramatics of John Henry Lewin, Sr. He was called into the case by John Hardwicke after the Circuit Court of Harford County had perfunctorily ordered the construction of a sewage treatment plant near the historic light house in the City of Havre de Grace at the head of the Chesapeake Bay. Mr. Lewin's Notice of Appeal, which ordinarily would have been one terse sentence, went on for two and a half pages, castigating the allegedly dastardly action of the lower court. Of course local politics were heavily involved, and we were in a free-for-all—every minute of which Mr. Lewin relished. He called me in to help and we had a riot. When I researched the case, I came up with a decision of the Court of Appeals of Maryland in 1901 on all "eights" with our case. Counsel in that one was Edwin G. Baetjer, Esq., "the Baetjer" of Venable, Baetjer and Howard. Justice prevailed, and the lower court was reversed. *Mayor and City Council of Havre de Grace v. State Board of Health*, 234 Md. 222, 198 2d 732 (1964). The practice of law can be fun.

CBR Jr.
Baltimore, circa 1926

16

HORSES

Both Mother and Father were ardent horse people. Mother had always fox hunted, with the old Elkridge Hunt, then based on Charles Street at the present city line. I have a picture of her at Elkridge in a horse show. Aunt Frances told me that she spent a winter, in 1908 or so, fox hunting in Ireland. She may have hunted with the Meath or West Meath. She stayed at a Lady Decies. In those days it was strenuous since the banks were not covered with vegetation, and the field used to charge them with twenty or more abreast, according to *Experiences of an Irish R.M.* by Somerville and Ross.

Father took up fox hunting after World War I. He and Mother were thrown together at the Jack Symingtons and the David McIntoshes. They and a big group of the Elkridge and Green Spring fox hunters went to England in March 1928 to see Mr. Howard Bruce's Billy Barton run in the Grand National at Aintree. They hunted in England before the races. Father said that one day they were hunting with the Duke of Beaufort's. There was a large field at the meet, and they had a wonderful day. When the hunt staff finally picked up hounds at the end of the day, Father looked around and the only ones left were the hunt staff and the Elkridge field. In the Grand National Billy Barton fell at the last fence, was remounted and finished second, the only other finisher besides the winner.

Father was on the Maryland Hunt Cup Committee, and for many years he was responsible for running it as Secretary. He also was MFH, Master of Foxhounds, of the old Elkridge in 1930–1932, part of the time as Joint Master with Mr. Howard Bruce. Father's particular responsibility was the Churchville country, which he always claimed was the best fox hunting country in America. It was like the "galloping shires" in England. It was mostly dairy farms and had some huge fences. Mr. Bruce hunted Billy Barton, and Father had Pigeon, a "seven-eighths bred" who was a wonderful jumper. Mr. Bruce and he led some merry chases. When Pigeon had to be put down he was 22. Father had him brought from the Elkridge-Harford at Monkton and buried at Long Quarter Farm, the former old Elkridge Hunt club house, off the Pot Spring Road.

I started going to the Maryland Hunt Cup in 1930. David and I are subscribers. As children we were allowed to stand on the tongue of the farm wagon which was the Committee's "finishing stand." Father used to say we would see much better from the top of the hill, but we wanted to be near the "seat of power."

Mother had started me riding with lessons from Charlie Hector in Druid Hill Park when I was three years old. After she died and the Depression arrived, Father took me riding only occasionally. I never had a pony and I didn't particularly enjoy riding on a large horse. I rode some with Tommy Ramseur when his father bought Loch Raven Farm on the Dulaney Valley Road above Pearce's Plantation. I also did some riding in the ROTC at Princeton and once or twice at law school from Elliwood Keith's.

In 1965 I had thought of going to Aintree to watch Jay Trump and Tommy Smith run, but I was working on the Millipore offering and some other things at the time, so I did not go. They won, the first completely American victory, horse, owner and jockey. I sent over some money with Bonnie White, "on the nose" at 18 to 1 through the mutuels.

When Tommy and Jay Trump ran in the "Grand Steeple" at Auteuil, the French equivalent of the Grand National, I made a spur of the moment trip with Cooper Wallker, for the weekend. It was at the height of de Gaullist anti-Americanism, but people could not have been nicer. They gave Jay Trump a great hand when he came in third, even though he had been an odds-on favorite.

In the Spring of 1974 I was at Maggie and Walter Brewsters' after the Maryland Grand National. Jimmy Stump was there and said that the horse that he was riding was just not good enough. I asked him if he would ride for me if I bought a horse. A couple of weeks later he called me and said that his mother, Louise, had advised him to call me and see if I meant it. I said "yes," and that started another delightful set of experiences. Some time later when I was visiting Maria (Grant) Hunter in Guys Hospital in London, she asked how I had entered the horse game. I told her that it "had all started at a cocktail party." She said, "Charles, don't most of the nice things in life?"

Jimmy, Louise, Kitty Hoffman and I drove to Leesburg, Virginia to Mr. Hunton Atwill's, a legendary Virginia horseman, to look at a good looking gray called "Danny Did." Jimmy liked him, and I bought him in early June. I had thought that Jimmy was going to train him at home, but he said he was going to work at Mikey Smithwick's that summer and would I mind if we put the horse there. In my naiveté and in abysmal ignorance of the prevailing charges for race-horse training, I said "fine," especially because Mikey was one of Father's godchildren. Although it nearly bankrupted me at times, it was the best thing that could have happened to me.

At first, when I came out to watch Danny Did "school," I would run around on foot. Mikey said I should get on a horse so that I could ride around more easily to watch. I soon did, and Mikey's employee Lynn Cox, who was a top-notch rider, specializing in the "puissance" event, took me in hand. She reminded me of my ski guide, Heidi Michel, at St. Moritz. She soon had me jumping and I loved it. Danny Did came along as a jumper, and Mikey ran him on Labor Day weekend at Fair Hill. He didn't do anything, but it was a thrill seeing him run in my gold-and-green colors. These were based on the Ivy Club colors and designed by Bonnie White, who had just bought Fox Fire Farm. It all began to come together. Sam Reeves, who came down with David, acted as tack boy with Willy Stump. I took the Stump family to lunch at the track before the races, and afterwards at Burley and Babs Cock's suggestion, I took David, Sam, Mikey, Virginia Guest, Doug Fout, Jr., who had just "broken his maiden" that day at Fair Hill, and Nina Fout to dinner at the Red Rose Inn.

At the end of September I had gone to Scotland to shoot at Revack for a week, described in more detail hereinafter in the "Shooting" section. I received a telephone call in Scotland from Aunt Frances that Mikey had decided to run Danny Did at Rolling Rock on Wednesday, October 2 and Saturday, October 5. I was coming home on the 2nd, so that meant that I could make it on the 5th. I drove out on Friday with the van, and early Saturday morning I was helping with the horses. J. B. Secor taunted Vivian Rall that I could not jump a certain fence beside the stable. I was on a "push button" horse of Mikey's, and Vivian took me out to practice over a post-and-rail fence. I cleared the fence but toppled off on landing. When I returned to the stable, Mikey's long-time groom, Speedy, diagnosed that I had a broken collarbone. They fixed me up with a figure-8 at the Clinic and I attended the races in a sling with "Don't ask" on it. Danny Did finished back in the field. After two days of racing, horse, jockey and trainer came home without a scratch on them. Owner came home in a sling with a broken collarbone.

I was still recuperating from my collarbone when Mikey said he had a fox-hunter for me. "Mikey, I don't want a fox hunter. The doctor told me not to ride." "Aw, Sprat, just ride her around

Mom's flower beds." This I did and ended up owning the horse, a mare, dark bay, about fifteen and a half hands, not a thoroughbred. Because of the last fact, Mikey said I had to name her. Without hesitation I said, "Violet." Mikey blinked and for once was speechless. Maria Hunter just a few days before had been telling me in London about her hunting days with the Pytchley and Quorn, looking "frightfully smart," veil and all with a bunch of violets, on a mare called Violet, who was not at all a shrinking one. Thus my Violet was named and went on to fame in "song and story" in the Elkridge-Harford annals.

When I had mended, I took up my regular riding again and was "tuteled" by Kurt Rosenthal, who had come down from Long Island. He taught me proper "flat work," figure eights, circles, diagonals, changes, etc. One day he complimented me on a "nice flying change." I hadn't even realized what I had done. That's the way I returned to horses, Lynn Cox taught me how to jump; Vivian Rall broke my collarbone; and Kurt Rosenthal taught me how to ride, in exactly that order.

I practiced all kinds of jumps and Mikey put me through some grueling paces. One drill that I did not like was jumping over a bar in the woods, nailed between two trees, on a downhill slope. Thank heaven Mike insisted on it because it became of great use on at least one occasion in the hunting field.

One March morning Mikey sent Kurt Rosenthal and me up to have a "bye-day" with the Elkridge-Harford. I acquitted myself satisfactorily by keeping out of every one's way. We had a fair run from the Club and ended up nearly at Madonna. I recognized the Schuster Road, when we crossed it. When we had to start home, Kurt, my "keeper" confessed that he did not know where we were. I led him back to the Club. As we neared it, below the Club woods, we heard the hounds circling back, waited a few minutes and viewed a lovely big red fox quite close. A nice beginning to my fox hunting days.

Thomas Akinson,
Middleburg, Virginia,
Charles B. Reeves, Sr.,
and S. Bryce Wing,
Maryland Hunt Cup
Paddock, 1948

Below:
Nancy Hall Stettinius,
CBR Jr, Patrol Judge,
Paddock, Maryland
Hunt Cup, circa 1955

100th Anniversary Elkridge-Harford Hunt Club
November, 1978
Front row: left to right: Rosalie Bruce Culver, S. Bonsal White, Jr., Jack S. Griswold Jr., (on lap), Mrs. W. Carrington Stettinius, Thomas Voss. Back row left to right: Joan McHenry Hoblitzell, CBR Jr., H. Turney McKnight, T. Courtenay Jenkins, Jr., Jack S. Griswold

"Violet" and CBR Jr.
Elkridge-Harford Old Fashioned
April, 1976

Bonnie White bought the old Tom Eastman place on the Jarrettsville Pike in June, and I moved Violet there. Jerry Stautberg gave her a lift in his van. Pat Combs took over as groom, and Bud Lytle, who ran the Hess Store, picked her up one day standing in the middle of the Pike after she had jumped out of her pasture.

Turney McKnight was MFH and he showed us wonderful sport. I went out on hound exercise toward the end of July 1975. One cool morning, July 30, Turney decided to take the hounds across the Jarrettsville Pike and work through Clinton Pitts' woods and over toward the Turner Road. Pat Combs was at the corner of Turner and Houck's Mill Roads when she saw a large red fox slink out of a cornfield. The hounds picked up the scent and away we went. Fortunately Violet was completely fit, and as the field diminished we stayed in the chase, which eventually went past the Frank Obers', into their woods, down into a low field where we jumped a plank fence half buried in weeds and eventually put him to earth in a drain in Rieman McIntosh's driveway. We were all dripping. Turney looked at me and said, "Sprat, you'll never get to the bottom of Violet." She served me well for many years.

Turney and Mikey asked me to come to Saratoga, and one blindingly hot morning about 6 A.M. I was helping Mikey with the horses and rode around the corner of the stable, where I suddenly bumped into Betty Bird. She looked up unbelievingly and said, "Sprat, I've seen everything now!"

On September 25, I know the date from the plaque, we had a wonderful morning all through the Sprouts, Jerry Stoutberg's and Bonnie White's, their "ancestral acres," and up to the old Dean Bradford property. We had a kill in the bottom, and Turney presented with me a "pad." Brother David told someone later that, when we had a lunch meeting that day with people from the bank, I was so excited that all I could do was talk about the fox hunt and the kill.

That fall I suddenly succumbed to a fever, similar to the subsequently discovered Lyme's disease, and came close to cashing in my chips. I spent three days in the GBMC ICU. It had no windows, and I told my doctor, Dooner Wilson, that, if he did not get me out of there, and if I pulled through, he would have to trot me across the hill to the neighboring institution, Shephard Pratt. He sent me to my room, where I could look out at the autumn foliage, and I pulled through.

I was terribly weak, and one time later that fall when I was acting field master, a position which I won in a raffle at the Club, Violet ran away with me. I had to pull her head around practically into my lap to get her to turn and run her uphill. Another time Clinton Pitts saw how tired I was when we had a check in Verdant Valley. He suggested that I go home before I was hurt. He was right. I hacked home through Verdant Valley, up the driveway, across the Jarrettsville Pike and into Bonnie's driveway. I was so tired that I did not think I could get off and even considered rolling off into the sand. But I managed to make it.

We had glorious hunting. On New Year's Day 1976 we had four to six inches of fresh snow. We went out and had a good hunt. Rieman McIntosh advised me to go into my fences a little faster than usual so that Violet would throw the snow and ice out of her hooves. One also had to watch out for the ice balls flying from the horses in front. Green Spring did not go out that day, so their members took their trailers and suddenly appeared with us, Frank Bonsal, Carey Jackson, et al. I thought I was seeing something when they appeared.

October 13, 1976 would have been Aunt Ella's One Hundredth birthday. I knew in my bones that we would have a good hunt. We met on the power line on Gorman's Mill Road. It was a cold morning, heavy frost. We moved off northeast up the power line, over a rise, turned left and jumped a chicken coop, frost everywhere in the shadows. We did nothing for about twenty minutes. Then as we neared Sybil Dukehart's and the Lemon Road, it began to warm up. The scent must have become good, and the hounds took off on a hot line.

We tore all over the upper country, Sybil Dukeharts, Turney McKnight's. The field began to thin out and when we finally picked up the hounds about 9:30, there were only Jack Graybeal, the huntsman, Mackie Griswold and I. It had indeed been a day for the book.

Benjie Griswold became MFH and I was elevated to Honorary Hunt Secretary. We had great sport. It was during Benjie's tenure that we had a great run all around Verdant Valley and Atlanta Hall, jumping everything. At the conclusion, Benjie carefully looked over Violet and me and said, "Sprat, anybody who can hang in on that run deserves his hunt buttons." I was like a child being given a Christmas present.

Doug Small succeeded Benjie, and my most memorable memory there was a day out cubbing. We had had a good morning, and about 9:00 o'clock we were in the School House Woods, just off Verdant Valley driveway. The only ones left were Doug Small, Jack Graybeal, Susan Worrall and I. Scent had been fabulous and Jack asked Doug if he wanted to go back across the Jarrettsville Pike and try there. Doug looked at me and said, "How about it, Sprat?" I knew what time it was and, in effect, said, "In for a penny, in for a pound." I might as well be hung for a sheep as well as for a lamb, so across the road we went. We hacked up Bonnie White's driveway and then towards the little stream between his place and the Sprouts. I don't know where the hounds found, but we ended up having the most fantastic run, all around the hidden valley north of the Hess Road and between Bonnie's, the old Bedford Place and Harford Hill. A lot of the time the hounds were only fifty or a hundred yards behind the fox in full view. Susan Worrall and I often reminisce about it.

We also did some traveling, quite a few times to Andrew's

Bridge, once to Unionville, and then an old fashioned hunting weekend at Wolver Hill, the Iselin place in Middleburg. When we were hunting with Orange County, John Warner, the Senator, very kindly took me under his wing. When he came in to the hunt tea, I rather disingenuously went over to thank him for his kindness to me in the field. He said, "Charlie, I would like you to meet my fiancee, Elizabeth Taylor." Out of the corner of my eye, I could see Nancy Marburg, Barbara Sears and Ginny White. They let me chat with Elizabeth Taylor for about ten seconds and then sprang across the room, sweeping me out of the way.

The "piece de resistance" of my fox hunting was a twelve day trip to Ireland with the Ben Griswolds. At a check one day near Charles Street and Fallston Road, Leith Griswold asked me if I would like to come to Ireland and hunt. This held a fascination for me because Father had said that one of the few regrets of his life was that he had not accepted Mr. Ambrose Clark's invitation to do that after Mother had died. At the next check I told Ben Griswold what Leith had said and asked if he thought I was up to it. He said of course I could. I wasn't so sure, but Nancy Marburg and some others encouraged me to go, and in January 1978 I found myself on Aer Lingus, headed for Shannon.

It was a fast flight, and I had barely put down my champagne glass after dinner when they said to buckle seat belts, put up trays and seat backs. It was still dark when I arrived, and the Griswolds had me met. When I arrived at Beechwood House, Ben asked me if I would like to go out that morning with the Limerick Stone Hall Harriers. It would be a good warm-up for Tipperary the next day. I really wanted to say, "No. I am tired, and scared. I just want to go to bed." But that would have hardly been sporting, or what I came over for, so I said that I would be delighted.

Sheila Jackson was there so she drove us over to the meet. I was hired a rough-and-ready cob, and he did the job well. I jumped my first bank, a lowish sort of thing, well overgrown with bushes, down in a swamp. I managed to survive although at the end I was so tired that I was hanging on the cob's mouth and made him refuse a fair-sized jump off a concrete road up onto a bank. I think the locals wondered what was wrong with him. It wasn't "him"; it was "me." Having had not a wink of sleep on the plane, I fell asleep in the car with Sheila driving and again into a sort of "double REM" when I reached the house and went to bed. When Ben woke me for dinner, I awoke with a yell. I thought the fox had me.

The next day we went out with Tipperary. We met at a pub, and when someone asked me if I would like a port-and-brandy, I readily accepted. The Griswolds had obtained for me the best hireling in the West of Ireland, Mary Carroll's Egbert, a big Irish hunter. It was just what I needed, and I let him do the job. We moved off and went down a wide lane with a low bank on the left. The hounds found almost at once, and Sheila Jackson decided to face the bank. I elected to stay with the field, and as they turned and jumped up on the bank, I looked to my left, and there was Sheila rolling like a bowling ball in the mud. There was no way that I could stop. I was swept along in the cavalry charge. I soon caught up to Leith laboring along on something the size of a large pony. "Where's Sheila?" she called. "Back there," I said nodding and holding on to Egbert for dear life. "Is she o.k.?" "I think so," and Egbert and I flew on.

Having lost my two "nannies" I stayed with the bulk of the field, and we soon found ourselves in an upland, a high altitude bog. Eventually I attached myself to a man in a green coat, who I assumed would know what he was doing. He did.

We had good sport, and at one time I found myself in line confronting a large bank, covered with brush and with trees showing on the far side. I suddenly remembered Walter Brewster's horrific account of a bank where the horse had to scramble up, turn right, go along the top a few yards and **then** jump off. Walter being an aggressive rider had gunned into it, the horse had had too much momentum, couldn't turn and jumped into the trees, with dire results. I said, "Eggy babe, it's up to you. Go for it!" He did. He took a huge spring, hooked his front legs on the top, scrambled up with his back legs and stood up on top. He turned right, walked down the top of the bank about twenty yards, turned to the left and sprang off. We made it.

A few days later we were on top of another big bank, but no turns, when I suddenly saw a taut strand of new, silvery barbed wire a foot from the face of the bank and two or three feet below the top. I shouted, "Wire, Eggy!" and he made a special leap out into the field. If a horse slid down and under the wire, it would not have been pretty.

One day with Tipperary we met at one of the Vincent O'Brien stud farms. We drew generally east with a bit of north, and suddenly the Rock of Cashel with Cormac's Tower came into view. It was like something in a dream.

The last time that I hunted with Tipperary we had a huge field, and when hounds finally got away, there was a traffic jam at a panel in a big hedge. I politely held back, and when I reached the next field, I was far back. About this time I saw a scarlet coat coming hell-bent for leather from my right and at right angles to the main line of pursuit. It was one of the whips. I wheeled to my left, and, something that I never should have done, I took off in pursuit of him. Leith and Sheila had gone off with the field, so I was on my own, playing hooky in the worst sort of way. Soon we were joined by another whip and the whip's girlfriend, so at least I had company in my crime.

We came to a check. We were right with part of the pack, which in turn was close to the fox. A whip said, "Go back down the road," a farm track on fairly high, hard ground, "a piece and look for the fox." I did as ordered, and after a minute or so they signaled me back. They had "viewed" and away we went again, the two whips together and the girl friend and I behind them. We came at a good pace to a low hedge. "Does that harse (*sic*) jump on the fly?" gasped the girl. "I don't know," said I, "but we'll find out." I had supreme confidence in Egbert, and he flew it like a steeple chaser over a "hurrl." We jumped the hedge once or twice more in our chase, and it began to be a bit trampled. Our path began to converge with the main body of the hunt. I saw Leith. She turned to chasten me. When she saw my entourage, she said nothing. And so I had my private fox hunt with the Tipperary Hounds.

We had one day with Duhallow, the oldest pack in Ireland, near Mallow. It was different from Tipperary, much more informal, "real Irish." I was mounted on a cob lent by Mr. Carroll Leahy, honorary MFH. The cob was tough and did the job well, particularly hammering around curves downhill on a concrete road, which scared me half to death. I hate to think what would have happened if he had slipped.

We also hunted a couple of times with Tady Ryan's Black and Tans. We went there to dinner one night with Mrs. McCalmot. The last day I hunted on a James Breen mount, very different from Egbert and the other hirelings. He gave me my only fall of the trip when he bucked me off as we turned off the road into a field. When I told Nancy Griswold, she said, "Sprat, that horse had probably never been out in the hunting field, but now that you've hunted him one day he's probably for hire as a 'seasoned hunter.'" I am sure it was true.

After Violet gave out in the early 1980's, I gave her to Pat Combs to hunt with the non-jumping field. "Just like giving her to me," snorted Bonnie White. I bought Shipmate, who did well when he wanted to and could jump anything, but he was moody. One year we won the heavy weight division of the Elkridge-Harford Old Fashioned, probably since everybody else had fallen down or had to pull up. The last hunter I had was a re-made show horse known as "Baby Dear" informally but possessing a high-toned thoroughbred name. She too was problematical but on occasion could get the job done. I finally hung up my tack in 1986 when I was hunting only on Saturdays because we had too much work to do downtown. I wanted to quit while I was ahead and not push my luck too far. I had had a wonderful time, but I was not getting any younger.

My final horse—or interest therein—was Body Music whom Fife Symington and I owned with Jay Griswold. He fell at the 4th fence in the Maryland Hunt Cup, in 1994, the One Hundredth Anniversary race. Fife and I had another one for a short time, who was very unsound but who we hoped might make it to the 1997 Hunt Cup. He didn't.

St. Ignatius Church, Baltimore
Restored, 1999
Rededicated, 2000

17

Golf

I have enjoyed golf since I was 14 years old. The lowest handicap I ever had was 11, and now I have a fairly realistic 26. I began when Mabel Whiteley encouraged Father to have me play. Zandy Harvey and I used to play at Elkridge, and Mabel had me take lessons from Andy Gibson, from Prestwick, Scotland, then stationed at Bonnie View on Smith Avenue.

After the war I took the game up again at Green Spring, which, as I said previously, I did not realize had only ten holes. I had an 85 before I left for the University of Geneva, and in Geneva I played a few times with Dave Sterling, a good player from Newport. We used to see King Leopold of Belgium out on the course. Dave and I went to Chamonix one weekend, and I remember shooting a 42-42-84. The perspective was confusing with the mountains rising sheer on all sides.

When I went to work, I played regularly at Green Spring and always played in the Elkridge-Green Spring tournament on Memorial Day weekend, first with Newbold Lawrence and later for years with Bill Douglas. Newbold and I finished second one time.

We also had the Bowles Cup tournament around Labor Day at Green Spring. In 1953 I had just returned from ten days at Fishers Island, playing the "Big Club" course in high winds. I had a good round the first day. I had a 21 handicap, and Rex Wheeler and Bob McDonald bought me in the Calcutta and brought in Roland McKenzie, a famed Walker Cup player in his youth. They sent me home early, and I came out and practiced in the morning. My three buyers made me play with them. Jim McHenry was the favorite with a 75-8-net 67 the first day. I had a 92-21-71. Redmond Stewart came out to "assist" his cousin, Mr. McHenry, who promptly blew up. When Redmond tried to come near me on about the 11th hole, my captors shooed him away.

On the old 16th hole, now No. 14, I put my drive in the then-shallow stream on the left. Roland coached me into hitting it out and I saved the hole. It was at this juncture that Roland had drinks sent out, low ball bourbons. I was so nervous that my arms ached inside the elbow. He made me take a sip of one of the drinks, and it did relax me. On the 17th tee I had to get down in 10 on the last two holes to beat Redmond Stewart by one stroke.

I promptly hit a "worm-burner" that did not make the fairway, but by brute strength I managed to get a 7. There was quite a crowd around the 17th green. I walked in silence to the 18th tee. I had to get a par.

I pulled my drive and it landed in the trap on the left. The sand was a bit wet and I was fairly close to the "lip" of the trap. The pin was close to our side of the green, not an enviable position. As I walked off the tee and up the short fairway, there was a deathly hush. I felt as if my three golf-mates had a gun in my back. I took out my sand wedge, I believe that we had them in those days, dug in my feet, kept my head down and swung. The ball hopped up and stopped about ten inches short of the hole. Afterwards Roland was reported as saying, "I'm glad that I didn't have to make that shot."

I sank the putt, and, as they say, "the rest is history." Redmond had to be called back from getting in his car with the trophy. Afterwards he often said, "You had no business beating me." My partners were jubilant, and we raked in our not-inconsiderable winnings in the Calcutta.

In my 1967 trip through Ireland I played Portmarnock outside Dublin and Lahinch, near Ennis. At the latter I hit a screaming low drive between two small hills. At exactly the wrong time, a sheep, one of those which then "mowed" the course, raised his head and I hit him between the horns. The ball went straight up about fifty feet. The sheep didn't even blink.

In 1992 Beverly Beall organized a Green Spring trip on which we played Ballybunnion, Tralee, Waterville, the Killeen course at Killarney and Lahinch. We had lovely weather except for the last, which we played in an increasingly heavy downpour and in a wind which eventually rose to about 40 mph. We quit on No. 14.

In 1994 we had a Scottish tour and played Turnberry, the Ailsa Course and the Arran, both of which I walked in one day, Prestwick, Carnoustie, North Berwick and Scots Craig near St. Andrews and Taymouth.

My last triumph was in 1996 when Alan Grace asked me down to play the Robert Trent Jones course at Manassas, Virginia. Frank Weller had done much of the design with Mr. Jones, including the club house, a magnificent edifice. We played with Cabell Maddux and a friend, both members.

At first it looked as if we would be rained out, but the weather improved after we started. It was lovely and warm by the time we reached the 11th hole, which is the "signature hole" of the course. The three young ones were playing from the blue tees and all hit their drives on the green. I went down to the white tee, took out a five-wood and hit a beautiful shot, straight as a string. It stopped about five or six feet past the hole. I was closest, so the others putted out. I hit my putt and it looked as if it would go past the right edge of the cup. At the last split-second it suddenly toppled in, for a birdie. I think Frank Weller must have tapped it.

The other three jumped up and down and said, "You've got to buy the picture." I said, "What picture?" and they said, "Of the signature hole." When I arrived at the golf shop, I bought the picture, showing the hole, with Mr. Jones sitting on a bench on the tee, and the club house. The pin is in the exact same position as on the day that we played. The picture, with the score card, framed under it, hangs in my office.

Golf has given me much pleasure over the years, meeting congenial people and playing beautiful courses. Bill Douglas invited me to play in the Onwentsia-Shore Acres tournament in the 1960's and 70's in Lake Forest, Illinois. Nancy Marburg had me invited to stay with Gertie Legendre at Medway Plantation in South Carolina in the 1980's to play in her tournament at Yeaman's Hall.

I now play at Green Spring with the T.A.G's—i.e. the Thursday Afternoon Group. We are nearly all superannuated high handicap golfers, and we have a good time. Some years ago Kathleen Nes, a former British Women's champion, was watching a group of us tee off on the first tee, adjacent to the club terrace. She asked her companion who we were and, when told the T.A.G.'s, asked what the acronym stood for. When duly informed, she said a bit caustically, "I thought it might be, 'Try Another Game.'" I was delighted to confront Kath with it at dinner one night.

18

Shooting

My shooting career started with Father at Blakeford, Miss Mary Thom's place on the Chester River near Queenstown. I had a 410 and amazingly brought down some ducks with it. I chiefly remember the cold. At night the bedroom seemed colder than outside. The river was full of ice.

Father next took me to the Philadelphia Club on East Neck Island, on the other side of the Chester, below Rock Hall. The shooting was excellent. It was just before and at the time of World War II. During the war we took the Love Point or the Tolchester Ferry to save gas. I also went down with Eddie Johnson to Ingleside, which his father had bought about 1937. It was quite luxurious and well staffed. That is where I first met Splint Downey.

After the war and just as I came to work in 1951, Mr. Johnson died and left Ingleside and Wickcliffe to Molly Brent White. I have referred to this briefly hereinabove in the "getting down to work" portion. We had fabulous times there and terrific shooting, including one memorable day in the fog at Ingleside with the geese coming over like bombers.

I was invited one time by Shanghai to come down and shoot Cedar Point, next to Molly Brent's, and the epitome of duck shooting on the Eastern Shore. We had good sport, lots of ducks, and by luck I was "on." Unbeknownst to me, Amos Waterfield came up behind our blind and as one duck came in, I dropped it. "That's what I like to hear" spoke up Amos. "One shot."

In 1969 Andre Brewster and Phil Hathaway organized a grouse shooting trip to Scotland. When Bobby Fenwick dropped out, they asked me to join. It was a riot. Bonnie White and his son Stevie and I met in London. After a trip on the night train to Inverness, we were on time before lunch at the Newton Hotel in Nairn to meet our hostess, The Lady Pauline, a violet-eyed, 26 year old soon-to-be-divorcée. We agreed that we would like grouse shooting.

After lunch when we went over to leave our guns at Revack Lodge, where we were to shoot, I rode over with Pauline in her Lotus, at just under the speed of light. As we flashed past a high demesne wall outside Grantown-on-Spey, I asked her what was inside it. "Castle Grant," she said. "Oh," said I in my American accent, "I used to know a Grant at St. Anton. Her married name is Maria Hunter." "Oh, Auntie Mary," said Pauline, "My mother's best friend."

We had good shooting. On the "home beat" the first day, after lunch, we had them flying around all over the place. My loader was John MacDonald, a stalwart young farmer. As we collided in the butt, he said "That's when the shooting gets good, bumping together in the butt." At one point, a small bird came over, very high. "Snipe," said John, "Shoot." I raised my trusty Purdy and fired straight up. One pellet must have hit the unfortunate bird, and he came tumbling down. "Good shot," said John. After the drive, when John mentioned it to Bonnie White, Bonnie said, "Don't you know, John, that Mr. Reeves is a brilliant snipe shot?" It was the first one that I had ever seen.

We had delightful lunches in huts on the moor. Often I would tarry with Pauline over a sloe gin after lunch—a "quick, quick sloe sloe" as she called it with scarcely disguised double-entendre.

One night, we had invited Pauline for dinner and Frank Downey, Bonnie's loader, said, "If I may make a suggestion, sir, it might be nice if you had a piper in for her ladyship." Bonnie asked me at lunch if I would like to split a piper with him and I said "Lay it on, Steve." When the piper marched in during dinner, there was pandemonium. Later on, some of the young officers from Fort William joined in with their own piper, and it was a madhouse.

One day a year later, we were to shoot Lochindorb, one of the Stuart moors, set on a long slope running up to a low mountain. Below was a lake with the castle set out from the shore, reached by a causeway three or four feet underwater. The approach from the main Nairn-Grantown road was over a low pass which dropped down to the lake, a remote and almost eerie site. The tales of the chatelain who lived there in old times were gory.

The head gamekeeper's son, Ronnie Douglas, was a piper, and we arranged for him to go ahead of us and to be playing the pipes as we left the trucks and trudged up the moor. The sound of the pipes, the skirl of the pibroch, was spectacular coming over the water. It gave us goose-pimples.

We shot there through 1973 and then in 1974 Pauline and her then husband, Sir William Gordon Cumming, invited me for a week as a guest. On my "bye day" I went stalking and bagged a stag, a 200 pounder, eight points.

In 1971 Fig Coleman asked me to join his shoot in Spain for the "perdiz roja," red-legged partridge. Bob Hill, married to Cecilia Bowdoin from Baltimore, was our ambassador to Spain. We started off with a magnificent dinner at the Embassy in Madrid. Afterwards we went to a flamenco dancing place, where I made the acquaintance of the local drink of Spanish brandy—Fundador—and anise—*chinchon*—known as "sol y sombra." Thereafter, I was known as the Conde de Sol y Sombra, from an ancient family of grandees with their seats at Salamanca and Valladolid.

CBR Jr., Conde de Sol y Sombre
Near Guadalmez, Sierra Morena, Estramadura, Spain
November, 1973

Perdiz Roja
Quartel Francisco Coleman, Guadalmez, Spain
November, 1973

Our shooting was far down in Estramadura near Badajoz and the Portuguese border, in the Sierra Morena, rough country with wild mountain birds. We stayed at a hotel in Puertollano, had to arise in the dark and had a long drive, about an hour-and-a-half, into the shooting site, near the small town of Guadalmez. When we arrived about nine in the morning, we would be met with a table, set with hot coffee, and *chinchon*.

The shooting was fabulous. Those were the days of Franco, the Spanish dictator, who exerted a strong control over everything. He himself was an ardent shooter, and while he was around, there was no poaching. I particularly remember one drive, the "Embudo Francisco Coleman," the Coleman Funnel. I was in the rear line, the *retranca*, where the funnel was narrowest. The birds came sailing off the hillside driven by the beaters. When they reached the first line, those that made it through speeded up. By the time they reached us, they were going like bullets. I was "on" that day, leading them a mile and those that I hit cartwheeled down to crash into the brush. I hit one and turned to aim at one farther back. For some reason, I looked back at the first bird, and there he was—tumbling end over end and headed straight for my chest. I stepped aside and he thudded into the ground. If I had not ducked, I would probably have been badly hurt.

One of our chauffeurs was so wild that nobody would ride with him except John Welsh and me. To compose ourselves for the return journey one evening, John and I had him stop in the little town of Alamillo. We found a dingy pub which seemed to have the only light bulb in town. When we reached our hotel, Phoebe Welsh and the other "girls" asked us where we had been. We told them that we had stopped in a small town and found a charming inn, much like a men's club, with portraits of grandees on the walls, etc. We laid it on so heavily that they insisted on coming to see it the next evening. We couldn't dissuade them. When they saw it, they were disgusted, and furious that they had been duped. I added to my titles, Duque de Alamillo.

I shot with Fig again in 1972 and 1973. At his suggestion, I stayed over extra days and had some delightful informal shooting and also a wild boar hunt.

I have not shot since those days and really have no desire to do so anymore. I remember when I was training to do the Finsteraarhorn in 1969 with Herman Steuri, he used to reminisce about his hunting days but said that as he had become older he did not want to do any more shooting. He liked to watch the game. I feel the same way.

Kenny and salmon
Ristigouche River
Canada

19

FISHING

I have never laid claim to being a fisherman as such, but I have had some good fishing.

My debut was crabbing with chunks of raw meat on a "dab line" in the marshes behind Cape May, New Jersey in 1929 and the early 30's. I remember scampering away, in my bare feet, from a mass of crabs dumped on the kitchen floor, skittering all over the place. Also, father took us gudgeon fishing in the Gunpowder River, where we caught masses of them.

John Kinder and I had beautiful trout fishing at the "real" Snowmass in Colorado, not to be confused with the ski resort of the same name near Aspen. Gaylord Clark and I had good fishing the next year in Canada. I landed a nice salmon on the Forde River in Norway in 1967. I recently had a bang-up day of striped bass fishing with Carl Barton in Nantucket, off Tuckernuck. We pulled in so many that I became tired and watched the others fish.

But the *piece de resistance* was my first day on the Ristigouche with Ollie Iselin in late June 1986. I will never duplicate that, and I would never try to. Ollie is a member of the Ristigouche Club, and on short notice he invited his sister Nancy to fill a cancellation and said, "Bring Sprat." I checked with then Chief Judge Alexander Harvey, and he said that under the circumstances, it was all right to miss the Fourth Circuit Judicial Conference for one year. I ran into Mr. Donald Sherwood, a famous fisherman who had written a book about his fishing all over the world. He said, "Charlie, do it, even if you don't catch a fish. It is worth it just to see the place."

Nancy and I flew to Presque Isle, Maine, where Ollie and Swannie met us. It was a long drive across Aroostook County and into New Brunswick. We passed Kedgewick and drove down to the bank of the Ristigouche River. We were met by the guides in boats and taken by outboard motor to Indian House. It was a cold drizzling day. The river had been low, but the guides told us that the rains had brought it up ten inches in the last couple of days. It sounded good.

Indian House is a dream fishing lodge with "chunk stoves" in the bedrooms and a beautiful view from a bluff over an S bend in the river, idyllic. The next day, we were assigned guides and I had Kenny, who was superb. He was big and stocky and could cast equally well with either hand. We drew for pools and Nancy and I drew the Patapedia, the "Millionaires' Pool." I am sure that today, it would be more accurately called the "Billionaires' Pool." Then they explained that there was an "Upper" and a "Lower" pool and Nancy allowed that she would take the Upper. I meekly took the Lower, completely unaware that it was the section where the Patapedia River comes into the Ristigouche.

We boarded our canoes and drove up river, a lovely trip, plenty of water in the rapids and with the sun shining. Nancy and her guide went to their section and Kenny and I anchored in ours. Ollie had lent me a graphite rod, and I tried a few casts, with a notable lack of success. I asked Kenny to show me what I should do, and he obliged by casting first to one side and then the other, gradually lengthening line so that he covered a fan pattern on either side, letting the fly, a wet one, drift down toward the stern.

It was about 10:00 or 10:30, and I said that I would try. Kenny was facing aft in the stern of the canoe and handed the rod back to me over his shoulder while I leaned forward to take it. Fortunately, we each had a hand on the rod when suddenly, in the middle of the transfer, it bent over. "You've got one," he said. "The drag is right. Play him." This I did for fifteen minutes. The fish was a lovely one and when he began to tire, we headed for the shore, beached the canoe and Kenny brought him in the last few feet, caught him in the net, worked the hook free, lifted him up to let me see him and released him. This was "catch and release" with a limit of four caught in one day, or two grilse, young ones, caught and "killed." "That's a nice one," said Kenny, "must be about 15 pounds. He's fresh from the sea. He has sea lice on him."

We paddled back to mid-stream and anchored. I began casting again, with improved dexterity. I hadn't made more than three or four casts when suddenly the rod bent over again. As the fish turned and began to fight, Kenny said, "You've got a big one this time." I began to appreciate what he meant.

I bent back and reeled in whenever I could. Then I would lose all my gains when the fish took off. The reel hummed and we were down to the "backing," i.e. most of the line was out in the river. From time to time, the handle would give me a crack on the hand as the line unwound. Kenny tightened the drag. The battle went on for 35 minutes. The fish made some powerful leaps. He was giving me a work out. At times, the outcome seemed to hang in the balance. I thought the fish might win.

Eventually, we brought him to shore and released him. During the battle, I had been bitten on the forehead by a black fly but didn't even feel it. I had this welt for a week. Kenny estimated the weight of the fish at 35 pounds.

We went back to midstream and I hooked one which "got away," not, however, without giving me a fight and a lovely show of jumping. Kenny estimated him at 18 pounds. One of his leaps was near the boat, and he seemed to hang in the air before slapping back into the river. He was the most spectacular one for jumps which I had on the line.

Before the morning was over, I had caught and released two more, one about 23 pounds and another 22. Thus, I had caught and released an estimated 95 pounds of salmon. I was "out of the river" by lunch time. That afternoon, I took a walk up the Mary Phipps Trail to the top of the hill behind the camp, no more fishing for me that day. I had had "my limit" and then some.

20

CHURCH

My earliest memories of church are of being a pest and a nuisance at St. Ignatius on Calvert Street in Baltimore. I must have been about 3 or 4, since I was there with Mother as well as Father. I vaguely remember sitting on his straw hat, a proper Baltimore Hopkins-hat-style "boater," denting it and then trying to put it on his head. A few years ago I happened upon a certificate recording my baptism at St. Ignatius. Ergo, I have been associated with it all my life.

We went to Sunday School at the old St. Mary's (Govans), then on Notre Dame Lane. Aunt Frances took me with her family and the Jenkins children, Courtenay, Chilly and Dottie. I made my First Communion there, and also was confirmed. I took St. George as my sponsor name. I am not sure of my status, since I believe that they subsequently "de-frocked" or de-sanctified my St. George in the general upheaval after Vatican II.

At Gilman the seminarians came over to give us some religious instruction and then, as aforesaid, I want to Canterbury, where we received a good grounding. At Princeton I had the usual spell of "doubts" in sophomore year, but I made up my mind that I had been through it all before and said, in effect, "This is it. Stop fussing."

One of my religious memories is of going to Mass on Sunday in the "field" at Fort Bragg, the only good day we had in two weeks when we were out on maneuvers. Everyone was going to Confession, as we did in those days. It would have been impossible for the priest to hear everyone so he gave us a "general absolution" and said to go to the priests on the base at our own convenience. I recall Father Currie at St. Ignatius saying many years later that "personal" confession came into the picture long after the Church was established. He said that it was "questionable." It looks as if it has gone out of favor, despite the Church's teaching.

I have clung to the Church over the years. It has meant a tremendous amount to me. I loved the French and English cathedrals which I visited. Matthew Kenny was the Dean of Killaloe, the old cathedral church near Ennis in County Clare, Ireland. George Kenny explained that this was the equivalent of being a bishop of the Catholic Church in the days of the Church of Ireland ascendancy. There is a plaque in his memory on the wall of the Church in Ennis.

In my far-flung travels I have always tried to attend Mass regularly, not that I think I will go to hell if I miss it on Sunday. I enjoy the spirituality and also it makes me part of the local community, not just the community of "the Faithful." It was satisfying assisting at Mass in 1996 in the Cathedral at Beijing, which had been closed when I was first there in 1982. Mass at the Cathedral in Nairobi, Kenya, in 1984, was impressive because the crowds were nearly all black with only a handful of whites. Mass at the little church in Derby, Western Australia was special with its aborigine acolytes and Pallottine priest from Germany. In foreign countries I usually speak to the priest after Mass, invariably a rewarding exchange. I have been lector in French and German in Switzerland; I was lector in Kathmandu.

At home we used to go to church at St. Vincent's with Father. Aunt Ella walked us over to the Loyola College Chapel on First Fridays. We went to our parish church, Sts. Philip's and James, and then to the new Cathedral of Mary Our Queen after it was opened in 1958. Mr. William Galvin, the Archbishop's lawyer who lived around the corner from us on Bedford Place, had his house and ours "gerrymandered" into the new Cathedral parish even though the boundary would logically have been at Cold Spring Lane, just to the north. The Rector, Tom Whelan, an old friend of the family and a member of the Ivy Club, said the funeral Mass for Anna Reeves O'Donovan Fenhagen at the Sacred Heart in Mount Washington.

When Aunt Ella found it difficult to get up the steps to CMOQ, we transferred our allegiance to St. Ignatius. We could drive into the old courtyard and park, and then she could walk to the elevator and go up to the church level. This was before Center Stage took over the old college and high school buildings.

John Sharp, who died at the age of 102 and who took care of the church for years, talked me into becoming a member of the Parish Council. This was a relatively new thing in those days for the Catholic Church. Father Drane was the Pastor, and I don't believe he was too fond of the new-fangled contraption. When I was President of the Parish Council, the Deputy Provincial of the Maryland Province of the Jesuits came to our meeting one evening. The church was saddled with the expenses of the buildings which were subsequently taken over by Center Stage. He had in effect come to tell us that the Order, the Society of Jesus, intended to close the church. I often say that if I ever manage to squeak into Heaven it may be because I helped save St. Ignatius Church.

We jumped him, to his evident surprise and dismay. Laity in those days, circa 1973, were docile. I led the charge. I explained that the church had a spiritual history and presence which should not be discarded. In the basement, before the Civil War, Mass had been celebrated for Afro-Americans, both free and slave. In that same basement Aunt Nannie and Aunt Ella in the 1890's had taught Saturday catechism classes, before the nuns took over.

Other members of the Council jumped in **seriatim**. Years later, when Father Henry was rector and I told him this story, he said, "Charlie, thank heavens you did." The Order had already told then-Cardinal Sheehan of their plans, and he was distressed. Fortunately, just after my tenure, Center Stage came along and took over all the superfluous buildings.

As the developments of Vatican II progressed, I became a lector, a task that I enjoyed tremendously. There is nothing like a lawyer infatuated with the sound of his own voice. I later became a Eucharistic Minister. One Sunday as Charlie watched me give out communion, he ventured that I had missed my vocation.

In due course, thanks to my partner, Herbert O'Conor, I became a Knight of the Order of Malta, in 1990 just before I went to Prague. The Maltese church was still locked up then, even though Charlie located it for me in Malastrana. I have enjoyed being a member—especially some of the "trappings," about which I have not been bashful. In 1997 I visited the re-opened Maltese church in Prague as set forth hereinafter.

A high light of my religious experience was the trip to Rome in late 1994 to witness the investiture of Archbishop Keeler as a member of the College of Cardinals. The details are set forth in the Special Trips section. Also the visit of Pope John Paul II to Baltimore on Sunday, October 6, 1995 was an extraordinary occasion. It coincided with our Kernan Centennial celebration, and Anne Reeves and I had good seats at Camden Yards ball park, in the bleachers just behind and slightly to one side of the altar set up in center field. Arrangements were made for everyone who wanted to go to Holy Communion. Afterwards the pope-mobile was in a parade from the ball park back to the Basilica.

In May 1997 I went on the Knights of Malta pilgrimage to Lourdes, in the South of France, where Aunt Nannie had been so active. I enjoyed it greatly. It had many aspects of a modern version of the *Canterbury Tales*. It is a lovely spot, near the Pyrénnées.

William Cardinal Keeler and CBR Jr.
Sala Constantina, Raphael Stanza, Vatican Palace, Rome
December, 1994

Left to right: T. Courtenay J. Whedbee, Truman T. Semans, W. Wallace Lanahan, CBR Jr. In background: Dorothy Pearre, Muffie Jenkins, Buddy Semans, St. Matthews Cathedral, Washington, D.C., April, 1992

CBR Jr., Palace of the Knights of Malta
Via Condotti, Rome, Italy,
December, 1994

When the Knights of Malta are there, they fly a huge Maltese-cross banner from the tower of the castle overlooking the town.

St. Ignatius has flourished under Father "Bill" Watters, whose energy is prodigious. The Radio Mass at 9:30 on Sundays is so popular that it has created a parking problem for us regulars at the 10:15 "high mass" who arrive early. Father Bill's Academy for disadvantaged inner city youths has been in existence for six years and has made a great name for itself. Several of the boys were invited this year (1999) by Peter Angelos to journey to Cuba for the Oriole baseball game against the Cuba All Stars. The St. Ignatius boys were favorably remarked for their deportment, courtesy and dress.

Father Watters has undertaken an extensive remodeling and redecoration of the church. I was delighted to be in a position to help. Unfortunately part of the project is an expansion of the altar area to take care of the acolytes, lectors, eucharistic ministers and other support personnel in the new emphasis on the participation of the laity. This means that Pew 5, the third from the front on the main aisle, on the left—the family pew of the Reeves family since the 1870's, where I always sit—will have to be moved. I chide Father Watters that I am being "hoist on my own petard"—an expression that purportedly comes from the Great Siege of Malta in 1565. It is a worthy cause, even if I am so hoist! Grandfather Kenny's pew was number 15, five rows farther back. Aunt Frances (Kenny) Goodwin and I occasionally sat there also.

At Mass on June 6, 1999 the organ and chorus, at my request, gave a beautiful rendition of the Sanctus from Gounod's *Missa Solenelle*. This was the music for the 11 o'clock High Mass on many Sundays at St. Ignatius when I was a child. It has become a custom to have it played at our family funerals, joyous as it is! It was a fitting close to the Reeves' occupancy of Pew 5 from about 1875 to just short of 2000—125 years.

I was dissolved by the music and the flood of so many memories from the years that I have sat in Pew 5. Father Braunreuther, on the altar with Father Watters, seemed similarly moved. After Mass, Father Watters gave a special blessing, with laying on of hands, to Mike Murphy, the architect for the restoration, and to the contractors.

The main church was closed for six months; the 10:15 Sunday Mass was held next door at Center Stage, the former home of Loyola High School and College. I am sure we had Peter Culman, the Director and brother of David's Canterbury friend, John Culman, largely to thank for this. At first we were in the main Pearlstone Theatre downstairs and later in the Howard Head Theatre on the fourth floor. Howard had been a strong backer of Center Stage. He became a Catholic at the end of his life. I got a kick out of seeing his portrait when we came out of Mass in his theatre. Life has some funny quirks and turns. I am sure that Howard must have had a kick out of seeing us there—assuming that he did!

The church reopened on Gaudete Sunday of Advent, December 12, 1999 with a lovely Vivaldi Mass.

21

Special Trips

In looking over these reminiscences, one might receive the impression that I was always taking trips, starting as a one-year-old with a summer on Penzance Point at Woods Hole. Come to think of it, maybe that's how I did get started, but I am not like some of my friends and acquaintances who can't stop traveling. I get "traveled out" and am delighted to flop down at home, crawl under a large flat stone for awhile, so to speak, and come out blinking into the sunlight some time later.

In Special Trips, I include those that were not taken for some special reasons, i.e. military service, skiing, climbing, fox hunting, golf, shooting, even "work," whether pure and simple or combined with one of the above "pleasures" or interests. These Special Trips were taken **qua trips**, for the pleasure [*sic!*] or interest of traveling to some unknown spot.

1982—China—Tibet—Mount Everest

I was fascinated by the accounts of the English expeditions of 1921, 1922 and 1924 to Mt. Everest, especially the mystery surrounding the disappearance of George Leigh Mallory and Andrew Irvine.*

I had seen the notice in a ski magazine of the proposed 1963 American expedition, and I toyed with the idea of applying as a cameraman because of the 16mm movies that I had made of skiing and climbing. However, I had just switched over in 1961 from Cross and Shriver to Venable, so I did not pursue the idea. Then at a law firm dinner one evening in the spring of 1982, I was seated next to Ronnie Reno's wife, Mary Ellen. "Charlie," she said, "you ought to be on the trip to China and Tibet that Ronnie and I are taking this fall." I found out that they were going on a Sierra Club trek which would take them to the East and North sides of Mt. Everest.

When I said I didn't think I could take the time, five weeks, Mary Ellen suggested that I look at the prospectus in Ronnie's office. At first I couldn't understand exactly where they were going, since the Tibetan place names were spelled in Pin-yin with lots of "x's," a method which made them indecipherable to me. Then I realized that they were going to the very places where the British had been sixty years before—Shigatse, Shegar, etc., as spelled in the Brewster method.

I made application, filled out the forms, took a complete medical examination, had a full stress test, (heart rate up to 205 as I recall), and early in October found myself in San Francisco with Mary Ellen and Ronnie. I might add that downtown San Francisco with its live sex shows looked tawdry compared to what I remembered from war-time days nearly forty years before.

We boarded CAAC—Chinese Airways, the only available flight in those days, and had a long flight to Shanghai, since we had to avoid Russian territory. We had a one-hour layover and then flew to Beijing, (I called it "Peking" in 1982), which we reached about

* As I finish this opus, I read that the body of Mallory has just been found 900 feet from the summit of Everest and buried, at the request of his family, on the mountain. No camera has been found, so no one knows whether he reached the top. The body of Irvine has not been found.

10:00 P.M. We bussed in to the Bei Wei Hotel, formerly reserved exclusively for Chinese. It was small but comfortable, and they gave us a hot dinner at midnight. There were banks of chrysanthemums around the front entrance.

The next day we walked to the Temple of Heaven and in the afternoon bussed to Tiananmen Square, the Forbidden City and the Cultural Palace. At the last I took one look at Marx, Engels and Company on the political side and opted for the historical side, which was well done, especially the horses, of which I took many pictures for the "run and jump set" at home.

We left early the next morning for Chengdu and had a tour there in the afternoon including the estate, under renovation, of the poet Dufu, exiled in the Seventh Century. I took pictures of the double moon gate for Bill McMillan at home since I always admired his single one looking over the Western Run Valley.

The following morning we left Chengdu for Lhasa, taking off before sunrise. We had an incredible flight. As Galen Rowell, the Tibetan expert and author, says, it is a flight over the wildest jumble of snow covered peaks, glaciers and precipitous forested valleys in the world. We landed about 9:30 A.M. The plane refueled, took on its return load and took off. They do this to take advantage of the good morning weather. If there is a cloud in the sky, they do not fly. There is no margin for error in that terrain.

We drove in to Lhasa, about 75 miles, since land for an airport is scarce in the mountains. We could see the Potala, the Dalai Lama's home and sanctuary, until 1959, from a long way off. We went to the "rest house" about three miles out of town, which must have been an army cantonment. When I walked up to lunch in the dining hall, I walked slowly, Swiss mountain guide pace, since we were at an altitude of 11,300 feet, the same height as the Jungfraujoch. A month later, after we returned from Everest, I could practically run up the slope.

The next day we drove in to Lhasa to take in the sights, Potala, Jokhang, etc. The tour of the Potala was long, and fortunately we started it at a relatively high level, driving up a road to a rear entrance, which meant that we did not have much climbing. It was filled with pilgrims and was a fascinating experience. We descended the long stairs down the front side. We saw the Dalai Lama's spartan living quarters and walked the roofs with their ornamentation.

I walked around the Jokhang, clockwise as required. I was impressed by the sturdy young pilgrims prostrating themselves around the temple. A charming old man with a prayer wheel respectfully stuck his tongue out at me. I replied in kind as we bowed to each other. This is the Tibetan "formule de politesse" about which we had been informed in our introductory literature.

The following day we drove in two mini-buses over two high passes to Shigatse. The road ran along the Yarlong Tsangpo, the Tibetan headwaters of the Brahmaputra, for a while, and then it turned left and hairpinned up to the Kamba La at 4794 m.u.m. or 15724 feet. After the first few turns on the gravel road and after passing crawling, ramshackle trucks crammed with baggage and people, we fatalistically resigned ourselves to the journey. From the pass, we descended to a large sapphire-blue lake, the Yamdruk Yamtsu, or Yamsho Yamco, depending on which map you are reading, and drove along its shore for some way. We then went over another pass where glaciers came down close to the road. From a reading years later of Peter Fleming's *Bayonets to Lhasa*, this must have been the place where the British force under Younghusband and the Tibetans had a famous battle in 1904, the highest ever fought anywhere in the world. This was the Karo La, 5045 m.u.m. or 16,551 feet.

We spent the night in Shigatse at another "rest house," fairly spartan but adequate. I met a young Dutch climber who had been caught in an avalanche on the slopes leading from Camp III to

Camp IV on the North Col of Everest. He was lucky to be alive. The little local hospital must have done a good job since his rib cage and chest cavity had to be opened to take care of his injuries. We were supposed to go to Camp III. I thought it was impossible, and fortunately for us it subsequently turned out to be so, thanks to a providential "unseasonable" snow storm.

The next morning, Monday, we stopped at the Monastery of Tashilunpo, the seat of the Panchen Lama, second to the Dalai Lama. They were having a religious service with chanting, and there was one basso super-profundo who would have made Chaliapin sound like a first tenor. One of our party, Marian, a photographer and protégé of Ansel Adams, was a Tibetan Buddhist by religion, which gave us an entrée with the lamas and monks. I have a photograph of some of the pilgrims in the courtyard, and the features could be American Indian, Eskimo, South American Indian, et al. They must have come over the Bering Sea land bridge or "coasted" down the Pacific Coast of the Americas about 25,000 years ago.

From Shigatse, we drove to Shegar, a distance of about 200 kilometers or 120 miles. The countryside was like an enormous Nevada, with a single telegraph/telephone line marching across the desert. There was no wild life, probably shot up by the communists. Vegetation was sparse. We crossed one pass, possibly the Tsuo La, 4500 m.u.m. or 14,760 feet, where we had a distant view of the Himalayas, a "rugged highland view" according to a more recent guide book. This was followed by an even higher one, where I really felt the altitude and moved very slowly when we walked around. It was cold and clear and a fair wind was blowing. This may have been the Jia Tsuo La, 5220 m.u.m., 17,226 feet. There were mounds of manestones and ragged prayer flags fluttering in the wind. We had our first magnificent view of Everest, forty or fifty miles away, that "great excrescent fang" as George Leigh Mallory called it. One thing that was puzzling was that our Chinese Mountain Association guide did not know the names of the huge peaks in the chain, which must have been Makalu, Everest, Lhotse, Nuptse, Cho Oyu, Melungtse, etc.

At Shegar we were again in spartan quarters but livable. It was difficult to realize that the line of ruins and rubble reaching up a low mountainside opposite us was all that remained of the famous Crystal Monastery which the British had visited in the 1920's and where they had befriended and photographed the head lama.

The next day we drove on by Red Army truck to Kadar on the east side of Everest. We camped in our tents in a meadow beside a fair-sized stream. I had the geodesic tent which I had bought with Gay Black before I left Baltimore. I had borrowed his sleeping bag which was supposed to be comfortable at -35° F.

The next day our luggage was loaded on yaks and we started the trek. There had been expeditions on the east side, but we were purportedly the first "trek" as such. We walked past a couple of small settlements and then trudged up a fairly steep dusty slope. The yaks came behind, bells ringing and the drivers whistling and calling to them. They didn't seem to go fast but they forged steadily ahead up the steepest parts.

We camped in a level spot with a few clumps of bushes around. The next morning we recommenced our trek. We must have been at an altitude of about 15,000 feet. The going was not difficult but it was a steady upward slope. In the afternoon, I was walking along beside our doctor, Steven Penrose. I felt perfectly all right, taking it easy at a "guide's pace." I turned to him and said, "Steve, I'm wheezing." He was not the official doctor. Our leader had not included one in his plans. But it's a good thing that Steve was along. He worked in the emergency room at a San Francisco hospital, and he studied pulmonary and cerebral edema before he left. "Sit down, Charlie," he said and took my blood pressure. "Stay absolutely still for twenty minutes." He took my blood pressure again and said to come on.

In about a half hour, the same thing happened again. The others had gone on and made camp. It was dark by now. I was beginning to feel weak. Steve had some of the group come back and practically carry me into camp. The next morning, I felt all right but Steve said, "Charlie, you have to go down and rest. I can help you now, but if anything happens, I can't do a thing for you. You know that we are at least three days from the nearest hospital."

They arranged for me to ride a horse down. Steve did not want me to walk. He insisted that one of the Tibetans accompany me. Then they left to climb up and go into the area under the east face of Everest. The horse came up the next morning. I would much have preferred to walk because the wooden saddle was most uncomfortable. But I followed doctor's orders. It's a good thing that I did because I now more fully appreciate what Steve was advising me to do. His advice was the same procedure set forth in detail by Jon Krakower in his recent book "Into Thin Air" about the 1996 catastrophe on the south side of Everest. There is now a small facility on that side of the mountain which treats cases of High Altitude Pulmonary Edema ("HAPE") and High Altitude Cerebral Edema ("HACE"), most of them trekkers.

My guide, Godju, who spoke no English, was going to sleep outside in the open, but I insisted that he come inside, especially since it was freezing the first night at the high camp. When he unrolled his fine sleeping bag, it had a leather name plate on it, "Messner." Godju was the Tibetan guide who had gone the farthest with Reinhold Messner on his solo climb of the north side of Everest in 1981. Heine Messner made Godju turn back, possibly on the North Col or North Face, and then he went on alone. I shook Godju warmly by the hand. I was with a "celebrity."

When we arrived "down," 12,500 feet above sea level, at the camp site by the river, I had my tent to myself and followed doctor's orders—"be a gentleman of leisure." Steve also gave me some hard candies to suck on. I ate with the Tibetans, much better fare than the Sierra Club provisions. I had yak, yak dumplings, chicken, etc. Fortunately, Braxton Mitchell had given me a paperback of *The Snow Leopard* by Peter Mathiesson, an account of his trip to Dolpo in far western Tibet with George Schaller, director of the American Museum of Natural History. I rationed myself in reading it. By the third day I began to be restless and walked around a bit.

When the others returned, I was fine. They looked noticeably thinner, and they didn't have much to say about their experiences. I think they must have had a tough time. Looking back on it, it is lucky that we all got off as well as we did because we did not have enough time to acclimatize properly, and later on the others all had bronchial problems. In the morning the noise from the tents sounded like "seal rocks" and I learned to recognize the individual coughs.

The next day we were due to travel to the north side. It was a raw, overcast day. I observed that it "felt like snow." I was vetoed with "it never snows at this time of year," i.e., toward the end of October. By the time we left, it had begun to rain. After we had turned the corner to the north side, we passed a dingy little settlement where we had a brief stop to see if we wanted to make any purchases. In the little store there was nothing to buy. As we climbed toward Rongbuk, it began to snow and soon we had three inches on the ground. We finally had to stop when the road became steep and a supply truck for a German expedition doing the North Peak, Changtse, had become stuck. We piled out and walked in the last mile or so. We passed the German camp, celebrating because they had just made their climb. Our equipment arrived later by yak, and we pitched camp in the dark. It was cold and miserable, but the sleeping bags were warm.

The next morning we awoke to brilliant sunshine and a foot of new snow. We had a meeting to decide what should be done. Our leader had his heart set on reaching Camp III, but it was out of the question. As soon as one left base camp, the snow was much deeper and the yaks could not have moved through it. Also our yak drivers and porters had inadequate or no shoes. We could go no higher, and we individually took independent treks. One day I walked up to about 19,000 feet. I tried to walk back without stopping, but it was impossible. My feet could feel the cold, the air temperature was below freezing, but the sun temperature was unbearable. The sun felt like a weight, beating down on one.

We had two young geologists with us. On the drive from Lhasa they had showed us the fault line where the Indian subcontinent was grinding up under Asia. One morning it felt particularly cold as I crawled out of my tent in my Gore-Tex suit, climbing boots and glacier glasses. I asked what the temperature was and they said that, depending upon which thermometer you believed, it was either -8° or -13° Fahrenheit. Fortunately, there was not a breath of wind. Since the Chinese had their entire country, including Tibet, on the same time, no zones, the sun did not hit our tents until about 10 A.M. We were at least three hours west of Beijing by sun time.

One afternoon when I returned from a walk I heard the two geologists talking. When I asked them what they were discussing, they said that they had walked along the stream that came down from the main Rongbuk glacier. It was mostly frozen over but open in stretches. They had seen a set of footprints coming down from the opposite side, from the direction of the Nepalese border. The tracks descended to the stream, then retreated a bit, came down again and finally rose toward the mountain chain. I asked them if they thought it might be a Himalayan blue bear. "I don't know what it was, Charlie," one of them said, "but I can tell you for sure that whatever it was, it was not walking on all fours." This was interesting since it was in the same area that the old lama of the Rongbuk monastery had matter-of-factly indicated to the British in the 1920's that this was where the yetis were located. I make no claims. I simply report the facts as given to me.

One day we walked to the ruins of the Rongbuk monastery. It was sad. Some of the frescos were still exposed to the elements. The Chinese blamed the Tibetans for the desecration, but obviously the Chinese directed it, although some of the disaffected Tibetans may have joined in. In Tashilunpo and some of the other monasteries, restoration of the buildings and the libraries had begun to a certain extent, but after 1987 the monks' revolts occurred and since then there has been continuing repression.

After a few more days, we returned to Lhasa via Shegar, Shegatse and Gyantse. At the last they were starting a two-day celebration because of the moon, and the two calendars, Tibetan and Chinese, were not in sync. It was November 1 and somewhat like our All Saints' and All Souls' Days. That evening in Lhasa, we went to the little celebration in one of our recreation halls. The Chinese left, there was one German from another trip and the rest were all Americans and Tibetans. I put on my best Elkridge Club dancing-class manners and had a fine time dancing to a recorder with tapes. As I started to try to speak a few words of Tibetan with a lady whom I had asked to dance, she put me at ease by saying that she spoke English. She had been educated in Darjeeling. She must have come from the "upper class" in the old days. She talked freely of the situation and at the end said, "... but the people are better off." It was a fascinating evening. I also danced with the Tibetan girl who had climbed highest with the Chinese expedition on their ascent of Everest. That was a bit like dancing with the Red Army truck in which we had been riding.

I made a final trip into Lhasa and managed to take a good photograph of the Potala across the pond, just cleaned of algae. The cleanup crew asked me in for tea in the gazebo in the middle of the lake. The people everywhere were invariably friendly, like the young people in Beijing who invited me to go rowing with them in the big park behind the Forbidden City.

We flew out of Lhasa early in the morning and I took some fantastic pictures of the mountains which we crossed. We landed at Chengdu under its ever-present cover of high fog. We had a trip out to the irrigation river control works, which were started about 200 B.C. We had lunch in a real Chinese restaurant, filled with "real" Chinese people. The food was excellent. I remember one plate made of vegetables arranged to look like a rooster.

From Beijing, we made a journey to the Great Wall at Badalong and also visited the Valley of the Kings. Our young female guide at the latter gave me a personal tour and was most intelligent and interesting. She had no desire to emigrate to the United States or elsewhere, but I felt that with people like her, China was bound to change. This was seven years before the Tiananmen Square riots.

The next day we flew to Shanghai and had a bit of a layover which gave me time to buy a red silk dragon-decorated dressing gown, on the enthusiastic recommendation of the Chinese in the shop.

We flew to Los Angeles. With tacit permission, Mary Ellen and I went into the empty business class section, and stretched out. We had an hour layover in L.A. while they cleaned the plane and made it ready for its return flight to China. We then flew to San Francisco. It was a sparkling clear day, we flew up the coast with the snow-covered Sierra Nevada to our right and commenced our let down above the Monterey Peninsula. We could clearly see the golf courses. I spent the night at the airport hotel and flew to Baltimore the next day. It had been an extraordinary trip.

Just prior to my departure, I had tried to buy a 35mm camera since we were advised that movies were forbidden. In San Francisco on the morning that I left, I managed to pick up one of the then-new automatic cameras. I couldn't believe that it took 35mm film. The salesman showed me how to use it. I never saw a picture until I had my films developed in Baltimore. I held my breath as I went to pick them up. They were perfect. As our Tibetan

Buddhist trekker said, "If a picture wants to be taken, it will be taken." In the winter I showed my slides to a packed house at the Maryland Club, freely heckled by Fife Symington, Kitty Hoffman and Courtenay Jenkins. A fitting finale.

1984—Africa

In the fall of 1983, Nancy Marburg called me up and said, "Sprat, we have a trip that you must go on." It was a trip to Kenya with her sister, Barbara Sears, her brother, Ollie Iselin and his wife, Swannie, her cousin, Bettina Dilworth, Fig and Julia Coleman, Doris Anderson and the Beebe sisters. "When are you going?" I asked. "February," replied she. "Nancy, you know I'll be skiing then in St. Anton." "Oh that's all right, you can arrange it."

So I called my travel agent, Ogden Gorman, and he said that I could cut my skiing a bit short and fly down direct from Zurich to Nairobi on Swissair. I checked back with Nancy, told her I thought I could work it out but, since I would be coming from the snow-and-ice clad Alps, "What will the weather be like?" Without pausing for breath Nancy said, "It's their coldest time of year." Naturally I took her at her word.

I had my skiing with Herbert Rofner in St. Anton, watching the Olympics on TV, etc., all as set forth hereinbefore. I took the train to Zurich, caught Swissair at midnight to Nairobi and deplaned about 8 A.M. in my heavy gray flannels and tweed coat. As the obliging porter wheeled my duffel bag to a taxi, I said, "I hear that this is your coldest time of the year," "Nah sir," he replied. "This is our hottest time." "She's done it again," thought I to myself. Actually, Nairobi being on the Equator at 5,000 feet has very little difference in temperature between the seasons.

I ensconced myself in the Norfolk Hotel, beetled around to Colpro's, had myself safari-outfitted and was seated comfortably in a wicker armchair on the verandah when the group came in the next morning. They chivvied me on my attire, and when the "white hunters" David Mead and Gillis arrived, they took one look and said, "Hemingway lives again!"

We had a wonderful trip, Meru, the Aberdares, Lake Naivasha, the Masai Mara. We had a "house giraffe" group which greeted us every morning at Meru. We saw the "wide" or "white" rhinos at Meru before the poachers slaughtered them and their keepers a few years later. We almost ploughed into the rear end of an elephant as we careened down a rain-slick road through the Aberdares. The natives reported seeing an elephant carefully step through our tents in the dead of night. We came alarmingly close to hippos on Lake Naivasha in a sputtering outboard motor boat. Our jeep was charged by a hippo as it suddenly came up out of the Mara River. We saw cheetahs run down a "Tommie," a Thompson's gazelle. We saw lions, zebras and wildebeest galore. We saw a leopard take her cubs out hunting. We went out at night to see the animals prowling around. The trip was fascinating and I would not have missed it for anything.

I teased the Iselin contingent because one morning I went to the vehicle and white hunter to whom I had been assigned for that day of game viewing. When I started to mount my vehicle, I was told it was "reserved for the Iselin Trustees." They were going to have a financial conference. My protests "but I am supposed to be in this vehicle" did me no good. I was outnumbered and outgunned.

After the group left, I flew up for a couple of days at George Small's place north of Nanyuki. Bill and Mary Marr from Baltimore were there. When I arrived, a lion had killed one of George's cattle the night before. The estate manager asked if I wanted to go with some of the natives to look for the lion that night. I of course had to accept. Fortunately the lion had left the area.

It is a good thing that I went to Kenya when I did. I have no desire to go there now.

Australia

In 1986, I was going to Hawaii to attend a State Securities Laws convention, the arrangements being made though United Airlines. I asked the "800 number girl" in Hawaii if it were possible to extend my trip to Australia, to visit Margaret Crawford and Frances McDermott. She replied in the affirmative since United had just taken over Pan American's Pacific routes. Accordingly, after the Hawaii meeting, with a day trip to Kauai, which I much preferred over Oahu, I embarked at midnight after the Securities dinner-dance in Honolulu and debarked at Sydney on Saturday, November 22, where I was met by Margaret and Frances.

Margaret whisked me to her flat on Darling Point overlooking the harbor, and then we went down to spend the weekend at Palm Beach with Rob and Jeannette Minter. The first thing we did was take a swim, which was heaven-sent after the all-night flight from Honolulu. After the weekend, Margaret drove me to Mayfield, Emu Swamp, near Orange, which was across the Blue Mountains and in the Central Highlands. When we drove into Mayfield, I fell in love with it since the gravel drive with the grass center looked just like the entrance to "the farm" at Mill Green.

It was a one-story house, which had been built by the uncle of Margaret's husband, James. He was Crawford biscuits in Liverpool, England and because of his health he had to leave England and Scotland in the winter. He spent six months each year at Mayfield. The countryside reminded me of the country around Upperville, Virginia. It is high, about 3000 feet, and, for Australia, quite green. The back road comes out at Lucknow, where gold was first discovered in Australia in 1849.

We had a lovely time, visiting Margaret's neighbors, including Jim and Sheila Thompson, near Bathhurst, and Mary Glasson, near Molong, where the land starts to descend to the Outback. The Thompsons have a lovely stone house, built in 1832, which is early for Australia, and Mary Glasson's garden, built entirely from earth imported is considered the "jewel in the crown" of Australian gardens, as I heard one visitor say. Her delphinium were unbelievable, and her roses superb.

Mary's daughter was there, and we looked up the area where she lived on the map, at White Cliffs on the far western edge of New South Wales, near the border with South Australia and the Northern Territory. Their property was 160,000 acres, but the map showed no roads into it. She said that she could not take it for the entire summer, when temperatures stood at 120° F. She had to come east to spend part of the time with her mother.

I met many locals, who couldn't have been nicer, one of whom was Max MacCarthy, owner of the best drug store, pharmacy, in Orange on Summer Street. Of Max, more later.

One evening Margaret and I went to see the recently released movie "Crocodile Dundee." The theater itself was worth the price of admission, on the second floor, up a steep flight of stairs, and would never have passed fire regulations at home. The manager appeared on stage, gave an introduction and explained that there would first be some "**try**lers." I asked Margaret what that was and she said "tr**ai**lers," short subjects and advertisements. She also warned me about not being able to understand the Australian jokes and comments in the movie, which was true. When the locals were cracking up over something, I would lean over and ask Margaret, "What did they say?" Then when everything was quiet and something was said on the American side, I would be rolling in the aisle and the locals would be looking at me as if I were crazy.

I shook the manager warmly by the hand as I was leaving, and told him that I was an American, "as if he couldn't tell!" hissed Margaret in a strong stage whisper. I suggested that Margaret and I go over to the King George Hotel and have a beer, for local color, but Margaret quashed the idea with "It's probably full of nothing but sheep shearers." Max McCarthy several years later had an appropriate counter-comment.

During my stay at Mayfield, I flew down to Sydney on the local airline to go to a party that Frances gave for me. There were lots of judges, lawyers, etc. I had a chance to get to know her husband, Charles, a wonderful person, a physician, former football player at 6' 4", and in his heyday a good golfer. Their house on Darling Point, near Margaret's flat, was charming. Subsequently, their sister Alison bought a flat in the house next door.

I flew back to Orange, and spent a few more days with Margaret. Then we drove to Sydney and visited numerous other friends, including Jane Ashton, a friend of the Alex Cochrans' in Baltimore. Jane's husband had been one of the four famous Ashton brothers who came over to the States and played polo against the likes of Tommy Hitchcock, Cecil Smith, et al. They financed their trips by selling their ponies when they returned home.

We went one evening to the Max Buchanans for cocktails. Both Frances and Margaret told me that in the old days Max was famous for rolling into town from his "property" way up in the north with his "wool check." I was delighted when Max said, "Charles, I'm sorry I didn't know you twenty years ago. We could have had a good time together!"

One day I took all three "girls" i.e., Frances, Margaret and Alison, to lunch at Doyle's, the famous fish restaurant, near the harbor entrance. The wind was howling and the sun was broiling, but they insisted that we sit outside. I was badly outnumbered.

Another day Frances took me to the RSGC, the Royal Sydney Golf Club, for lunch. She was hailed by a Mrs. Cherry Jackaman, and after introductions Mrs. Jackaman asked where I lived. When I said Baltimore, Maryland, she said that she had a friend who lived near there, and when I asked "where," she said, "Oh you would never have heard of it. It's a little place out in the country." I persisted and she said, "Monkton." I exclaimed, "Monkton! What's the name of your friend?" She began to reply "Alva Sargent ..." and I added "Robinson Flanagan." She and Mrs. Flanagan had known each other in Biarritz in the 1930's and on a visit to her flat a couple of days later, she showed me a scrapbook, which included pictures of Poppett Robinson Pitts, aged about two. Small world.

On my last day, Frances took me to her beach club at Bondi, the "clothed" end of the beach. The water was lovely, on December 13. After lunch she drove me to the airport, and I took off on UAL about 2 P.M. It was a brand new Boeing 747-400, half-full. I was able to stretch out in the back and after dinner slept a good night's sleep. At Los Angeles in the morning we had the usual change to the domestic terminal. The flight to Chicago was spectacular on a clear afternoon, particularly the deserts and the Grand Canyon. Coming over the Rockies I could clearly make out Aspen, Snowmass Mountain, the real one, not the ski area, and little Snowmass Lake in its glacial cirque, where John Kinder and I had camped in 1949. I was dreading a three or four hour layover in Chicago, but instead I ran from one terminal to another and caught a Baltimore flight just as they were closing the doors. I walked off the plane at BWI about 7 P.M. I had had two Fridays but the elapsed time was only about 18 hours.

1989

In 1989 Margaret Crawford was staying with me in Baltimore and said that Max McCarthy had told her that he would like me to come back to Australia so that he could to show me the "real Australia," the Outback. I took him up on it and as I arrived in Sydney, all the airlines went on strike. I took the train to Orange, since Margaret and her sisters had conveniently fled to Europe. I stayed in Max's apartment over the drug store and saw local, country Australian life, not "high society," as in Sydney, with the Stephens girls.

Max and I drove north to Cunnamulla, across the border in Queensland. We stayed with his lady friend, Cynthia "Tinty"

Brandon, in a little house above the Warrega River. When we arrived, Cynthia congratulated us on the timeliness of our arrival, and when we asked "why?" she said we had come just in time for the Engonia Races and Polo Week.

The polo was rough, tough Outback style with strong riders and ponies. The Engonia Races were straight out of Banjo Patterson and Henry Lawson, the poets and balladeers from the turn of the Century, "Waltzing Mathilda," "The Man from Snowy River," etc. There was one day of racing, on a dirt track with practically no fencing, a rickety grandstand and a "club house" shack where everyone repaired for beer. People arrived, in their private planes, from miles around. The ladies were smartly dressed as at our spring steeplechases. The races themselves were a series of sprints, run clockwise, in a cloud of dust, and were respectable, a far cry from Pimlico or Belmont but good fun.

On the way to the races I spotted a sign marked "Bellale" and asked Cynthia's sister-in-law, Dorothy Gordon, what it was. She said that Will Ogilvie had lived there for several years as a young "jackaroo," i.e., cowboy. I suddenly remembered his books at home, which Mother and Father had bought. He was a Scot who had come out to Australia for about nine years and many people said that his finest literary work was done in Australia.

Max and I had intended to drive out to Broken Hill, but since "Tinty" said she would like to join us, we changed plans and did the "Channel Country." We drove out to the Jackson Oil fields and went through Quilpie and other towns that were straight out of "Breaker Morant" and other Australian films. I really saw the Outback, but I was cautioned on one thing, and that was to not expect it to look like this if I came back again. There had been lots of rain and the land was carpeted with wild flowers, in some places fields of yellow flowers, stretching for miles.

1990—Prague

In 1947 George Kennan, using the pseudonym "Mr. X," wrote an article in the Foreign Affairs Quarterly setting forth the need for the United States to contain communism world-wide but particularly vis-a-vis Russia. In 1989 Mr. Kennan, who incidentally lives in Princeton near the Reeves house at 28 Olden Lane, wrote an article for the *New York Times* Magazine Section of February 5 entitled *After the Cold War.* In it he stated, "What we are seeing today is, in effect, the final overcoming of the Russian Revolution of 1917." I could not believe my eyes and showed the article to Bill (Levin Gale) Shreve, a past president of the Maryland Club and a long time officer of OSS and CIA. Bill said that he agreed with the article whole heartedly. He also added that he rarely received publications of the "Agency" because of his retirement, but that in the material which he did receive, the CIA had begun expressing great concern about the possible "break-up of the Russian Empire." I thought that I knew a fair amount of Russian history but I was puzzled by this categorization of "Empire." It was a little more than two years later, in 1991, that the Russian Empire did break up, first the Baltic States, Estonia, Latvia, Lithuania; then the Ukraine, Belo-Russia (BeloRus), and Moldavia; and simultaneously Inner Asia, Kazakhstan, Uzbekistan, Kyrgyzstan, Turkmenistan and Tajikistan. "Outer" Mongolia, i.e. Mungolia, had obtained independence in 1990. Parenthetically, my nephew, Charlie Reeves had had an opportunity to take a trip with a group from the University of Wisconsin in March, 1989 to the "—stans" and says that at that time no one even mentioned the possibility of such action.

In November 1989, the Berlin Wall came down with surprising suddenness, and at the same time the "Velvet Revolution" occurred in Prague with Vaclav Havel becoming President of the new Republic of Czechoslovakia. In his article Mr. Kennan had stated, with prescience, that the new Russian leaders had to relate themselves "not just to the post-1917 revolutionary period but to the entire span of Russian history. What they are creating, and what we must now face, is another Russia entirely identifiable neither with the revolutionary period nor with the centuries of czarist power that preceded it."

With that as background, Charlie obtained a job in Prague the summer of 1990 teaching English to Czechoslovakians, who had some previous knowledge of English. He lived with a Dr. and Mrs. Pavel Rossman in a flat at the end of the "C" Subway Line, beyond Vizograd. I flew over at the end of Charlie's stay and his mother, Anne, also came over. I stayed at the recently opened Diplomat Hotel, built by Austrian interests and conveniently located at the end of the "A" Subway Line. Charlie and the Rossmans' son, Zdenek, showed us around. The city was lovely, practically untouched by World War II since the Nazis had taken over in 1938 and then the Russians had come in 1945. Very little had been done to up-date the city since 1945, except for a handful of hotels, mine included. The Russians did, however, build the excellent subway line.

The Rossmans invited Anne, Charlie and me to dinner, and we had a fine time. Mrs. Rossman spoke very little English but we got along admirably. Dr. Rossman was a microbiologist or other high technologue. Zdenek, one of their two sons, was 17 and finishing school. They had given Charlie a bedroom for himself. The flat was typical Communist-era construction, located in a new town but with attractive surroundings.

We invited the Rossmans to have dinner with us at U Psi Strossu, the Three Ostriches, at the end of the Charles Bridge in Malastrana, opposite the Old Town, Stare Metzka. We had to take the early seating and had a lovely time. We left about eight o'clock when the second seating came in. We strolled across the Charles Bridge in the twilight. The bridge was jammed with people. The Rossmans told us that a year before the police would have dispersed everyone.

In talking about the changes of the past year, Dr. Rossman said that a year ago they could not have had us to dinner with them, and they could not have come out to have dinner with us. Zdenek described how two or three days after the "Velvet Revolution" in November 1989 the students had tried to march over the Charles Bridge from Old Town and up to Hradcany, the Castle, government headquarters and Cathedral. The police stopped them on the bridge with a solid phalanx of shields, but no arms.

When we reached the Old Town end of the bridge, there were five young musicians in the square medieval tower, playing classical instruments, violin, cello, clarinet, bass, etc. We all gave them a little money. Dr. Rossman began to dance with joy. They were playing music from his native Moravia. Mrs. Rossman later told Zdenek, who told Charlie, that she had not seen her husband so happy in twenty years.

After Charlie's teaching ended, we drove across then Czechoslovakia. It was a beautiful drive, reminiscent of the countryside of rural Pennsylvania and Iowa. We spent the first night in Olomos, the old Olmutz under the Austro-Hungarian monarchy. It was a beautiful old town, with lovely gardens through which we walked a long way beside a small river to a sort of amusement park. Our hotel, the Eden, was old-fashioned. I had a corner room with a ceiling that must have been a least ten feet high. We had dinner downstairs, ran into some people who could speak English and had a thoroughly amusing time. The next day, Sunday, we went to Mass in the lovely old cathedral, sitting in a pew with a nice looking lady and her children. They looked poor.

That day we drove east with the Carpathians beginning to appear on our left. We reached Poprad, now in the Slovak Republic, a large industrial town. We headed north toward the mountains and filled up with gas so that we would have a full tank before we reached the Polish border. We had heard, or read in the papers, that it could be difficult to obtain gas in Poland because it came from Russia and there were problems over payments by the Poles.

We continued up into the foothills, now looking for a hotel, without success. We passed one that did not look bad but thought we could do better. We went through the last town before the border, Javarina. It looked Swiss or Austrian, with mountain guides sitting on a low wall. It was a beautiful spot with the High Tatra towering over us. We were about to turn back when I saw a large edifice up the hill. We at first thought it might be a monastery, but it was of recent construction. I told Charlie to keep on and we came to a sign which said, "Hotel—Open." We turned in. There was a low stone building on our left, which looked like a sentry post and barracks. We drove to the front entrance of the hotel. There were only two or three cars there and a handful of people strolling. I told Charlie to wait while I went in.

There was a woman at the desk, and I asked if she had any rooms. "Yes." "Two singles?" "Yes." "With bath?" "Yes." I forget what the price was but it was reasonable. I beckoned Charlie in. We had two nice big rooms with balconies which looked down a long slope, over the village and to the High Tatra cliffs above a pine forest. Deer were grazing at the far edge of the field. It was idyllic, and I wished that Charlie had had more time so that we could have gone walking with the mountain guides. It reminded me of Mürren or Zermatt, but many years ago.

Charlie took a walk before dinner, and I had a snooze. When we went down to the dining room about eight o'clock, our waitress told us the hotel had been open only since April. She did not volunteer any information. We had an adequate dinner and turned in early after taking a short stroll up past some other buildings farther up the hill. We were a bit puzzled.

The next morning the situation was clarified by our waiter at breakfast. He readily answered our questions. The place had been a recreation spot for members of the Communist Party, like

Honniker's shooting lodge in East Germany. When we returned to Prague, Zdenek filled in the gaps. It was for **high** party members and there had been incidents hushed up, such as shooting out of season, illegal game, accidents in which people had been shot and/or killed. But it was a lovely spot and I wished that we had had more time to enjoy it.

Leaving the hotel after breakfast, we drove to the pass, two or three kilometers away, then down to the Czech-Polish border in a pine forest. Border formalities were no problem. Then we had a beautiful drive through the forest on the Polish side. At one point we took a wrong turn and encountered a youth religious festival in a national park. We drove into Zakopane about noon.

We looked at a hotel in town and did not like it. We decided to take advantage of the good weather and drove to the cable car station for Karposi, the ski mountain. We took place numbers and waited. We decided to have a coffee. It was terrible and I thought it was robbery at $3 a cup. But I had misplaced a decimal, and at 10,000 zlotys to the dollar, it was thirty cents.

When we finally entered the lift, I had a strange case of déja vu. The cable car held only about twenty or twenty-five persons, and the car itself looked old and shabby. Suddenly I remembered; it was exactly the same as the Galzig-bahn in St. Anton in 1948. They had both been built at the same time, 1937 or 1938, by the same people, the Nazis. St. Anton's had been upgraded every few years and now held about ninety people; Zakopane's had remained the same, thanks to the Communists.

We had lunch in the restaurant at the top of the lift. They had no alcoholic drinks, not even beer, just alcohol-free beer. I like the native specialties so we settled on "golonka," pig's knuckle. It looked unappetizing when it came. I ate part of mine with my alcohol-free beer, which was bilge, but Charlie rebelled. He pointed out that they hadn't even shaved his golonka.

At the top of the lift we had a lovely view and walked farther to the subsidiary summit. There were lots of people there, and we had a good time talking with them, especially when they found out that we were American. One couple with children from Gdansk told us about a hotel outside of town, very expensive. It sounded right to us, and when we came down, we drove out to it. It was fine, had good rooms for us, with beautiful views to the mountains. We stayed a couple of nights and had some lovely drives in the surrounding countryside, particularly in the evening just before dinner when the cattle were being driven home. The farmhouses were handsome wooden ones, looking much like pictures of Russia or the Ukraine.

We drove to Cracow, and toured the Wawel, the fortress and cathedral. We left the car where we had parked it, since it already had a parking ticket on it. When I returned home I paid the parking fine of 9,000 zlotys by sending them a one dollar bill. Whether the dollar ever made it to the city treasury I do not know, but at least my conscience was clear. We walked through the park to the Old Square, had lunch, saw the steeple crier-of-the-hours in St. Mary's Church, did our sightseeing and departed for Czestachowa. By the map we were not far from Auschwitz (Ozwiciem) but did not go there.

Arriving at Czestachowa, we booked into a hotel at the bottom of the hill. We obtained some gasoline, with the helpful directions of the manager, at a station near us, without too much trouble, although there were short lines, and then we visited the monastery and the cathedral. We saw the Black Madonna and afterwards followed a group of young seminarians on the ramparts as they sang the Stations of the Cross. They were fine looking young men.

The next morning we went to Mass at one of the side chapels with a group of German pilgrims. I enjoyed talking with them in German. It was a moving ceremony. We visited the Rittersaal,

Knight's Hall, before leaving, and I spotted the Knights of Malta flags and emblems.

We drove to Wroclaw, the old Breslau, a Hanseatic city leveled in World War II but now restored. It could be anywhere on the North German coast. From there we continued to Zelena Goria, where we again stayed in a brand new hotel. The weather had turned hot, but it was lovely.

The next day we drove through the old Sudentenland to the Karkenosi and took an old ski lift to the summit ridge. This is the Czech-Polish border, and there was a big electronics installation on the peak of the ridge which had been marked "off limits."

We drove to the head of a long pass leading back to Czechoslovakia. Toward the top we could look down into a high valley where there was an industrial plant, possibly for the manufacture of cellulose. As Charlie had warned me, the forest was denuded by pollution. Crossing over into Czechoslovakia, the environment was better. As we descended through the low mountains, Charlie said that he had been in the area on a weekend outing with his English class.

The next day Charlie returned to the States to reenter the University of Wisconsin while I went down to Mürren to have a little "rest and recreation" in the Alps. On reflection, it seems unreal that on August 2, as I was about to leave for Prague, Saddam Hussein overran Kuwait and threatened Saudi Arabia. George Bush, as President, rallied the Coalition to stop him. The "land war" of the Coalition did not start until February 1991, by which time I was in St. Anton. People used to ask if I weren't afraid to fly during those times, but I answered that it was probably safer because of the increased security.

1991—New Zealand

In 1991 Charlie and I flew to New Zealand in Mid-August for three weeks. We landed in Auckland, rented a car at the airport, took a couple of days getting acclimated and then drove south, wandering along the secondary roads. We spent a night at Hawkes' Bay with the Glazebrooks, friends of Margaret Crawford and Frances McDermott. They have 7,000 acres with lovely views of the mountains. They also have a vineyard, which makes excellent wine, including port. Since it was on our way to Wellington, they said not to miss Mt. Bruce to see the birds, kiwis and other nocturnals for the most part, all threatened with extinction since they had no predators until man and his cats and dogs came along.

Charlie and I became separated in the exhibits of Mt. Bruce, and I was having a cup of tea at a table outside the cafe when a flightless bird walked up, looking for food. He was a "pokicka" and had been found hurt on the road. He wandered around freely and jumped up on my table. I sat still and he began to make a cooing noise. I answered him and we had a conversation of sorts. We were communicating. It was uncanny. Mt. Bruce was written up in the *New York Times* recently, since it is a sanctuary for native birds that are becoming extinct with the increase of development.

We arrived in Wellington, stayed at a hotel on the harbor and the next day took the ferry across the Cook Strait to Picton on the South Island. We had been advised by the Automobile Association to take the train from Picton to Christ Church, a beautiful trip along the ocean with mountains on the right. At one point I said to Charlie that I thought I saw a whale spout a couple of hundred yards off the beach. About five minutes later the stewardess said to be on the lookout because we might spot a whale.

In Christ Church we stayed in the Quality Inn, a comfortable hotel, not like the gaudy Japanese-built one across the street. The Glazebrooks had handed us on to Judy Gould, who showed us her place in the horse country. We had dinner there with her family and later returned the hospitality with dinner at a trendy restaurant in Christ Church.

We drove to Queenstown, passing the bungee jumping bridge on the way. We stopped for a while and watched the jumpers, dropping 185 feet on their long lines, stopping short of the surface of the river. We settled into the Quality Inn, and since it was afternoon I told Charlie we should go to Coronet Peak and enroll him in ski school. This we did, and when I asked for a private guide the next day, they were not sure. However, a guide stepped up and said he would take me if everyone was booked. This turned out to be Michel Marchand, a Suisse Romand, born near Neuchatel, teaching skiing in Leysin in their winter and head of the ski school at Coronet Peak.

I skied with Michel for a couple of days and we had a good time. As we were going up the lift one afternoon I said I was sorry that the weather had been bad when Charlie and I stopped at Mt. Cook and could not do the Tasman Glacier. He said, "Would you like to do it? I have the day off tomorrow." For a split second I thought of the possibly hideous expense involved, flying both of us back to Mt. Cook, mountain guides on the glacier for two, etc. But it was a chance of a lifetime so I said, "Sure."

Michel worked it all out, and since the weather was good the next morning, away we went. A beautiful flight took us to the Mt. Cook airport, where we changed into ski gear, met the guides, were briefed, with a group of other tourists, Japanese, etc., and then flew to the top of the glacier. The weather was good on the eastern side of the glacier, but to the west clouds boiled up over Mt. Cook and the range running north. We had a special flight since the guides wanted us to see everything, particularly for Michel, head of a neighboring ski school. We flew over the range, skirting the heads of the Fox and Franz Josef Glaciers. It was spectacular as we looked down through the clouds on the Tasman Sea side into a cauldron of black mists.

We landed near the top of the glacier and walked a couple of hundred yards to the cornice on the north edge. The guides cautioned us not to get too close because it dropped off thousands of feet on the far side. On our right we could look up the cliffs a few hundred feet and see a compact mountain-climbing-club hut perched on an aerie.

The guides obviously wanted to show Michel the best, so as we started our ski descent with our guide, we stayed on the left side of the glacier. We first had two or three runs in powder snow, then traversed high over to the left again and had a succession of beautiful spring snow descents, linked by traverses. I hadn't had spring snow skiing like that since years ago in St. Anton with Benno Rybizka. The remainder of the group, including most of the Japanese, stayed with the other guide and took a more mundane descent toward the center of the glacier.

When we reached the bottom, the plane met us and flew us back to another spot, more westerly, at the top of the glacier. There we had lunch, with champagne, and had a nice run down on the right side of the glacier. Toward the bottom the clouds closed in from the Tasman Sea and we had to "crappel" down part way in bad light. Fortunately we had reached the "flat" but I still took it steady.

The small plane flew us back to Mt. Cook airport and we changed into the commercial plane for Queenstown. On the flight back I asked Michel for "la douloureuse," i.e., the bad news, the bill. To my astonishment he told me that the airline had flown him up and back free for "public relations." The guides had done likewise, for Michel's portion of the mountain glacier tour. When I asked him how much I owed him for the day, he said it was his "day off," so all I did was pay for myself.

I forgot to say that just before we left the hotel in the morning, Charlie had asked if he could use the car while I was gone, and I of course said "yes." Then he asked me if he could have an extra fifty dollars. "Why, Charlie?" "I want to go bungee jumping." I thought, "My God, here I am worried about falling into a crevasse on the Tasman Glacier, and now Charlie wants to go bungee jumping. What would Anne say?" I gave Charlie the fifty dollars. He made his jump and loved it. He said that as he leaped out off the bridge in the approved fashion of a swan dive, his long drawn out exclamation as he fell in a descending arc was, "O-o-o-o-h shi-i-i-i-it!"

We had wanted to take Michel and his part-Maori wife, Hiné, out to dinner, and we decided to do it that night. We four went up to the Alpine restaurant on the cable car, overlooking the lake, the mountains and the lights of the town. We waited for a window table, had a delicious dinner and then it turned out that Hiné used to sing there before she married Michel. We had her sing after the crowd thinned out. We had a ball.

1993—Alaska

In August 1993, the Gourmet Group decided to take a trip to Alaska, from Seattle via the Inside Passage to Juneau, Sitka, Glacier Bay, etc. The group consisted of Helen and Bob Thomas, Beau and Dottie Pearre, Frank and Alice Ober, Glenn and Fan Whitman, Hurst and El Purnell, Marna Hopkins, Courtenay Whedbee, Sheila Jackson and I. Cocktails were a movable feast each evening in a different stateroom. We dined together in the late sitting at two or three contiguous tables, had good weather and a thoroughly good time. It was a nice group. I took every extra day trip that I could, including flying over and landing on the Mendenhall Glacier. Glacier Bay was spectacular as we came quite close to the glacier. Great icefalls "calved" off giving birth to huge icebergs and making sizable waves. The mountains in the background, the Mt. St. Elias Range, were spectacular, rising to 12,000 feet.

1994—Australia and New Zealand

I had retired from the practice of law as of December 31, 1993, and I took full advantage of my first year of retirement. In January 1994 I had a lot of free mileage amassed with United Air Lines, some of which ran out that month. I accordingly booked a trip to New Zealand and Australia, to use everything up, first class. As the year wore on, other things came up, to fill out my schedule rather fully. When Margaret Crawford came to stay with me in June, she brought various brochures about things which I could do in Australia in her absence. She was flying to Europe again. We settled on the "Bill Peach Great Australian Air Cruise." I called them on the phone and made arrangements on the spot.

I again flew to New Zealand and to Queenstown, stayed in a hotel outside town near Marcel and Hiné's new house, and baby. I skied a bit on the Remarkables, including one day when Marcel took me outside the regular ski area. We skied down the ridge overlooking the lake and reached the road quite far down. It was far different from skiing anywhere else, Europe or America.

I took the jet boat trip from Glenorchie, at the end of the northern arm of the lake, as far up the Dart River as we could go, under the shadow of Mt. Aspiring. It was spectacular.

We went over to Wanaka one day and sampled the wines at the southernmost vineyard in the world. We went over the back way, a beautiful drive and had lunch in Arrowtown, the old mining town that has been restored and is attractive, somewhat arty.

From New Zealand I flew to Melbourne, was put up by Jilly Laycock in the South Yarra Hill Suites and had three days or so seeing the city and surroundings, including the wonderful Botanical Gardens. One night we went for dinner at the home of some friends of Jilly. At the end of dinner they began reciting Australian poetry, Henry Lawson and Banjo Patterson, including "Clancy of the Overflow." This is one of my favorites and contains the lines:

"Clancy's gone to Queensland droving
And we don't know where he are."

This is one of the most famous quotes in Australian poetry. Someone then recited "A Bush Christening," another famous one, and Jilly leaned over and said, "That was my grandfather Maginness."

From Melbourne I flew to Sydney, stayed at the airport hotel since the "Stephens girls" had fled to Europe at the advent of my arrival, and the next morning I took off on the 12-day "Bill Peach Air Tour" all around the far north and west of Australia. It was fabulous since we went to all the out-of-the-way places I wanted to see. The majority of the participants were Australian, with only a few Americans mixed in, so it was a "native trip."

Our first stop was Longreach, the site of the Stockman's Hall of Fame. We flew over the country that I had toured with Max McCarthy three years before and the "Channel Country," famous in droving days, the first location of the Duracks, the subject of "Kings in Grass Castles." That's where Clancy was, "droving." We passed by Winton, where Banjo Patterson wrote "Waltzing Mathilda" while he courted his wife-to-be. Max had told me that Banjo was born in Orange.

At Longreach we of course saw the Hall of Fame, a museum, which was fascinating with its memorabilia of the old days of the cattle industry. We witnessed an exhibition of dog and horse work at Longway Station in the country and then had dinner there under the trees in the open. It was charming. We saw all sorts of game on the way out.

The next day we flew to Mount Isa, the site of one of the largest mines in the world, silver, lead, zinc, copper, etc. Only seven of us could go down into the mine itself, and one of the older ladies, who had drawn a place, gave up her spot to me. This was kind of her, but also fortunate since the trip was strenuous.

We changed into mine overalls at the mine entrance, including helmets and miners' lamps with heavy batteries, and then embarked in a pickup truck which was stripped to the bare essentials, e.g., no windshield, windows, roof, except over the cab. They asked for a volunteer to ride in the cab with the driver, a rather cramped spot, and since no one spoke up, I volunteered. It was by far the most interesting place to be. We drove onto the mine elevator, they locked the cage and we descended three thousand feet, rapidly but with no sensation of speed.

Down in the mine it was a bit hot but not stiflingly. Everything was pitch dark in the tunnels, except where men were working. We had to be careful to give the mine trams and trucks right-of-way in the tunnels. We could see their headlights coming a long way off on the straight-aways and their reflected beams coming around corners. They showed us mine faces where they were preparing to blast. We drove down to the 3500 foot level. They explained the enormous ventilating and cooling system to us. Without it the heat in the mine would be unbearable. It was a wonderful experience and I understand how someone could get wrapped up in it, at least for time enough to make a lot of money and then clear out before becoming captivated by it.

From Mount Isa we flew the next day to Katharine, where we went through the gorge on boats. We had lunch on our boat between two river-lakes. We flew on to Kakadu where we stayed in a modern hotel in the shape of a crocodile, owned by the aborigines. On the way in to Kakadu, we flew low over the forest or jungle so as to see the "escarpment" and Arnhem Land, which I remembered from "Crocodile Dundee." I was in the rear of the plane, in a seat by myself. It was hot, as we flew in at tree-top level. The plane was bouncing all over the place from the thermals and some of the people were sick. As I snapped my pictures I felt as if I were in a bomb run over New Guinea or a German city. I could hear Shorty, the head pilot, saying over the intercom, "... and now we'll come in again for another look at the esc**aah**pment," in a real Beantown, Charles River accent. It was wild, like coming in for another bomb run and "damn the flak!"

This is the real "Crocodile Dundee" country. We took small boats in the afternoon on the Yellow Waters Lagoon. We saw one big croc on a bank, and the waters swarmed with others, just submerged. The fresh water crocs are supposed not to attack humans, but I wouldn't want to give them the opportunity.

The next day we went to Nourlangie and Ubirr to see the painted rocks, which are thousands of years old. From the top of Ubirr we could see the valley where many scenes of "Crocodile Dundee" were shot. At the end of the afternoon we flew on to Darwin, a modern city, the capital of the Northern Territory, established in 1869. I had forgotten that it was bombed by the Japanese in World War II and suffered much damage. Our hotel was luxurious, the Beaufort, and I admired the trailing vines in the interior atrium growing down six or seven stories.

From Darwin we flew west to the Kimberleys, where the Duracks ended their fantastic odyssey after leaving their lands in Queensland. We flew over some of the most desolate country that I have ever seen. We crossed the Gulf of Arafura, with the Timor Sea north of that. We came to the mouth of the Victoria River and flew across Victoria River Downs, the largest station or "property" in Australia. I asked the second pilot if he knew its size in acres. Using his calculator to convert square kilometers, he said it was 8,300,000 acres. For the most part, it was miles and miles of mud flats with sluggish rivers and inlets. It must swarm with crocodiles. Not a very nice place to have to put down. They muster the cattle by airplane, with a fleet of 26, a colossal operation, that dwarfs even our King Ranch.

We flew at low level over the recently discovered Bungle Bungles, a weird group of beehive shaped hills in the middle of the desert. We also flew near the Kimberley diamond mine, supposedly the largest in the world. We could see the huge trucks crawling around the various slopes but it is kept very "restricted." We landed at Kununurra and took a cruise on the Ord River, to the dam which holds back the lake. We toured the reconstructed home and graveyard of the Duracks, including that of the famous aborigine servant, Pumpkin, the original homestead being beneath the lake.

We flew on that afternoon to Derby, a town I liked because it seemed like the real, unspoiled West Australia. It was Saturday and, knowing that we would have a full Sunday morning, I asked if there was a Catholic Church in town. They said there was and that Mass would be shortly, at six. The daughter of our hotelier drove me down to the little church. It really was Outback. The priest was a German Pallottine, the acolytes aborigine.

The Australians on our tour did not particularly like Derby. It was too primitive for them and that's exactly why I liked it. The hotel was simple but nice, the food adequate. They had a bar where I could get my Bunderberg rum. The family who ran the hotel couldn't have been nicer.

The next day we saw the port with its huge cattle pier, no longer in use. We saw the *beobab* trees, not indigenous to Australia, but whose seeds may have blown across the Indian Ocean from Africa. Then we flew on to Broome. We stayed in a hotel in town, and instead of taking the planned tour, I took a taxi out to the resort on the beach, built by an English lord who went broke. It was lovely. I took a swim. I wished we were staying there. The group came out late in the afternoon to have champagne and cocktails and watch the sun go down over the Indian Ocean, very pleasant living. We had dinner at the Club.

The following day we were to fly out, but something did not check out with the pilots and they had to send back east for a part. They transferred us to the beach club, and we had another lovely day there.

CBR Jr., skiing "The Remarkables"
Queenstown, New Zealand
August, 1994

Margaret Crawford and CBR Jr.
Mayfield, Emu Swamp, Orange, N.S.W., Australia

CBR Jr. in the pub at Birdsville,
Northern Territory, Australia
September, 1994

On the way back we flew to Ayers Rock and the Olgas; then on to Alice Springs; and then to Birdsville for lunch en route to Sydney. I had wanted to go to Birdsville after seeing the Engonia Races. We went to the pub, which used to be the only building there, on the Birdsville Track. Now there are a handful of other buildings. The land is as flat as a pancake in all directions. It is surrounded by four "properties," each of a million acres.

From Sydney I flew the next day to Bathhurst to visit Jim and Sheila Thompson, great friends of Margaret's, whom I had known before. They were going through a terrible time because they had had four years of drought, with no rain in sight. We took a drive up to see the Hunter Valley and stayed in the heart of the vineyards. They drove me back to Sydney, through the smoke of numerous brush fires. We had a delightful farewell dinner at the Royal Sydney Golf Club with Max Buchanan and others.

When my plane was delayed the next day, I took a water taxi out to Doyle's and gave myself a proper lunch. The delay meant that I had to "overnight" in Los Angeles, and Neily Reeves came out to have dinner with me.

Chile—Patagonia

Ollie Iselin, Nancy Marburg's brother, a Harvard alumnus, had put both of us on the mailing list for tours arranged by the Museum of Comparative Zoology (MCZ) of the Harvard Museums. Their trips are top-notch, to all the corners of the earth and in first class style. Accordingly I signed up for the Patagonia trip in November 1994. Before I left, I went to dinner at the Owen Dalys', and the guest of honor was Archbishop Keeler who had been recently notified that he was being elevated to the College of Cardinals. They were just beginning to organize a trip to Rome, which would leave two days after I returned from Patagonia. I said to sign me on.

I had always wanted to go to Patagonia, and this trip, my first with the Harvard museums and John Constable, met all my expectations. We assembled in Miami and then flew Ladeco, the second Chilean airline, to Santiago, arriving in early morning, Sunday. I went to High Mass at the Cathedral. The celebrant was the Archbishop, soon to be made a Cardinal in Rome at the same time as Archbishop Keeler.

We toured Santiago, spent a day at Las Pingues, a couple of hours towards the coast, a beautiful ranch from the old days. We flew to Puerto Montt, half-way down the coast to Patagonia. From there we took a beautiful trip through the lakes, Llanquehue and Todos los Santos, past Orsono, the Fuji-like, snow-covered volcano, to Puella, near the Argentina border. We did not have time to go over to Bariloche, the ski resort in Argentina.

From Puerto Montt, we flew to Punta Arenas. We visited a rookery of Adelie penguins en route to our first stop at Puerto Vallerta. Then we had a long trip into Argentina and across the pampas to Calafate and Lago Argentino. We had a fabulous lamb lunch the first day at a little inn at Rio Verde, where they had a pet *guanaco*. The next day we had a similar lunch at Esperanza, with whole lamb cooked over an open fire. After lunch, we had a long afternoon traveling across the pampas, and although it was tiring, it made us appreciate how vast these areas are. Finally, we began to see mountains on our right and eventually topped a pass and had Lago Argentina spread out below us. It was huge, with the snow covered Andes in the background. It was cold with small icebergs floating in the lake.

The hotel at Calafate was simple, but nice. One day we drove an hour and a half to a landing where we took a small ship up the lake to the glacier. As I took a last picture on the dock, a tall tourist next to me, also taking last minute pictures, looked down at me and said, "Don't I know you from St. Anton?" It was Heiner Glauer from Munich, with whom I had often been at the Alte

Post. Small world.

The trip to the glacier was fantastic, like Alaska. The brochures claim that the ice field is the largest in the world. The glacier was continuously calving small icebergs, that eventually floated down the lake past Calafate.

Another day we took our bus to see the Petito Moreno Glacier, with an unusual aspect in that it periodically blocks a river, causing it to eat through the ice dam after a large lake has built up behind it, cutting off the access road, etc. We were able to drive to a point about 200 yards from the main body of the glacier, where we saw continuous crumbling of the ice and calving of icebergs.

On Sunday, I went to Mass at the little church. The priest was a young man, with a choir of the native children. It was a warm and friendly gathering. Calafate is tiny in winter when there are no visitors. Founded about 1927, it is remote.

We motored back into Chile and into the Torres del Paine, the needle-like peaks featured in all the travel posters. The approach was spectacular and when we reached the national park, we stopped to watch the *guanacos*. They could jump the Maryland Hunt Cup course with ease.

We stayed at the new hotel, on the lake, a spectacular setting with a waterfall from the outlet river. We drove around to Lago de Gray to take a cruise to its glacier, but the wind was so strong that we could not do it. When we departed from our hotel, the wind must have been blowing close to 50 miles per hour, a standard performance for those parts. It whipped up sheets of spray from the lake.

We drove back to Puntas Arenas and flew via Puerto Montt to Santiago. The view of the Andes on the right side of the plane was stupendous. The weather was mostly clear and we had good views of Mount FitzRoy and its surrounding peaks and later of Orsono, the snow-capped volcano. The next day, Saturday, I flew to Miami and to Baltimore on Sunday. That same afternoon Don Joyce from UMMS came in to brief me on the groundbreaking for the construction of the new Montebello-at-Kernan facility to be named for Governor Schaefer and scheduled for the next day, Monday, a tight schedule. I was coached on making a short speech but later teased Steve Schimpff that he stole my lines and I had to "wing it."

Rome—Papal Consistory

On Tuesday, I boarded a chartered Alitalia 747 at BWI with Courtenay Whedbee and 350 other Pilgrims to fly to Rome for Archbishop Keeler's elevation to the College of Cardinals. Another 100 went by TWA from New York. Courtenay and I were lucky since we were billeted at the Hotel Parco di Principe, behind the Borghese Gardens and next door to the Villa Taverna, the residence for the United States embassy.

We had a non-stop schedule in Rome. The Consistory was in the Nervi Hall. 41 cardinals were consecrated, including one from Albania who had been imprisoned by the Communists for 21 years and Yves Congar, the French theologian who had been in disrepute for many years because of his advanced thinking. There was also a Scot who had his bag-piper and girl folk-dancers. After the Consistory, we went to the North American College for a buffet lunch.

After lunch we walked down to St. Peter's and I stayed on for the private reception in the Apostolic Palace. We had a long wait outside in the Bernini Loggia as it grew dark, and then I had a long walk up staircase after staircase in the Vatican until finally I recognized the Raphael Stanza. Cardinal Keeler was receiving in the Sala Constantina, containing the magnificent murals designed by Raphael and painted after his death by his pupils, including the Battle of the Milvian Bridge.

From there I tore back to the hotel to clean up and Courtenay and I went to the Cardinal's dinner at the Columbus Hotel on the Via della Conciliazione leading to St. Peter's. We had truly "made the cut" since there were only about 70 guests and seven of them were Cardinals. It was a most impressive evening.

On Sunday we attended the Papal Mass in St. Peter's. We had to be in our seats by 9:00 since Mass began at 10:30 and lasted for two hours, but no one noticed the time. We were on the right, in the transept, quite near the Bernini high altar, and behind the new Cardinals.

After Mass I took a taxi to Jeanne van der Valk's, on the Via dei Delfini, near the Forum. We had champagne and then I took her to lunch at a restaurant near her flat. After I left her, I walked around for a bit on the Campidoglio and in the Forum, then took a taxi home. That evening Courtenay and I and Pierce and Mary Anne Flannigan went out to have a "light supper." We ended up by having a delightful evening in a restaurant specializing in game, with plenty of vino rosso.

On Monday, Cardinal Keeler said Mass in the chapel behind the main altar in St. Peter's. It was special. We had a huge farewell dinner that evening in the Pamphilia Doria, a converted palace. We flew home on Tuesday. It was the experience of a lifetime for all of us.

1995—India—Bhutan—Nepal

When I was in Patagonia, I had asked John Constable if there were any chance of a trip to Bhutan. He said it was difficult to arrange but they were beginning to work on it. I said to sign me on. Thus, in November, I found myself flying KLM (Northwest) to Amsterdam and on to Delhi.

We assembled in Delhi, put up at the Taj Palace Hotel, and

had a sight-see around, including Sir Edwin Lutyen's Regal Lodge. I even made it to Mass at the Catholic Church. The beggars swarmed around as we came out.

We flew to Paro, Bhutan, on Druk Air, Royal Bhutan Airways, with a Scottish pilot. He allowed me to come into the cockpit when we neared the Himalayas. We had spectacular views of Everest (far off), Kanchenjunga and Chomolhari. We flew up a long narrow valley before landing at Paro. As in Tibet, there is not much room for an airport in Bhutan. It is all mountains.

Our hotel was top-notch, in a lovely location up a steep hillside. That afternoon we went to the ruins of a fortress-monastery, Drugyel Dzong, from which we could see Chomolhari, the Bhutan sacred snow peak on the Sikkim (Indian) border. I could feel the altitude as we walked up to and around it. I walked at "guide's pace," since our hotel was about 7,000 feet and this must have been about 9,000 feet above sea level.

The morning that we were to leave Paro, I noticed filmy clouds coming into the crystal clear sky from the southwest. "Is the weather changing?" I asked, harking back to our experience in Tibet in 1982. "Oh no," I was told, "The weather never changes at this time of year." By the time we reached Bumthang, our farthest east, two days later, it snowed. The storm was the remnant of a typhoon which came in off the Bay of Bengal and blew up to the Himalayas. Gradually, the stories came in about the trekkers who were trapped in the mountains, including some in Bhutan. It was catastrophic in Nepal, where they had six feet of snow at Gokyo pass near Mount Everest. The snow buried a party of Japanese trekkers and Sherpas in their tents. We subsequently heard that a German trek had taken their Sherpas' advice and did not push on. The Japanese had overruled their Sherpas and about 65 people died. I was reminded of the Germans pushing the ski guides at St. Anton into situations which they did not like.

We had a lovely drive through the mountains and river valleys, although the road itself was narrow and the vehicular traffic like that in Tibet, in other words hair-raising. Although it was November, the poinsettia trees, both red and white were in bloom, and also a few cherry trees which bloom in autumn as well as in spring. The old monasteries were fascinating. I could understand that only thirty years ago there were no real roads in Bhutan.

We stopped at the Dochu La (pass) which had a little tea room and a powerful telescope. The view of the distant Himalayas on the Bhutan-Tibet border was incredible, 200 miles of summits, according to our prospectus. We realized that to date nobody had been able to approach them and try to climb them. We heard that a Japanese expedition was seeking permission.

When we were on the pass we could see high cirro-stratus clouds approaching slowly from the south. Although we did not know it at the time, this was the leading edge of the typhoon. The long range of peaks to the north was still bathed in brilliant sunshine.

We had a brief stop at Thimphu, the capital, then continued to the guest house at Mendegang where we stayed in outlying cottages. John Constable and I took advantage of the "Bhutanese Stone Bath," a combination sauna and hot tub, fed by hot springs. Afterwards I sat out on the porch of our cottage enjoying the view. We had dinner outside around a roaring fire. These fires are a Buthanese custom since they have so far preserved the forests, which provide plenty of firewood.

The next morning we visited the manor house, quite luxurious for Bhutan and miles away from anything. It had an altar room filled with statues and paintings. We were fascinated by the blooming poinsettia trees, many about 20 feet tall.

From there we drove to Tongsa, the "seat" of the royal family of Bhutan and the site of the Tongsa Dzong, the largest in Bhutan. From there we had a long circuitous road through the forests to the Pele La, at an altitude of 10,825 feet above sea level. The rhododendrons were huge but of course had no blooms at this time of year. There was a large *chorten*, i.e., religious monument, at the top of the pass with many prayer flags.

In the afternoon we reached Jakar, in the Bumthang Valley, our farthest east. We put up in a rather remarkable sort of Swiss chalet across the river from town, owned and run by a somewhat eccentric young Swiss. It had become cold, and drizzling. We were lucky that we had made our reservations far in advance since Professor Thurman, the acknowledged expert on Bhutan, and his group which included his daughter, the actress Uma Thurman, had to live in tents near the town. Everything, if there was anything, was full because of the Jambey Lhakang Druk, i.e., castle festival, that we had come to see.

When I awoke next morning and looked up the hillside, I saw that wet snow was falling and there were two or three inches on the green meadows above us. By this time I had picked up a stinking cold, probably from sitting out in the evening chill after the hot springs bath of Mendegang, so I stayed in and let it snow. The others went into town and said the temples were lovely in the snow. We were supposed to take a walk up the valley, reputedly the most beautiful in Bhutan, but it was too cold and snowy, and the festival was canceled for that day.

The next day the rain let up, and we decided to go to the festival if it could be held. Gradually they put the festival together. I bought my little temple bell and *dorji* from a lady who was spreading out her wares on a blanket on the ground. One of our party came up with the usual, "Oh you can do much better than that in Katmandu." Fortunately, I paid no attention.

The sun came out bit by bit, revealing lovely snow-capped mountains through puffy clouds across the valley. The festival commenced with dances, not by professionals but skillfully put on by the local citizens. The costumes were beautiful. The festival was organized by Chakar Lam, "Lord of the Iron Castles" and a descendant of King Sindhu Raja who ruled the region in the Eighth Century. He had invited Guru Rimpoche to Bhutan, who introduced Buddhism to the Kingdom.

We left after a couple of hours and drove to a nearby school where we watched more dances by the students and eventually joined in with them in round dances, changing partners, etc. Some of the girls were quite pretty, and there was one who was particularly good looking and a ball of fire dancing. Pretty tough on an old man. I later heard that she was some connection of the royal family, but then in Bhutan nearly every one is. The population is only about a million-and-a-half, and the young King has four wives, all sisters.

When we left the school, most of the boys were outside and one of our party urged me to give them the ceremonial salutation or blessing, traditionally given as when crossing a pass with its *chorten* and prayer flags—"Lha gyelo" ("May the god always win!") This I did three times, like a cheer, and we left the place in an uproar, flashing the traditional Tibetan (Bhutanese) thumbs up sign —"Yapooray!"—which in Tibetan means about the same.

We were lucky to have been able to leave Bumthang since the road back had been blocked by snow and mud slides. We crossed the Pele La with lots of snow still around. We wound down through the forests to Tongsa and put up at the very attractive guest house across a small valley from the Tongsa Dzong. The manager was a bit of a character, and as I was looking at a picture of the previous King, the father of the present King, he said his name was Dorjie. He laughingly indicated the same for me as a sort of nick-name. I asked what it meant, and he said, "Thunderbolt." That was the little instrument that I had bought in Bumthang along with my temple bell. It is turned from side to side in the left hand while the bell is rung with the right hand. I was delighted and I took it as a compliment.

The next day was fascinating, almost a focal point of our trip under the aegis of the Museum of Comparative Zoology. We were due to go into the hidden valley of Phobjika to view the black-necked cranes which winter there. We left Tongsa and detoured off the main road on a dirt and gravel road "completed" only in the 1980's. We ascended by various hairpin turns through the forest and over a pass and into a beautiful hidden valley, surrounded by pine-clad mountains. The valley itself was quite broad, maybe a half-mile to a mile. As its head was the Gangteng Gompa, purportedly one of the oldest and wealthiest private monasteries in Bhutan, a lovely location.

We drove on down the valley to our "rustic guest houses" a couple of miles away. The whole area was strongly reminiscent of a Swiss valley, the wooden architecture strikingly chalet-like. Our quarters were a bit spartan but livable.

On the way in to the valley we had spotted a couple of cranes in a field below the road and some more were farther away. After settling in, we went in search of cranes and split into groups. The most energetic of our party elected to walk up the center of the valley to the Gompa, looking for cranes, and the least energetic elected to ride the mini-van to the Gompa. I joined the compromise group which rode part way back, walked down into the fields to look for cranes and then rode up to the Gompa. We were the lucky ones since we spotted quite a few cranes in the fields with scattered ones flying in. I had my field glasses up when a bunch of "things" flew past. "Damned pigeons," I thought, but then I realized that pigeons did not fly with their legs stretched out backward. I took my glasses down and there must have been forty cranes coming in to feed and roost.

When we assembled at the Gompa, we made a careful composite count and figured that we had seen a total of 100 cranes. We had thought that we would be fortunate if we saw only a handful since the date was November 12 and the cranes were not expected to arrive until the 15th. There are less than 800 in the wild and about 200, recently discovered, are thought to winter here. We were lucky indeed. Perhaps the typhoon and the resultant snow in the north had brought them down early from their summer grounds in Tibet.

The next day on our way out of the valley we tried to approach some cranes that were below us, on a rough hillside leading into a meadow. They eluded us, but we must have come fairly close to one in the undergrowth because it let out a bugle of warning that made us jump, a beautiful call, very strong.

We drove out of the valley, a real Shangri-La, and hated to leave it. I sat in the front seat on our way down the forest road, a real treat with the snow-covered mountains to the north showing through the trees. We stopped several times to watch lemurs crossing the road or swinging through the trees. We rejoined the main road, two lane macadam, below a little settlement that looked like a remote Swiss village. I was continually reminded throughout Bhutan of its similarity to Switzerland.

We were headed back to Thimphu, and some of the crowd elected to go directly so that they could go shopping and get ready for our dinner with the Foreign Minister. I elected to go with the other group to Punakha, and I am glad that I did. It was one of the most beautiful sites that I have seen anywhere.

It was a lovely afternoon, clear, cool, crisp, with a warm sun. We branched off the main road to the right and descended to the Chhu River. We drove a short distance and reached Punakha Dzong at the confluence of the Po (male) and Mo (female) Chhu rivers. One was light and the other dark, very much like the confluence of the Schwarz and Weiss Lutchine at Zweilutchinen, downstream from Grindelwald and Lauterbrunnen, in Switzerland. Probably the same sort of geology at the sources caused the different colors.

Punakha Monastery and Summer Palace
Bhutan, November, 1995

Syangboche Airstrip, "Everest Villages"
Nepal, November, 1995

CBR Jr. near Khum Jung, "Everest Villages"
Chumbu Valley, Nepal
November, 1995

CBR Jr. with hiker and guide looking toward Macchupuchare ("The Fishtail") in the vicinity of the Annapurna Massif, Nepal.
November, 1995

Father Ooki, S. J.
Pokhara, Nepal
November, 1995

Taj Mahal
Agra, India
December, 1995

We walked over the suspension bridge to the monastery and had a thorough tour, even seeing the novice monks at their chants. Flowers were everywhere; there was a gorgeous tree in the middle of the main courtyard. The whole scene was one of beauty and serenity. This used to be the ancient capital of Bhutan. The body of monks moves in from Thimphu for the winter months. On our drive we passed a smart black car with a revolving-type beacon on the top. It was one of the leading monks or lamas, on reconnaissance for the winter move, I suppose.

We drove on to Thimphu and stayed at the Druk Hotel, the lap of luxury compared to our quarters since we had left Paro. That night we had dinner at an inn on the edge of town, with cocktails around a blazing fire in a courtyard. The foreign minister was there with other potentates and we were firmly warned by John Constable not to try to initiate a conversation with them. I meekly sat on my little stool by the fire and did not dare to approach the mighty. When we entered the inn for dinner, buffet style, I was awaiting my turn toward the end of the line when I found myself beside a fairly stocky man who turned and asked me how I liked Bhutan. I told him that I liked it very much but that I had one regret. "What is that?" he asked. I replied, "I am sorry that I did not have a chance to meet Father Mackey." I was talking to the foreign minister, and I had struck exactly the right chord.

Father Mackey was a Canadian Jesuit, stationed in Darjeeling, who had died about a month before our trip. The King of Bhutan had invited him to come in to modernize the educational system, but before Father Mackey accepted, the King told him that there was one condition to his coming. "What is that?" asked the priest. "That you do not try to make one convert." To which Father Mackey replied, "I have never believed that entry into the Kingdom of Heaven depended on having water poured on one's forehead."

The minister asked me if I had read Father Mackey's book, and I said that I had not but that I wanted to. He then said, "That book is probably thirty percent about me. I was Minister of Education then, and Father Mackey and I worked together putting the education system in place." We had quite a chat and then to my utter surprise he said, "You know there are two Jesuits in Bhutan now." He said that one of them was a Father Van who was settling up Father Mackey's affairs in Thimphu.

The next day I skipped a temple visit and decided to find Father Van. Our Bhutanese guide, Sharma, located him through his tour office. I called and took a taxi out to meet him at Father Mackey's house. We had tea, and I had a most interesting visit. Father Van was straightening matters out, including the house, and was due to meet the Queen of Bhutan for lunch after I left. The status of the Jesuits in Bhutan was a matter of considerable uncertainty, and further Van told me about the identity of the other Jesuit who was then in Bhutan and whom I did not meet, a fascinating story.

It seems that one of Father Mackey's best Bhutanese students went through the school system in Bhutan and then wanted to go to college in India. He obtained the permission of the King, graduated, received his degree and returned to Bhutan to go into business. He was successful, but not satisfied. He asked for permission to return to India to study for the priesthood. He was again granted permission, became a priest and then entered the Jesuit order. He had just returned with Father Van in order to visit his family in Bhutan. The Holy Spirit moves in mysterious ways.

The following day we drove to Paro, past the confluence of the two rivers where there is a sentry station with a barrier. The next day we had our hike up to Taktsang, the "Tiger's nest," a monastery perched on unbelievable cliffs. Pictures of it are in every type of advertisement or poster for Bhutan. I climbed as far as the tea house, which was a long slog of about three hours. I did not attempt the last bit to the monastery. It looked quite "airy."

An amusing episode occurred that night at Paro. We had drinks before dinner in the courtyard around the roaring fire. The Thurman party with Uma Thurman was also there, and we were cautioned not to speak to them. Instead, during dinner, some of them came over to our table to find out who we were.

We flew to Katmandu the next morning, a flight even more incredible than the one from Delhi to Paro, since this time we were flying almost due west with all the giants of the Himalayas on our right, Chomolhari, Kanchenjunga, Makalu, the Everest group, Cho Oyo, et al. We put up at the Yak and Yeti Hotel, quite an establishment, incorporating some of the Rana palaces, and we were on the special fourth floor, with a sitting room for cocktails, reading and other amenities. It was like a club, most pleasant. That night we had dinner in the Rana theater in a wing of the Yak and Yeti and were entertained by Nepali dancers.

The next day we flew to Tiger Tops in the Royal Chitwan National Park and did the usual game viewing, river cruise to see the garwahls, a sort of crocodile, and elephant ride. We saw many rhino but no tigers, par for the course. We stayed at Tiger Tops about four days. It was a lovely place and the views to Manaslu and the Annapurna massif were wonderful, from our level of about 1,500 feet to the tops of the Annapurnas at 25,000 feet.

On our return, we toured Katmandu and Bhaktapur, the nearby medieval city. We had a farewell dinner, and I bade good-bye to our group the next day as they set off for Delhi and home. We had had a good time together.

As is my wont on long trips, I took advantage of the long flight from home with its brutal time changes and, rather than return immediately, hooked on to a trek, supposedly "moderate," to the Everest Villages. I wanted to see the Nepal side of Everest after having been on the Tibet side in 1982.

The group was nice, seven in all, and they too were staying at the Yak and Yeti, although not in the fourth floor club suite. We were supposed to fly in the morning to Lukla, one of the Sir Edmund Hillary landing strips at 9,400 feet. There was something wrong with the first helicopter which we loaded into, a rather ugly, orange-colored job, a veteran of the Russian army, which had seen service in Afghanistan. We had to wait for several hours and eventually took off in another about one o'clock. We sat along the sides in bucket seats and the center was crammed with duffel and freight.

The flight to Lukla was uneventful, and we had lunch in a small hotel. We started the trek about three-thirty, much too late. We walked down about an hour to the Dudh Kosi River, then walked up to Phakding. This was supposed to take about 2½ hours, but it became dark and we had quite a grind to the camp site, with the river roaring in our ears. I had one of the Sherpas, Ram, to myself, and he succeeded in getting me there about seven o'clock. We slept in tents. We had supper in a sort of mess hall, spartan.

We took off the next morning for Namche Bazaar, a long, long slog, supposed to take about six and a half hours. I made it in three hours to the little settlement where we had lunch in an inn. After lunch the going was slow since some of the trail was like a stone staircase. There was quite a bit of traffic, some trekking groups, many local villagers and one young porter carrying a large wooden beam for construction, that must have weighed over one hundred pounds. Everybody greeted one another with "namasté," meaning, according to our guide book, "the divinity within me welcomes the divinity within you," a salutation similar to the Austrian "Grüss Gott," shortened by the Swiss to "Grüezi," meaning "Greet God."

I plodded on, wondering if I would make it. Thank heaven I took John Constable's advice and had Ram carry my little day pack. Fortunately Sona Hise, our head Sherpa, and his crew must have sized me up because even our prospectus had characterized the grunt up to Namche as a "long and challenging day with many ups and downs." [*sic!*]

About an hour or so out of Namche a horse appeared, and I rode the rest of the way into Namche Bazaar, passing many of the groups which had passed me earlier in the afternoon, including the porter. We all greeted each other warmly with "namastés." Namche is at 11,300 feet and I was delighted to get there. My trusty steed and I rode through the town, scrambling up a steep and stony lane to the inn, which was set on the far edge of town. It was Thanksgiving Day, November 23, 1995, and I was thankful to be there. My ride into Namche Bazaar was a bit different from the Thanksgiving Day hunts which would be held that day, several hours later (by our time) at the Elkridge-Harford and Green Spring Valley Hunt Clubs.

One amusing aspect of the grind to Namche Bazaar is that the youngest member of our group was a jogger or runner. The day before he had "flashed it," i.e., walked very fast, from Lukla to Phakding, arriving hours ahead of me. On this day he had also flashed it, first to the lunch spot, then up to Namche. He had not seen me arrive on the horse, and when I sauntered in to the inn quite fresh, he looked up surprised, if not with consternation. "Where are the others?" he asked, and I casually answered, "Back on the trail." He was puzzled. Then he offered me a drink, an offer which I wisely refused, with memories of our trek on the Tibet side in 1982. I suppose the others must have told him about the horse when they arrived. By this time, I had gone out to take a shower, primitive but pleasant.

An interesting sidelight is that when everyone returned to Katmandu, I having preceded them as hereinafter set forth, they told me that the young man was not quite well the rest of the trip. I believe that, although he was in excellent shape, he did not fully appreciate high attitudes. Also, alcohol at these altitudes is a "no-no" since it burns up oxygen. When we were in Tibet in 1982, even though I had a plastic bottle of high-proof rum with me, I never touched it. None of us had even the slightest desire to have a drink.

The next morning we walked up to a hilltop above the town toward Everest and had a marvelous view of the Himalayas. Everest was visible over the shoulder of Lhotse. It was impressive, although not as over-powering as it is from the north side where it towers directly upward 12,000 feet above the advanced base camp, which is a little over 17,000 feet. I gather that on the south side one has to reach base camp to really come to grips with it because of the deep valleys and surrounding peaks. Ama Dablam was the most spectacular and beautiful peak in the area. Also the peaks behind us above Namche, rising to about 20,000 feet, were imposing.

We did a lot of picture taking, including a group of girls trekkers from Singapore, and then walked down. On the way, since I felt so well, I was ahead of Ram and took a nasty slide on the path, fortunately enclosed by low walls. I had come off the hard-frozen ground and hit the ground which had thawed out and was greasy. I pulled something in my thigh that made me feel quite sick for a bit, but I recovered and had no further trouble. I was lucky that I had slipped straight ahead and came up against the walls. When I returned home the doctors at Kernan and Billy Neill said that I had torn my quadriceps muscle, and I have a hole in the front of my right thigh to show for it.

The next day, while the others passed the morning shopping in Namche, I took off with Ram for Khunde since I wanted to have plenty of time. First we had a switchback trail straight up out of Namche for about 1,000 feet in altitude. We had spectacular views down into Namche and could see the crowds packing the Saturday bazaar. Then the path leveled off a bit and we walked up through scattered pine trees and eventually reached Syangboche, which is another Hillary airstrip. We walked across it and up through scattered pines, and also scattered patches of snow. By the time we reached Khunde we had about a foot of snow on the sheltered sides. This was the result of the storm which we had had about two weeks before in Bhutan. The views of Ama Dablam and the other peaks were fantastic, and Everest clearly showed over the shoulder of Lhotse. Here in Nepal Everest is known as Sagamartha; in Tibet, Chomolungma.

On the way our yak train caught up with us and I was amused when the yak with my duffel bag acted up a bit and crashed through the branches of a pine tree. The bag stayed firmly in place and was not in the least damaged, thank heaven.

I was delighted with the way that I had walked up. I was becoming conditioned and acclimatized since Khunde was about 13,000 feet. Hisé suggested that I go down to Syangboche the next day and fly to Kathmandu and I readily agreed. I had accomplished what I had come to see and, although I am sorry that I did not get to see the monastery of Thyangboche, I am just as glad that I didn't. That night at Khunde was cold as hell, down to about 22° F, and when the rest reached Kathmandu they said that the remainder of the trek had been more of the same, grunting up and down steep trails. They said that when I left the next morning the comments were something like "That s.o.b. will be back in the Yak and Yeti this evening," obviously enjoying the amenities.

The Sherpas set off at a blistering pace early the next morning, about eight A.M., since the chopper was due in about 9:30 and it was supposed to be about an hour's walk. We made it in half that time. I was determined to keep up with them. Appa, the Sirdar, came with me and carried my day pack. Ram carried my duffel bag with ease. I found out that Appa had already climbed Everest seven times and was supposed to climb the next spring with a Japanese expedition on the north side. He explained how the

Sherpas are allowed inside Tibet without formalities, but no more than twenty-five miles, or about the distance of Shigatse from the border. After all they originally came from eastern Tibet.

I said good-bye to Ram and Appa at Syangboche, and they put a kata, a white, gauzy cloth, around my neck as a symbol of good fortune. Appa said he would see me again, and when I looked a bit quizzical he indicated that he meant the hereafter. I hope so. The chopper came in and away I went to Kathmandu, arriving in about an hour and a half, quite a change from the British expeditions in the 1920's toiling up from Darjeeling to the Tibetan plateau to get to Everest or even the ones in the 1950's and 1960's grunting up and down the Nepali "hills" and valleys to Namche Bazaar and in to the Everest base camp.

Back on the fourth floor of the Yak and Yeti, I arranged to take a flight out from Kathmandu to Mt. Everest. It was well worth it. It was not too bumpy as we reached Everest, and I could clearly see our landing strips at Lukla and Syangboche. I took some good pictures.

I also arranged to fly out to Pokhara and stay in the Fishtail Lodge, a lovely location on the lake, surrounded by tropical gardens and flowering poinsettia trees. I walked up a local mountain one day to get the stunning views of Dhaulagiri and the Annapurna massif. I also had a fascinating visit with Father Ooki, a Japanese Jesuit, whose mentor in Japan had been Father Arrupe, later General of the order. Father Ooki runs a school for somewhat retarded Nepalese children. He had been a Kamikaze submarine pilot at the end of the war. We concluded that we would probably have faced each other if the Allies had had to invade Japan. Both he and Father Arrupe were in Hiroshima when the first atomic bomb dropped. He showed me tracks in his garden, on the outskirts of Pokhara, where a leopard had been prowling around trying to catch his dog. I have been trying to keep in touch with him, but the mails are unreliable.

I returned to Kathmandu, had a farewell dinner with my trekking friends, and when they headed back to the states, I flew to Delhi, stayed in the Taj Palace and took a short trip with a car and driver to see Agra, the Taj Mahal, and Jaipur. I had a good guide in Agra. En route to Jaipur, he took me on an interesting tour of Fatehpur Sikri, built by Akbar and extensively rebuilt in modern times. My guide in Jaipur was also good and we saw the usual sites, including the Amber Fort and the Maharajah's palace. On the way back to Delhi we had some trouble with the car so that I had a chance to relax by the wayside for about an hour or two and watch India flow by, trucks, buses, motorcars, motorcycles, motorbikes, scooters, bicycles, ox-carts, all forging along together.

At Delhi I had Rahul, one of our guides in Bhutan, come in for lunch with his sister. I left about midnight for Amsterdam, arrived there in early morning, couldn't find a bed at the airport hotel, so slept for about four hours on a comfortable settee. I caught KLM to Dulles, and was mercifully met by my transportation service. It had been a fabulous trip, but I was glad to be home.

As a sidelight, when we reached Delhi at the beginning of the whole trip, I went down to buy some postcards in the Taj Palace hotel shop. I noticed that they also had a beautiful rug shop. I thought of the tattered rug in the upstairs hall at home over which I had been tripping for at least thirty years. There didn't seem to be any compelling reason not to replace it, and I ended up buying two rugs. I had them carefully vetted by Sylvia Constable and Margaret Nalle, a member of our trip, before I bought them.

When I reached Kathmandu from Bhutan, I found a small shop in the street to the Yak and Yeti which had Tibetan rugs, not the rough home-made ones that we had seen in 1982, but rugs that looked somewhat like the Chinese one which I have in the living room at home. When the Tibetan weavers came out of Tibet after 1959, the merchants in Nepal gave them patterns with Tibetan motifs which would be salable on the world market. I immediately spotted one with a sand-colored background that would fit on the landing going up to the second floor. I later bought two more regular-sized rugs. I was such a good customer that my rug-merchant, who was not at all a hard-sell man, gave me a small runner of panels in the old Tibetan type with stylized yaks. This is now in the sun parlor.

1996—The Silk Road

On September 20, I flew to Detroit, Michigan and joined a group from the Harvard MCZ to do the Silk Road by private trains from Beijing to the far northwest corner of China, then into Inner Asia, Kazakhstan, Uzbekistan, Kyrgyzstan, and finally across Russia into Moscow.

We left Detroit on Northwest Airlines about 3:30 P.M. We arrived in Beijing at 5:55 P.M.—a long afternoon of about 14 hours, —but when we landed it was September 21! I don't remember it as a particularly harrowing journey. I must have dozed a bit. The most interesting thing on the flight was crossing from America to Asia.

We had been flying over an overcast as we crossed northwest Canada, and I figured that we must be getting somewhere near Alaska and the Bering Strait. Fortunately, it began to clear and I saw a coastline stretching north and west. As we began to cross open water, I gradually saw two coastlines far ahead one stretching southwest–northeast. I spotted a large island, which must have been Big Diomede, and a smaller one, Little Diomede. We were crossing the International Date Line and I could clearly see America and Asia with the Bering Strait between.

It was further interesting that this time we crossed over to the snow-covered wastes of Siberia and flew directly down to China via Harbin. This would have been unthinkable in 1982.

We put up at the Grand Hotel Beijing, in the new addition, adjacent to Tiananmen Square. It was a far cry from the little Bei Wei Hotel in 1982. It was the equal of any luxury hotel at home. The next day, Sunday, I went to 10:00 A.M. Mass at the Catholic Cathedral. The Mass was said by a Chinese priest and I had an interesting time talking to him and another priest afterwards. He asked me to come back the next Sunday and be the lector. When I was in Beijing in 1982, the cathedral was locked tight.

That afternoon we went to the Temple of Heaven. The grounds looked much better kept up, bright with flowers, etc. By contrast, two days later, I thought the Forbidden City looked grungier, with sales stands, etc. Also the smog from the vastly increased traffic was noticeable. It was not as bad as Delhi, the year before.

On Monday we went out to see the Great Wall at Mu Tian Yu. It was a nice drive to the mountains, and I liked it much better than the wall at Badalong. It was cleaner, airier, etc. The pestering sales concessions were in marked contrast to 1982, and we rode up to the wall itself in a modern ski-lift type gondola like the First lift at Grindelwald.

The next day we commenced our train journey after lunch on the ninth-floor terrace of the hotel and a champagne reception at track-side, in a special section of the railroad station. The train itself was impressive, the China Orient Express. It was twenty cars long, and we had the entire train, about 85 of us. It had been built in the 1950's for Mao Tse Tung to make his official tours of the country. It was comfortable, connecting roomettes or compartments with washing facilities in between and toilets at either end of the car. There were no shower facilities, as on the next train, the old European Orient Express with its shower car. In the dining cars we were provided with chopsticks. I could get along a bit with my Japanese experience after the war, but I usually asked for knife and fork.

We were overnight on the train. I had single accommodations and was comfortable. The next morning we alighted at a way station east of Xian, and went to see the terra cotta army, discovered in 1974 by two farmers digging a well. It is truly incredible, with its thousands of life-size human figures and horses. The figures themselves are protected by high air-conditioned sheds. The surroundings are lovely, with mountains in the background.

We went to stay overnight at the comfortable Hyatt Hotel. I skipped some of the museum trips but had an informal tour of the Wild Goose Pagoda and then was escorted to the colossal city wall by a nice student at a nearby school, who picked me up to practice her English. Times have indeed changed.

Back on the train at Xian, we started up the Lanzhou Line which follows the valley of the Yellow River toward the northwest. The land becomes more and more arid, with rich cultivation in the river valley by irrigation.

At Jiayuguan we reached the western limit of the Great Wall and the end of the "Celestial Kingdom." After we had toured the Ming Fort outside the town that looks toward the vast reaches to the west, I went into the little shop and ended up buying a yellow-background scroll of the "Hundred Wives." It now hangs on my staircase.

We climbed the wall, the top of which was not quite as far off as it looked. The top gave an incredible panorama of the desert. I walked at my usual "guide's pace" and was amused at the ones who would race past me for a way and then have to stop, out of breath.

After spending the night at the Great Wall Hotel, we reboarded the train and traveled to Liuyuan. From there we drove 80 miles across the desert to Dunhuang. We took a camel ride at the Mingsha sand dunes, and spent the night at the Dunhuang Hotel. The next day we drove out to the Magao Caves, which are crammed

Terra cotta soldiers excavated near Sian, China
September, 1996

CBR Jr on Defensive Wall at Jiayuguan, the gateway to the deserts of Western China.
September, 1996

CBR Jr at Aletao, China, with official at the border of Kazakhstan, near junction with Russia and Mongolia. China Orient Express on left; European Orient Express on right.

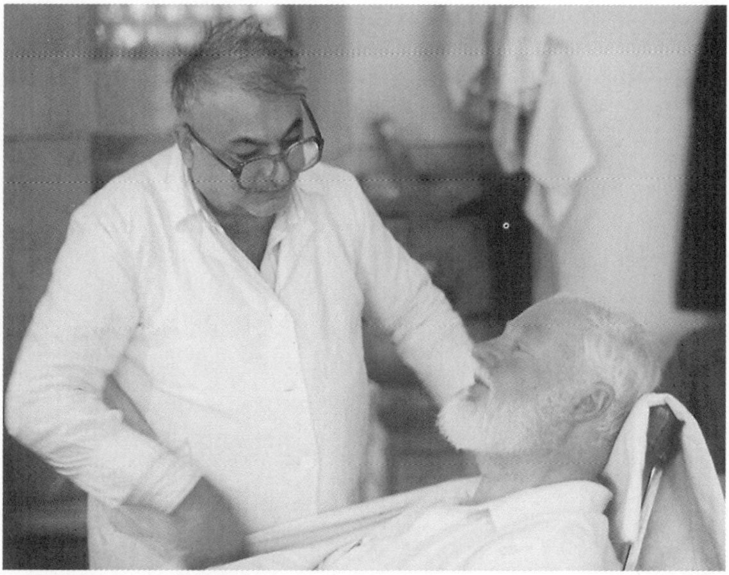

CBR Jr having beard trimmed at
Madresseh in Bokhara, Uzbekistan

Bokhara carpet
bought by CBR Jr in Madresseh

with Buddhist paintings and statuary. One Buddha reaches up several stories inside the caves, which themselves are carved out of sandstone cliffs. They were discovered by Westerners at the beginning of this century.

There is apparently an ancient irrigation system because there were acres of cotton fields being harvested. Trucks piled high with cotton were lined up waiting to be weighed and presumably the cotton baled. It is this cotton culture both in China and the former U.S.S.R., particularly around the Aral Sea in Kazakhstan, which has ruined a large part of the area and destroyed the water resources, somewhat like ours in Virginia and the Deep South.

At Dunhuang we were taken to see some native weaving. I went back into the extensive store, spied a heavy silk rug with red-crested, black necked cranes and snapped it up. One of the sales ladies assured me that cranes mean good luck and longevity. I hope so. I also picked up a second scroll.

On the drive back to the railroad station, we crossed part of what must have been a military airstrip. I assume that this whole area would have been off limits a few years ago since it is near Lop Nor, which was, or is, the center for the secret Chinese military work, missiles, etc.

On the train again we traveled toward Turfan, in the heart of the Taklhamakhen Desert. We visited the ruins of Jiache, that the Mongols destroyed in the Thirteenth Century. There was a little gift shop, and Sarah, one of the party who lives in Norfolk, Connecticut, and I were surprised to find some nice-looking silk rugs hanging on the wall. I eventually bought the one that we liked the most for about one-half the original asking price. Sarah was my bargainer.

We drove on into Turfan, on a gravel strewn plain, dropping down to one of the "deepest waterless depressions on earth" according to the brochure/prospectus for our trip. It is in the Uighur Autonomous Region. We visited the Bazaar and also some of the

Uighur houses. It was colorful because there was some sort of festival on and the old streets were filled with little donkey carts, piled high with goods and family.

We reboarded the train and traveled overnight to Alatao, on the border with Kazakhstan. En route, about 11:00 P.M., we passed through Urumqi, where they have recently had ethnic riots against the Han Chinese. I waived good-bye to our Chinese piano player, who left us there. It was her home, and she would catch the train on its return journey to Beijing.

This part of the line was opened only in 1992 and is at the knot where China, Mongolia, Russia and Kazakhstan meet. Alatao is about 5,000 feet above sea level and cold, even though this was only October 2. We could see the snow-covered Kun Lun Mountains across the desert to the south of us and the Alai Mountains to the north and west. I wish that we had had time to explore around a bit, since there are some remote valleys in the mountains which are beautiful with pine forests, lakes, rivers, etc.

They had warned us that it would be a tedious day, and so it was. We arrived promptly at 10:30 A.M. and were moved into our dining cars while the rest of the train was readied for the new crowd coming in from Alma Ata, etc. They were late, finally arriving at 2:30 P.M. The formalities took forever, and finally we swapped trains. They came over from the "Nostalgic Orient Express," the old Orient Express which had been built in the 1930's and was the scene of "Murder on the Orient Express" and other thrillers, Alfred Hitchcock, et al.

One amusing incident occurred when both trains were waiting side by side at the platform. I went outside, took some pictures and then went inside, as instructed. Suddenly a Chinese military-looking official came in and beckoned me to come outside. I thought, "Uh oh. What have I done now?" My anxiety departed when I found out that the various officials wanted to have their pictures taken with me. I went inside, got my camera and had them take pictures of me with them.

We finally pulled out at 7:30 P.M. and crossed the no-man's land into Kazakhstan. We had caviar with dinner and a talented Russian piano player in the bar car. The next morning we were rolling south across the Kazakhstan desert, with the snow-covered Tien Shan curling down on the left to keep us company. Some of the river valleys, which were like long oases, were beautiful.

We reached Alma Ata in the late afternoon, and again I wish that we had had more time there. The section where the Russians lived is attractive. A great many of them left after the break-up of the Russian Empire in 1990, such as Inna who works as a waitress at the Green Spring Club. We saw some of the handsome party and public buildings, with the snow-capped Tien Shan in the evening light, a beautiful background.

We had dinner at a fancy hotel with a dance band. Returning to the train, we left for Tashkent, the capital of Uzbekistan. After a long day's train ride, we had dinner the next night in Tashkent, at a restaurant atop a sky-tower, like the one in Seattle.

The next day, October 5, we arrived in Samarkand early and had a full day of sightseeing, Tamerlane's Mausoleum, Registan Square, etc. The Blue Mosque is covered with scaffolding, and has been for years, according to Charlie who was there in 1989, but it is beautiful with its fantastic blue tile work and inlays.

We went to the enormous market adjacent to the Blue Mosque. I have never seen so many melons in my life. After lunch in a modern hotel, we visited the monument and ancient observatory of Ulug Beg, Tamerlane's grandson and a leading astronomer in the 15th Century.

We did not have too long a train ride that night to Bokhara, but sometime around 1:00 A.M. our sleeping car attendant woke us. We had an electrical fire on our car, fortunately while the train was stopped. We had to be evacuated to other cars and I was lucky because I had to move only into the next car. Frank and Sally Gray, from Baltimore, had a scary time since the fire was next to their compartment. I was at the other end of the car.

Since I did not get to bed in my new compartment until about 5:00 A.M., I took it easy in the morning while the others went touring "mosques, minarets, medressehs and fortresses" as our prospectus described it. I had an amusing time writing some postcards, watching the train crew shunt the damaged car to the rear of the train and took pictures of the local citizens in their colorful native dress.

I joined the main body for lunch in a hotel with native dancers and music. We visited a *medresseh* after lunch and in one of the shops a typical "Bokhara" rug struck my fancy. The original asking price was too high for me, and I left and went to a barber shop in the *medresseh* to have my beard trimmed. I did not mean it as a ploy, but it worked as such since the owner sent his emissary to the barber shop to offer a much lower price, and the deal was clinched. The rug, a "double elephant's foot," is in my upstairs hall. I have been told that actually Bokhara rugs are made in Turkmenistan. Be that as it may, I love it.

From Bokhara we went to Khiva, a fascinating place with a huge fortress, mosque, etc. Thereafter, we had the longest and most tedious part of the trip. Anticipating it, I stayed up quite late with Robert Amstutz, the young Swiss who ran the passenger aspect of the train. I slept late the next morning as we ground across the great Kazakhstan desert. It reminded me of West Texas, only multiplied about ten times.

We crossed the Volga at Saratov the next afternoon, a most impressive scene, and that night we had our gala dinner with everyone wearing whatever native dress they had picked up, particularly hats. At the end, our tour hostess, Micheline, from Paris, took over the piano from the Russian and amused us well. On Thursday, October 10 we reached Moscow early in the morning.

We had a tour, took in the Pushkin Gallery, where I reveled in the early Impressionists, had lunch at a delightful restaurant and then checked into the Penta Hotel, a modern luxury built for the Olympics which Jimmy Carter boycotted. We had a gala farewell dinner, and the next day most of the group disbanded for home, some via Copenhagen.

I had opted for the St. Petersburg extension, along with about twenty others. We had a good flight on Aeroflot, were ensconced in the newly refurbished Grand Hotel and had a wonderful three days there. We saw all the sights, Peter and Paul Fortress, Cathedral, Hermitage, Winter Palace, etc. We went one day to Petrodvorets on the Gulf of Finland, the summer palace of Peter the Great. That day at lunch a group of Cossack dancers entertained us. In the evening of the last day, we visited the Yusopoff Palace, including the room where they started the murder of Rasputin. We had dinner in an excellent restaurant in the gate house, purportedly the best in St. Petersburg. It was our final farewell.

I loved St. Petersburg and would very much like to go back there. It would be interesting to see it in winter. It is impossible to realize how it was devastated during the Nazi siege, the "900 Days." The monument marking the nearest approach of the Nazis is now inside the city limits.

The next day we visited the cemetery where all the musicians are buried, Borodin, Rimsky-Korsakov, Tschaikowsky, et al., and the cathedral, packed with people at Mass. About twenty of us left for Copenhagen.

That night I invited Michilene to dinner at Krogh's, the fish restaurant. I dined royally on the special three types of herring first course and then had a delicate baked or boiled cod with lots of sauces. It was almost like a "cod fondue."

The following day I flew home on SAS to Dulles. It had been a wonderful trip, around the world.

1997—MONGOLIA—LAKE BAIKAL—YENISEY RIVER

In 1997 I managed to combine two trips sponsored by The Harvard MCZ, now the MCNH, Museum of Cultural and Natural History. At first they said it could not be done, but I showed them that the two trips dovetailed exactly.

On Sunday, June 8, I flew to Newark, New Jersey and at midnight we took off on Korean Air for Seoul. There were only seven of us, plus our leader John Constable and his brother Giles, who lives in Princeton and knows the Reeves family. My nephew, Charlie, had done some work for Giles. We were all in business class, in the upper deck. It was cozy and comfortable, and since John and Giles wanted to sit together, I had two adjoining seats and after dinner had a nice sleep. We had a long fueling stop in Anchorage, Alaska, a welcome break in the trip, so that we would not arrive in Seoul before 6 A.M., in order to comply with noise restrictions.

A lay-over in Seoul until ten A.M. was tiring but then we boarded Korean Air again and had a three and a half hour flight to Ulan Bator, now spelled Ulaan Baataar. We flew up the Yellow Sea between China and Korea, and on the right I could make out the Ongjin Peninsula where the Russians had given us so much trouble immediately after World War II. We gave North Korea a wide berth.

When we reached Mongolia, the land looked flat and arid, with little puffs of cloud. We arrived at Ulaan Baataar on a beautiful day, lovely desert air, about 1:30 P.M. It was by now Tuesday, June 10. It had been a long flight, but I didn't feel too badly.

The airport waiting area was a bit primitive. We mini-bussed into our hotel, the Ulaan Baataar, which was "Russian massive" construction, on a small park. It is around the corner from the main ceremonial square, which looks a bit like Admiralty Square in St. Petersburg or Tiananmen Square in Beijing.

We used the hotel as base headquarters, from which we forayed out into the countryside by helicopter or by airplane and then mini-van. I originally was assigned to a "broom-closet" in the hotel, but since the water did not run, I upgraded to a suite, that I kept for the remainder of the stay, to avoid packing up every time we went out on an expedition and then unpacking on return.

The first foray took us to Amarbayas Galant Monastery, established in the 17th Century. We had an uncomfortable flight in a government helicopter but the last part was beautiful up a broad, green upland valley with a small river in the middle. The Tibetan Buddhist monastery was lovely. We descended from the helicopter into a field filled with dwarf Siberian irises.

We spent our first night in a "ger," known as *yurt* in the Russian days, a round structure covered with white felt with a hole for the stove pipe and a cover which could be closed in bad weather. The next day we stopped first to see waterfowl, then flew to Karakorum, the remains of Kubla Khan's "stately pleasure dome" in Xanadu. The Chinese had leveled it centuries before in retaliation for what the Mongols did to them in the 13th Century. There are only a few odd stones which have been collected from the countryside, plus a huge stone tortoise about a quarter-mile away in the "semi-arid" desert. The Erdene Zuu Monastery, which is supposed to date back 1,000 years, is located within the mesne wall, which encloses approximately a square mile.

On another trip we had three nights in a *ger* in the Gobi Desert, reached by Mongolian Air and then mini-van. We visited the Flaming Cliffs where Roy Chapman Andrews in 1922 discovered the first dinosaur eggs. We also went down to the Altai Mountains, saw the remains of a snow field and had a picnic and some good walking. It was at the Gobi *ger* that we had a dust storm one evening that slowly advanced across the desert and surrounded us for about two hours.

Our third air trip was to Moron, pronounced Morou, in the

CBR Jr
Altai Mountains, Mongolia

Yak herder
Lake Hovsgol, Mongolia
June, 1997

CBR Jr's bunk
in Ger (Yurt), Mongolia

CBR Jr with giant tortoise
outside of Karakorum ("Xanadu"), Mongolia

CBR Jr with guide fishing on the Ak River,
near Lake Hovsgal, Mongolia
June, 1997

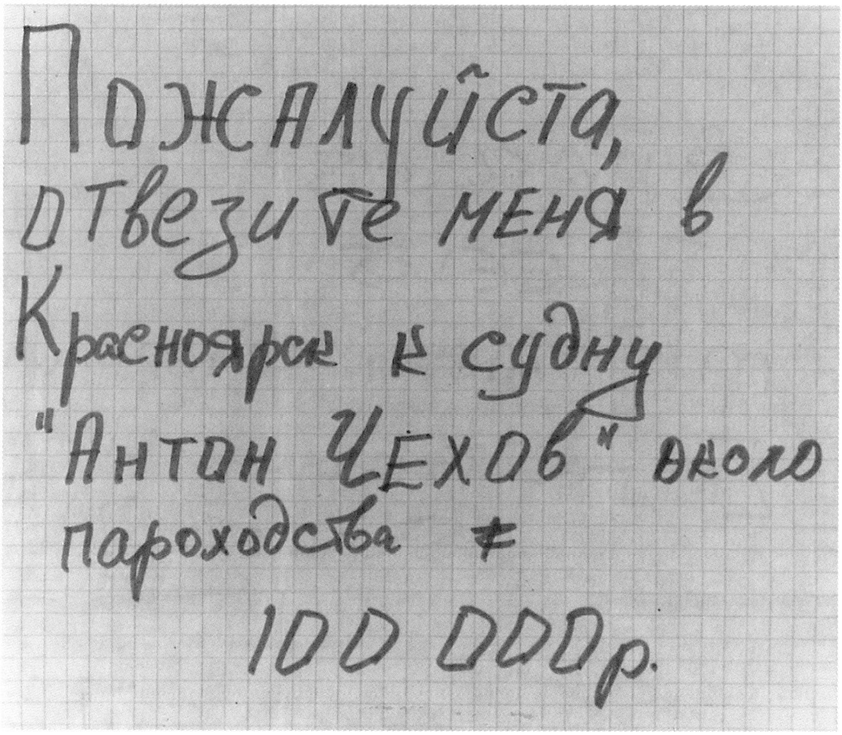

Sign lettered by my travel agent, Yourie in Irkutsk, Siberia, asking someone to get me a taxi in Krasnoyarsk and drive me to the "Anton Chekhov"
Suggested fare –100,000 roubles
June, 1997

north, with a long land-rover ride into Lake Hovsgal, near the Siberian border. The roads across the desert, really prairie, were almost non-existent, and we followed tracks. As one of our party remarked, it was much like a safari. We eventually came to pine forests mixed with hardwood, and the last hour was beautiful as we first climbed up a ridge through the forest and then descended to the lake. The lake itself reminded me of Lake Champlain, as it must have looked 400 years ago. There were mountains behind us and also in the distance across the lake.

We went fishing in the lake, without much success, but it gave me practice for our day on the Ak River, a three-hour drive to the east. John Constable, Giles, Dana Hamel and I went, with our "guide," who simply wanted to fish himself. Our fishing spot was in a spectacular plateau surrounded by mountains with beautiful larch forests. The air was like champagne, the river looked as if it were in the movie "A River Runs Through It," and the fishing was superb, trout, grayling, taimen, a type of land-locked salmon. Lacking boots and wanting to reach good fishing spots, I waded out into the river up to my knees. The water was lovely and cool. My clothes dried out at lunch on the river bank, where we cooked and ate some of the fish we had caught. We had 50 or 60 in all and would have had many more if we had had a real guide like a Scottish ghillie.

We did a lot of flower walking in the hills since the area was blanketed with them, including wild azalea, wild orchids, etc. We also had a delightful ride to the yak-herder's home on the lake and had yak yogurt. It was strong but good. On the last night the *ger* staff put on a dance show with native costumes.

Returning to Ulaan Baataar, we drove one day to Bandshir Monastery in the Bogadon Strictly Protected Area. It has been protected since the 13th Century and has lovely pine forests. The monastery was badly smashed, partly destroyed, by the Communists in the 1930's but the main temple has been rebuilt. It is a bit frazzled but attractive. We saw a crowd of young monks in their red robes, studying to be lamas.

Another day we had a long drive to the Hustain Nuruu National Reserve, where we were lucky to see the native Przewalski Horses which had become almost extinct. The Dutch saved some and have reintroduced them to Mongolia. On the way into the Reserve we stopped, then slowly walked up a hillside and managed to approach quite close to one herd of them.

Our group broke up on June 24 in Ulaan Baataar, and I tearfully saw them off. We had had a good time with such a small group. The next day I flew from Ulaan Baataar, on Mongolian Air, an hour and a half to Irkutsk in Siberia, which is near the Buryat Autonomous Region. I was met by Yourie, my local travel guide, who did not speak much English but was a mountain climber who had climbed to 7,000 meters. We changed $300 in express checks at a local branch of the only bank in Irkutsk that exchanged currency. Yourie explained that my hotel was prepaid for bed and breakfast but that everything else had to be paid in cash at Lake Baikal. At the then prevailing rate of exchange, before the 1,000-to-one devaluation in the fall, I received 1,700,000 rubbles, about 5,800 to the dollar. Shades of Poland in 1990.

After obtaining funds, we had a short drive around Irkutsk, looking at the wooden architecture. The trees in the city were impressive and a sort of cottonwood blossom was falling off and drifting everywhere. We drove out to Lake Baikal through birch forests that looked like Canada. We drove up to the hotel overlooking the lake, and after a late lunch, I took a walk along the lake shore.

The next day my guide, Evgeny, showed up. He turned out to be excellent, and I enjoyed being with him the next few days. He was 25 years old, a University of Irkutsk graduate, well versed in history, an independent thinker and pleasant. Our first outing was to walk up to Chersky's Peak, a gradual ascent to a wooded summit overlooking the outlet of the lake into the Angara River. It was a lovely sight. The lake reminded me a bit of a mountainous Lake Michigan. It is 400 miles long, and from where we stood it was 25 to 30 miles across. Evgeny explained that on our shore, the western one, there was a shelf extending out only about 100 or 200 yards. Then it plunged down a mile deep, or about 1,400 meters. This is why, although Lake Superior has a larger surface area, Lake Baikal has the largest cubic capacity of fresh water of any lake in the world.

After a visit to the Limnological Museum, we walked to the main road and took a bus to Listvyanka, a village stretched out along the lake. The old wooden houses, brightly painted, were attractive. It looked just like a Siberian village should, a picture postcard. We had lunch in Yourie's summer house, on an open air porch, with his two sons and Tamara, who cooked a specialty for us, meat in a cabbage leaf. We then walked to the edge of town. The outskirts were ramshackle, including a brick building which was originally started as a hotel that couldn't be finished. One of the "New Russians," i.e. new rich, took it over as a house. This was typical of the Siberian economic chaos.

The following day we took a hydrofoil north on the lake to Bolshye Koty, a picturesque town. One particularly nice house on the shore near the pier belonged to the person who ran the prosperous glass works in Tsarist days.

We walked north up the shore, but as the bluff became higher and the gravel path more uncertain I told Evgeny that I did not think it wise to continue. If I had tripped or slipped, I would have gone headlong down the steep slope over the cliff. It reminded me of those walks with Fritz Stäger around Mürren, when we would come to a sharp corner over a beetling precipice, a "nose," which I did not like at all.

We retraced our steps, walked past the southern edge of town and had a picnic lunch on a grassy spot among the pine trees overlooking the lake. It was cold and there was a stiff breeze out on the lake.

We took the hydrofoil back to Listvyanka and walked through the town to see the Orthodox Church. It had been built as a thanks offering by a rich merchant or ship captain in Tsarist days. It was a lovely church, wooden, of course, with beautiful icons. It is amazing how places like these survived the 75 years of Communism. Probably, in a remote place like this, most of the people must have clung to their religion, or at least the old culture and traditions.

When we retraced our steps to the lake shore, we were moseying along looking for the jitney bus, when I spotted a small restaurant. I told Evgeny that I felt that a beer was in order and he agreed. As we crossed the road, I noticed an elderly Mercedes with a sign on its side proclaiming "Paris to Peking Rally, 90th Anniversary, 1907–1997."

When we sat down to have our beer, we nodded to two people at the next table, eating *shaslik*, who turned out to be German and the crew of the car, a 1951 Mercedes sedan, which, as the sign said, was part of a recreation of the 1907 "race" or Rally from Paris to Peking. They were interested when they found out that I had just come from Mongolia because they were en route to Ulaan Ude on the east side of the lake and then into Mongolia. I thought that they could probably make it in their car with their support team in a truck. But I wondered about the team that was attempting it in an MG. I remembered all those loose rocks in the tracks across the prairie or desert.

When we returned to the hotel, we had a glass of wine on the terrace and the couple at the next table turned out to be a Dutch team on the Rally. They told us that one of the German team was in the construction business in Germany, specializing in repairing old buildings. During the coup in Moscow in 1993 by the militarists against Gorbachev, in which Yeltsin stood on the tank and defied them, the White House across the bridge from the Ukrainia Hotel was badly damaged. I remember the television pictures showing the artillery shells hitting six or seven floors up.

The Russians hired this German to repair the White House, a task he performed beautifully. I saw it about three weeks later. Yeltsin befriended him, and when the Rally reached the Russian border, they were met by a police escort that stayed with them all across Russia.

The same afternoon some people came in for a drink on the terrace from the Trans-Siberian Orient Express special train, that had arrived from Ulaan Baataar and was parked on the tracks at the outlet of the Angara. They turned out to be from Philadelphia, and we had mutual acquaintances. Again, small world.

That evening in the dining room I had fun speaking to a group of Germans who were passing through. I also offered to take a picture of a group of young Russian Army officers at the next table, and they invited me over for vodka and *blinis*, with good, fresh caviar.

On Saturday, June 28, we drove back to Irkutsk. Evgeny wanted to leave promptly because the Duma, which was on tour from Moscow, was coming in and he did not want to be held up by the army sentries along the road. We stopped at the Museum of Wooden Architecture, which was interesting, starting with structures that looked like American Indian teepees and continuing through log houses, fort and church. When we reached my hotel in Irkutsk, the Angara, Evgeny asked me if I had noticed the men on the sidewalk, about to get into automobiles. He mentioned one in particular and I went back to take a look at him, circumspectly. The men were members of the Duma, about to go down to "Baikal," as the Siberians call it. The one in particular, a medium-height, rather powerful-looking man, had been involved in the coup against Gorbachev and Yeltsin, but he was still in the Duma.

In the afternoon we toured Irkutsk, including the Zenemensky Monastery with memorials to the man who extended the Russian Empire to Alaska and California. Evgeny and I had dinner that evening in an excellent new restaurant across the park from the hotel.

Sunday, June 29, was the feast of Sts. Peter and Paul, and Evgeny went with me to High Mass, with two Polish bishops, at the Polish Roman Catholic Cathedral a couple of blocks from the hotel. The church was packed and it was a lovely service. Evgeny said he would never have seen it unless he had been there with me.

That afternoon we did more sightseeing, including the Troubetskoye House, the museum of the Decembrists of the 1820's. They had been exiled by the czar for plotting against him and trying to put in someone more enlightened. Evgeny said Russian history might have been different if they had succeeded. We went to the Irkutsk Museum, with its interesting Buryat artifacts. The Buryats are closely related to the Mongolians. We took a short boat ride on the Angara. That night I had dinner in a nice restaurant recommended by Evgeny, with music and entertainment.

The next day Yourie took me to the airport and saw me safely off to Krasnoyarsk, two and a half hours west across the Siberian fields and forests. I felt like a "daring old man on the flying trapeze" as I swung from my Mongolia-Baikal-Irkutsk MCNH trip to the MCNH trip, "The Majestic Yenisey River." Yourie had made me a sign in Russian saying that I wanted a taxi to the M/S Anton Chekhov at dockside in Krasnoyarsk. Seeing not one soul in the airport who spoke English, I went to the "?" bureau, Information, where there was a helpful young lady who had my bags collected and hailed a taxi for me. The driver was a character and we hurtled across the countryside in a half hour to the city, which has 1,000,000 inhabitants and later that summer was the site of the Russian-Japanese "summit" talks. It was chosen as the site since it is midway between the east and west borders of Russia.

We drove up to the big Stalinesque transportation building, and I told the driver to go around it to the pier. We drove down to the gangplank of the Chekhov, and I was glad to hear those "Amurrican" voices. The "daring old man" had completed his leap, without the benefit of a net.

The Anton Chekhov was a large vessel, of shallow draft, built in Austria, transported by rivers and canals to the Yenisey, crewed and staffed by Russians with a Swiss purser and owned by a Swiss-Russian consortium. I checked on board, went to my single stateroom and changed in time for the welcome cocktail party. The main group had come via St. Petersburg the day before. We were 125 in all, organized primarily by the American Museum of Natural History, with 25 in the Harvard MCNH group, led by Karl Liem, professor of ichthyology and a delightful person, with his wife, Hetty. When people asked where I had come from, dropping out of the skies as it were, I calmly said Mongolia and Lake Baikal. They were puzzled.

The next morning we had a trip by hydrofoil to a huge dam, part of a colossal hydro-electric complex in central Siberia. Our group returned by bus, and that afternoon we set sail.

The following morning we were sailing through lovely farming and dairy type country with plenty of trees. The weather was fine, bright sun with puffy clouds. It was July 2, brother David's birthday.

In the afternoon we went ashore at Yeniseyek, a nineteenth century gold mining town. In Tsarist days, 90% of Russia's gold passed through it, and the museum in a merchant's house showed how rich it must have been. We visited the local monastery, fallen into disrepair, but we were shown around by an attractive, relatively young monk-priest, who explained that they are trying to restore the building. Another big church with elaborate icons was nearby. The glory days must have passed when the capital was moved to Krasnoyarsk, on the Trans-Siberian railway.

As we were walking down a street to the long stairs leading down a bluff to the dock, a group of young girls, 14, 15 or 16 years old, approached some of us, and one of them held out a small watercolor painting. I thought, "Oh good heavens, they're trying to sell it." Not at all. They said "present, for you." I took it and had some one take a picture of us. The water color framed, hangs in my dining room. Every time I look at it, a painting of a typical Siberian wooden house with a wooden fence, I like it better. It is a nice picture. I wish I had the young artist's address so that I could thank her. When we sailed from Yeniseyek, I stood on the top deck and waved good-bye as long as I could.

In the morning of July 3, we reached Vorogovo, a nice little town, and went through one of the houses and a simple little museum which also serves as the local bakery and shop. We then sailed to Komsa where we took a short walk through the taiga, reminding me of a forest in New Hampshire or Maine with spongy soil, bushes, dried leaves from trees, etc., and **clouds** of mosquitoes. They had warned us to be well covered up, trousers stuffed into stockings, etc., and dowsed with bug juice. I was well prepared, but I was glad to reach the beach again.

We had a picnic dinner on the shore, colorful with little tables and benches set up and little American flags everywhere. It was hard to believe that we were in the heart of Russia-Siberia. We had sturgeon soup and traditional Siberian dishes, a Russian-style barbecue, with music, squeeze box, etc. It was a lot of fun. Karl Liem was a good leader.

On July 4, we arrived at Verashagino, but I finessed it since the tour started a bit early. Later that morning we practiced up our skit for the evening's entertainment. In the evening we took a diversion up the Tunguska River which had narrow passages through cliffs and forests. It was lovely in the evening light, as the daily "Voice" said it would be. All the staff were dressed up as pirates at dinner, playing at having shanghaied us. Some of the waitresses

CBR Jr with water-color given by local girls
Yeniseyek, Siberia
July, 1997

M/S Anton Chekhov
Yenisey River, Vorogovo, Siberia
July, 1997

Karel Liem, Harvard professor of Icthyology
Picnic ashore near Komsa, Siberia
July 3, 1997

Dance company performing at Dudinka,
Tamyr Penisula, Siberia
July, 1997

Russian Orthodox priest at monastery
Yeniseyek, Siberia
July, 1997

St. Basil's Cathedral
Moscow
July, 1997

were very cute, particularly Natasha, our usual waitress. After dinner we had a ceremony of Crossing the Arctic Circle and put on our skits, with dancing afterwards. It was an amazing Fourth of July at the Arctic Circle in Siberia.

The next day we reached Igarka, a bleak but interesting place with its former slave labor camp, now being made into a memorial, complete with barbed wire. Stalin had decreed that a railroad be built across the tundra, but it was never completed because of the permafrost. At least 5,000 prisoners died there. Stalin himself had been exiled there by the Tsar in 1913–1916.

We also visited the Permafrost Institute, with its various exhibits. We bundled up warmly to go down 45 feet into the permafrost. It was unbelievable, like a huge deep freeze. It made us all realize what it must be like to live there. We were informed that here the permafrost reached down only 500 feet because there is comparatively little snow fall, being so close to the arctic desert. They told us that in the Baikal area the permafrost goes down to 1500 feet because of the deep snow cover in that region. I recalled Evgeny telling me that Baikal in winter was covered with black ice except for the outflow into the Angara that was always open since the current was swift and the outlet relatively shallow. He said that thousands of waterfowl congregated there.

In the evening we had a fine Russian Folklore Concert on board with a group from Igarka. The next day we had lectures as we were approaching the "delta," the mouth of the Yenisey, with no place to go ashore. It was cold, probably in the thirties, and there were banks of snow on the river bank to the east, nearest us. There was a stiff wind and a small ground swell. We did not venture into the open ocean, although the river mouth almost amounted to it, since the Anton Chekhov is a river boat with shallow draft. Cape Kristovsky was our farthest landfall, low and flat. Our farthest North was 71° 03.92, 1140 miles from the North Pole.

On the evening of our farthest north, I decided to stay up and see the "midnight sun." We were not on the true meridian since the actual time of the sun's lowest descent toward the horizon was at 2:10 A.M. I persevered and took a couple of pictures of the sun above the horizon. Some low clouds made it possible to shoot directly at the sun.

We turned back and reached Ust-Port the next day, a forlorn-looking settlement on the river bluff, with trash strewing parts of the river bank. I did not plan to go ashore, but I am glad that later in the morning I did. The population is 600, many of them the native Nenets. We saw men on the shore with their fishing boats, but walking through the town we saw few people. Bog water was everywhere because of the tundra and the underlying permafrost, and we were told that conditions were actually better in winter when everything is frozen. The temperature drops to -50° F.

I visited the little hospital with one of the doctors from our group. The "locum tenens" was glad to greet a colleague. The hospital was simple but clean. The "log" which they sent us later said that the doctor was going to leave, since there was too much alcoholism among the people. Small wonder. There is practically no industry, and it must be depressing in the dark of winter. It did not look too cheery even on July 7, mid-summer.

We had a Captain's Farewell Dinner that evening. The captain did not speak any English, as far as I could tell, but he was there to greet us at cocktails. The crew, all in costumes, put on a show after dinner, which was hilarious, and then we danced. I was picked up by a buxom Russian lady who turned out to be the head chambermaid on our deck. We had a good flirtatious dance. The chief engineer, a strapping fellow, cut a wide swath with the ladies. It could not have been more fun.

The following day we reached Dudinka, the northernmost port kept open in winter. I don't see how the ice breakers do it. We took a tour of the town, a forlorn sort of place, with a population of 30,000. There are many empty buildings that have subsided because of the permafrost. The newer ones, however, seem to have solved the problem, with modern engineering techniques, and we were proudly shown a building nine stories high that is habitable.

This area is the Taymyr Peninsula, and a folk dance group, "Keiro," put on an excellent show for us in the attractive auditorium. They give performances all over the world, and their sprightly dances, spirited singing and bright costumes are in marked contrast to the surroundings.

Wednesday, July 9 was a **long** day. Our first wake-up call was at 3:30 A.M. I had packed and put my bags outside my stateroom door before going to bed, thank heavens. We finished breakfast by 5:00 A.M. and debarked for the buses at 5:30 A.M. The crew and staff lined up on the pier to bid us good-bye. When I came down the gangplank and put on my Mongolian hat, I was given a rousing cheer. I was quite touched.

Our three buses drove past the line of big cranes on the docks, through the huge railroad yards and some factory buildings, and then came out onto the undulating tundra. There were a few ponds and some birch trees in the hollows, but this soon gave way to bare tundra with occasional banks of snow as we headed for Norilsk where we were to take our chartered plane on Krasnoyarsh Air Lines, "Kras Air."

Although it was not meant to be an attraction, the two-hour drive to Norilsk turned out to be so. We followed the railway line across the tundra, mile after mile. The line would run straight for a long way and suddenly it would drift to one side for a few yards and then drift back again. This was on account of the permafrost. Also at one point we passed what obviously must have been a slave labor camp. The barbed wire and the dilapidated watch tower were stark reminders.

At one point we climbed a low ridge, with snow banks on both sides, and in the far distance, to the east one could see high ground, the Central Siberian Massif. As we neared Norilsk we could also see billowing clouds of steam, from the smelters over the horizon. They were located at a huge deposit of nickel and other ores, and that is why Dudinka and Norilsk continue to exist. A few years ago they would have been strictly off limits to "westerners," especially Americans.

The airport is still military. A guard would not let one of our party take a picture as we waited to board our plane. The main waiting room was chaos, but we were sent upstairs to an adequate room. We took off at 8:30 A.M. on a comfortable plane and they served us a nice breakfast, far better than our American air lines. We flew for four hours, crossed the snow covered Urals and landed at Domodedovo airport, the charter and local airline field for Moscow out in the country, at 8:30 A.M., a four hour time change.

The bags were sent to the Penta Hotel and, since our rooms would not be ready, we took a tour, the Kremlin, Red Square, St. Basil's, etc. I finessed most of the exhibits at the Armoury since I had seen it a year ago. The cathedrals looked even whiter and the domes more golden than the year before since the energetic mayor was sprucing Moscow up for its 850th anniversary in October. Also, in contrast to the previous year, when it was autumn and raining, this year we had bright summer sunshine.

We had lunch in the Ukrainia Hotel in the same dining room as the year before, and afterwards I looked across the river at the gleaming White House that our German acquaintance from Baikal had repaired for Mr. Yeltsin. I collapsed that afternoon and surfaced just in time for the farewell dinner, which was excellent. I remember particularly the lovely lettuce in the salad and nice fresh vegetables.

The next day 20 of us flew to Copehagen. I checked in at

Angleterre, where they took excellent care of me. I had a beautiful fish dinner at Krogh's, including my favorite herring.

The next morning at breakfast I ran into Bob and Justine Keidel, "TAG" members from Green Spring. Once again a "small world." I caught SAS to Newark, arriving in the early afternoon, was met by Mark Thistel of Freedom Services, my transportation agency, and driven to 4406 Greenway. It had been a fabulous trip, but I was glad to be home.

Prague, Vienna, Budapest

Nancy Marburg urged me go on a "reunion" trip in September, 1997 of our 1984 Africa group, namely Barbara Sears, Ollie and Swannie Iselin, Fig and Julia Coleman, Bettina Dilworth, Louise Bodine, Nancy and I.

We assembled in Prague and were met by our tour director Vary Kemeny, a Hungarian countess. Mike Rainey from the Prague Order of Malta Priory also met us since I had been in contact with him by phone about seeing the Malta Church, Embassy and Priory in Malastrana, all of which had been tightly locked in 1990.

We drove to Zemka Castolovice, now owned by Diana Phipps, a Czech who had taken back her family place at the urging of Vaclav Havel. Mike Rainey rode with us, a mine of information, far better than our guide and an amusing companion. He was enchanted with the castle. As I wrote Diana after the trip, staying with her was like a house party. She entertained us royally. We sight-saw neighboring castles galore.

After four days we drove to Prague, stayed at a small hotel, the Krale Karla, on the side road leading to Hradcany, and did all the sights, including a boat ride on the Vlatava, the Moldau. I enjoyed going to the Malta Embassy and being shown around by the Conseiller, Count Mensdorff-Pouilly. Zdenek Rossman, who had been working on the flood damage in Moravia, came in and had a nice visit with me. He is studying to be a doctor.

We next moved for three days to Cseske Krumlov, a medieval town in southern Bohemia. From there we had a beautiful cold, early morning drive to the south up the headwaters of the Vlatava (Moldau) River, through the forests and with the mists rising from the river. We visited Roszmberk Castle on its aerie, near the border with Upper Austria. We then drove down to Grein, Austria on the Danube. We took a boat to Durnstein, a beautiful trip through the vineyards. We stayed at the Schloss Hotel, where I wrote a card to Ollie and Nancy Reeder on the terrace where we had sipped Durnsteiner white wine in 1969.

The next day Barbara Sears, Nancy Marburg, Julia Coleman, and I took the train to Vienna, since we were scheduled for a three-day extension there. We stayed in the Rommisher Kaiser Hotel, had a wonderful "high light" tour of the art museum with a friend of Vary's, went to Grinzing, etc. One evening we went to the ballet, followed by a late dinner at the Sacher.

I bade Barbara, Julia and Nancy good-bye, and then I went by hydro-foil down the Danube with Vary to Budapest. I passed by Esztergom and Visograd with nostalgia. We were met in Budapest by Ella Borocz, by birth a Szechenyi, a superb guide, most agreeable and a student of history.

We checked in to the Gellert, where I "took the waters" and had a lovely view of the Danube from my room. We took a tour out to Esztergom and came back by way of Visograd, with lunch at the game restaurant on the mountain. We stopped at Szentendre, the artists colony, a quiet town in 1982 but now booming. We visited 12A Szechenyi Rakpart, where Kitty Hoffman had stayed with Marian and Ross Titus. We visited the newly restored part of Budapest Castle, which had been a mass of rubble when I was there in 1969. We took in High Mass in the Coronation Church on the Var, unchanged since 1969, and visited the Knights of Malta Chapel.

Thus, in a sort of dénouement, we knitted up the loose ends of years past. We even were able to see the inside of the courthouse at Esztergom, thanks to a nice guardian, although it was closed for Saturday. I found the court room, sat on the bench where I had been during the trials and told the story of Kitty's plea for a grace period, the immediate assent of the president of the court and the suppressed fury of the party apparatchik.

In particular with Prague and Budapest, it was difficult to take in how quickly they had been rejuvenated, albeit with plenty of modern, economic problems. Esztergom was the most changed. The Communists had deliberately neglected it on account of the Church. The bridge over the Danube, destroyed by the Germans in 1945, had still not been rebuilt. The other side had become the Slovak Republic. The town of Esztergom had been spruced up, painted, refurbished with a nice park, flowers, etc. We visited the Cathedral where Cardinal Mindzenty was reburied in 1991. After his fifteen years of asylum in the U.S. Embassy in Budapest, his final years were passed in exile in Austria. The Pope had made a special visit in 1991, probably as a sort of peace offering for the Vatican's insistence that he leave Hungary so that there could be a rapprochment with the Communists.

On my way home I stopped off in Amsterdam and had my friends, the van den Biesens, in for dinner at the Amstel—Harry and Therèse, Lisette and Joleen. I had stayed with them in Joppe to see the Vermeer exhibit at the Mauritshus. We reminisced about my earlier visit to Holland in 1958 and our fond memories of Harry's sister, "Auntie Jeanne" and her house at St. Anton. Thus we knit up another loose end of times gone by.

1998—Republic of Georgia, Azerbaijan (Baku)

If the trip to Prague, Vienna and Budapest can be characterized as a dénouement, then the 1998 trips would probably be a Coda since they covered new territory but also contained a sort of gathering up of old strains in a new form.

On September 8, 1998, I flew to Zurich and went up to Mürren to acclimatize and absorb six hours of time change. We had summer weather, then we had four inches of snow in the town and, when it became lovely again, I walked with Fritz Stager—perfect training.

I flew from Zurich to Tbilisi, Georgia on September 19, arriving at 3 A.M. My lady guide from Caucasus Travel arrived at 10 A.M. Since it was Sunday and I could not get to the Roman Catholic Mass, we went to Sioni Cathedral, which is Georgian Orthodox. This is the same as Russian Orthodox but with the liturgy in Georgian. We lucked into a service being celebrated by the "Catholicos," the primate of the Georgian church. The place was packed, the heat intense and the singing—particularly the male choir—magnificent. It was a wonderful introduction to Georgia.

We took in other churches, Russian Orthodox, Roman Catholic, St. David's and the grotto on the holy mountain, and generally saw the sights. My Harvard Museum guide, Micheline de Bièvre, took me to dinner that night on the roof-top restaurant of Betsy Haskell's small hotel. Originally from Ruxton, Betsy is at the hub of Tbilisi foreign society.

The next day my guide, Irakli, and my driver, Besso, picked me up and we drove into the Caucasus mountains. We diverted up a narrow gorge where Irakli and I alit and had a "trek" of about three hours to the plateau, walking past old stone towers originally built for protection from the north. Besso met us and drove us to Gudauri, a modern hotel built for heli-skiing, now run by Swiss and Austrians.

The next day we drove up to Kazbek and trekked about two hours to the St. Nicholas Church, from which there was a stupendous view of Mount Kazbegi, snow capped and glaciered, 16,500 feet high. This according to Greek legend is where Prometheus was chained in punishment for his having stolen fire from the gods to bring to mankind. After lunch we drove down the Dariali Gorge to the Russian border.

Two days later I met the Harvard Museum group. Our leader Michele is married to a Georgian Zoldistani and we covered the country. At Kutaisi to the west toward the Black Sea we visited the "dig" and small museum at Vani with gold artifacts dating from Scythian times and Hellenistic artifacts. The latter substantiate the reality of the legend of Jason, Medea and the Argonauts. It occurred probably in the Eighth or Ninth Centuries B.C.

At Dmanisi, near the Armenian border, we saw the excavation of a medieval complex of fort, church and town where the "dig" had broken through a stratum of volcanic ash and lava into a settlement dating back about 1,500,000 years. The recovery of a hominid mandible was the basis of a recent seminar entitled "Humans at the Gates of Europe."

We visited many Byzantine churches dating from around 1100 A.D. when Georgia was flourishing under David the Builder. This was all set against a modern backdrop of 300,000 native Georgians driven by Russians from Abkaisia in northwest Georgia into refuge in Tbilisi hotels, "ethnic cleansing." The whole picture is also made dramatic by the discovery of the vast oil and gas reserves of the Caspian Sea region, Kazakhstan and Turkmenistan. The problem of getting it to markets all over the world and the location of the necessary pipe lines and tanker routes has become a new "Great Game" between the major powers.

We helicoptered one day to Shatili, a stone village in the depths of the Caucasus, only a few miles from Chechnya. The inhabitants have been resettled in modern housing close by, to keep the area occupied.

We drove through eastern Georgia to Azerbaijan, which is

Islamic. We stayed in luxury at a Hyatt Regency in Baku. Thus we had a kaleidoscope of civilizations and cultures 1,502,000 years in extent. No wonder that the region has been a door mat for invasions from all sides as it sits between the Caspian Sea to the east and the Black Sea on the west and between Europe to the north and Asia to the South. The gene pool must be vast.

MALTA

In December the tapestry of my life was further enriched by a pilgrimage to the Island of Malta for the 900th Anniversary of the founding of the Sovereign Military Order of the Knights of Jerusalem, Rhodes and Malta. Clad in our long black robes with the Maltese cross embroidered in white on the front and wearing our Maltese cross decorations, we marched in procession each day to magnificent high masses in the Co-Cathedral of St. John in Valetta, the Conventual Church of San Lorenzo in Birgu, now Città Vittoriosa, and the cathedral in the old capital of Mdina. All this was interspersed with lectures, lunches, receptions and sight-seeing. On the flight back, I read an illustrated history of the Great Siege of 1565, when 500 Knights of Malta beat back the navy and army of Suleiman the Magnificent, thus saving Europe in "The Last Battle of the Crusades."

1999

I took my "fin de siècle" Harvard museum trip in July as part of a Lindbad expedition on the Caledonian Star. We flew from New York to Edinburgh, boarded at Leith and sailed for the northern Scottish isles—the Orkneys and Shetlands—en route to northern Norway and Svalbard (Spitsbergen). This trip, at the end of the millennium, was again a knitting up of loose ends and a putting of things in place, by returning to ethnic origins, i.e. Picts, Celts, Danes and Norsemen. Our Harvard lecturer was Karel Liem, who was with us in 1997 on the Yenisey River trip.

Our trip historian, Scott Pearson from Stanford, gave a fascinating lecture on the great European migrations, and I was intrigued by the origin of the Celts in the region southeast of the Caspian Sea, where I had been in 1996. Also, when he showed a map of the old Viking voyages and invasions, I noted with great interest that one broad arrow came out of Denmark, skirted our location north of Scotland and came to rest in southeastern Ireland—in the vicinity of Wexford. George Kenny in 1967 told me that the Kennys had settled there in the Ninth or Tenth Century after coming down as Danish Vikings. Scott Pearson placed them about 975 A.D. George was "right on the money."

I was intrigued by the Lofoten Islands since I remembered them from geography lessons at Calvert School. There were tales of the notorious "Maelstrom," the huge sea whirlpool. In the days of sailing ships, it was a menace.

We sailed up the Geiranger Fjord with the spectacular Seven Sisters waterfalls—eight this year because of the abundant rain —and the smaller and narrower Troll Fjord where Captain Skog actually touched the sheer wall so that a naturalist could reach from the bow and pluck a speciman of flora. We stopped at Tromso, Gateway to the Arctic and Paris of the North, saw the Polar Museum, the Catholic Church, the Planetaria film on the Northern Lights and had a glass of the locally brewed Mack beer.

Then we entered the Arctic, sailing the North Polar Sea with a stop at Bjornoya (Bear Island) before entering the region of drifting sea ice. We made our landfall in Svalbard (Spitsbergen) at Halvmaneoya. We were particularly fortunate in that this was a "light ice year" which meant that we could enter the Hinlopen Strait at its southern entrance, usually blocked by pack ice, and circumnavigate the entire island of Spitsbergen, the largest in the archipelago. Late in the evening, still in broad daylight, we had our first full view of a polar bear as he alternately walked across the ice floes and swam the leads. We followed alongside him for quite a long way. That “night” I sat up to see the midnight sun which reached its lowest point in blazing daylight at 12:55 A.M. We were at Latitude 79° North.

We had to be especially careful of polar bears on our zodiac trips ashore. Many of the bears had been stranded on islands when the pack ice went out early. Each time we went ashore, we were split into small groups, each led by a naturalist or crew member, armed with a shotgun loaded with solid ball. On one island, Reinsdyrflya, we had not seen a bear who was lying in a small hollow about a quarter mile away from our walk. When he stood up to look at us, we retreated to the zodiacs and then watched him from the mothership.

That evening, the captain took the ship as far north as he could, until he reached the pack ice. We were at 81° 32.88' North, 507 nautical miles from the North Pole. I was delighted since, as a child, I had been fascinated by the accounts of the discovery of the North Pole by Robert E. Peary. It is now questioned by some, but my faith has not been shaken.

The next day we visited Moffen Island, north of Spitsbergen, where there was a large colony of walruses. We watched through binoculars for a long time, from the ship. We went ashore at Danskoya, the site of Danish whaling and the starting point for expeditions by balloons and airships trying to reach the North Pole.

On the day that we visited the Monaco Glacier, we took zodiac trips quite close to the face of the glacier in the afternoon. We sailed close to it in the ship after dinner. Captain Skog was thoroughly enjoying himself and it may be that he was trying to make the vibrations of the ship's engines induce “calving” of the glacier. In any event, a few small ice falls came down and then a huge one, several hundred yards wide and about 150 feet high. It made a roar and produced quite a wave. The loudspeaker cautioned all hands to hold on. Olle Carlsson, one of the lecturers, from Sweden, said that he had never seen a larger calving in Svalbard.

Toward the end of the trip, we went ashore on one island which had been scouted for bears and declared safe. As we walked up to an abandoned hunter's cabin, one of our group spotted a bear browsing a quarter of a mile away. I was with Olle, watching through my field glasses, as the others went back to the zodiacs. When the bear looked at us and took a few steps towards us, we too departed. Apparently, they can move like lightning and are not to be taken lightly.

We stopped at the polar research station at NyAlesund, took a long walk and then sailed for the capital, Longyearbyen, where I was able to buy Sir Martin Conway's history of Svalbard. I was particularly interested in this because he was a famous mountaineer at the end of the 19th Century and named the Wellenkuppe (White Cap) at Zermatt. Josie Petrig and I climbed it in 1959, along with its sister peak, the Obergabelhorn.

We flew in the afternoon to Oslo, stayed at the Grand Hotel on the Johnannsgate, bringing back memories of my trips to the Olympics with Bruce Baetjer in 1952 and in 1967 with Eddie Johnston. I took Karl Liem and Karl, Jr. to a fine fish dinner at the Lofoten Restaurant on the harbor, looking over at the Aarhuis, the town castle and fortress. The next morning we flew to Newark, where I was met by Mark Thistel's service and driven to Greenway. Thus, another trip ringing down the century's odyssey—but, as always, I was glad to be home.

22

MILLENNIAL YEAR—2000

"TAKE A COOKIE WHEN THEY ARE PASSED"

It is now generally accepted that the Twentieth Century did not end until December 31, 2000, and the Third Millenium officially began on January 1, 2001. This has given me an excuse for a Revised Edition of *Carpe Diem* in which I could correct mistakes in family genealogy, fix typographical errors, take care of other slips and extend the narrative through the millennial year. In so doing I have stretched the year a bit to cover my trip to St. Anton in 2001 to attend the Alpine Ski World Championships, celebrating the One Hundredth Anniversary of the founding of the Ski Club Arlberg, the oldest ski club in the world, of which I have been a member since 1953.

This extension has enabled me to knit up loose ends, not in the Shakespearean sense of the "raveled sleeve of care" but in rounding out my experiences into an account of "seeing [my] life as a part of a larger drama, as a variant of some archetypal tale," to quote Professor Kotre. See Preface, page xi.

I have appended a subtitle to this millennial addition—"Take a cookie when they are passed"—an expression often used by my friend Trafford Klots. In this year, mindful of advancing age, I have taken advantage of a number of opportunities that presented themselves. I have been fleshing out my "life review" as recommended by Professor Kotre before attaining the age of eighty.

As the plate has been passed, I have helped myself to a few more cookies, as you will see.

To ring out the old century, Nancy Marburg, Kitty Hoffman, Isabel Klots, Catherine and Ham Allen, Natalie Brengell, Fife Symington and I did it fittingly at a dinner dance on New Year's Eve 1999 at the Elkridge Club. True to form Kits Hoffman and I closed it up. We then followed up on New Year's Day 2000 with a member's reception at the Maryland Club. We all wanted to be at home with old friends and amid familiar surroundings—no junkets to far off and exotic places as a number of people did.

In February I took my annual ski trip to Europe. I spent the usual two weeks in St. Anton and two weeks in Mûrren, skiing with Herbert Rofner and Bruno von Allmen respectively. In both places we had lots of snow but not too much as in the previous year. In St. Anton work was being pushed feverishly to move the railroad tracks and station from the middle of town to the other side of the river, The Rosanna Fluh. All this was being done in preparation for the 2001 Ski World Championships.

Also Franz Tandl had made extensive alterations and additions to the Alte Post. I had a new room—Number 203—on the north side of the hotel and looking up the ski slopes. This removed me from the din of the "Café Village," the ice bar with its booming rock and roll. I must admit that I do not mind it when I stop by the café after skiing to have a glass of wine and chat up the barmaids. But when I want my nap after skiing, I prefer quiet.

My ski trip was a bit early since I wanted to return in time for the Rededication of St. Ignatius Church on March 3, the last Sunday before Lent. Before I left I told Father Watters that I would sponsor the Gounod *Missa Solenelle*, the St. Cecilia Mass, that we used to have at the eleven o'clock High Mass when I was a child. He pulled out all the stops—choir, organ, brass, strings, soloists. Jacques Kelly, who writes for the Baltimore *Sun*, wrote me afterwards that it was a proud day for Catholicism in Baltimore.

The music was overpowering, particularly the solo rendition of the Gounod *Sanctus*. There was not a dry eye in the house. Father Braunreuther said that he went through two handkerchiefs. Father Casciotti gave his usual trenchant and amusing sermon, remarking that Father Watters was fortunate in having such supportive parishioners. Rather it is we who are blessed in having such a dynamic spiritual leader as Father Watters. The renovated church looks magnificent. Mike Murphy and his contractors and workers have done a superb job. Some have said that it is now the most beautiful church in Baltimore, and it has begun to win many professional awards. After Mass we had a reception in the Center Stage auditorium.

Anne Reeves, Emily and Charlie had come down for the rededication, and it was wonderful to have family fill up the pew. This time we sat in Pew 15, Grandfather Kenny's pew, where Mother used to sit and that Aunt Frances, Frances and I occasionally used. Father Watters saved the brass marker from Pew 5, the Reeves pew, and at my suggestion added it to Pew 15 so that now the pew memorializes both grandfathers. I am sure that the members of both families who sat there years ago heartily approve. Eddie Dunn joined me on Gaudete Sunday, Advent 2000, for a special Mozart Mass. He was puzzled by the two markers on one pew. I explained the provenance.

Since I was scheduled to go on a trip sponsored by the Harvard Museum of Natural History entitled "Backroads China" in April, I asked the permission of the respective Boards of Trustees of the Warfield Fund and the Kernan Hospital Endowment Fund to hold our annual trustees' meetings earlier, in March.

At the Kernan meeting we approved a gift of Three Million Dollars to the University of Maryland Medical School to help endow a separate Department of Orthopedic Surgery and a professorship named for James Lawrence Kernan. This was a proud moment for Kernan.

At the Warfield meeting I bowed out as president and turned the reins over to Braxton Mitchell, who had orchestrated the move of the office to Ruxton and its modernization and computerization. The Board presented me with a copy of *The High Mountains of the Alps* by Helmut Dumler and Willie P. Burkhardt, beautifully illustrated and thoughtfully inscribed. On the cover of the dust jacket was a stunning picture of the Finsteraarhorn, that I had climbed with Hermann Steuri in May 1969.

When I looked up the section on the Zinalrothorn, I found a brief paragraph on the Kanzel Grat, that Josie Petrig and I had climbed in August 1958. I was stunned to read, "This provides an excellent rock climb with several pitches of VI+." Josie and I had sure done a real one!

I hated to miss the April steeplechase season in Maryland, but as aforesaid had signed up for the Harvard Museum trip "Backroads China" April 7–23 and arranged for an extension to the Three Gorges of the Yangtze and Guilin on my own. It was a fabulous trip.

China

I flew to Los Angeles, "overnighted" at the airport, left for Hong Kong, business class, on April 7, on Cathay Pacific, had a room at the Hong Kong airport hotel for a few hours for a shower and brief lie-down and flew to Kunming in the afternoon, arriving April 9. That was a long haul. We stayed at the Green Lake Hotel, near the park most comfortably. The focus of the trip was Yunnan Province in far southwest China, part of the China-Burma-India (CBI) Theater during World War II.

We took in the sights around Kunming and had an excursion by train out to the Stone Forest, an area of large granite outcroppings. We traveled on the narrow-gauge railway which had been built by the French to connect Vietnam and Yunnan. It was an amusing ride with the locals. The Stone Forest was unusual, with an ultra modern hotel and a native village where I bought a cute, hand-made jacket for Charlotte Reeves, Sam's daughter. On the way back by bus, it felt sultry, and I asked our guides if they ever had thunderstorms. The answer was "not at this time of year," shortly after which we had a cloudburst, with violent lightning and thunder. It was fortuitous since thereafter we had clear cool days. We had been warned that we could have had lots of rain on our trip, particularly as we reached the mountains.

From Kunming, elevation 6,000 feet, we proceeded north by bus, part of the way on the old Burma Road and part on a modern version. We stayed en route at Chuxiong (Shoushong) and continued on to Dali, an attractive city at 9,000 feet, famous for its marble. It is on Lake Erhai with the 13,000 foot Cangshan Mountains to the west. We visited the three famous pagodas, bought marble pictures and decorations, saw the marble works and one evening had a charming private concert by a group of local professional people playing the ancient musical instruments. We took a boat trip to an island fishing town. We did quite a bit of walking to temples and pagodas in the mountains. The wild flowers, particularly the azaleas, were beautiful.

Dali at night, the old town, was charming with restaurants and cafés. We settled on the Tibet Café, where we ran into all sorts of world wanderers. We also went to an internet shop where we caught up with the stock market, via Yahoo.

From Dali we had a beautiful trip by bus through the fields and orchards to Lijang. The catalpa trees were in full bloom. As we neared Lijang on a new highway we suddenly saw the Jade Dragon Mountain, the summit of which is snow and ice covered and tops out at 18,300 feet. Our luck with the weather continued since it was beautiful with cumulous clouds. On one side trip we drove up to a viewing area that was being developed—Yak Meadow—where they had built a ski lift up to about 11,000 feet and were

Jade Dragon Mountain
Yunnan Province, China

Tiger Leaping Gorge
Yunnan

putting in tourist facilities. We were glad that we were among the first visitors. We had a lovely walk up over the meadow to a spot where we ate our sandwiches and had spectacular views over an evergreen forest to the cliffs, glaciers and snow capped peaks of Jade Dragon.

On one of our excursions we passed a sign commemorating the Flying Tigers, an American volunteer group of pilots who had an airfield there and had had air battles with the Japanese in World War II.

From Lijang we had a fascinating drive around the back of Jade Dragon with lovely views, then went over a pass and descended to the Yangtze River, just below its "first bend." We drove along the river to the entrance to Tiger Leaping Gorge, with the snow capped Jade Dragon on the right and other snow-capped peaks on the left. With the river at approximately 6,000 feet above sea level, that meant a total drop of about 12,000 feet from the tops of the mountains.

We crossed the Yangtze and had a spectacular drive, at first alongside a fair-sized tributary river and then branching off to the right up a narrow gorge with dizzying drops. We ascended through varying levels of vegetation until finally we reached a lovely hardwood and conifer forest. The Chinese now forbid lumbering in this area since the forests were being destroyed with disastrous results to the ecology of the countryside downstream—floods, etc.

Passing the forests we emerged on the Tibetan Plateau, still Mainland China but looking exactly like Tibet, children, people, houses, etc. It was cold since we were at 11,000 feet at least. We stopped at a drab little town strung along the road for a late lunch. The restaurant was unprepossessing, but our leaders, David Huang and Jim Ellison, had been there before, and to our surprise we had a delicious meal. From there we drove to Zhongdian, the chief town of the district presenting many contrasts.

We first drove in to a brand-new ultra modern hotel on the outskirts of town to see if we were booked there. It had a well stocked, western type bar, so several of us had a whiskey. This was not our hotel, so we went to another in the center of town. This too was good, but we returned to the first one for dinner, a hot one, Sichuan style.

At Zhongdian, we drove out to the old town, climbed the steep stairs to the Tibetan Buddhist temple, which is being restored and enlarged, and also went to see a local village and school. I tried my "tashi dalay"—Tibetan for "hello"—that I remembered from 1982, and was understood, to the amazement of David Huang, who did not know what I was saying. The school children were surprised since they did not know if I could really speak Tibetan.

We also went to the Napahi preserve to see if there were any cranes or other birds, but we were disappointed. They had all migrated to Tibet or Siberia for the summer. The cranes are a sad tale since they used to be everywhere and are greatly revered for good luck and longevity. They used to flock to Lake Erhai at Lijang in great numbers but are not seen there any more because of the destruction of their nesting grounds for agriculture.

On leaving Zhongdian we returned by the same road but stopped in the gorge to take a long walk along the road. After lunch in an attractive restaurant in the town overhanging the river, we drove to Tiger Leaping Gorge. A road has been built to a viewing point and descent to the river. I was skeptical of the descent since it was a long series of stairs, but we had done so much walking that I was able to make it down and back without trouble. The river upstream is several hundred yards wide but in the gorge it narrows to a torrent of about fifty yards. In the narrowest part there is a large rock to which the tiger reportedly leaped when he was being pursued and then jumped to the other bank. It looks as if it could have happened.

It is a spectacular setting and is now being made into a tourist attraction by the Chinese. Formerly it was remote and difficult to reach. I walked through a tunnel past our viewing point and continued a bit to get views and pictures, then walked back to the bus where I rewarded myself with a nice Dali beer, our favorite of the local brews. Chinese beer is good, having originally been brewed by the Germans in their concession in Tsing-tao about 1900.

From the gorge we drove back along the river, over the pass behind Jade Dragon and down to the Lijang Valley. In the hotel that night we had our first farewell party since four of the group were flying out in the morning.

The next day we drove to the airport down the valley from Lijang. I took my last wistful look at Jade Dragon Mountain. There was a good shop where I bought a scroll of horses, quite forceful. We flew back to Kunming, about an hour. That afternoon, since I had accumulated so many scrolls, marble ornaments, etc., I bought a suitcase in the big department store. I had a priceless time getting there and back by taxi and negotiating the purchase with my English-Chinese phrase book and dictionary. After another farewell party and dinner at the hotel, I made my usual visit to the mezzanine bar and listened to the piano player. Some of them had been talented musical students. David Huang joined me later to brief me on my extension trip. The next morning he gave me cash to pay the local travel agents at Chungking and Guilin. I told him it made me quite nervous to carry so much money. David was an exceptionally good tour director, a most pleasant fellow. We did not have a chance to discuss the current situation of China but I would have liked to. Our female guide was also good, and she did tell us of the harrowing times which her family lived through during the Cultural Revolution in 1966–1976. Part of the time they lived in one room and slept under her mother's concert piano, a prized possession that they were somehow able to keep.

David took me to the airport at Kunming and from there I flew to Chungking. My guide had arranged for me to have lunch near the airport, but I told him that it was Easter Sunday and that I wanted to attend Mass if at all possible. He took me to the Catholic Church, in English country gothic style, in the center of the city. We met the Chinese priest who spoke no English, but said there was a second Mass at 3 P.M. This suited me perfectly, so my guide and I went across the street to a nice hotel, had lunch and came back for Mass. They ushered me to the front pew, and it was touching to see all the devout old people. There were also a few young.

After Mass my guide led me on a bit of sightseeing, including the house of an industrialist that was Chiang Kai Shek's headquarters during the war. He and Mao Tse Tung had had dinner together in the dining room.

The next morning the guide took me to the boat, located with some difficulty in the huge and ramshackle waterfront. Once on board, the purser-cruise director, a young Australian, gave me a good stateroom next to his and across the hall from a friendly older lady who turned out to be the owner of the shipline. It was a beautiful modern ship.

We took off fairly soon and cruised down the river under the usual murky skies. At Fengdu we took a chair lift up to a temple devoted to the dead, with restored carvings of ghoulish characters. There were markers on the hillsides about 500 feet above the present level of the river which show where the level will be after the huge new dam is completed. It is a colossal project that will flood the river as far back as Chungking. Although there are skeptics, the experts claim that it will work and point to the dam at Ginzhou as proof on a smaller, trial level.

The gorges themselves were interesting, but the Little Gorge on the second day, that we ascended in sampans, was prettier. Even the atmosphere was clearer, as evidenced by my pictures. On the

Buddhist Monk
Zhongdian Temple
Tibetan Plateau, Yunnan

Guilin, China

Water Buffalo
Guilin

Rice Paddies
Guilin

second night we had delightful games of mah-jongg where I was directed by members of the staff, including the maker of my "chop" and the artist of my scroll, "The Hundred Cranes" (Bai He).

The next day we disembarked at Shashi and had a long bus ride to Wuhan, a large industrial city, that we reached after dark. Although the surrounding country was flat, it was not a dull trip since the countryside was green with all the crops and had many trees. There were frequent canals. I flew early the next morning to Guilin, where I was met by my guide, Nancy, an attractive 24-year-old Chinese.

We visited the grottos, that seemed to me over-decorated; then had a drive around the countryside—"real" south China, lush, warm, rainy. In the afternoon we walked around the university, and I bumped into some of my mah-jongg friends from the boat. They strongly recommended a watercolor of an ancient house that I bought in the gift shop. It was about the only worth-while object since everything else looked like "tourist junk" to me. That evening Nancy's boss had arranged for us to have dinner at the big Hotel Guilin. I found it a "tourist trap" with poor food and our dining room full of dull-looking Americans. We fled to my hotel, the Dangui, where we had dessert from the buffet and a glass of wine.

The next day we took the boat to Yangshou along the Li River. This was the height of the tourist season, but we had a nice boat, generally congenial people and a beautiful trip down the river through the granite hills that one sees on every postcard of China. It was the epitome of Chinese tourism but worth every minute of it. Every turn of the river gave another beautiful view, and I burned a lot of film.

Landing in late afternoon, Nancy suggested that we stay in Yangshou, rather than returning by bus to Guilin. I heartily agreed, and we took a pedal taxi, driven by a woman, to The Golden Leaves Hotel. This was a bit simple but clean and had rooms with bath. I was in the back where it was quiet. Dinner was a bit plain, but it enabled us to finish quickly, take a motorbike taxi to the waterfront and go out on a cormorant fishing excursion, at night with flares. In later conversation with the fisherman we learned of his attachment to his birds, five in number. He said they lived to be about twenty years old.

We walked back along West Street, that we christened "the best street," and found the Café Under the Moon, run by an attractive Taiwanese. We made this our headquarters for dessert, coffee, drinks, and just watching the passing parade.

The next day we hired a real "automobile" taxi and toured the countryside, including a drive to one of the river towns that we had passed on our voyage down the Li. We had a long walk through the rice paddies, with the granite hills reflected in the water and the farmers plowing with oxen. It was quintessential China.

That evening we had the local specialty, duck cooked in beer, at a huge local restaurant. There were practically no tourists. We then repaired to the Under The Moon for dessert. I heartily approved the quotation on the back of the Café's business card:

> "I should like to spend the whole of my life traveling,
> If I could anywhere borrow another life to spend at home."

The next afternoon, we motored back to Guilin and after a rest at the hotel, Nancy saw me off at the airport for Hong Kong. She had been a top-notch guide and reminded me a bit of the guide that I had had in 1982 at the Great Wall and the Valley of the Kings. They were both attractive and intelligent young women.

The contrast between Yangshou and Hong Kong caused "cultural shock," but I managed to adapt. I put up at the Harbor View Hotel, that was right on the harbor, with excellent views. I went by bus to the downtown American Club for lunch the next day. It has reciprocity with the Maryland Club. The dining room on the

42nd floor had even better views. I took a taxi out to the country club after lunch and caught a bus back. That evening I had dinner at a Chinese buffet restaurant with both Western and Oriental dishes. I was the only American there, and it was most amusing. The next day I took a morning tour of Kowloon and then took a taxi out to Happy Valley to see the racetrack.

That evening I had dinner in the revolving restaurant on the 66th floor of the Hopewell Enterprises building. Hopewell is Gordon Wu, a Princeton graduate and benefactor, and I left a note for him. The next day I packed up, had lunch at the American Club, rested in the afternoon and took Cathay Pacific at 11:00 P.M. for Los Angeles, where I again "overnighted," and flew home the next day.

Thus ended my third trip to China. This one pulled many strands together since I was able to see a part of the country which was near Chengdu, our point of departure for and return from Tibet in 1982. It also enabled me to see the tremendous economic progress made by China in general and how they are handling their re-annexation of Hong Kong. I was amused that in Hong Kong they would not accept mainland yuan, only their own dollars. When I tried to change my yuan in the hotel they would take only 100 yuan notes and larger. I could not change my smaller currency even in the banks. I finally worked a deal with the hotel's bellboys since they went back and forth to the mainland and could use yuan. I took loads of pictures, that were enthusiastically received by a large audience at the Maryland Club on October 5.

I took in the Fourth Circuit Judicial Conference at the Greenbrier at the end of June, played golf and at the banquet with the Washburnes and Stichels had a fine time with a group from Charlotte, North Carolina. Robin Hinson asked me for a copy of "Carpe Diem," which he evidently enjoyed. We plan to meet at Hot Springs next June. Zandy Harvey first invited me to the Judicial Conference in 1972, and I have enjoyed it ever since. It is the sort of professional activity that appeals to me since it is held in alternate years at the Greenbrier, in White Sulphur Springs, West Virginia, and at the Homestead in Hot Springs, Virginia. I have a ritual stop-over every year with the Washburnes at their house above the Cascade's golf course at Hot Springs.

I went to Nantucket on July 6 for my usual week at Dexter Tutein's Wood Box, residing in my spacious downstairs suite in the Annex, under the aegis of George and Betty Constable. I attended the Wharf Rats Club on Old North Wharf nearly every morning with George. From there, I flew to Hyannis, picked up a car, drove to the Nautilus Inn at Woods Hole, where I stayed under the aegis of Shang and Charlotte Goodwin. I have the privileges of the Quamquissett Beach Club. Shang was in full glory in his second year as Commodore of the Quissett Yacht Club. It was all a throw back to my youthful days of the 1930's and '40's.

Canadian Arctic

At the end of July, I flew to Ottawa and joined another Harvard Museum trip, this one to the High Arctic of Canada. When asked why I wanted to take the trip, I replied that as a child I had been fascinated by Robert Peary's voyages and his discovery of the North Pole. I had also devoured David Binney Putnam's tales of his trips to "Baffin Land," etc.

We flew about three hours by regular jet from Ottawa to Iqaluit, formerly Frobisher Bay. The northern area has been turned over to the Inuits, formerly Eskimos, and is now known as Nunavut. All of the places names are being changed. From there we flew another hour and a half on a smaller jet to Cape Dorset.

The next day we took an excursion by boat to a neighboring island and explored the ruins of a pre-historic structure consisting of a low ring of stones surrounding what must have been a sort of tent dwelling. It was cruder but it reminded me a bit of the structures that we had seen the previous summer in the Orkneys. We had a picnic of freshly cooked arctic char, that was delicious. We were supposed to fly out by chartered plane the following day, but fog at Iqaluit kept our Twin Otter from taking off. Thus we had a taste of the uncertainties of arctic weather. The water and the air temperatures are so close to freezing that any minor variation can affect the conditions. Fog is a constant threat that can come up suddenly.

After a day of enforced idleness at Cape Dorset—that I did not mind at all—we took off the next day in our Twin Otter for the trip around the Far North. We flew to Hall Beach, had lunch and then I took the opportunity to sit in the co-pilot seat on our leg to Resolute. When we flew over the Brodeur Peninsula of Baffin Island, one could see what was meant by the Arctic desert. I took a couple of pictures, and if Margaret Crawford sees them, she will swear that they were taken over the Australian Outback.

It was a beautiful day and of course there was no sunset or darkness since we were so far north of the Arctic Circle. After dinner at Resolute, the leaders decided to make up some lost time and take our excursion to Beechey Island to see the site of the ill-fated Franklin expedition in 1841. It was a short hop in broad daylight, and, after "dragging" the beach in approved liaison pilot fashion, we landed on the shingle near the four graves of the sailors who had died there.

We had seen a tape of the most recent exhumation of one of the bodies. The remains had been perfectly preserved by the permafrost. The setting of the tragedy was a lovely spot in such perfect weather. An ice breaker came in and anchored between us and Devon Island. It helps keep the channels open for the ore boats, tankers and other craft to the huge mine at Resolute.

The next day we flew to Isaachsen on Rignes Island. Taking skelter from the arctic wind, we had lunch in a large sled/trailer that had been abandoned some years ago by a mining enterprise.

We were greeted by a young scientist and his girlfriend who were there for the summer.

We then flew to Axel Heiberg Island and had a spectacular flight over its ice cap. We crossed a fjord and reached a barren desert area with interesting geologic strata. Again we "dragged" a landing strip in a dry valley between hills and landed on dirt and grass, liaison pilot style.

We climbed up one of the hills to the stratification, consisting basically of preserved wood, not calcified or fossilized. It was aged, disintegrating wood with stumps a foot or so high, said to be 40 million years old. It is puzzling how it arrived there—continental drift, tectonic plate shift, etc. Our geologist, Charlie Burnham, did not have an answer. We had a short hop to Eureka Weather Station, on Ellesmere Island, the northernmost of the Canadian archipelago and just west of northern Greenland.

The weather station is quite large and comfortably accepts a limited number of visitors. It is situated on a bluff over the Slidre Fjord, an arm of Eureka Sound, that in turn opens into Nansen Sound and Greeley Fjord. There was a spectacular view up the Fjord to a range of snow covered mountains in the distance. The weather was clear, cold and windy. Icebergs floated in the fjord. It was the "real" Arctic.

Charlie Burnham, our geology professor, and I bunked together that night, and when I looked outside at 4 A.M., there was a blazing mid-day sun. Rather than go chasing birds and musk oxen in the morning wind, I rolled over and slept late, then wrote postcards. After lunch, I rode up to the airstrip and had a long walk down its length to where it dropped off into the tundra. I had been told where the musk oxen were in the morning, and sure enough, I picked them up in my small field glasses. I could count twelve, about a mile and a half away. I watched them for a long time until I looked up at my shadow as I sat and was surprised to see the shadow of a bird hovering near me. It was a "jaeger." I tried to shoo it away by waving my hat and even pegged stones at it but it was adamant. Finally I retreated ignominiously up the airstrip. I don't think there was a nest nearby. Jaegers simply are aggressive.

In the evening after dinner, we drove up a steep hill to the joint Japanese-Canadian Astrolab where they are conducting some sort of astral scientific research. The wind was howling, but the outlook was spectacular. I would hate to have to drive that road in winter, up or down.

The next day, Thursday, August 3, we flew to Nansen Sound, then hopped over a narrow peninsula to Otto Fjord, the most spectacular scenery of the entire trip—and that is saying something! The north side of the fjord is sheer, and the land on both sides is arid, brown wasteland. At the eastern end of the fjord, a huge glacier descends from the ice field to the water's edge, where it calves myriad icebergs and floes. The fjord is choked with them. We could not land on the glacier but we circled it and the upper end of the fjord and its icebergs from every angle. I obtained beautiful photographs. We then flew across the ice cap to Tanquary, where we landed on the airstrip beside the fjord.

There were two young Canadian wardens at the park station, a base for campers, hikers, kayakers, etc. It is located at 81° 21' North, about 5–600 miles from the North Pole. We saw the small museum of Inuit artifacts, had lunch and then departed with the enormous Agassiz Ice Cap on our right. I keep using the word "spectacular" because there is no other word to describe it. We were due to fly to Alert on the far northeast corner of Ellesmere and then swing down the coast to Grise Fjord. Unfortunately, the latter was in fog, and fog and sleet were moving down from the north.

I have subsequently read that a low pressure system has been sitting for some time over the Arctic Ocean and the strait between Greenland and Ellesmere Island. This affects not only that area but has a far-reaching effect on the Atlantic Ocean currents and weather, that in turn have an important effect on winters in northern Europe—i.e., my skiing trips in Austria and Switzerland. Modern science and meteorology are also making it a small world.

Since there is no margin for error with fuel in these vast uninhabited reaches, we had to fly direct to Pond Inlet, a long flight down the coast and across long stretches of open water with drifting sea ice. At the beginning we could look across the Nares Strait to Greenland, indistinct in the patchy fog and haze. As we neared Pond Inlet, we had good views across Bylot Island, a bird and animal sanctuary.

We spent the next day at Pond Inlet, saw the new Visitors Center and Museum, built to resemble an iceberg, and the Catholic Church where Father Guy Mary-Rousselière was a missionary for many years, as well as being a renowned geologist. The Center has a good library and place to study, overlooking the fjord with its stranded icebergs. Here they drift down on their regular route from Greenland to menace the North Atlantic shipping lanes.

We had a long walk up the beach to Salmon Creek, then cut back across the tundra and the airstrip. In the evening they put on a folk dancing show with throat singing, eerily reminiscent of Mongolia and Siberia. All these northern peoples are said to be related—Lapps (Samis), Nenets, Buryats, Aleuts, Inuits, etc.

On Saturday we had a long flight down the coast of Baffin Island and then cut inland across the Cumberland Peninsula and the National Park. We flew through spectacular fjords rimmed with mountains, over glaciers and ice caps, and up a continually narrowing pass with lowering clouds until we reached Cumberland Sound and landed at Pangnirtung. This last part of the flight brought back memories of my flight with Beverly McVeigh to Yokohama in 1946.

After a long pause for a late lunch and a visit to the extensive native art gallery and museum, I tried to buy a picture of a bird returning a man's mitten—a sort of folk tale—but neither the artist nor the manager was there. I had run into the same difficulty at Cape Dorset where we were warned not to buy from itinerant sellers, advice that I took to my regret when I passed up an excellent soap-stone carving of a polar bear.

We then flew over Frobisher Bay to Iqaluit and were put up comfortably at the Navigator Hotel. We walked to a restaurant for a farewell dinner of delicious Arctic char. Some of us had fried narwhal for hors d'oeuvres.

On Sunday morning I walked to the Catholic Church for Mass. The priest turned out to be Father Fred Homann, a Jesuit who had taught at Loyola College in Baltimore and was a friend of Father Watters. Small world! His sermon on the Transfiguration was excellent, and since the date was August 6 he compared it to the flash of the atomic bomb at Hiroshima. Fifty-five years ago I was at Fort Sill in the Department of Air Training, waiting to be shipped to the Pacific for the invasion of Kyushu, Japan scheduled for November 1, 1945. The atomic bombs, horrible as they were, put an end to that. Thank God!

We flew to Ottawa, had another delightful farewell dinner at the Chateau Laurier, and the next day dispersed for home. I turned around a few days later and flew up to Manchester, New Hampshire to join the Reeves family at Rockywold. The camp was déja vu of Camp Wallula in the 1930's. We seemed to be out to cocktails every night, which everyone said was unusual. I made the ritual climb of Rattlesnake Mountain behind the camp. Charlie Reeves and I had a non-stop tournament of backgammon, in which he slaughtered me, to my chagrin. One rainy day I showed my slides of the Arctic—unedited but kindly received. Bradford Washburn, skier, climber, explorer and photographer was in the camp but unfortunately I missed him. It would have been fun to talk to him about our trip to the Arctic.

Leaving Rockywold for Manchester, I took the back roads, skirted Mount Kearsarge, my first mountain climb at age eight, and drove to New London, Little Lake Sunapee and the site of Camp Wallula, now guest cabins, that I had not seen since 1933. I was agreeably surprised to find how little things had changed. It was still a beautiful area.

On the first weekend after Labor Day, I drove to Wernersville, near Reading, Pennsylvania, to the Jesuit Center for Spiritual Growth. This was formerly the Jesuit Novitiate, which Newbold Lawrence had briefly attended. Our object was the St. Ignatius Church Retreat, organized by Gail Baker and conducted by Fathers Braunreuther and McGauley. I am not a "retreat person," although we had good ones at Canterbury. This one was low pressure. I enjoyed it greatly, particularly since I was able to do a lot of walking around the spacious grounds. The Novitiate was a gift of Mr. and Mrs. Nicholas Brady (not Nick's parents) in the 1920's and now houses a few retired priests besides serving as a spiritual center for outside groups. I was glad to have been there with memories of Newbold. The chapel is beautiful and I visited it often.

On October 13, Braxton Mitchell, Ken Spence, Davis Sherman and I met at the University of Maryland Medical School and presented to Dean Don Wilson the first of the checks for the new Department of Orthopedics and the James Lawrence Kernan Hospital professorship. Mort Rapaport and Steve Schimpff were present.

The next day, October 14, I attended Mass at 9:30 at St. Ignatius, presided over by Father General Peter-Hans Kolvanbach, S.J., Superior General of the Society of Jesus, formerly referred to as the "Black Pope." I met him briefly after Mass. He is Dutch but I did not have a chance to ask him if he knew the Vanden Biesens. It was the Feast of Saint John Ogilvie, S.J., a Jesuit Priest and Martyr at the time of the Reformation.

Rome—Jubilee Year

That evening Carter and Betty Beese, Rowland and Deedie Morrow, Margaret Wheltle and I were driven to Dulles Airport where we took Air France via Paris to Rome for the Jubilee Year convocation of the Knights and Dames of the Order of Malta. In Rome we had an evening reception at our Hotel Metropole, in the Cavour district. The next morning, Monday October 16, we walked in our robes to Santa Maria Maggiore where we marched in procession through the Porta Santa, opened for Jubilee 2000, the Holy Year. As we were forming up I ran into Heine and Ludmilla Kyborg, acquaintances of many years at St. Anton. Once again, a small world!

The Mass was presided over by Cardinal Laghi, Patron Cardinal of the Order of Malta, formerly Apostolic Nuncio in Washington. It was beautiful. I had broken ranks and was seated next to a Frenchman, the Cappellmeister at Versailles, and near a knight from Neuchatel, Switzerland, as well as a group of Canadians. After lunch we went to Villa Malta on the Aventine with its famous view of St. Peter's dome through the keyhole of the entrance portal. In the late afternoon, we returned to Santa Maria Maggiorie for a lovely Benediction, the first I had attended since Vatican II.

On Tuesday we took a bus to St. John Lateran for Mass, again presided over by Cardinal Laghi. We then went to Tivoli for lunch with a tour of Hadrian's Villa and the gardens of the Villa d'Este. I had visited the latter with the Foxcroft girls in 1948, but I had not seen the former. The fountains were playing in the gardens, and it was beautiful. Since it was a clear late afternoon, we could see the dome of St. Peter's in the distance. That evening we had dinner at an excellent restaurant at Castel Gandolfo and came home late.

On Wednesday we went by bus to San Paolo Fuori Le Mura. The presiding celebrant was Cardinal Szoka and we were surprised at first to hear English (American) until we learned that he was from Detroit. Large parts were also in Latin, Italian, French, German, Spanish, and Portuguese. That afternoon I relaxed, had a glass of wine and wrote postcards outside at the little Washington pub on the corner. In the evening there was a reception for our group, The Federal Association, at the residence of the Ambassador to the Vatican, Lindy Boggs, widow of Congressman Hale Boggs. She is the mother of Barbara Boggs Sigmund, Charlie Reeves's godmother. Anne Reeves had stayed there in the spring and I had a chance to have a long talk with the Ambassador, whom I had met two years ago in Malta. She was lovely to us and showed me Barbara's portrait as a child. It had been ten years since Barbara died.

On Thursday October 19 we had a 7:40 A.M. start for St. Peter's, where we assembled in the square. As with the other basilicas we proceeded through the Porta Santa. The last time I had been through it was with Aunt Ella in 1950. I managed to maneuver myself next to the barricade by the aisle and thus had a good view of the proceedings. Mass was at 9 A.M. presided over by Cardinal Sodano, papal Secretary of State.

At the end of Mass a white chair was placed before the high altar, and after a half hour wait the Pope came in from the west in his gliding chair. He came quite close to me, blessing as he went. I thought his color was good and one of our doctor knights agreed. He is of course quite lame, unable to do much walking and suffering from Parkinson's, but his voice was strong and he gave quite a long homily. He departed by the north transept, on the left.

From there I went to the Via Campo Marzio, where I met Sandra Malfatti. I had located her through a telephone call to Herbert Rofner in St. Anton. He had obtained her address and telephone number from Bimpy Kertess of St. Anton. I had telephoned Sandra in advance from the States. We had a wonderful time reminiscing of old days at St. Anton, Bruce Baetjer, etc. I did not meet her

CBR Jr
St. Peter's, Rome,
Knights of Malta Pilgrimage

John Paul II
St. Peter's
Knights of Malta

husband Antonio "Tonino" Grassi, but had an amusing telephone conversation with him. We had lunch at a local restaurant near her flat.

In the late afternoon we bussed to St. John's Hospital, for the Grand Master's Reception. It was jammed, but amusing. We were all given a commemorative medal. That evening several of us had dinner at the Café Terme Dioclezione, near the Metropole, part of its structure being a wall of the Baths of Diocletian. We had a delightful time and our waiter faked a fall that would have spilled dishes on me, a bit of pantomine that had us in stitches. It was a nice ending to our "pilgrimage."

Burma (Myanmar)

The next morning, Friday October 20, the main group departed early. I took my time, packed, having given my robe and various accoutrements to Carter Beese to take home for me, then went over to the Vatican photograph office to order some pictures. I took the shuttle to the airport and boarded Thai Air for a 3:40 P.M. non-stop flight to Bangkok. Because of the length of the trip, I went business class, a wise decision. I had a comfortable flight, arrived early the next morning, was hit by the heat, sent a FAX to Charlie in Quito, Ecuador (since he had FAXed me in Rome) and then flew Bangkok Air to Rangoon (Yongan), Burma (Myanmar).

I was met by "Joe," our young Burmese guide, taken to the Pansea Hotel and collapsed. It was a lovely place, located in the embassy section of Rangoon, with spacious grounds, pools, scattered living quarters, etc. I had dinner in the garden despite the warmth. Joe came in later with Chris Gold, our AsiaTranspacific Journeys guide, born in South Africa, British by birth, educated at Oxford and now living in Chiang Mai, Thailand. They looked like, and were, an excellent team.

The next day, Sunday October 22, I went to Mass at a church in the city and had a nice chat with the native priest afterwards. I met the wife of the Italian ambassador, who had sat beside me. That afternoon the group began to trickle in, and I took it easy in my air conditioned room. Kay and Dana Hamel, who had been with me in Mongolia in 1997, arrived as did Arthur and Camilla Blackman and John Constable, our leader, with whom I had also traveled in Patagonia, Bhutan and Nepal.

On Monday we went to a monastery in the outskirts of Rangoon, where we had made a donation for the war orphans and where they had a large sign to greet us. Joe had arranged this since there are 1400 monks, about 800 of whom are orphans from the age of about five. They filed out in a long line with their begging bowls, and we were asked to fill them from huge vats of rice with smaller serving bowls. Our ladies did it at first, and then they asked all of us to do it. I was a bit reticent at first, but then I caught the spirit of the occasion and was deeply moved. It was a remarkable experience especially when viewed in context with the religious events that I had encountered in Rome.

We watched the monks eat at long, low refectory tables where they added a small soup to their rice. We also paid a call on the head abbott and his assistant at their lunch. On the opposite side of the compound were the young nuns, about two hundred. The whole episode was touching.

We lunched at a restaurant in a park with a view of the Schwedagon Pagoda, then drove out into the country to a park and game preserve with an outdoor zoo. On the way out we stopped at the British military cemetery where over six thousand British war dead are buried, with memorials to another twenty thousand. These were the casualties from World War II when the Japanese swept up from Malaysia after their capture of Singapore in 1942.

The next morning we made a long visit to the Schwedagon Pagoda, a spectacular main spire with literally tons of gold contained

John Constable
Buddhist Monastery
Rangoon, Burma

Procession of Monks

Rice for Monks

CBR Jr
Distributing Rice

in the main structure. We took our shoes and stockings off at the bottom level, went by elevator to the main level and walked around the main pagoda and through the various shrines. I rested at one point and played with the children who were fascinated with my beard. A nice-looking, well-dressed man came up and talked with me and then offered to show me around. We visited the shrine of the Buddha's footprints, which are filled with holy water, Buddha's tears. My guide asked me what my "sign" was, and when I said that I did not know he asked me on which day of the week I was born. Again I did not know. He brought out a century dictionary and found out from my year, month and day that I was born on a Wednesday. The sign is an elephant, which delighted me. He asked if I knew the exact time that I was born, which of course I did not, so I will have to look it up on my birth certificate. He was typical of the friendliness that we found from the Burmese people throughout the trip.

Since we were at the pagoda on Tuesday, I did not join the pilgrims sweeping the vast marble floors. If I had been there on my "sign day" Wednesday, I would have joined them. My guide finished off my tour with a visit to the elephant pagoda. I was ringing wet from walking in the heat, and at lunch the restaurant owner lent me his son-in-law's shirt so that I could change. When we departed from Rangoon, I left a note with the shirt, using what Burmese I had picked up.

We had an early morning flight of an hour and half to Bagan the next morning. We toured the various temples and pagodas, which are legion, thousands of them scattered across the dry dusty plain. Some are being restored, much against UNESCO's recommendation, and a lot of them are crumbling which gives a greater atmosphere of antiquity.

On the next day we had an all-day excursion to Mount Popa, an extinct volcano about 5000 feet high. On the way we stopped at a grove of totty palms where a young boy was driving a bull in a circle crushing peanuts for oil. The proprietor climbed a palm to show us how they collected coconuts, from which they make a delicious sugar and also a liquor that is clear and quite smooth. I had some even though it was only about ten o'clock.

We stopped in a village at the foot of Mount Popa which was luxuriant with tropical trees and flowers, mostly orchids. We drove up a winding road giving views of the temple complex and its golden spires. We finally came to a resort development that had just been built about half way up. We all wanted to walk, and I went along with the main group up a road in the woods toward the summit. I turned back after about 45 minutes, and, since I had brought my Murray's Toggery, Nantucket bathing suit, I took a lovely swim in the modern pool with a water-level view down to the temple. It was idyllic. We were high enough to be a bit out of the valley humidity. The water was cool. A nice gin and tonic was quite soothing, and after the various groups returned, we had lunch in an outdoor dining room. A tropical downpour moved across the scene, casting the temple in a fantasy light against the gray and black backdrop of the storm.

We left the scene reluctantly, since it was a beautiful spot. On the way back we had to wait about a half hour for a torrent to subside in what had been a dry stream bed when we came up in the morning. We arrived in the outskirts of Bagan in a misty golden light of evening, which made the decaying pagodas even more attractive. We paid a brief visit to Joe's family, most attractive, in their new house, since the government had moved them out of the area where their forebears had lived for hundreds of years. We had dinner in a large restaurant with local music and dancers and an athletic, attractive Burmese girl who performed amazing feats of balance with a small soccer-like ball on her feet. It looked as if she would be a good candidate for the Austrian ski team.

Early the next morning we flew to Mandalay, took a short tour and then went to our boat the R.V. Pandaw, built in Scotland in

Monastery, Mount Popa
Bagan, Burma

R.V. Pandaw
Irrawaddy Flotilla Company
Burma

1947 and owned by the Irrawaddy Flotilla Company, incorporated in 1865. I was assigned a stateroom on the lower deck with John Constable, Chris, Joe and Jake, the manager/steward of the boat. After lunch and a snooze in the heat of day, we paid a visit to a "living monastery" where the monks were most friendly and enjoyed talking.

We remained tied up that night near Mandalay but were underway about 5:00 A.M., sailed upstream and crossed the river to Mingun. There the King about 1810 had built a huge chedi or pagoda, supposed to be 500 feet (150 meters) high but never completed because of financial and other difficulties. Some of the more adventurous of our party went ashore early to climb to the top. I went ashore about 9:00 A.M. The structure has an enormous crack in it from an earthquake, in 1838, the epitome of a by-gone oriental age. We walked through the town on the one main street with boards over the mud puddles. Children and animals, including bullock carts, were everywhere. A smaller pagoda allegedly had the largest hanging bell. We rang it for luck with wooden mallets.

I bought a little water color of a rustic scene at a shop, but when I showed David Hamel, he scooped me when he found a nicer one of the Mingun Pagoda, crack and all. As we went down to the boat landing, we passed two huge elephant gates with trees growing out of their tops. It was a colorful sight, and I saw that I would be using far more film than I had counted on.

We sailed about 10:30 and proceeded up stream. I sat outside my stateroom on the lower deck and enjoyed the scenery and the water gliding by. Fortunately, the late monsoon weather which we had been suffering seemed to break since it was noticeably cooler and less humid.

Having been told of George Orwell's *Burmese Days*, available in the ship's library, I sat on deck reading it and sipping a single-malt Laphroig fancying myself in the days of the Raj. George Orwell had been posted to Burma in the British police after World War I, and we finally found out that the place where he was stationed was Katha, where we were headed. I did not like the book at first since it disparaged the British colonial types, but aside from that it put me in a fantasy world of seventy-five years ago. I became part of the scene, immersed.

We tied up that night at Sathe and the next morning, Sunday October 29, we went ashore at Nwc Nyin near Kyauk Myoung to see the pottery works. There was obviously no Catholic church available for Mass. But we did get to a native wedding where the bride and groom in a small tent set up on the village street obligingly posed for photographs. There were loudspeakers blaring hideous music, a sort of Burmese rock and roll. We had a walk and the pottery works were interesting. Some of their products were huge and well ornamented. Throughout our visit we were surrounded by masses of children.

At lunch time we reached the Third Defile where the river narrows and the water becomes more than 100 feet deep. Heretofore, the river had been at least a mile wide, full of shoals and sand bars, with a depth of three to six feet. There were low hills on each side, and it was here in the 1980's that a sister ship of the Pandaw was sunk by KIA (Kachin Independence Army) mortar fire. When the Pandaw was taken over for refitting by the Irrawaddy Flotilla Company she still carried armor plating. Fortunately, we did not need any.

On Monday, we went ashore in the morning to visit a monastery sheltering many orphan children. They were all togged out for us and were cute in their formal dress. Late in the afternoon we tied up at Inn-ywd, a cluster of houses on the western bank, where many of us took a short "jungle" or forest walk. We walked up a hill on a good path, but then it turned out to be a bit longer than anticipated. I was ringing wet from perspiration when we reached the boat at dusk. Some of the women had most inappropriate footwear, but every one made it, and the "roughing" brought the group together. It was good for morale.

The next day at Khannyaut we walked through the town to a "nat shrine" where a pair of priestesses put on a show for us, shaking, smoking two cigarettes at once, drinking orange pop. They seemed to be enjoying it, not taking it too seriously. As our summary of the trip described it, "No Irrawaddy captain would dare pass here without paying his respects."

Twenty miles farther on in the afternoon we reached Tapaung, described in the ship's daily schedule as the "birthplace of the Burmese nation." We climbed to a pagoda perched on a hill top overlooking the river, having left our shoes and socks at the entrance to the "gaung dan," a long stair hall up the hill to the pagoda. The views up and down the river were lovely.

After dinner we saw a movie of World War II in Burma, a largely forgotten segment of the war. I am glad that we had seen the British military cemetery outside Rangoon. The movie was British, reflecting their slant of the China-Burma-India (CBI) Theater, a view was not too favorable to "Vinegar Joe" Stillwell, who was a controversial figure at best. In April when I had been in Yunnan Province, China I saw the memorial to our Flying Tigers outside Lijang, all part of the same war.

On Wednesday, November 1, All Saints' Day, I dutifully read my Mass prayers from the leaflet missal which I had filched from St. Ignatius. It reminded me of All Saints and All Souls Days in 1982 when we were returning from Mt. Everest and Shigatse to Lhasa and had that remarkable evening at the little Tibetan festival in the rest camp outside Lhasa.

We reached Katha in the morning and had a walk around town, through the markets. This is the town where George Orwell was stationed as Eric Blair in the British colonial police, on which he based his novel "Burmese Days." After lunch we took a cramped native bus to a teak farm where they were training elephants to work in the forest. After dinner a troop of native dancers in lovely native dress gave us a lively show on the upper deck.

On Thursday, November 2 we paid a visit to more of the extensive native street markets. Then we had a long drive to Indaw Lake through dense teak forests and stands of tall ironwood trees. Passing the elephant farm we had seen the day before,we arrived at Indaw, a large lake with no development and a "prolific population of bird-life, including the Chinese pond heron, crested goshawk, coreather, blue-eared kingfisher, red-whiskered bulbul and the white-vented myna" according to our trip brochure. There were also lots of egrets resting in the reeds and our group walked through the rice paddies to get closer to them for pictures. Rather than retrace my steps, I kept going and eventually reached high ground after flushing quail on the way. The egrets roosted in the trees and I was able to take some photos of them on the wing. As I reached the road, I encountered some agricultural implements used in the fields that could have been in use centuries or even millennia ago.

Near the lake, after crossing by foot a fragile bridge as the bus drove across, we visited a school where we disrupted the routine but had a delightful time taking pictures of the children and chatting with the teachers. On the riverbank I took a picture of two young boys, naked in the broiling sun, bringing a boat across the river. Their mother motioned for me to come back and join some funeral festivities in the village with loud music. I waved back and declined. It reminded me of the time I was in Lhasa at the large pond below the Potala. The workers who had cleaned this pond invited me for tea in the gazebo in the middle. Also the young Chinese in Beijing in 1982 had invited me to go boating with them on one of the lakes adjacent to the Forbidden City.

On our return we stopped in the outskirts of Katha by some houses from the colonial days, one of which must have been

George Orwell's. They are across the street from the police station. We took pictures of the houses, but not the police station because of "security." We had to be careful not to offend the military dictatorship.

Fittingly, that night after dinner, we saw "The Bridge on the River Kwai." Keith Hyland had been a prisoner of the Japanese for four years and I had heard from Margaret Crawford that he possibly had worked on the bridge. I never asked him. He later had been a prisoner of the North Vietnamese for eleven months after the Tet Offensive in Hanoi—Ho Chi Minh City—in 1969. He did tell me about this captivity when he had been kept in a pit and was almost deafened by our B-52 bombers.

We left Katha in the late afternoon in order to go as far upriver as possible by night fall. As the Daily Schedules put it, "The Route from Katha to Bhamó is unchartered waters for the Irrawaddy Flotilla Company in its present incarnation, and we must take due care for some difficult navigation over the next part of our journey." Between Mandalay and Bhamó we used five or six different sets of local river pilots. One day I watched from the bridge as they took soundings, a scene straight out of Mark Twain. We had ten feet of water at the spot where I watched.

As we left Katha the lead male dancer from the previous night's entertainment put on a spectacular show on the upper river bank. In my best Burmese, I called "Pýan dáwme" (good-bye) and waved as long as I could. Our spectators on shore replied in kind.

We were delayed by fog the next morning, but cast off after breakfast, arriving at Schwegu at 1:00 P.M. We took a walk through town in the middle of the day and my notes say "sun hot as hell." Schwegu's chief claim to fame is pot making.

In the late afternoon we entered the Second Defile, another spectacular spot. The riverbanks are "lush with bamboo and other flora and the Irrawaddy passes through steep, rocky gorges," reminiscent of the gorges of the Yangtze. Small pagodas were perched on unlikely outcroppings.

That evening we tied up at dusk on a mud bank. Joe went ashore and located a village of the Lisu tribe. After dinner, the crew set a square of candles on the bank, and a group of local dancers performed. The square was surrounded by villagers, including many children who were vivacious, ingenuous, and highly amused. It was a remarkable spontaneous performance.

The next morning the tribesmen entertained a number of our group in their village at a breakfast of river prawns and grasshoppers. I would have gladly gone but I was a bit "off my feed" and demurred. When we cast off we were serenaded by a chorus of good-byes and waving. I gave them my best "pýan dáwme," much to the amusement of the crew, who mimicked me and joined in the chorus.

We sailed the rest of that morning, Saturday, November 4, to Bhamó, the farthest point that large river boats can go. Looking at the map, I saw that there were airfields at Mitkyina—of Merrill's Marauders fame in World War II—and Patao in the far north near the Himalayas. Things are evidently opening up a bit since Joe said it would be possible to fly there but it would take about two weeks to get permission. I would have loved to make the trip.

We reached the Bhamó landing at lunch time, quite a distance from town. When we disembarked we took individual pony carts. I went to see the so-called "Irish Church" that turned out to be a large one built around 1950 by a Catholic bishop from Dublin. The two native priests were most accommodating and said there were 6,000 Catholics in the area. They had no "vigil" Mass on Saturday, and I could not attend the Sunday Mass at 7 A.M., since it was too far from the boat and we were due to go to the airport to fly to Mandalay. The rest of our crowd appeared on the scene and we took a picture outside the church.

Transporting Elephants
Irrawaddy River
Burma

“Official Version”

The priest had mentioned that they had had an All Souls' Day service on November 2 at the nearby cemetery. He recommended that I drive down to see the place, but the overseer of the pony carts overruled it, again for "security" reasons. At Bhamó we were only thirty miles from the Chinese border, near Riuli, the home town of David Huang, director of our April trip. The security evidently tightens the farther north one goes with India-Assam to the west and China to the east.

We had a nostalgic drink that evening in the saloon and our final dinner on board. We settled up our accounts, and I was touched when the quartermaster, Tonto, said good-bye and how much he and the crew had enjoyed my attempts at speaking Burmese.

The next morning we disembarked early for the airport and reluctantly left the RV Pandaw on our tenth day. I can think of no better way to sum it up than to quote the excerpt in the Daily Schedule from The Irrawaddy Flotilla Company Handbook, 1935:

> "Further on will be found a short description of the various places of call on the river, but while all of these possess their own particular interest, scenic or otherwise, the principal charm of a trip lies in its complete restfulness. Without any effort on his part, the traveller is enable to survey the beauties of his surroundings, the life of the river, the customs and habits of a delightful people and the products and industries from which the country's wealth is derived. There is no hustle nor is there the monotony of a sea voyage, for something of interest is always in site [*sic*]."

I had enjoyed every minute of it and felt that I had become part of the scenery.

At the airport we met the Stanford University group that was due to take over the Pandaw and go down river to Bagan in five days. I preferred our upstream course. They were a nice crowd and there were a few mutual friends among our crowd. We gave them a good report of what to expect.

After a good flight to Mandalay and a pleasant lunch, we checked in to the Sedona Hotel, a most luxurious hostelry across from the grounds of the former royal palace. I opted for afternoon Mass at St. Francis Xavier, a native church with the Mass in Burmese. The congregation sang beautifully and I enjoyed it.

On Monday we went to a temple where the men, but not the women, were allowed to affix gold leaf to the main statue of the Buddha. We then went to the national theatre where the company put on a fine show of native dances. This had been especially arranged by Joe. In the afternoon we took in the goldsmiths and tapestry works and I bought my small elephant tapestry. Elephants and cranes are now my favorites.

On Tuesday we drove down the banks of the Irrawaddy to see the Ava Bridge, the only one across the Irrawaddy, and also to climb barefoot up to the pagoda with its lovely river views. From there we went to the U Bein bridge, about a mile long, a teak foot bridge to an island with a crumbling old pagoda in a forest. The walk across took about fifteen minutes and I did it quickly, nonstop to avoid the heat.

We had lunch in the garden at a charming lakeside restaurant and then came home via the bronze and marble works. I picked up two small elephants of blue jade, of "poor quality" according to Joe but I liked them. I had a lovely swim in the huge hotel pool.

On Wednesday November 8 we had an early start, flew to Heho and then drove over a range of hills and down to Inle Lake surrounded by the Shan Hills. We took small boats down the lake to our hotel, an attractive cluster of buildings at lakeside, had a quick change and then went immediately by boat to buildings in the middle of the lake. There they put on special boat races for us by crews of men and women, using the unique standing one-legged system developed by the fishermen. A crew of girls dressed in blue was the best of the lot, and we cheered them on as the Yale crew. After the prize awards we had lunch in the main hall and were entertained by native dances afterwards.

Tuesday, November 7 had been Election Day at home. During most of our trip we were out of touch with the outside world with no television, radio, or International Herald Tribune but Joe had obtained a small transistor radio and at cocktails before dinner he held it to my ear. I could hear the announcer say that Bush had won. Then we began to hear confusing reports of a narrow margin in Florida of about 200 votes and the decision to have recounts. We hoped we would be home in time to hear the final result. None of us could have guessed what lay ahead. Thus for me on Inle Lake, Burma began that amazing period of 36 days with its recounts, court cases and Florida and United States Supreme Court cases which finally ended in the Bush win and the Gore concession on December 12. We were home in plenty of time to see the final result.

On Thursday we again had an early start and took a 50-minute boat ride down the lake, turned right up canals and a river, through a lake town and finally landed at a remote village. From there we hiked up to a temple dating from the eighteenth century surrounded by crumbling stupas. It was fascinating, particularly since we were the only non-natives. It was a beautiful, remote spot with a view of untouched forests on the Shan Hills.

After a late lunch at the hotel, I had a nice lazy afternoon with a snooze and then watched the birds, including quite a few egrets, from the back porch of my bungalow.

On Friday November 10 we arose at 5:45 A.M., went by boat to the end of the lake, by bus to Heho and were in Rangoon about 11 A.M. There the group broke up, some going directly to Singapore. The rest of us had lunch in the garden at LePlanteur, an

"Yale Crew"
Inle Lake
Burma

excellent new French restaurant run by a Swiss from Martigny. Shades of my trip with Bruce Baetjer staying in Martigny in 1947 and then years later with Michele Marchand passing through en route to Finhaut to helicopter up to the Col du Trient. Most of our group had departed by afternoon, and Chris and I had dinner at Panseco. We agreed it would be fun to take another trip together. He is a top-notch guide.

The next morning, Saturday November 11, I arose at an ungodly hour and caught the 7:30 plane to Bangkok; had a comfortable lay-over in the preferred lounge; flew to Siam Reap, obtained my visa in the airport without trouble; and met my guide, Lay Noy, and driver for Angkor Wat. I checked in at the Grand Hotel which has been redone and expanded by the Raffles group and is first class.

After a quick change, we drove to Angkor Wat and had a long tour. Although there were throngs of tourists, it was fascinating. We did not climb to the top of it but still covered it thoroughly. It was most impressive.

That evening I ate in the buffet dining room and then took a motor-bike-taxi ride around the summer palace and a part of the town.

On Sunday I finally found a simple chapel in a house on the river road near the hotel. Mass was just ending but I had a brief chat with the priest, a Spaniard. We then had a long ride on a terrible road out to the Citadel of Women, but it was well worth it. We visited another temple on the way back.

My itinerary called for a boat ride on the lake, Tonle Sap, but I said I had had enough of that in Burma and went instead to the temple which has been only partially reclaimed from the jungle with huge Banyan trees everywhere. We also visited Bayon, with its magnificent display of carvings.

At dinner that night in the formal room I ran into Tim Gibson

Angkor Wat
Cambodia

Jungle Temple
Angkor Wat

who had been the TCS representative on our trip in 1997 down the Yenisei and also Micheline who had been with us on the Orient Express trip in 1996. Also a tennis group from Baltimore, some of whom I knew, appeared on the scene. More examples of the small, small world.

On Monday November 13 we went out in a different direction from Angkor and saw an early temple with three towers. In the afternoon on the way to the airport I tried to see the modern hospital near the hotel run by a Swiss doctor, a protégé of the royal family. I was unable to get in—which I understand is the usual practice—but my guide took me around to the "Japanese" hospital, originally founded by a well-known Japanese photographer but now largely supported by Americans. I was warmly received by the director and shown around. It is simple but obviously doing good work.

We paid a brief visit to the centuries-old reservoir near the airport. The roads were lined with people who would stay there all night to see Jang Zemin, the president of China, due the next morning. I flew out about 8 P.M. to Bangkok, where I put up at the Amari Airport Hotel.

The next morning I collected my extra bag at "Left Luggage" and caught Thai Airways, business class. We had a stop at Narita, the new Tokyo airport, and I was glued to the window as we flew up the south coast of Japan in the late afternoon. I had a clear view of the Kobe-Nara area and the Yamato peninsula and then the coast from Nagoya up toward the Ise peninsula that Beverly McVeigh and I had circumnavigated in the spring of 1946.

We reached Los Angeles the next morning, still November 14, and when I arrived at the Sheraton Gateway I collapsed until dinner. The waiter that evening recognized me from my visit in April.

The next afternoon, Wednesday November 15, I flew United Airlines first class to Baltimore, was met by Freedom Services and was delighted to be home. A fantastic trip.

I barely had time to catch my breath since on Saturday Frank Bonsal threw a birthday bash for Fife Symington's 90th. Humpy Stump and I did some light emceeing but mostly we just let the good time roll. It reminded us old-timers of the way the Hunt Ball used to be after the Maryland Hunt Cup.

New Year's Eve was quieter than the year before but a great way to celebrate the true Millennium. Our regular group was a bit dispersed but Nancy Marburg and I went to Fife Symington's and Natalie Brengell's for dinner where we met Rudolfo and Goga Riedel, formerly from Argentina. Rudolfo was Ambassador to Trinidad-Tobago at the same time that Fife was from the United States. We had a far ranging conversation covering a good bit of the world and worldly events. I was home in time to see on TV the descent of the great ball in Times Square. Thus truly ended the Twentieth Century for me.

As aforesaid, a bit of editorial license permits me to extend this treatise into the Third Millennium, the year 2001. On Saturday, January 20, I journeyed by bus with a group invited by Bank America (formerly Maryland Trust, Equitable Trust, Maryland National, NationsBank, et al) to attend the presidential inauguration of George W. Bush. We had a good time and superb location in their building, the former Security Trust, at the corner of 15th Street and Pennsylvania Avenue. The Bushes obligingly dismounted for us at the corner to make their way on foot.

Reflecting on the inauguration, I can remember Aunt Ella telling me years ago that she had attended the inauguration of William McKinley—including the one inaugural ball—with the Robert Garretts in 1901. They had traveled on the Garretts' private train on the Baltimore & Ohio Railroad, the nation's first, which no longer exists. A century has passed.

Eleu fugaces, Postume, Postume,
Labuntur anni. Nec pietas moram
Rugis et instanti senectae
Afferet indomitaeque morti.

—Horace, Odes, Book II, No. 14.
"Alas, Postumus [a friend of Horace to whom the ode was addressed], the fleeting years slip by. Nor can piety [i.e. right living] delay wrinkles, approaching old age and indomitable death."

St. Anton

The Alpine Ski World Championships were held in St. Anton, and although I had intended to avoid them because of the crowds, I had been firmly advised by Herbert and Marcella Rofner and others that I had to be present since I was part of the scenery. There was poetic justice in this. My first visit to St. Anton in 1948 was after the Winter Olympics in St. Moritz in order to attend the Hannes Schneider Pokol ("Cup"), the first major ski races held in Austria after World War II. As set forth in an earlier chapter, the Tirol was still "occupied territory" by the French and I had to obtain a Military Permit for the French Zone to attend. See page 71, infra.

St. Anton had obtained the games—Ski Alpine Weltmeisterschaft—held under the aegis of the F.I.S.—Federation Internationale de Ski—because 2001 was the 100th anniversary of the founding of the Ski Club Arlberg. Benno Rybizka's father was one of the founders.

I took my regular Swissair flight at Dulles, on Thursday, February 1, arrived at 8 A.M. at Zurich and caught the 9:33 train to St. Anton, arriving a little after noon at the new station. Ensconced in the Alte Post and with the help of Herbert Rofner, I organized skis and boots at Rudi Tschol's and had my ski clothes from Herta Fahrner. Gary Black, working on the F.I.S. public relations committee, had left me a pass to USA House, the United States team open house at Bobo's Bar. So I was all set.

The U.S. Team was staying at the Alte Post, and Daron Rahlves, who had won the Super-G the day before, was across the hall from me. We met out in the street watching the parades surge by the hotel. The people doing the daily picture paper for the races took a snap of me. When they brought it by later in the evening, I had them join me for dinner and regaled them with tales of St. Anton and "*Singendes, Klingendes Österreich*"—singing and ringing Austria.

It began to snow that evening, as a result of which the men's and women's downhills were postponed from Saturday and Sunday, respectively. That meant that the place was a mad-house with 40,000 people on hand and no races. I came home from the Platzl one evening and there was a full-blown brass band playing in our bar.

They finally held the men's downhill on Wednesday, and Herbert Rofner and I had "*stehplätze*" in the stadium along with 35,000 people. Hannes Trinkl of Austria nosed out Herman Maier for the gold. We could watch the races from the start on a huge television screen in front of us. The announcing was deafening.

After the races, Herbert and I went up the Galzig to ski. We made our customary two or three turns and then commenced our usual schuss. Since most of the piste machinery was busy on the race courses, there were ruts or bumps that Herbert shouted back to me to watch out for. It was too late. My skis accelerated, I hit and down I sent, twisting my left thigh and crashing on my right shoulder. I sorted myself out, skied down to the Tanzboden lift, went up it, skied down and over to the Galzigbahn and took it down. I was going to have a hot bath and massage—the worst possible thing I could have done—but Herbert recommended that I go to Dr. Knierzinger. The leg began to swell, they x-rayed me, no breaks, and I had therapy.

About two days later neither Dr. Knierzinger nor I liked the look of things, so on Saturday, the day of the men's salom, I went by ambulance to the hospital at Zams, next door to Landeck. Getting through the crowds at St. Anton was quite a job, since there were more than 50,000 people on hand that day, but we made it. Among the spectators was Vladimir Putin, President of Russia. He stayed at the Hospiz at St. Christoph. He skied with Karl Schranz. Herbert saw him on TV and gave him good marks since he had "skied parallel."

The hospital—St. Vinzenz Krankenhaus—could not have been nicer. I had a large corner single room looking out on the "Sound of Music" scenery, and the somewhat austere dietary regime made the pounds melt off me. Dr. Hanno Pall was an excellent doctor, and I had a good old fashioned "rest cure"—probably just what I needed after all the rushing around of the previous year.

I watched Mario Matt from Flirsch (the home town of Franz Tandl) win the slalom and then the closing ceremony on TV from my hospital bed. Franz Farhner would have been a part of the ceremony if he had been alive. He had done many things over the years for St. Anton.

After the closing ceremony, I watched with interest a round table discussion on skiing, including emphasizing the combination of downhill and slalom instead of one-event specialization and curbing the extreme "carving skis." The participants included Karl Schranz who had given honorary ski school caps to Father Leo and me in 1982; Herbert Sprenger, Burgemeister of St. Anton, who had presided over my ceremony as 35 time guest; Adolf Ogi, former President of Switzerland, in whose parents' house I had been a guest with Fritz Stäger in Kandersteg; Gian Carl Franco, President of the F.I.S. to whom Gary Black had me send a copy of my book; Toni Sailer whom Bruce Baetjer and I had seen win three gold medals in the 1956 Olympics in Cortina; etc. It was "old home week" and somehow humorous but fitting that I watched it from a hospital bed. I had been brought down to earth!

Herta (Schneider) Fahrner was also in the hospital, so we had a good time talking on the phone and visiting.** I had cancelled any plans to go to Mürren since skiing was out for the year. Herbert Rofner picked me up on the following Saturday. After a couple of days at St. Anton, I took the train to Zurich, spent the night at the Airport Moevenpick and flew back to Dulles, upgrading myself to business class on the plane before take-off for about half of what a ticket would have cost. I was met by Freedom Services, and since it was late afternoon we avoided the Capital Beltway, went home via Leesburg, Point of Rocks and Frederick, and then, when we saw the Baltimore Beltway jammed up, I guided Chuck across town via Kernan, Rogers Avenue and Northern Parkway to Charles Street. We made it in an hour and thirty minutes. The next day, true to form, we had a snow storm, about four or five inches.

And so endeth this tale of my wanderings over the course of more than three quarters of the Twentieth Century and a small sliver of the Twenty-First. It has included the Roaring Twenties, although I was too young to "roar"; the Great Depression; World War II; the Cold War; the introduction of television, jet travel, computers and the Internet; the sudden end of the Cold War with the destruction of the Berlin Wall; the collapse of the Soviet Empire; the wars in the Balkans, Bosnia, Kosovo and Serbia; the Russian troubles in Chechnya; etc.

—♦—

** As I was correcting proof for this Revised Edition on March 27, 2001, Gary Black phoned me from Sun Valley to let me know that he had just heard that Herta had died in her sleep in St. Anton. I knew that she was in failing health, and I am thankful that I had those visits with her in the hospital. I called her nephew Christoph in St. Anton, and we had a long talk reminiscing about the old times. Her death truly marks the end of an era in St. Anton, and I was lucky to have been a part of it.

As the century and the millennium end, the United States, as the "sole great power" at this stage of the game, faces many threats and challenges. Hopefully there will be no more worldwide wars, and we will take action with NATO, the United Nations and other local consortia only where it is in our interest and practical. We cannot micro-manage the World—e.g. Tibet and the Chinese; Georgia and the Abkesians.

It looks as if there will always be trouble as long as there are human beings to stir it up. Still I remain an optimist and a long term "bull." After all, I am a Taurus.

"Staubbach Kurt" von Allmen
and Kuh Hirt group
Dorffest, Mürren
circa 1985

Fritz Stäger and Charlie
Eiger North Wall
1983

Grutschchilbi,
Mürren, Switzerland
1983

CBR Jr
Base Camp, North Side of Mount Everest
Tibet, 1982

The Potala
Lhasa, Tibet,
1982

EPILOGUE

Ellie Kann was a delightful, outspoken friend. She said that you ought to live life so that you would not want to change anything, but on the other hand you had lived it so fully that you would not want to repeat it.

Gernie Underdue worked for Aunt Ella and me for a number of years after we moved back to 4406 Greenway. I remarked to her one time that I was possibly attempting to do too much. Her reply was, "Oh, I don't know, Mr. Charles. You might as well 'cause this is one place that once you go through it, you can't come back to pick up something that you forgot."

A similar remark to John Flattery, the golf professional at Green Spring, elicited the observation: "Oh, I don't know, Mr. Charles. You might as well as long as your health and your pocketbook hold out."

More poetically, the words of Wislawa Szymborska, 1996 Nobelist in Literature, from *Nothing Twice* (1957):

> Nothing can ever happen twice.
> In consequence, the sorry fact is
> that we arrive here improvised
> and leave without the chance to practice.

Even if there is no one dumber,
if you're the planet's biggest dunce,
you can't repeat the class in summer:
this course is only offered once.

It has been a good course—challenging—fascinating—rewarding. I have been a very lucky person. God has been good to me. My Guardian Angel deserves "flight pay!"